SHOOTING WAR

WRITTEN BY ANTHONY LAPPÉ
ILLUSTRATED BY DAN GOLDMAN

GRAND CENTRAL
PUBLISHING
NEW YORK   BOSTON

THIS BOOK IS A WORK OF FICTION. IT IS INTENDED AS COMMENTARY ABOUT THE STATE OF JOURNALISM AND THE WAR IN IRAQ. EXCEPT AS DESCRIBED BELOW, ALL THE CHARACTERS IN THE BOOK ARE THE PRODUCT OF THE AUTHOR'S IMAGINATION AND ANY SIMILARITY TO ACTUAL PEOPLE OR EVENTS IS UNINTENTIONAL. THE USE OF NAMES OF REAL CELEBRITIES AND LOCATIONS IN THIS FUTURISTIC SATIRE IS DONE IN A WHOLLY FICTITIOUS MANNER, IN ORDER TO CONVEY A REFERENCE POINT FOR THE INTERSECTION OF CELEBRITY, BRANDING, WORLD EVENTS AND THE BUSINESS OF NEWS IN OUR TIMES. THE AUTHOR DOES NOT INTEND TO IMPLY THAT ANY SUCH USE IN THE BOOK IS BASED IN FACT, AND ALL SUCH APPEARANCES ARE TOTALLY IMAGINARY.

GRAND CENTRAL PUBLISHING
HACHETTE BOOK GROUP USA
237 PARK AVENUE
NEW YORK, NY 10017

VISIT OUR WEB SITE AT WWW.HACHETTEBOOKGROUPUSA.COM.

PRINTED IN MEXICO

FIRST EDITION: NOVEMBER 2007
10 9 8 7 6 5 4 3 2 1

GRAND CENTRAL PUBLISHING IS A DIVISION OF HACHETTE BOOK GROUP USA, INC. THE GRAND CENTRAL PUBLISHING NAME AND LOGO IS A TRADEMARK OF HACHETTE BOOK GROUP USA, INC.

LIBRARY OF CONGRESS CONTROL NUMBER: 2007927397

FOR CLARICE AND LILLI

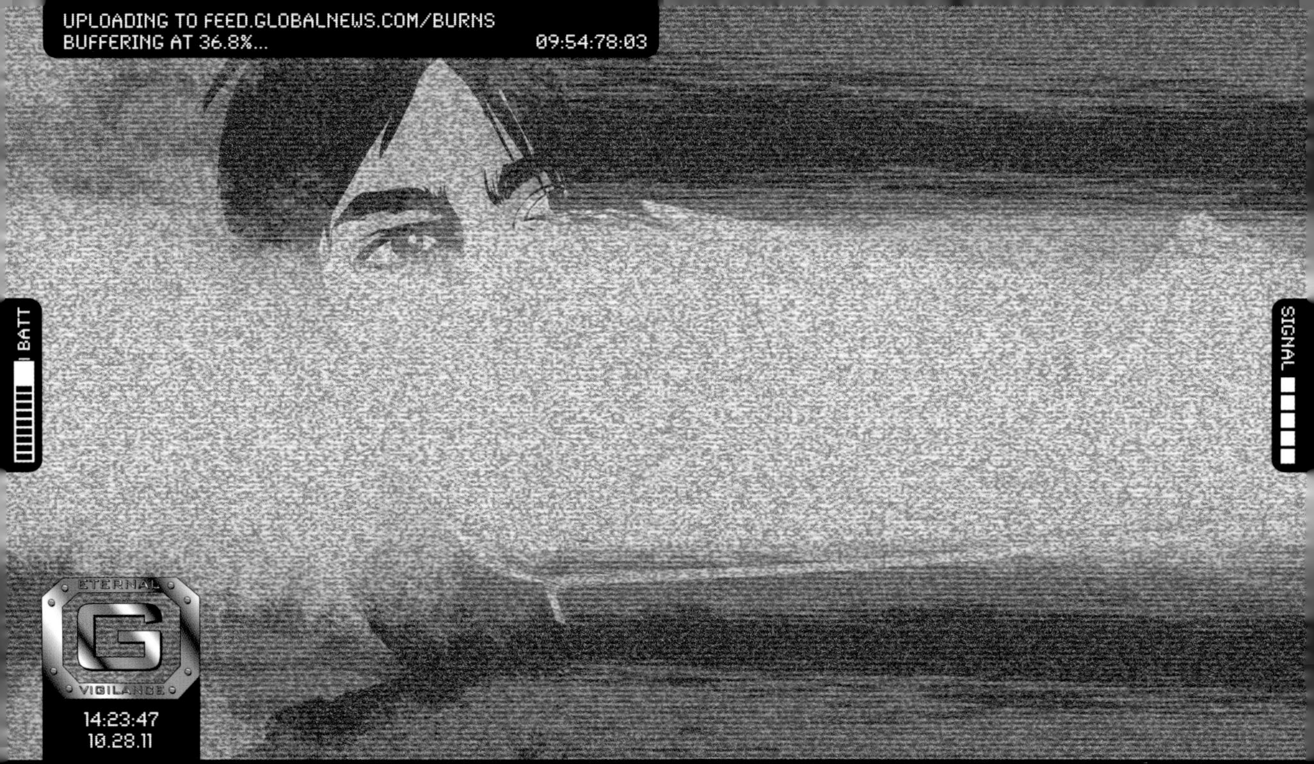
UPLOADING TO FEED.GLOBALNEWS.COM/BURNS
BUFFERING AT 36.8%...
09:54:78:03
BATT
SIGNAL
ETERNAL
VIGILANCE
14:23:47
10.28.11

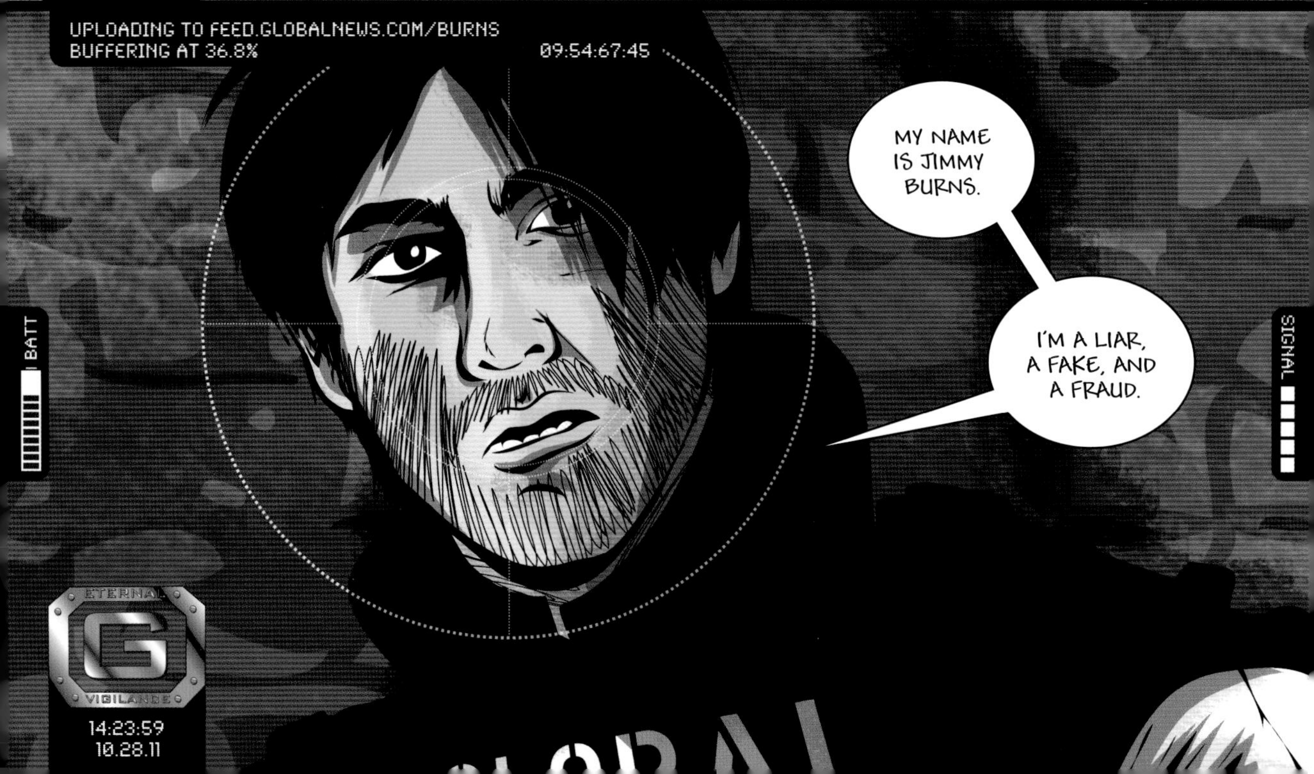
UPLOADING TO FEED.GLOBALNEWS.COM/BURNS
BUFFERING AT 36.8%
09:54:67:45
MY NAME IS JIMMY BURNS.
I'M A LIAR, A FAKE, AND A FRAUD.
BATT
SIGNAL
ETERNAL
VIGILANCE
14:23:59
10.28.11

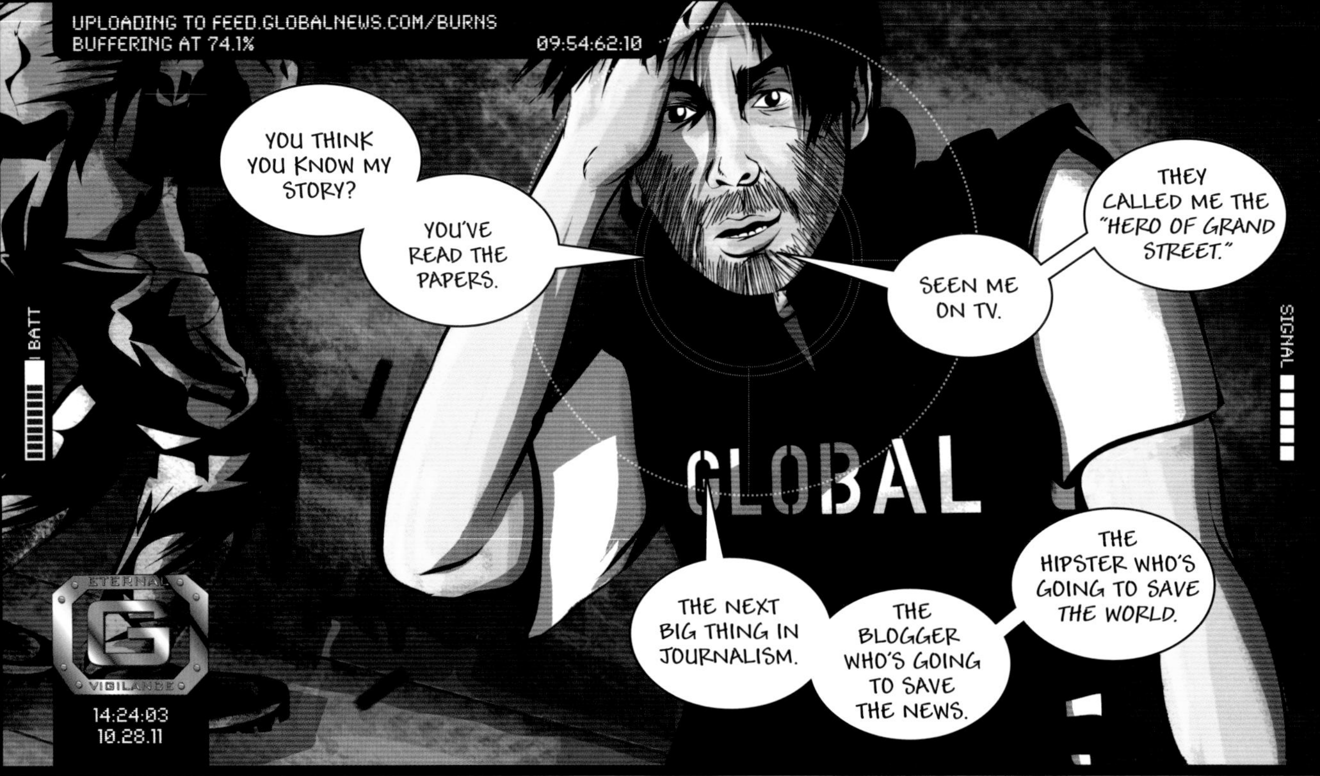
UPLOADING TO FEED.GLOBALNEWS.COM/BURNS
BUFFERING AT 74.1%
09:54:62:10
YOU THINK YOU KNOW MY STORY?
YOU'VE READ THE PAPERS.
SEEN ME ON TV.
THEY CALLED ME THE "HERO OF GRAND STREET."
THE NEXT BIG THING IN JOURNALISM.
THE BLOGGER WHO'S GOING TO SAVE THE NEWS.
THE HIPSTER WHO'S GOING TO SAVE THE WORLD.
BATT
SIGNAL
GLOBAL
ETERNAL
VIGILANCE
14:24:03
10.28.11

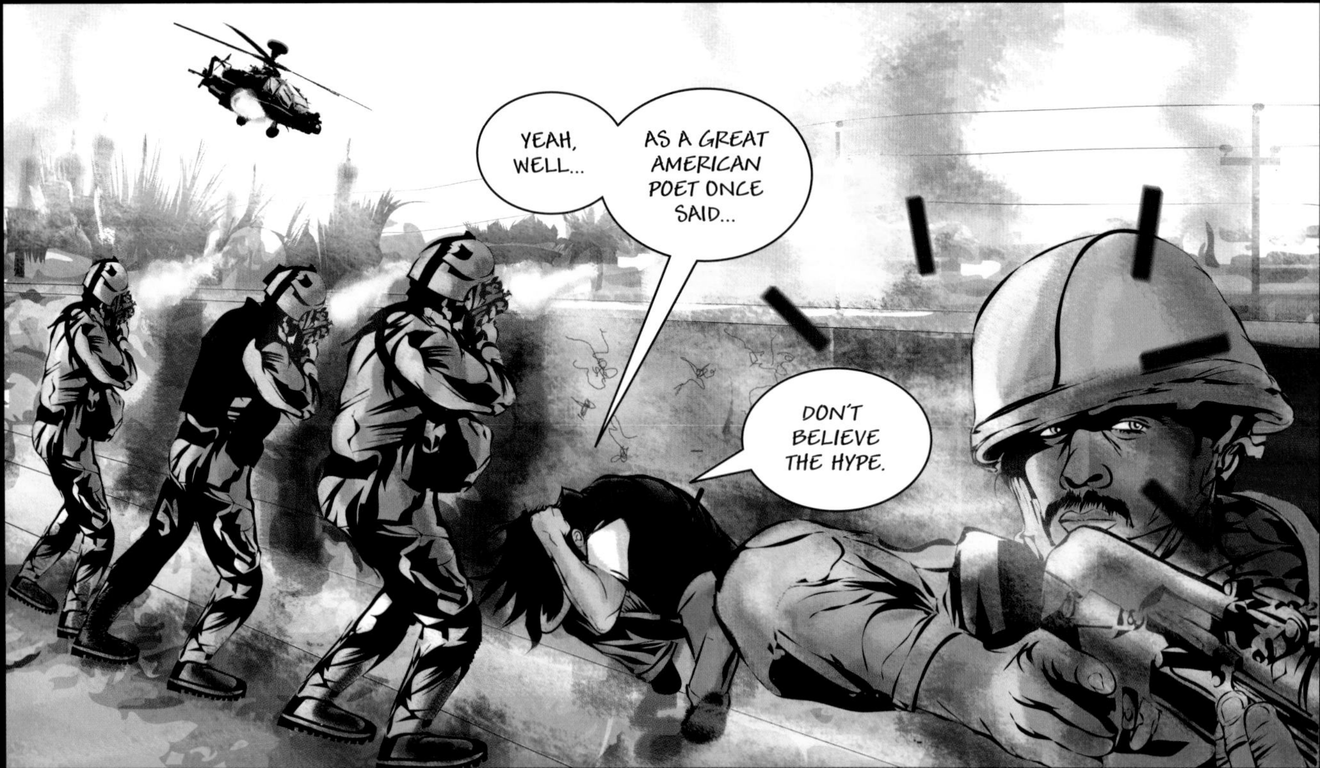
YEAH, WELL...
AS A GREAT AMERICAN POET ONCE SAID...
DON'T BELIEVE THE HYPE.

SHOOTING WAR

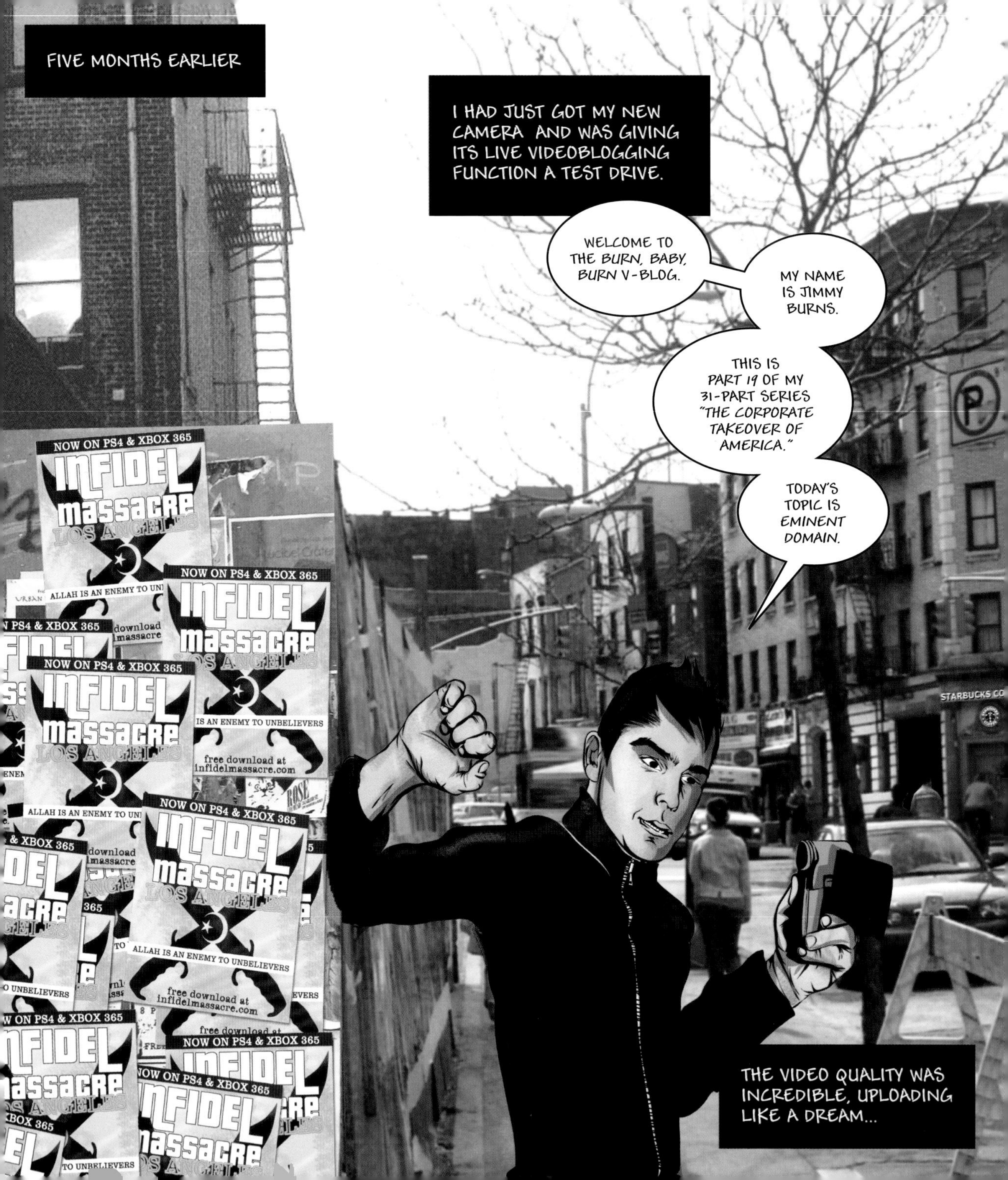

FIVE MONTHS EARLIER
I HAD JUST GOT MY NEW CAMERA AND WAS GIVING ITS LIVE VIDEOBLOGGING FUNCTION A TEST DRIVE.
WELCOME TO THE BURN, BABY, BURN V-BLOG.
MY NAME IS JIMMY BURNS.
THIS IS PART 19 OF MY 31-PART SERIES "THE CORPORATE TAKEOVER OF AMERICA."
TODAY'S TOPIC IS EMINENT DOMAIN.
NOW ON PS4 & XBOX 365
INFIDEL massacre LOS ANGELES
ALLAH IS AN ENEMY TO UNBELIEVERS
free download at infidelmassacre.com
STARBUCKS CO
THE VIDEO QUALITY WAS INCREDIBLE, UPLOADING LIKE A DREAM...

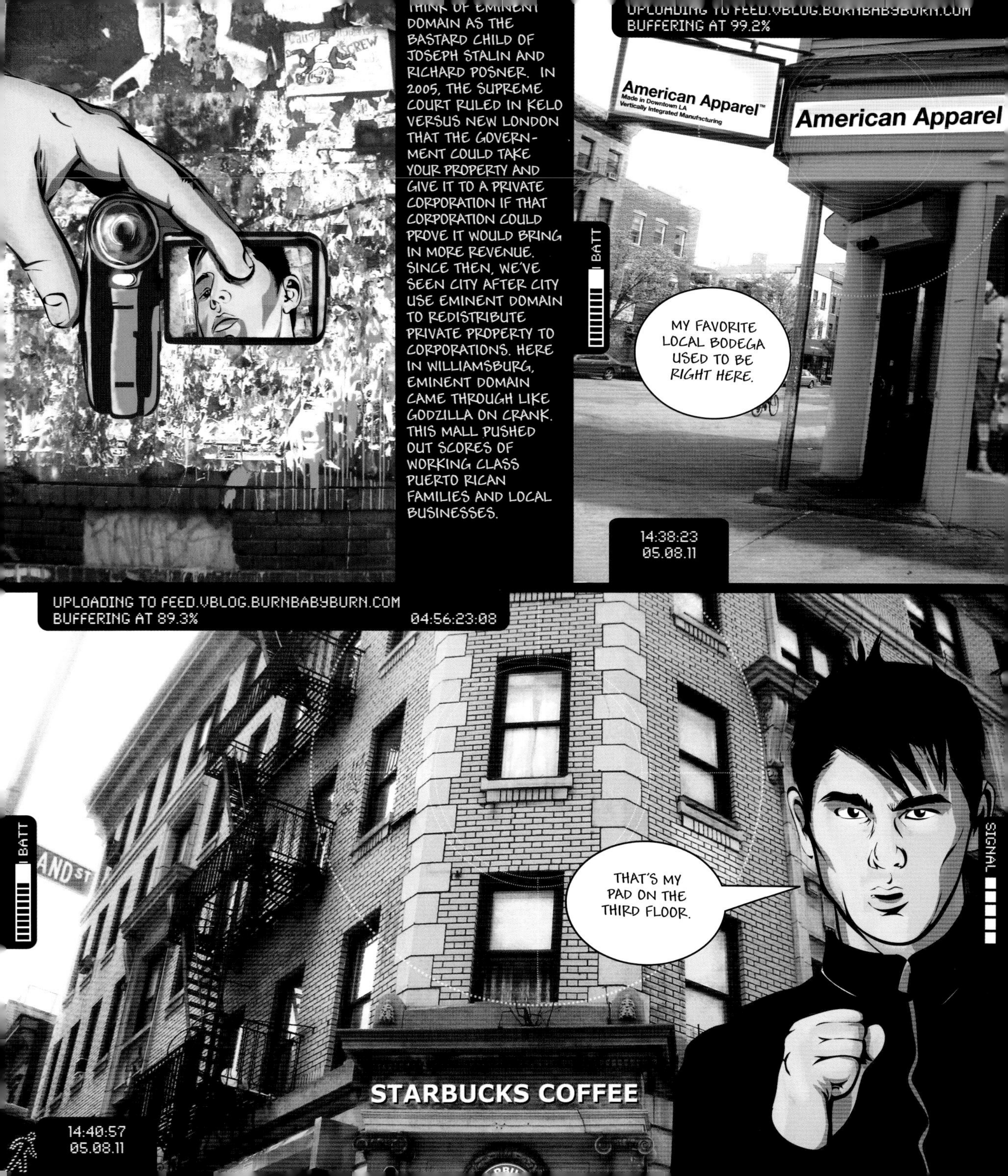
THINK OF EMINENT DOMAIN AS THE BASTARD CHILD OF JOSEPH STALIN AND RICHARD POSNER. IN 2005, THE SUPREME COURT RULED IN KELO VERSUS NEW LONDON THAT THE GOVERNMENT COULD TAKE YOUR PROPERTY AND GIVE IT TO A PRIVATE CORPORATION IF THAT CORPORATION COULD PROVE IT WOULD BRING IN MORE REVENUE. SINCE THEN, WE'VE SEEN CITY AFTER CITY USE EMINENT DOMAIN TO REDISTRIBUTE PRIVATE PROPERTY TO CORPORATIONS. HERE IN WILLIAMSBURG, EMINENT DOMAIN CAME THROUGH LIKE GODZILLA ON CRANK. THIS MALL PUSHED OUT SCORES OF WORKING CLASS PUERTO RICAN FAMILIES AND LOCAL BUSINESSES.
UPLOADING TO FEED.VBLOG.BURNBABYBURN.COM
BUFFERING AT 99.2%
American Apparel™
Made in Downtown LA
Vertically Integrated Manufacturing
American Apparel
BATT
MY FAVORITE LOCAL BODEGA USED TO BE RIGHT HERE.
14:38:23
05.08.11
UPLOADING TO FEED.VBLOG.BURNBABYBURN.COM
BUFFERING AT 89.3%
04:56:23:08
BATT
AND ST
SIGNAL
THAT'S MY PAD ON THE THIRD FLOOR.
STARBUCKS COFFEE
14:40:57
05.08.11

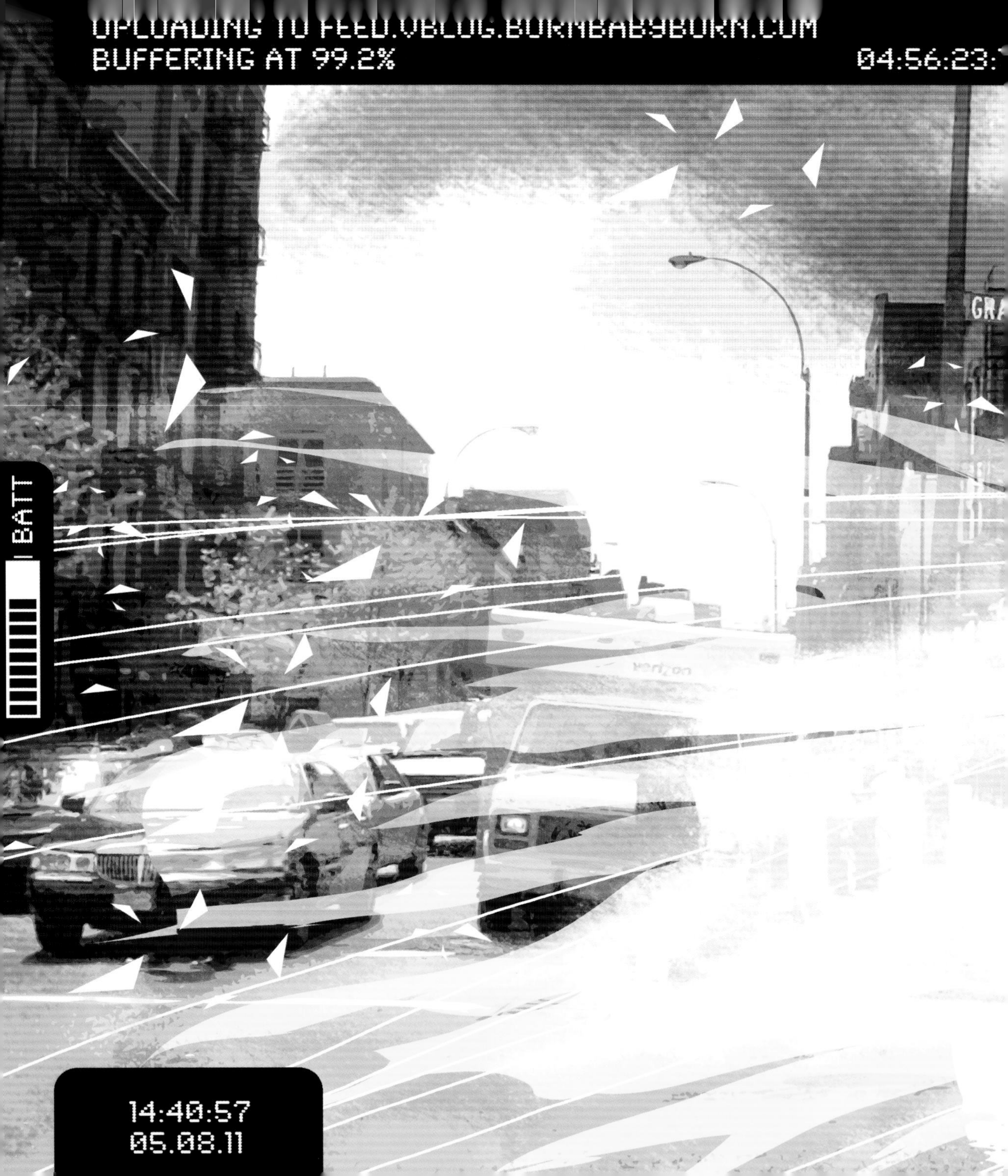
UPLOADING TO FEED.VBLOG.BURNBABYBURN.COM
BUFFERING AT 99.2%
04:56:23:
BATT
14:40:57
05.08.11

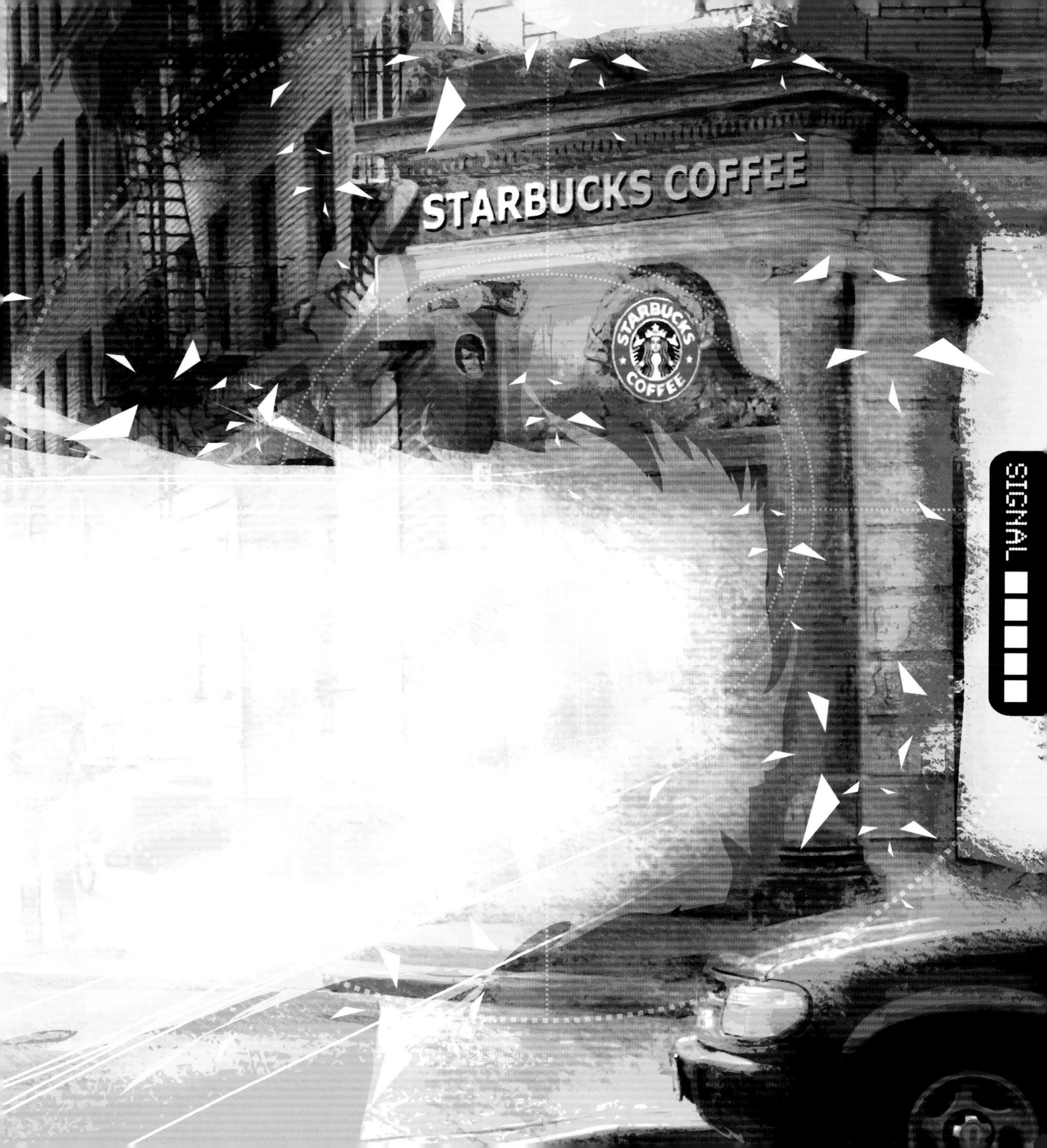
STARBUCKS COFFEE
STARBUCKS
COFFEE
SIGNAL

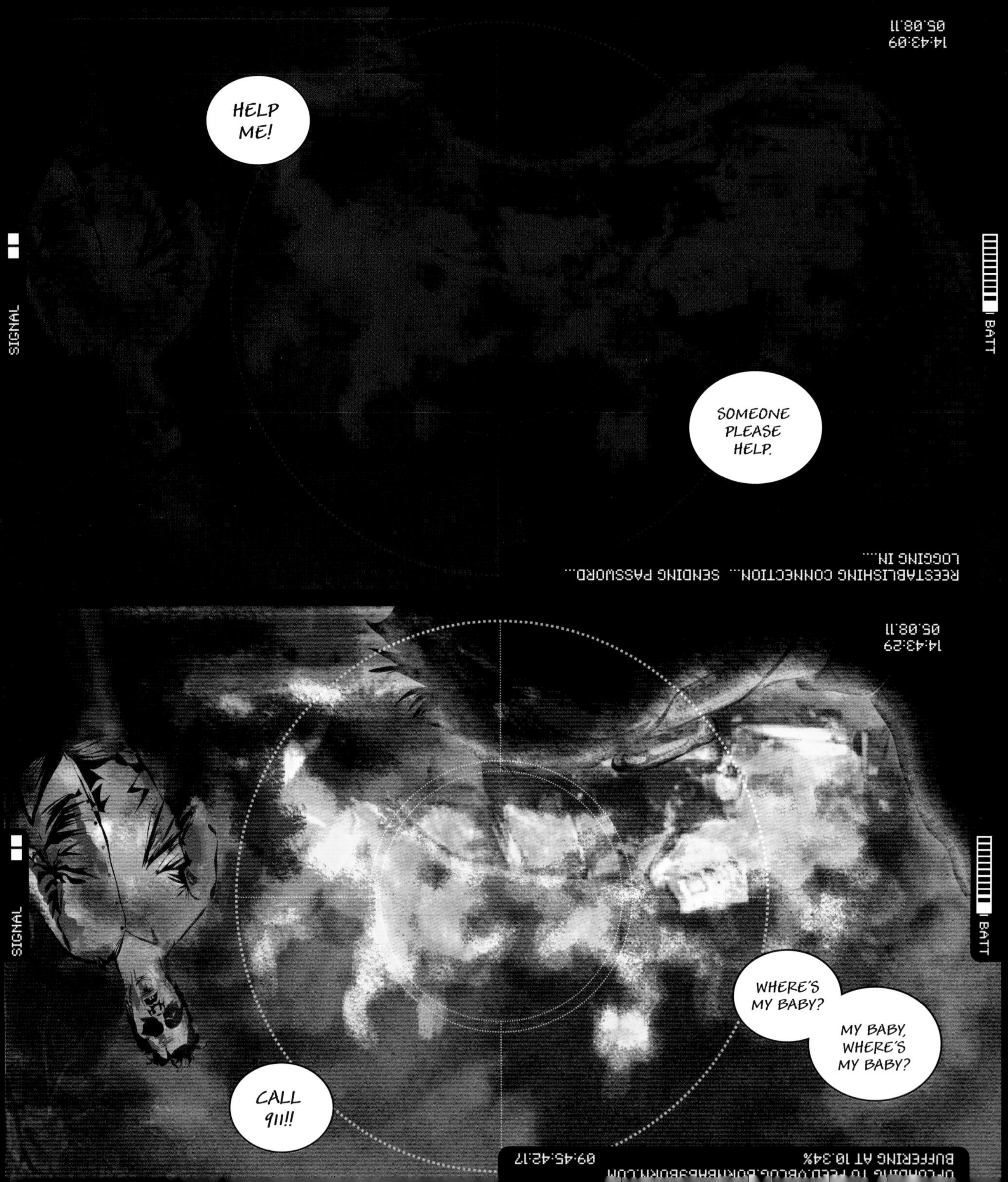

14:43:09
05.08.11
SIGNAL
BATT
HELP ME!
SOMEONE PLEASE HELP.
REESTABLISHING CONNECTION... SENDING PASSWORD...
LOGGING IN....
14:43:29
05.08.11
SIGNAL
BATT
WHERE'S MY BABY?
MY BABY, WHERE'S MY BABY?
CALL 911!!
BUFFERING AT 10.34%
09:45:42:17

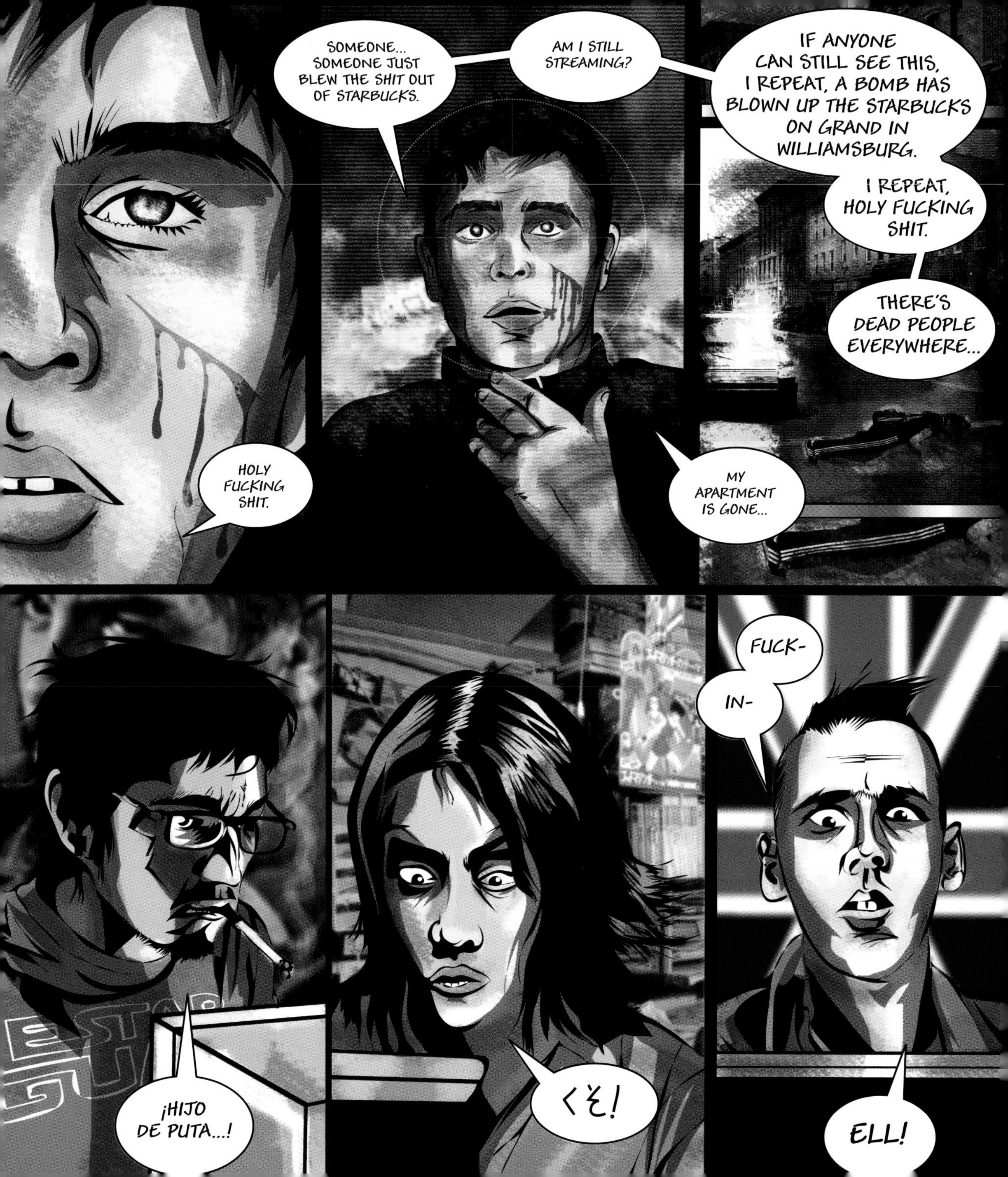
SOMEONE... SOMEONE JUST BLEW THE SHIT OUT OF STARBUCKS.
AM I STILL STREAMING?
IF ANYONE CAN STILL SEE THIS, I REPEAT, A BOMB HAS BLOWN UP THE STARBUCKS ON GRAND IN WILLIAMSBURG.
I REPEAT, HOLY FUCKING SHIT.
THERE'S DEAD PEOPLE EVERYWHERE...
HOLY FUCKING SHIT.
MY APARTMENT IS GONE...
¡HIJO DE PUTA...!
くそ!
FUCK-
IN-
ELL!

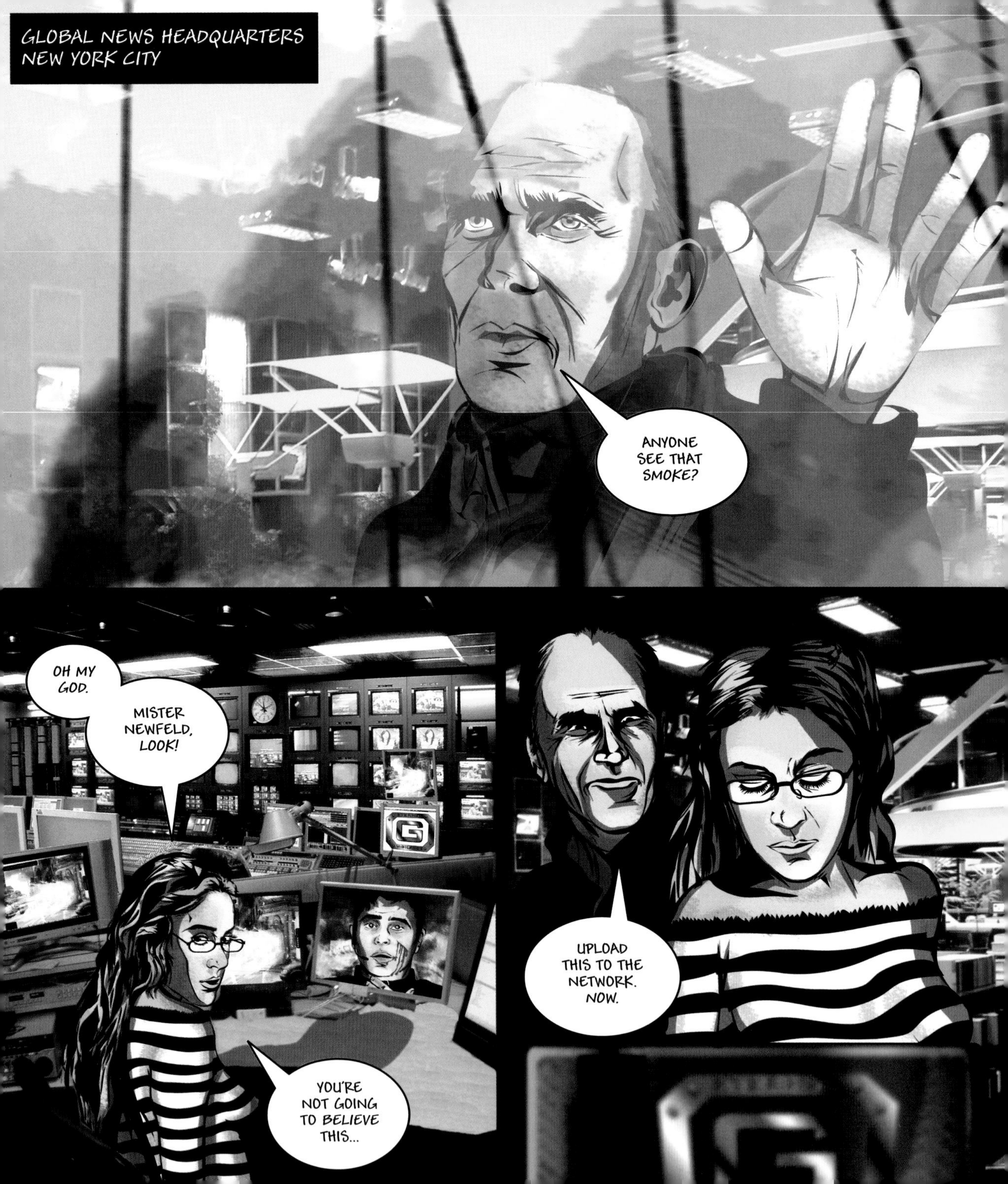
GLOBAL NEWS HEADQUARTERS
NEW YORK CITY
ANYONE SEE THAT SMOKE?
OH MY GOD.
MISTER NEWFELD, LOOK!
YOU'RE NOT GOING TO BELIEVE THIS...
UPLOAD THIS TO THE NETWORK. NOW.

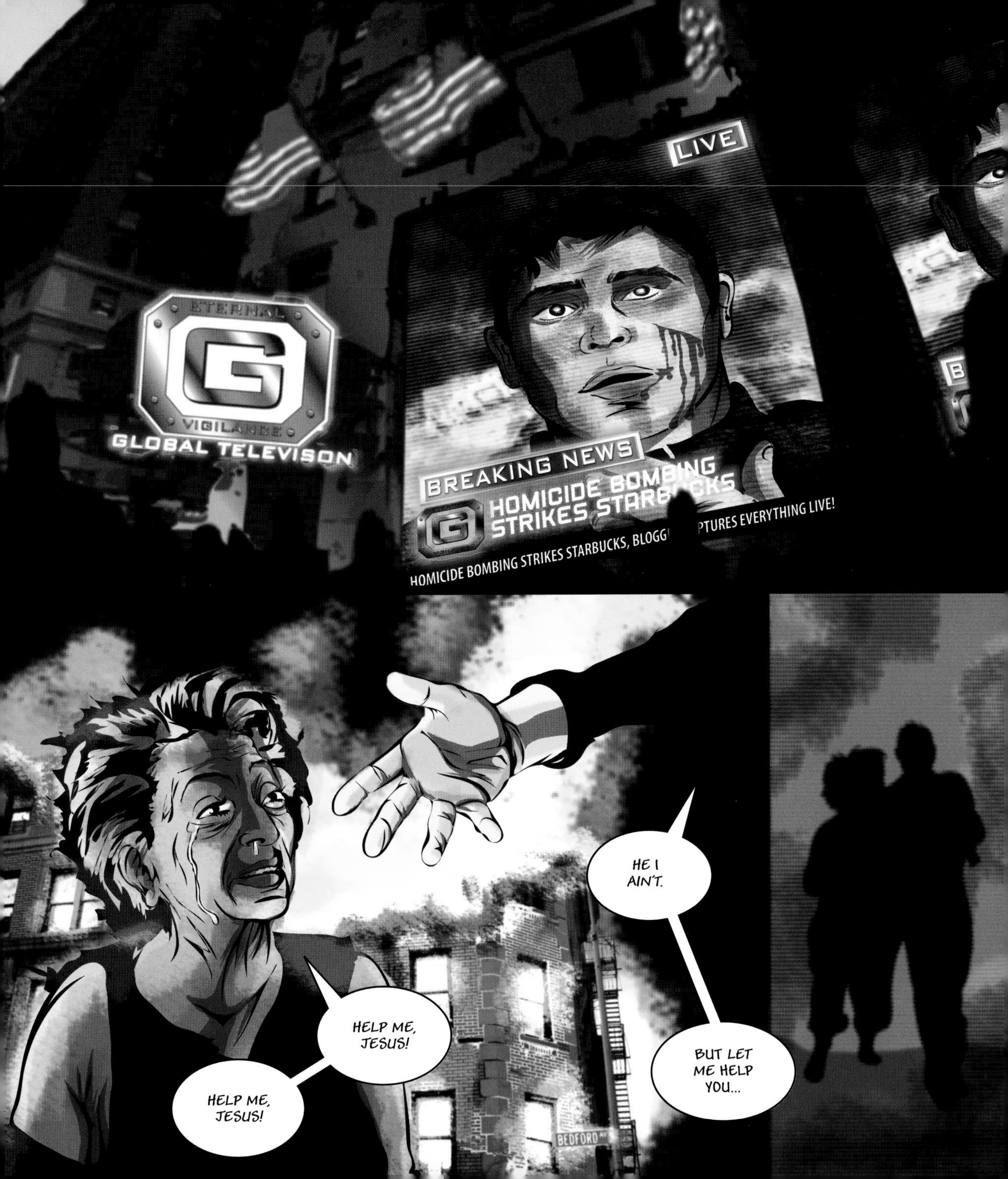
LIVE
ETERNAL
VIGILANCE
GLOBAL TELEVISON
BREAKING NEWS
HOMICIDE BOMBING
STRIKES STARB CKS
HOMICIDE BOMBING STRIKES STARBUCKS, BLOGG PTURES EVERYTHING LIVE!
HELP ME, JESUS!
HELP ME, JESUS!
HE I AIN'T.
BUT LET ME HELP YOU...
BEDFORD AV

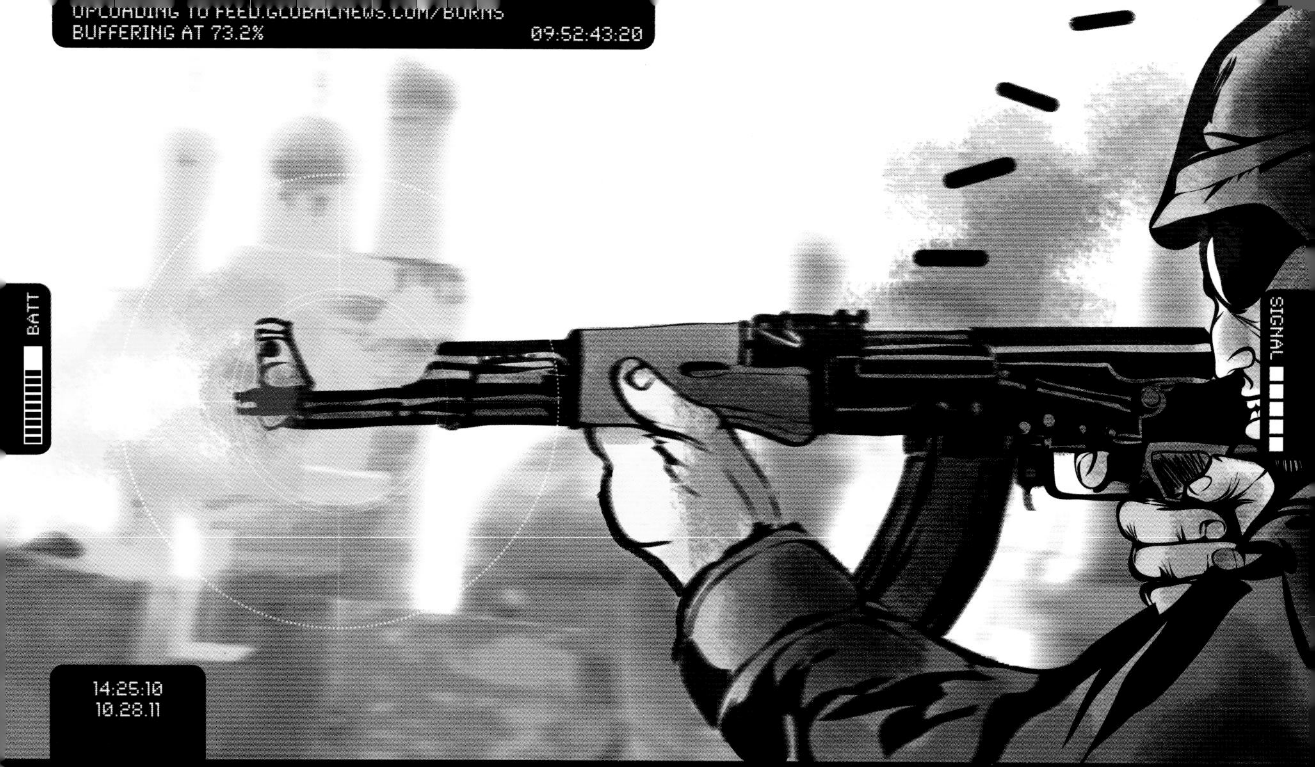
UPLOADING TO FEED.GLOBALNEWS.COM/BURNS
BUFFERING AT 73.2%
09:52:43:20
BATT
SIGNAL
14:25:10
10.28.11

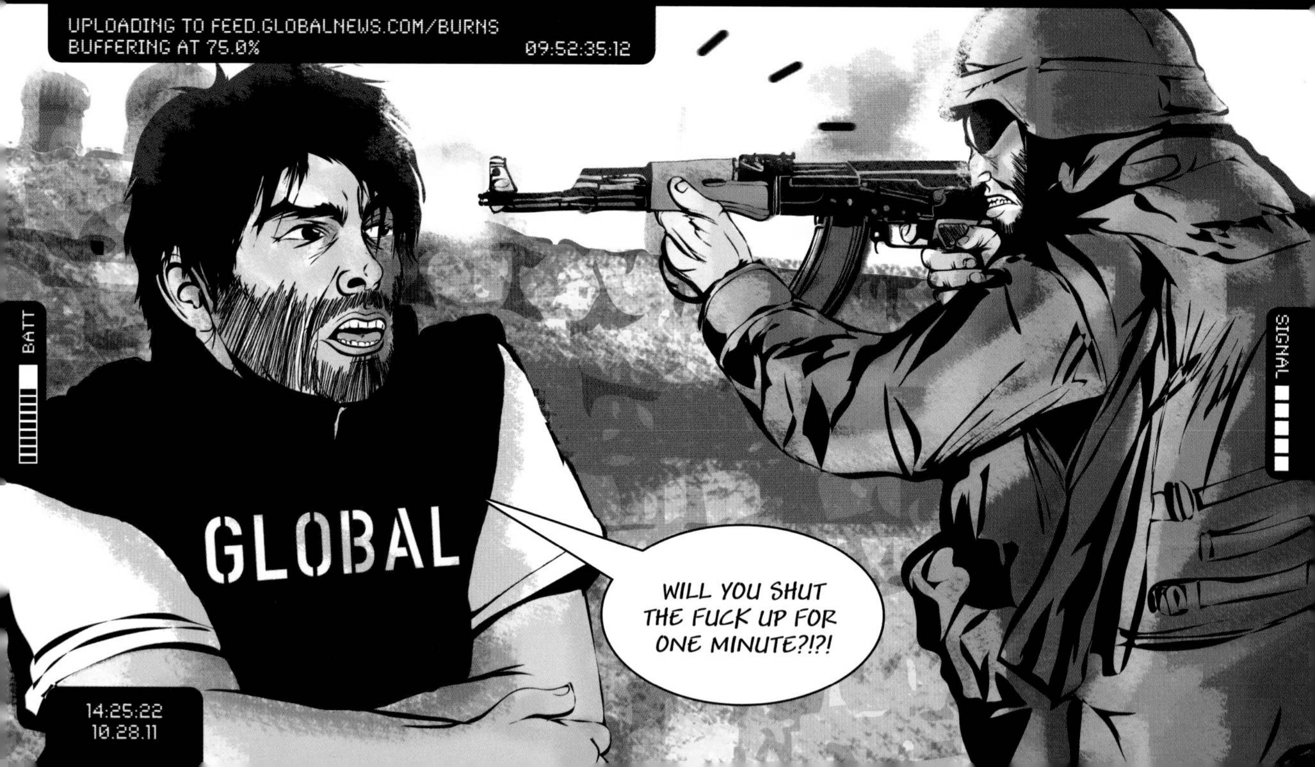
UPLOADING TO FEED.GLOBALNEWS.COM/BURNS
BUFFERING AT 75.0%
09:52:35:12
BATT
SIGNAL
GLOBAL
WILL YOU SHUT THE FUCK UP FOR ONE MINUTE?!?!
14:25:22
10.28.11

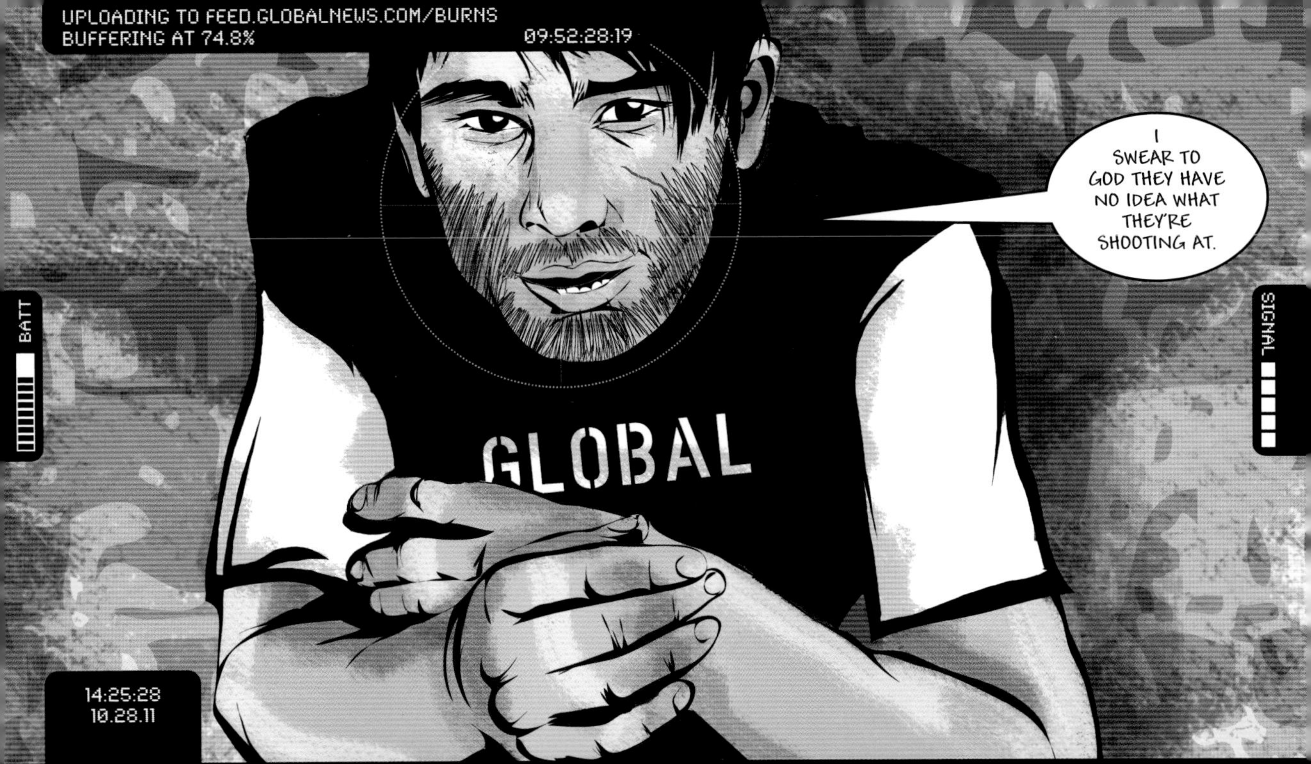
UPLOADING TO FEED.GLOBALNEWS.COM/BURNS
BUFFERING AT 74.8%
09:52:28:19
BATT
SIGNAL
I SWEAR TO GOD THEY HAVE NO IDEA WHAT THEY'RE SHOOTING AT.
GLOBAL
14:25:28
10.28.11

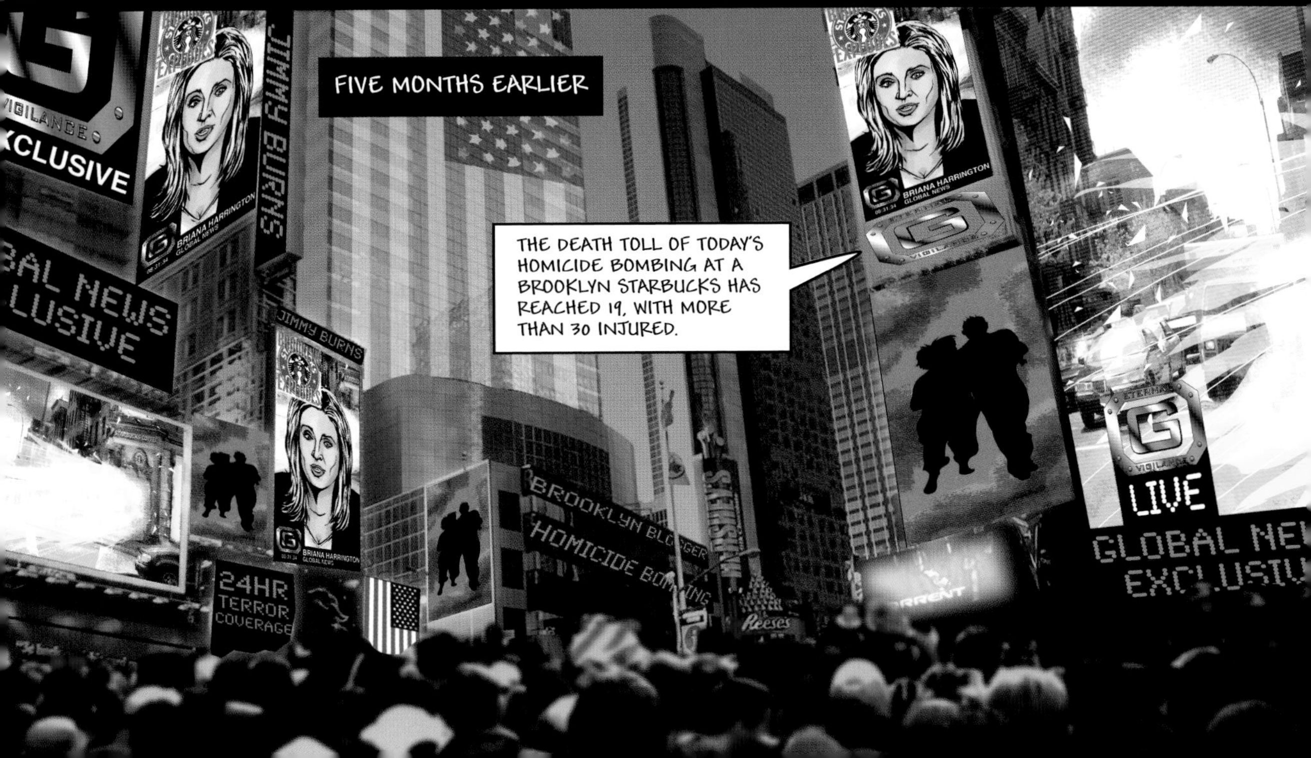
FIVE MONTHS EARLIER
EXCLUSIVE
JIMMY BURNS
BRIANA HARRINGTON
GLOBAL NEWS
THE DEATH TOLL OF TODAY'S HOMICIDE BOMBING AT A BROOKLYN STARBUCKS HAS REACHED 19, WITH MORE THAN 30 INJURED.
BAL NEWS
LUSIVE
BROOKLYN BLOGGER
HOMICIDE BOMBING
24HR
TERROR
COVERAGE
LIVE
GLOBAL NEW
EXCLUSIV

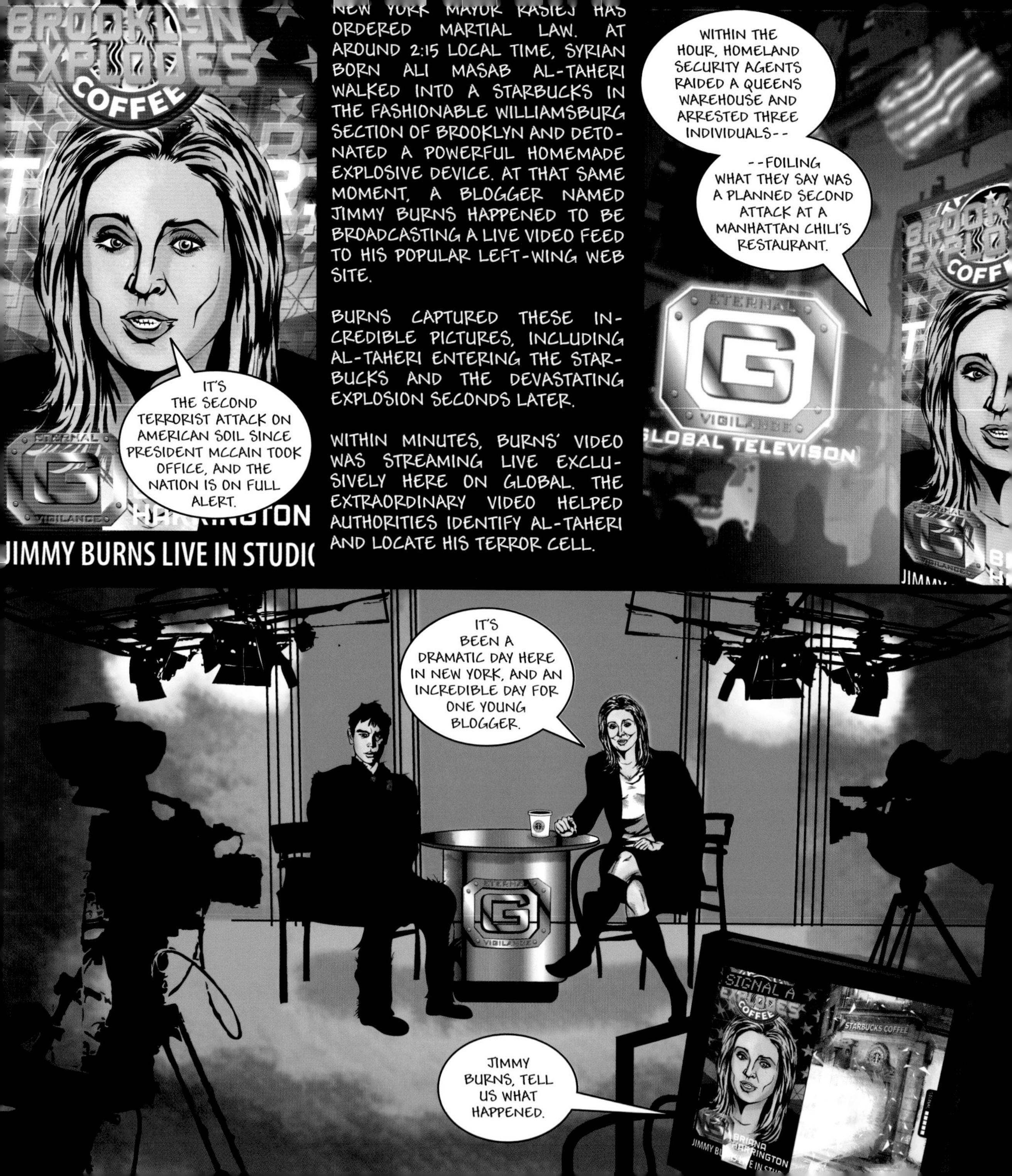
BROOKLYN EXPLODES
COFFEE
IT'S THE SECOND TERRORIST ATTACK ON AMERICAN SOIL SINCE PRESIDENT MCCAIN TOOK OFFICE, AND THE NATION IS ON FULL ALERT.
ETERNAL VIGILANCE
JIMMY BURNS LIVE IN STUDI
NEW YORK MAYOR KASIEJ HAS ORDERED MARTIAL LAW. AT AROUND 2:15 LOCAL TIME, SYRIAN BORN ALI MASAB AL-TAHERI WALKED INTO A STARBUCKS IN THE FASHIONABLE WILLIAMSBURG SECTION OF BROOKLYN AND DETONATED A POWERFUL HOMEMADE EXPLOSIVE DEVICE. AT THAT SAME MOMENT, A BLOGGER NAMED JIMMY BURNS HAPPENED TO BE BROADCASTING A LIVE VIDEO FEED TO HIS POPULAR LEFT-WING WEB SITE.
BURNS CAPTURED THESE INCREDIBLE PICTURES, INCLUDING AL-TAHERI ENTERING THE STARBUCKS AND THE DEVASTATING EXPLOSION SECONDS LATER.
WITHIN MINUTES, BURNS' VIDEO WAS STREAMING LIVE EXCLUSIVELY HERE ON GLOBAL. THE EXTRAORDINARY VIDEO HELPED AUTHORITIES IDENTIFY AL-TAHERI AND LOCATE HIS TERROR CELL.
WITHIN THE HOUR, HOMELAND SECURITY AGENTS RAIDED A QUEENS WAREHOUSE AND ARRESTED THREE INDIVIDUALS--
--FOILING WHAT THEY SAY WAS A PLANNED SECOND ATTACK AT A MANHATTAN CHILI'S RESTAURANT.
ETERNAL VIGILANCE
GLOBAL TELEVISON
IT'S BEEN A DRAMATIC DAY HERE IN NEW YORK, AND AN INCREDIBLE DAY FOR ONE YOUNG BLOGGER.
JIMMY BURNS, TELL US WHAT HAPPENED.
STARBUCKS COFFEE

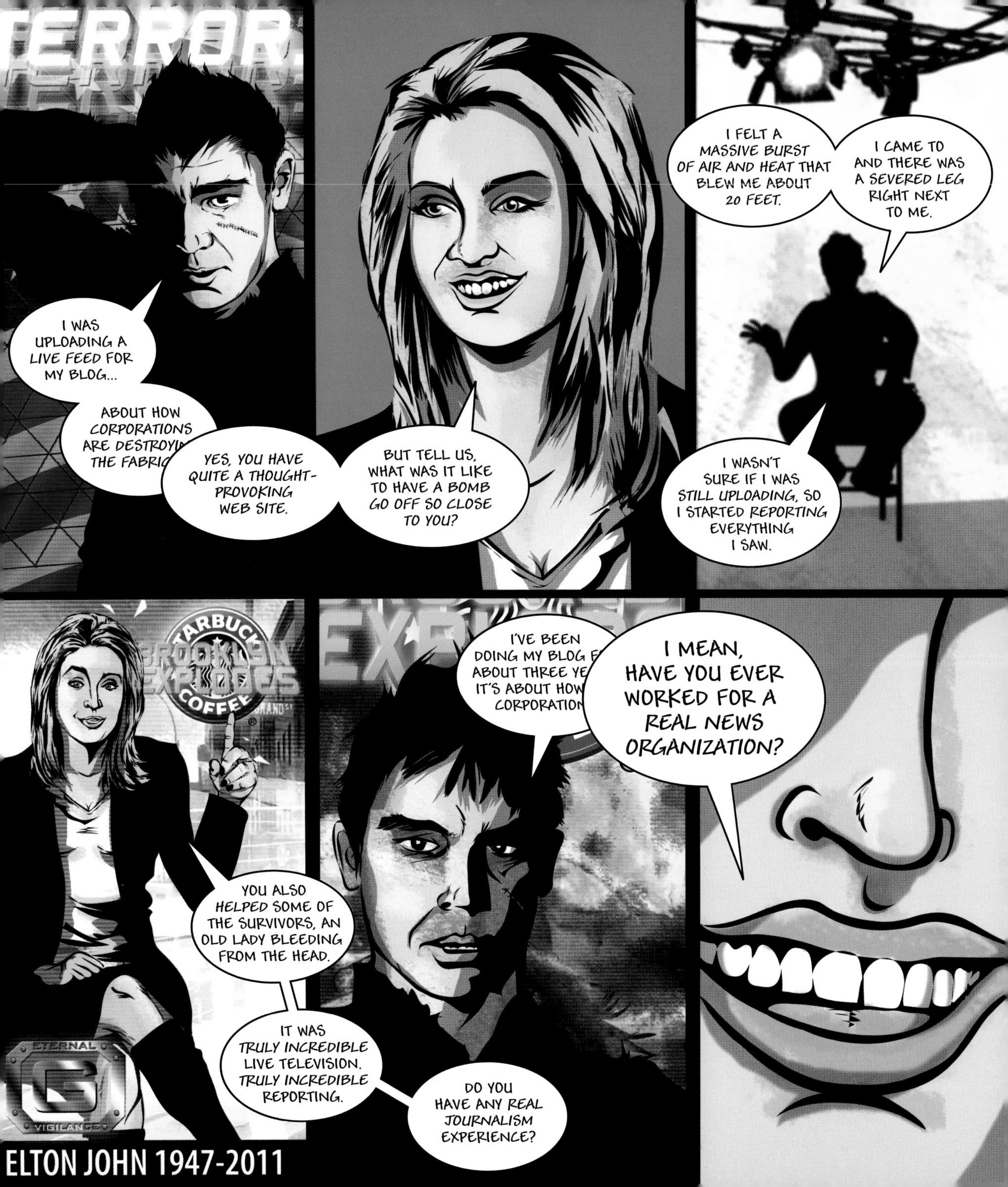
TERROR
I WAS UPLOADING A LIVE FEED FOR MY BLOG...
ABOUT HOW CORPORATIONS ARE DESTROYIN THE FABRIC
YES, YOU HAVE QUITE A THOUGHT-PROVOKING WEB SITE.
BUT TELL US, WHAT WAS IT LIKE TO HAVE A BOMB GO OFF SO CLOSE TO YOU?
I FELT A MASSIVE BURST OF AIR AND HEAT THAT BLEW ME ABOUT 20 FEET.
I CAME TO AND THERE WAS A SEVERED LEG RIGHT NEXT TO ME.
I WASN'T SURE IF I WAS STILL UPLOADING, SO I STARTED REPORTING EVERYTHING I SAW.
STARBUCKS COFFEE
BROOKLYN EXPLODES
YOU ALSO HELPED SOME OF THE SURVIVORS, AN OLD LADY BLEEDING FROM THE HEAD.
IT WAS TRULY INCREDIBLE LIVE TELEVISION. TRULY INCREDIBLE REPORTING.
DO YOU HAVE ANY REAL JOURNALISM EXPERIENCE?
I'VE BEEN DOING MY BLOG F ABOUT THREE YE IT'S ABOUT HOW CORPORATION
I MEAN, HAVE YOU EVER WORKED FOR A REAL NEWS ORGANIZATION?
ETERNAL
VIGILANCE
ELTON JOHN 1947-2011

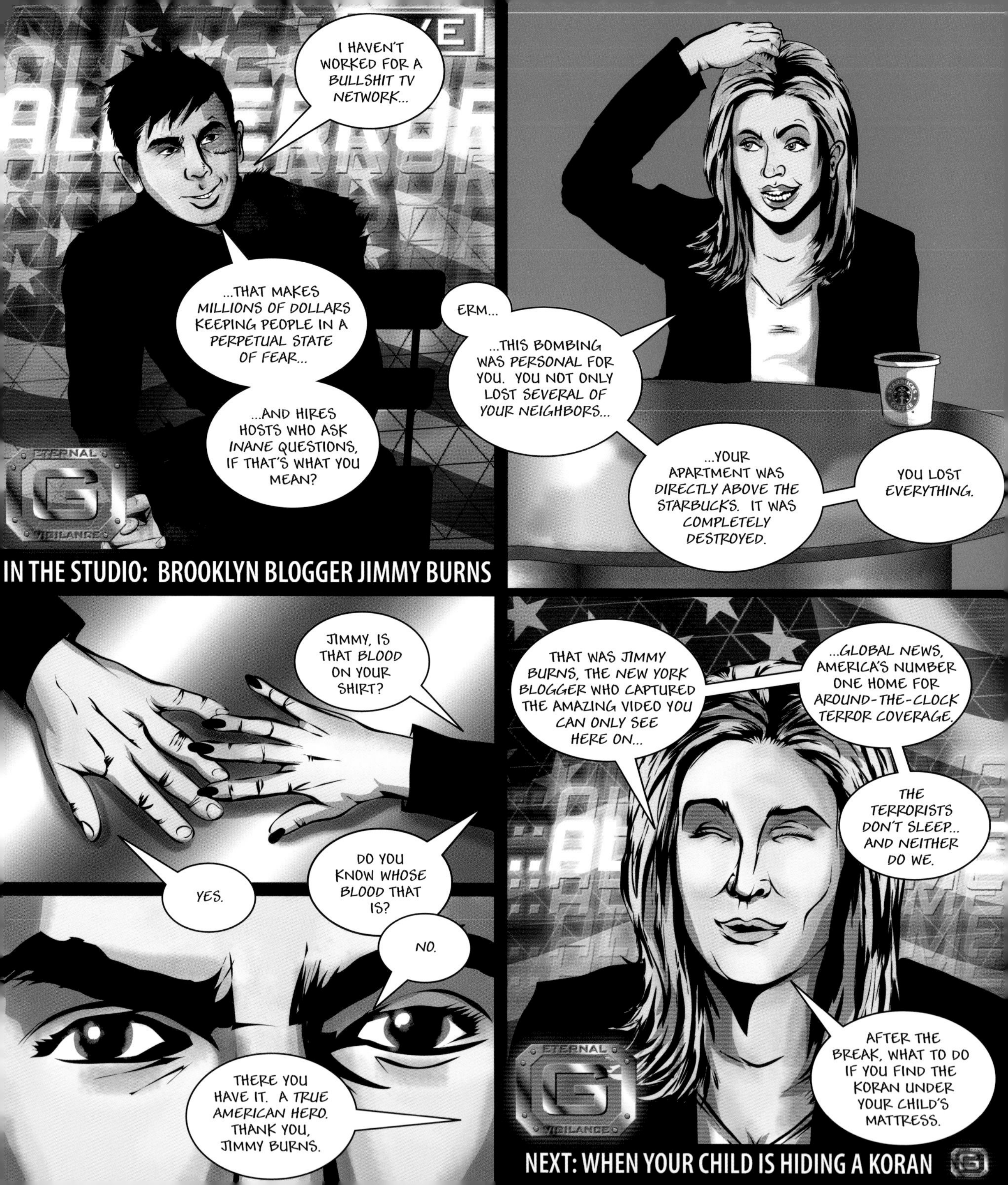
I HAVEN'T WORKED FOR A BULLSHIT TV NETWORK...
...THAT MAKES MILLIONS OF DOLLARS KEEPING PEOPLE IN A PERPETUAL STATE OF FEAR...
...AND HIRES HOSTS WHO ASK INANE QUESTIONS, IF THAT'S WHAT YOU MEAN?
ETERNAL VIGILANCE
IN THE STUDIO: BROOKLYN BLOGGER JIMMY BURNS
ERM...
...THIS BOMBING WAS PERSONAL FOR YOU. YOU NOT ONLY LOST SEVERAL OF YOUR NEIGHBORS...
...YOUR APARTMENT WAS DIRECTLY ABOVE THE STARBUCKS. IT WAS COMPLETELY DESTROYED.
YOU LOST EVERYTHING.
JIMMY, IS THAT BLOOD ON YOUR SHIRT?
YES.
DO YOU KNOW WHOSE BLOOD THAT IS?
NO.
THERE YOU HAVE IT. A TRUE AMERICAN HERO. THANK YOU, JIMMY BURNS.
THAT WAS JIMMY BURNS, THE NEW YORK BLOGGER WHO CAPTURED THE AMAZING VIDEO YOU CAN ONLY SEE HERE ON...
...GLOBAL NEWS, AMERICA'S NUMBER ONE HOME FOR AROUND-THE-CLOCK TERROR COVERAGE.
THE TERRORISTS DON'T SLEEP... AND NEITHER DO WE.
AFTER THE BREAK, WHAT TO DO IF YOU FIND THE KORAN UNDER YOUR CHILD'S MATTRESS.
ETERNAL VIGILANCE
NEXT: WHEN YOUR CHILD IS HIDING A KORAN

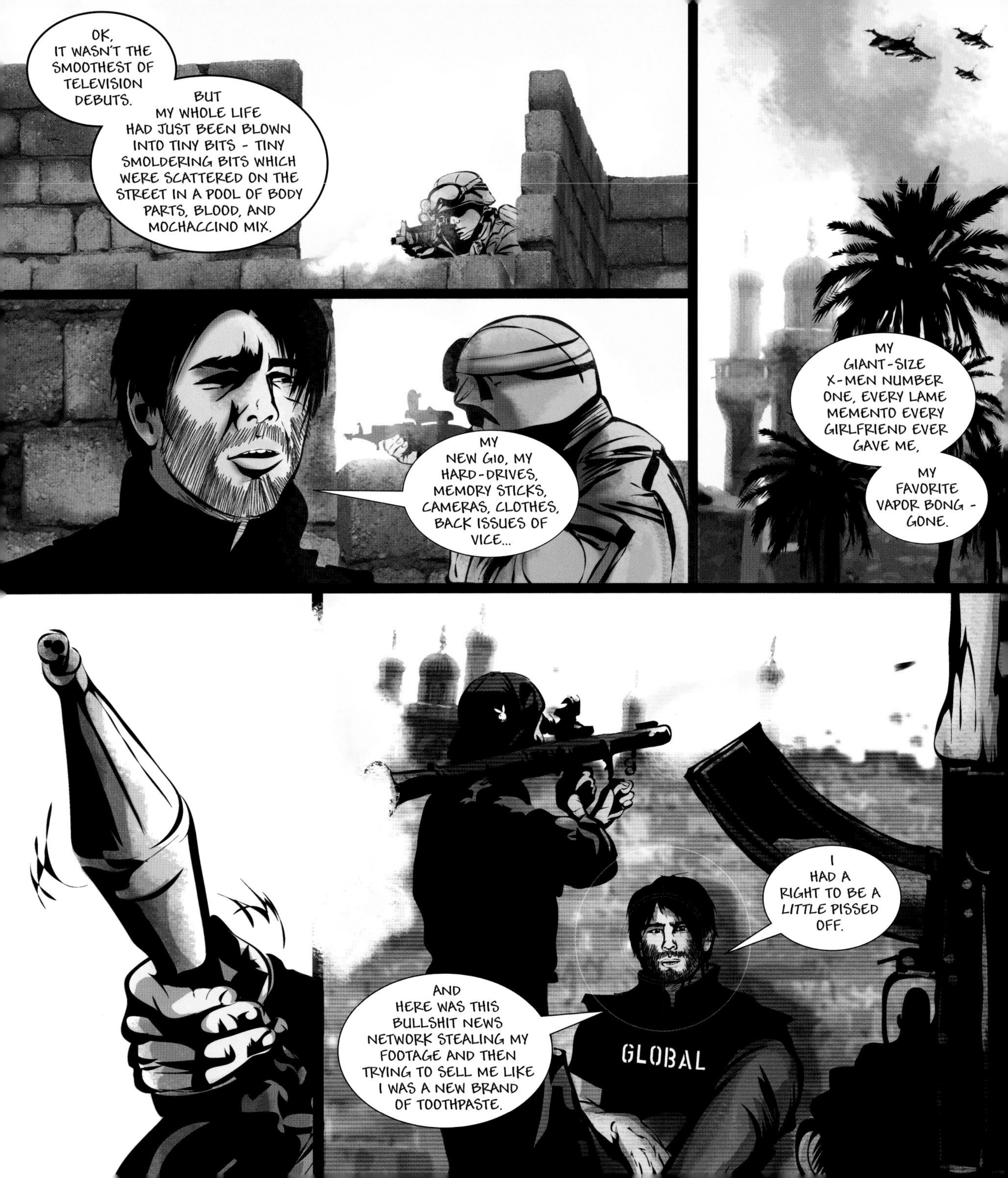
OK, IT WASN'T THE SMOOTHEST OF TELEVISION DEBUTS.
BUT MY WHOLE LIFE HAD JUST BEEN BLOWN INTO TINY BITS - TINY SMOLDERING BITS WHICH WERE SCATTERED ON THE STREET IN A POOL OF BODY PARTS, BLOOD, AND MOCHACCINO MIX.
MY NEW G10, MY HARD-DRIVES, MEMORY STICKS, CAMERAS, CLOTHES, BACK ISSUES OF VICE...
MY GIANT-SIZE X-MEN NUMBER ONE, EVERY LAME MEMENTO EVERY GIRLFRIEND EVER GAVE ME,
MY FAVORITE VAPOR BONG - GONE.
I HAD A RIGHT TO BE A LITTLE PISSED OFF.
AND HERE WAS THIS BULLSHIT NEWS NETWORK STEALING MY FOOTAGE AND THEN TRYING TO SELL ME LIKE I WAS A NEW BRAND OF TOOTHPASTE.
GLOBAL

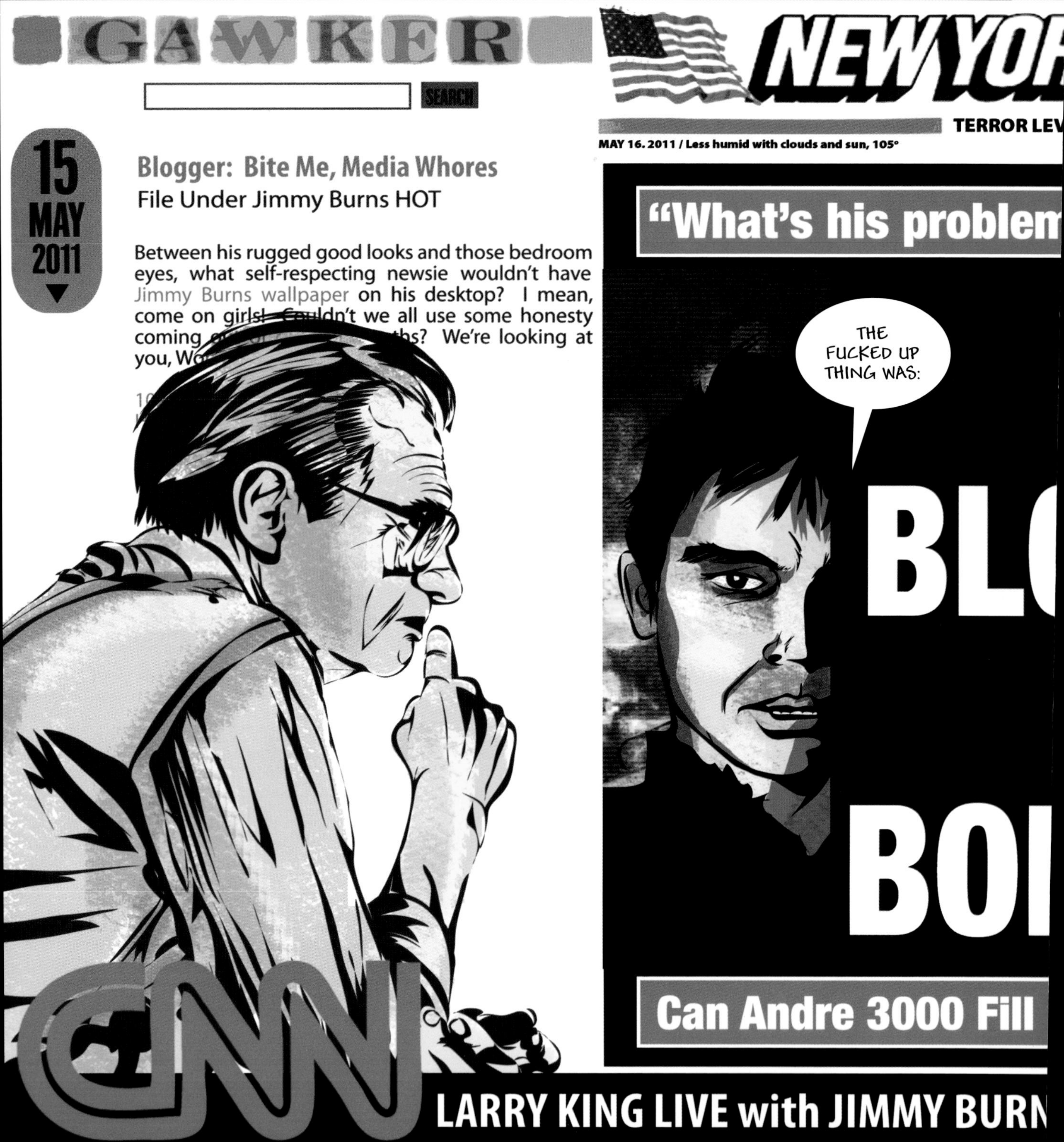
GAWKER
SEARCH
15 MAY 2011
Blogger: Bite Me, Media Whores
File Under Jimmy Burns HOT
Between his rugged good looks and those bedroom eyes, what self-respecting newsie wouldn't have Jimmy Burns wallpaper on his desktop? I mean, come on girls! Couldn't we all use some honesty coming
ths? We're looking at you, Wo
NEW YOR
TERROR LEV
MAY 16. 2011 / Less humid with clouds and sun, 105°
"What's his problem
THE FUCKED UP THING WAS:
BL
BO
Can Andre 3000 Fill
CNN
LARRY KING LIVE with JIMMY BURN

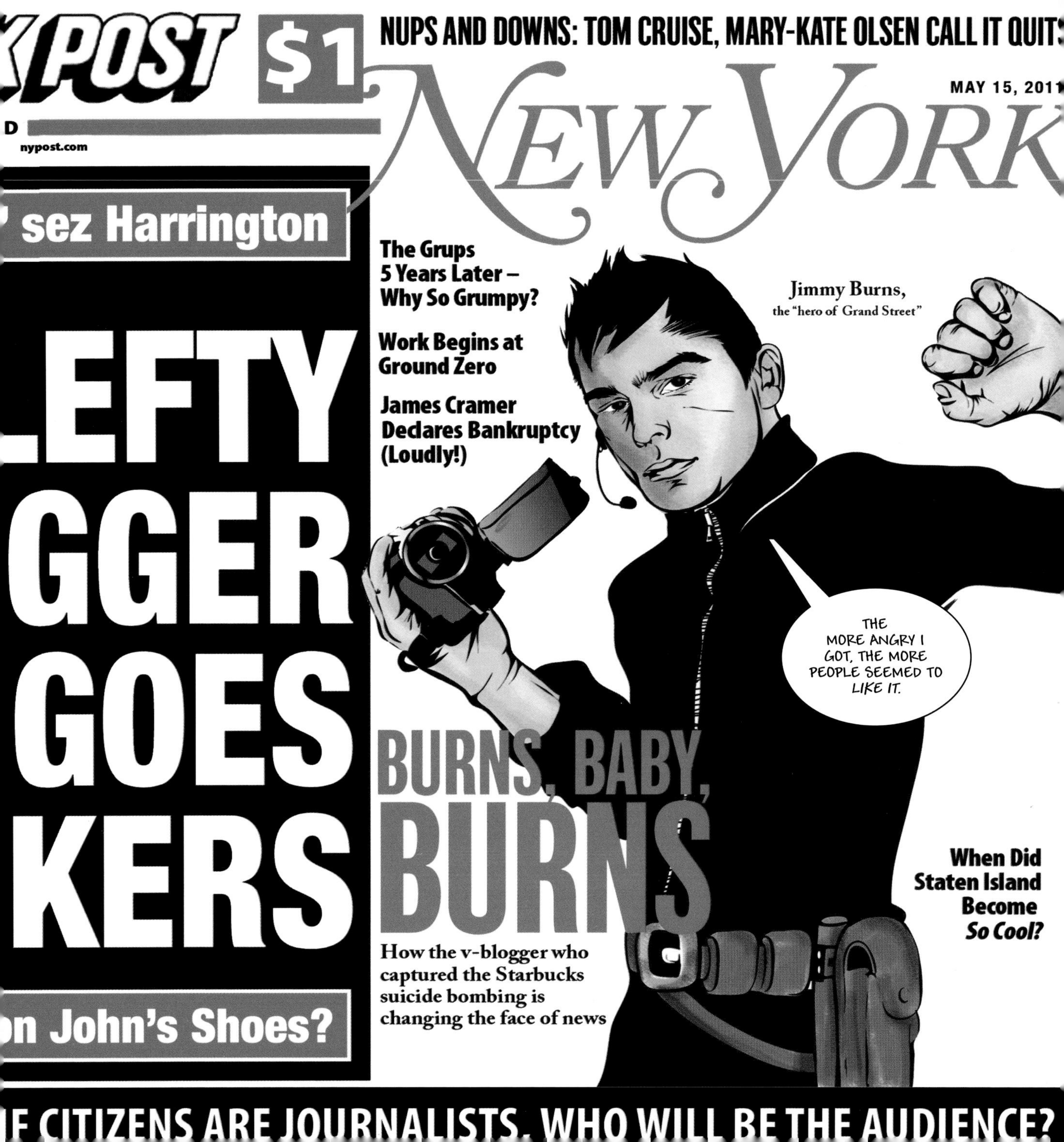

POST
$1
D
nypost.com
sez Harrington
LEFTY
GGER
GOES
KERS
n John's Shoes?
NUPS AND DOWNS: TOM CRUISE, MARY-KATE OLSEN CALL IT QUIT
MAY 15, 2011
NEW YORK
The Grups 5 Years Later – Why So Grumpy?
Work Begins at Ground Zero
James Cramer Declares Bankruptcy (Loudly!)
Jimmy Burns,
the "hero of Grand Street"
THE MORE ANGRY I GOT, THE MORE PEOPLE SEEMED TO LIKE IT.
BURNS, BABY, BURNS
How the v-blogger who captured the Starbucks suicide bombing is changing the face of news
When Did Staten Island Become So Cool?
IF CITIZENS ARE JOURNALISTS, WHO WILL BE THE AUDIENCE?

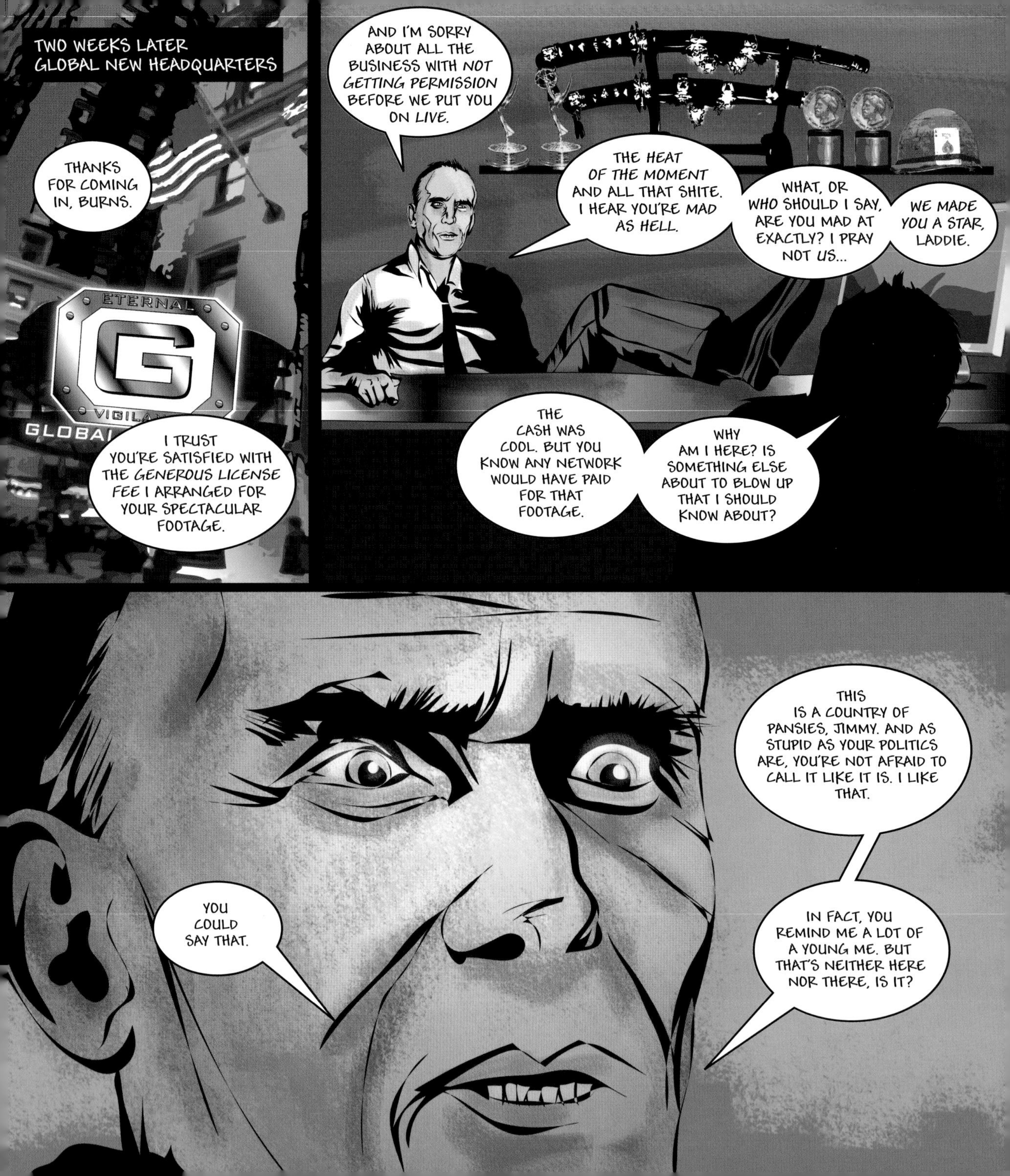
TWO WEEKS LATER
GLOBAL NEW HEADQUARTERS
THANKS FOR COMING IN, BURNS.
ETERNAL
VIGILAN
GLOBAL
I TRUST YOU'RE SATISFIED WITH THE GENEROUS LICENSE FEE I ARRANGED FOR YOUR SPECTACULAR FOOTAGE.
AND I'M SORRY ABOUT ALL THE BUSINESS WITH NOT GETTING PERMISSION BEFORE WE PUT YOU ON LIVE.
THE HEAT OF THE MOMENT AND ALL THAT SHITE. I HEAR YOU'RE MAD AS HELL.
WHAT, OR WHO SHOULD I SAY, ARE YOU MAD AT EXACTLY? I PRAY NOT US...
WE MADE YOU A STAR, LADDIE.
THE CASH WAS COOL. BUT YOU KNOW ANY NETWORK WOULD HAVE PAID FOR THAT FOOTAGE.
WHY AM I HERE? IS SOMETHING ELSE ABOUT TO BLOW UP THAT I SHOULD KNOW ABOUT?
THIS IS A COUNTRY OF PANSIES, JIMMY. AND AS STUPID AS YOUR POLITICS ARE, YOU'RE NOT AFRAID TO CALL IT LIKE IT IS. I LIKE THAT.
YOU COULD SAY THAT.
IN FACT, YOU REMIND ME A LOT OF A YOUNG ME. BUT THAT'S NEITHER HERE NOR THERE, IS IT?

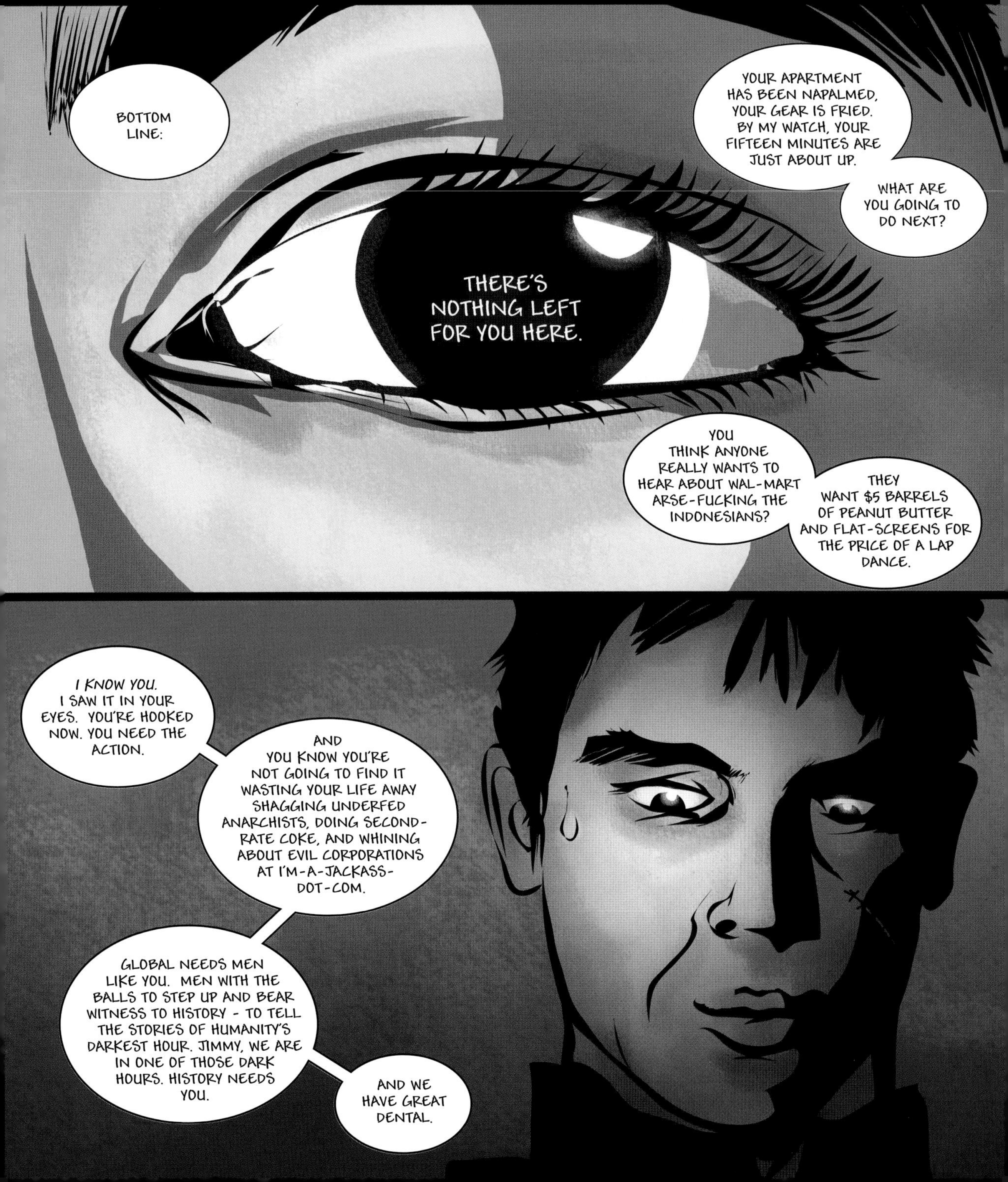
BOTTOM LINE:
YOUR APARTMENT HAS BEEN NAPALMED, YOUR GEAR IS FRIED. BY MY WATCH, YOUR FIFTEEN MINUTES ARE JUST ABOUT UP.
WHAT ARE YOU GOING TO DO NEXT?
THERE'S NOTHING LEFT FOR YOU HERE.
YOU THINK ANYONE REALLY WANTS TO HEAR ABOUT WAL-MART ARSE-FUCKING THE INDONESIANS?
THEY WANT $5 BARRELS OF PEANUT BUTTER AND FLAT-SCREENS FOR THE PRICE OF A LAP DANCE.
I KNOW YOU. I SAW IT IN YOUR EYES. YOU'RE HOOKED NOW. YOU NEED THE ACTION.
AND YOU KNOW YOU'RE NOT GOING TO FIND IT WASTING YOUR LIFE AWAY SHAGGING UNDERFED ANARCHISTS, DOING SECOND-RATE COKE, AND WHINING ABOUT EVIL CORPORATIONS AT I'M-A-JACKASS-DOT-COM.
GLOBAL NEEDS MEN LIKE YOU. MEN WITH THE BALLS TO STEP UP AND BEAR WITNESS TO HISTORY - TO TELL THE STORIES OF HUMANITY'S DARKEST HOUR. JIMMY, WE ARE IN ONE OF THOSE DARK HOURS. HISTORY NEEDS YOU.
AND WE HAVE GREAT DENTAL.

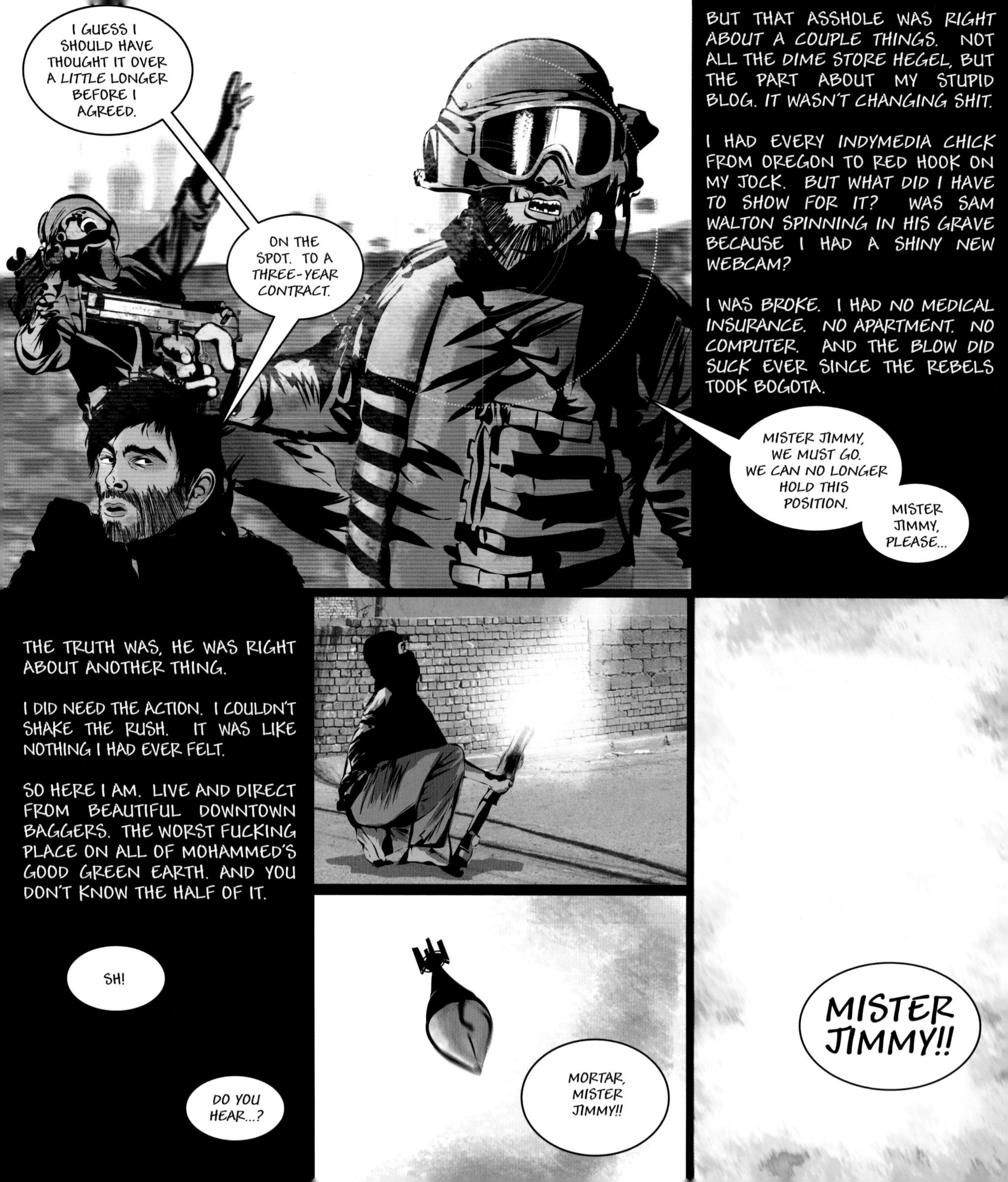

I GUESS I SHOULD HAVE THOUGHT IT OVER A LITTLE LONGER BEFORE I AGREED.
ON THE SPOT. TO A THREE-YEAR CONTRACT.
BUT THAT ASSHOLE WAS RIGHT ABOUT A COUPLE THINGS. NOT ALL THE DIME STORE HEGEL, BUT THE PART ABOUT MY STUPID BLOG. IT WASN'T CHANGING SHIT.
I HAD EVERY INDYMEDIA CHICK FROM OREGON TO RED HOOK ON MY JOCK. BUT WHAT DID I HAVE TO SHOW FOR IT? WAS SAM WALTON SPINNING IN HIS GRAVE BECAUSE I HAD A SHINY NEW WEBCAM?
I WAS BROKE. I HAD NO MEDICAL INSURANCE. NO APARTMENT. NO COMPUTER. AND THE BLOW DID SUCK EVER SINCE THE REBELS TOOK BOGOTA.
MISTER JIMMY, WE MUST GO. WE CAN NO LONGER HOLD THIS POSITION.
MISTER JIMMY, PLEASE...
THE TRUTH WAS, HE WAS RIGHT ABOUT ANOTHER THING.
I DID NEED THE ACTION. I COULDN'T SHAKE THE RUSH. IT WAS LIKE NOTHING I HAD EVER FELT.
SO HERE I AM. LIVE AND DIRECT FROM BEAUTIFUL DOWNTOWN BAGGERS. THE WORST FUCKING PLACE ON ALL OF MOHAMMED'S GOOD GREEN EARTH. AND YOU DON'T KNOW THE HALF OF IT.
SH!
DO YOU HEAR...?
MORTAR, MISTER JIMMY!!
MISTER JIMMY!!

http://burnbabyburn.com

Google Images

LATEST: THAMES BARRIER BREAKS, LONDON FLOODS...GLOBAL WARMING BLAMED

JIMMY BURNS

Jimmy is currently on assignment for the *GLOBAL NEWS* network as embedded vlog correspondent in Baghdad.

Live sat-cam feed here: *feed.globalnews.com/burns*

VLOG ARCHIVE:

Corporate Takeover of America series:

Part 19: Eminent Domain Disasters

Part 18: Your DNA, Their $

Part 17: ChoicePoint: They're back

INTO THE BELLY OF THE BEAST

I picked a brilliant time to head into the belly of the beast. Back home, the oil crisis is just hitting its crescendo. After the U.S. and Israel hit Iran's nuke plants, the mullahs teamed up with the Islamic junta in Nigeria and Chavez in Venezuela to cut off oil to the West. The Saudis' oil facilities were under near daily attack. Gas hit $8 a gallon and the U.S. economy spiraled into recession.

Everyone, left, right, and middle, is screaming to get out of Iraq. But McCain appears trapped. The "enduring bases" were built to *endure*. Too much blood has been spilt to give it all away now, the hawks sqawked like tone-deaf parrots.

The oil fields in the north are still under the control of our last friends east of Jericho — the Kurds. But the rest of the country is beyond Thunderdome.

In '09, a desperate McCain disbanded the Interior Ministry and purged the army of Shia extremists. The army was reconstituted with our old allies, the Baathists, whose leadership in the insurgency had been overtaken by foreign jihadists.

It was a bold move. There weren't many "secular nationalists," as McCain liked to call them, left — alive. The 10,000 American troops still in country are the most battle-hardened, ruthless mothers the Pentagon could muster. But even with the gloves off, they can't stem the bloodletting.

In Baghdad, a DMZ barely puts a dent in the ethnic cleansing of the city's last mixed 'hoods. In the western badlands, Al Qaeda and its competitors battle for supremacy.

ALLIES LINKS

Guerrilla News Network

TalkingPoints Memo

Information Clearing House

Crooks and Liars

Sploid

Huffington Post

Gawker

Metafilter

Antiwar

Truthout

War in Context

DailyKos

Treehugger

Show Me the War

Iraq & Afghanistan Veterans of America

ACT-I-VATE

Antiwar

Wonkette

Guardian

The Nation

Doc Searls

Village Voice

AlterNet

Entertainment Weekly

Independent Propaganda

Rolling Stone

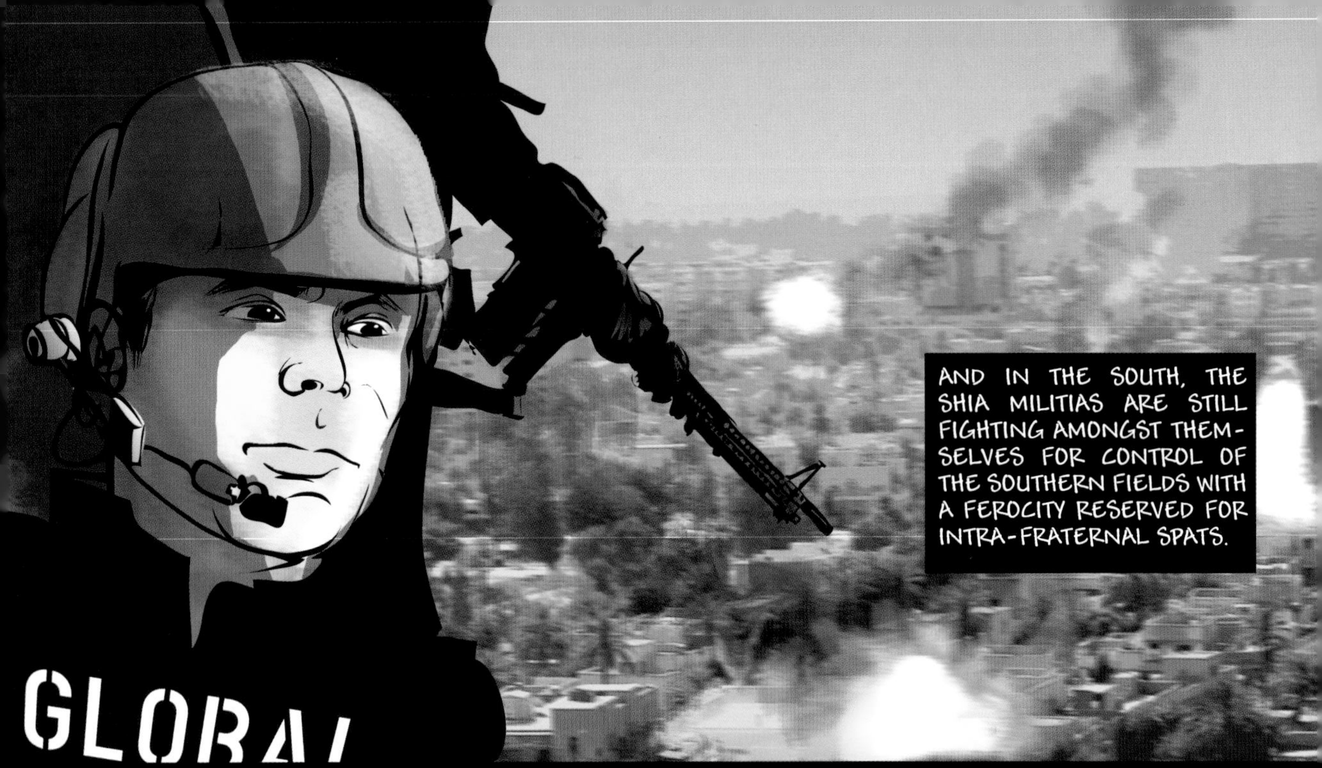
GLOBAL
AND IN THE SOUTH, THE SHIA MILITIAS ARE STILL FIGHTING AMONGST THEMSELVES FOR CONTROL OF THE SOUTHERN FIELDS WITH A FEROCITY RESERVED FOR INTRA-FRATERNAL SPATS.

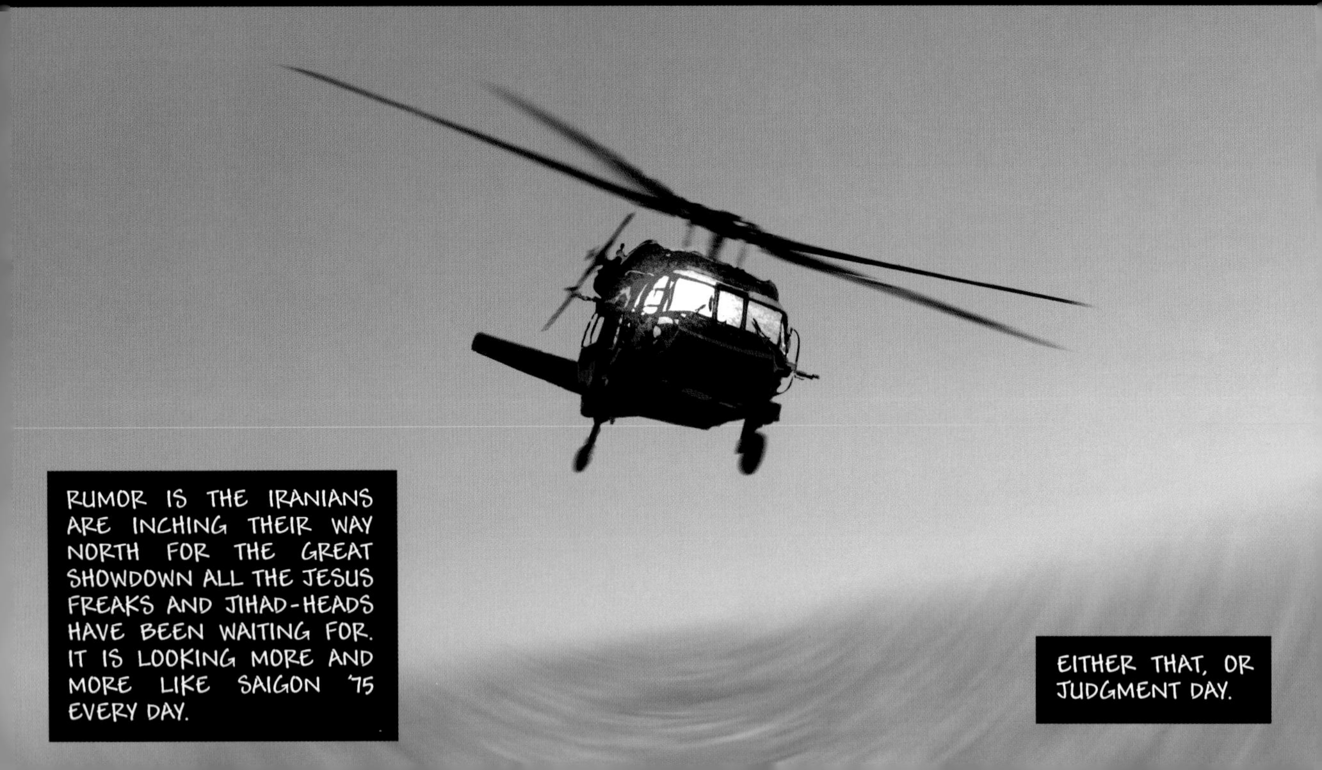
RUMOR IS THE IRANIANS ARE INCHING THEIR WAY NORTH FOR THE GREAT SHOWDOWN ALL THE JESUS FREAKS AND JIHAD-HEADS HAVE BEEN WAITING FOR. IT IS LOOKING MORE AND MORE LIKE SAIGON '75 EVERY DAY.
EITHER THAT, OR JUDGMENT DAY.

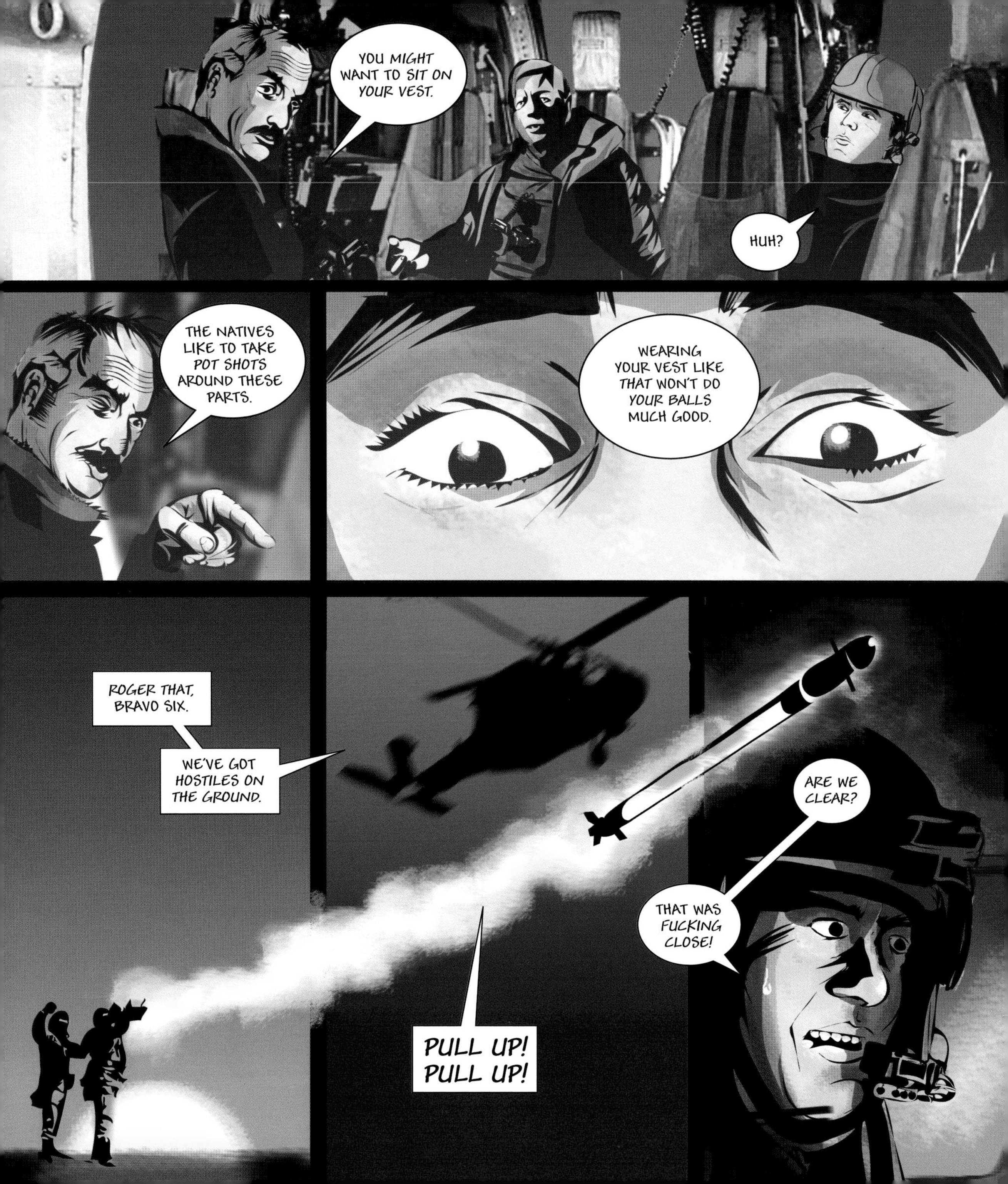
YOU MIGHT WANT TO SIT ON YOUR VEST.
HUH?
THE NATIVES LIKE TO TAKE POT SHOTS AROUND THESE PARTS.
WEARING YOUR VEST LIKE THAT WON'T DO YOUR BALLS MUCH GOOD.
ROGER THAT, BRAVO SIX.
WE'VE GOT HOSTILES ON THE GROUND.
PULL UP! PULL UP!
ARE WE CLEAR?
THAT WAS FUCKING CLOSE!

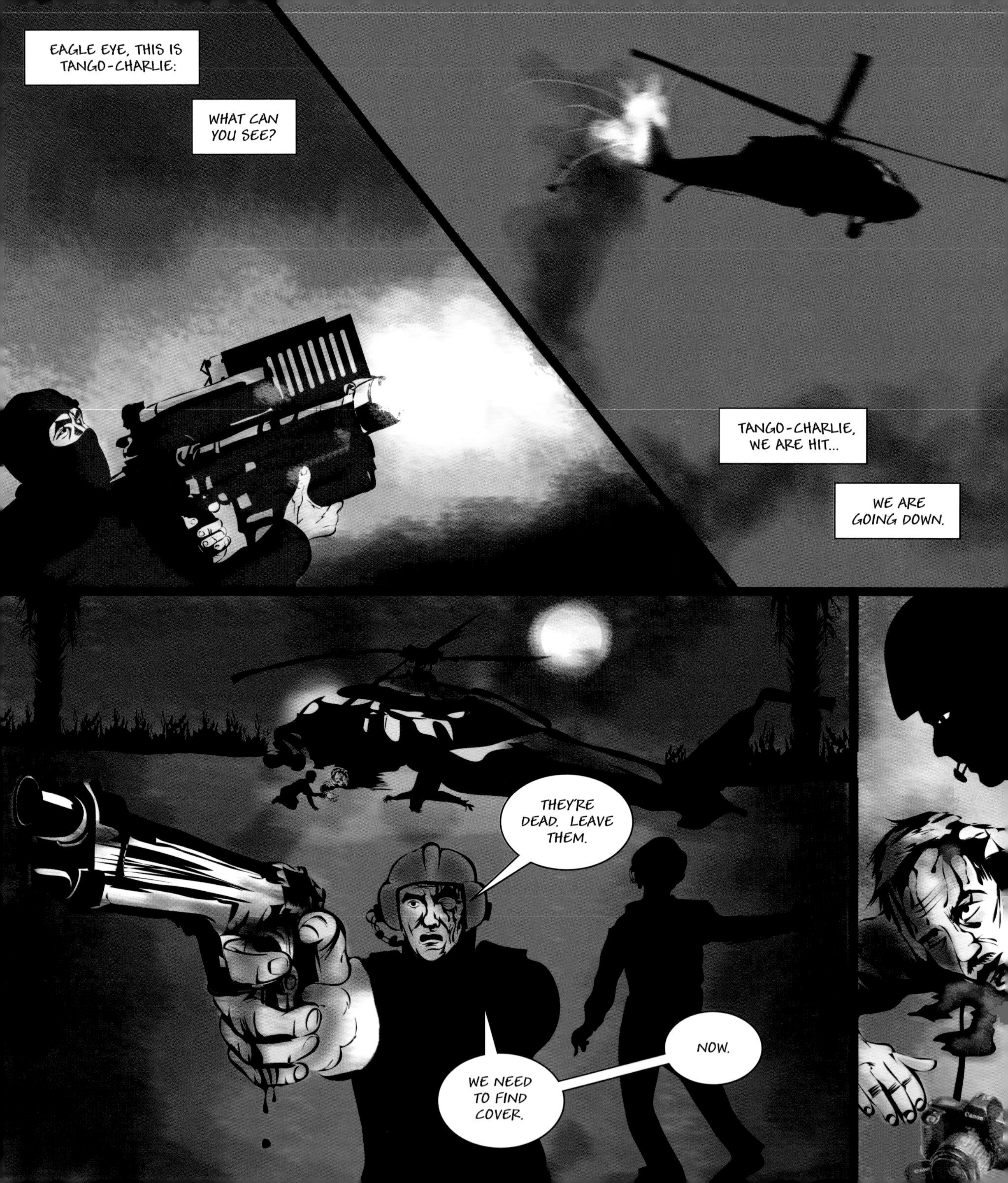
EAGLE EYE, THIS IS TANGO-CHARLIE:
WHAT CAN YOU SEE?
TANGO-CHARLIE, WE ARE HIT...
WE ARE GOING DOWN.
THEY'RE DEAD. LEAVE THEM.
WE NEED TO FIND COVER.
NOW.

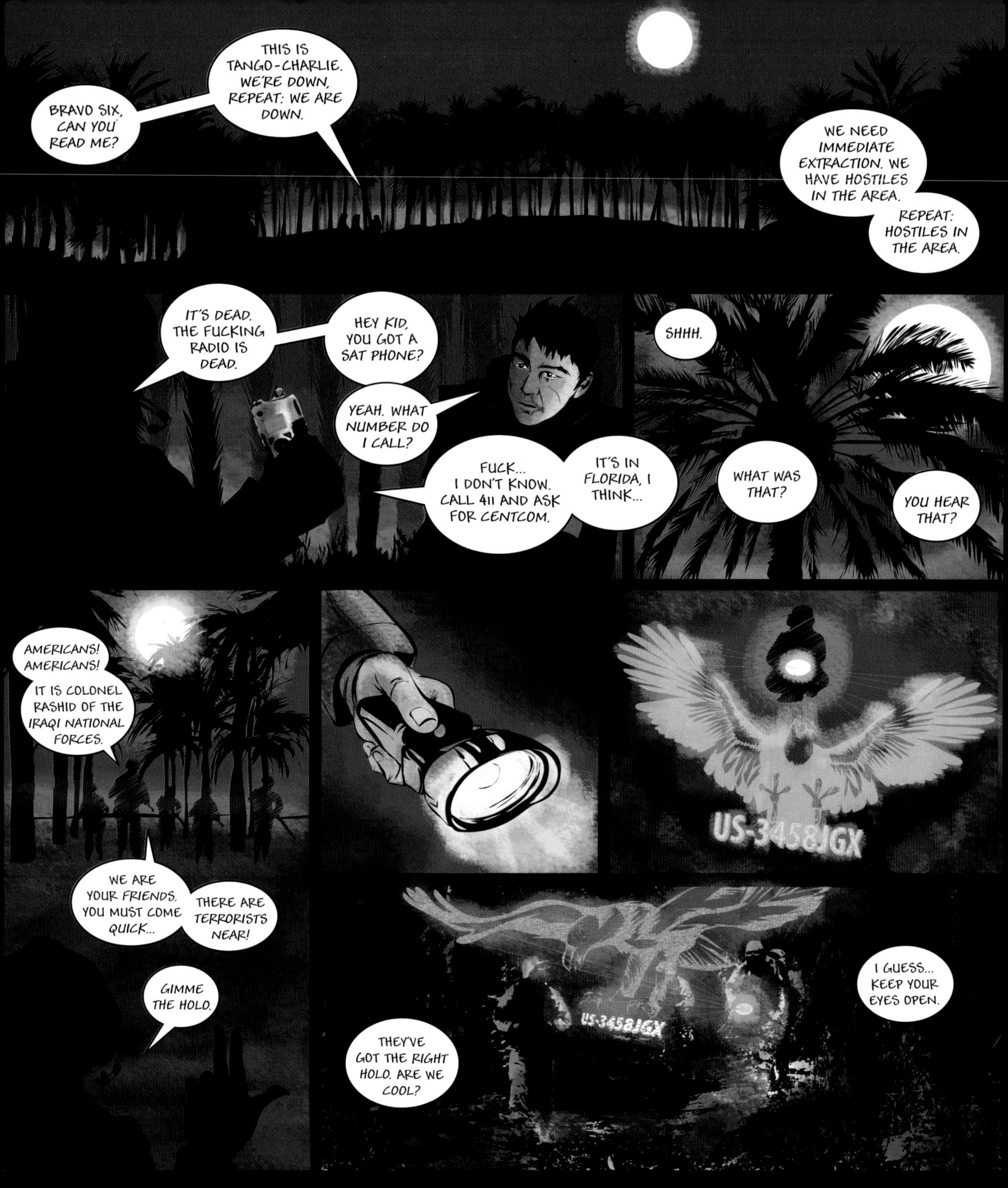
BRAVO SIX, CAN YOU READ ME?
THIS IS TANGO-CHARLIE. WE'RE DOWN, REPEAT: WE ARE DOWN.
WE NEED IMMEDIATE EXTRACTION. WE HAVE HOSTILES IN THE AREA.
REPEAT: HOSTILES IN THE AREA.
IT'S DEAD. THE FUCKING RADIO IS DEAD.
HEY KID, YOU GOT A SAT PHONE?
YEAH. WHAT NUMBER DO I CALL?
FUCK... I DON'T KNOW. CALL 411 AND ASK FOR CENTCOM.
IT'S IN FLORIDA, I THINK...
SHHH.
WHAT WAS THAT?
YOU HEAR THAT?
AMERICANS! AMERICANS!
IT IS COLONEL RASHID OF THE IRAQI NATIONAL FORCES.
WE ARE YOUR FRIENDS. YOU MUST COME QUICK...
THERE ARE TERRORISTS NEAR!
GIMME THE HOLO.
US-3458JGX
US-3458JGX
THEY'VE GOT THE RIGHT HOLO. ARE WE COOL?
I GUESS... KEEP YOUR EYES OPEN.

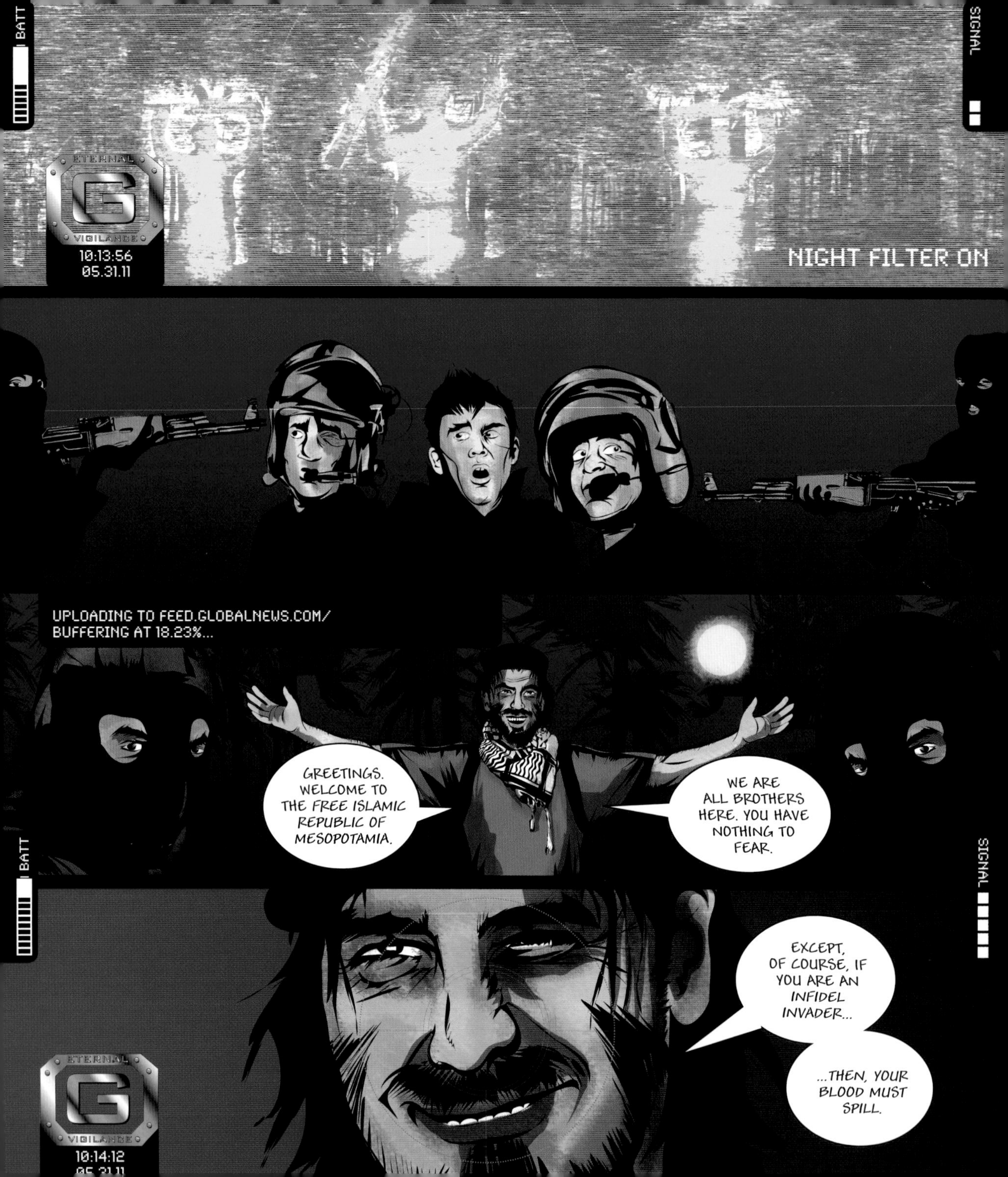
BATT
SIGNAL
ETERNAL
G
VIGILANCE
10:13:56
05.31.11
NIGHT FILTER ON
UPLOADING TO FEED.GLOBALNEWS.COM/
BUFFERING AT 18.23%...
GREETINGS. WELCOME TO THE FREE ISLAMIC REPUBLIC OF MESOPOTAMIA.
WE ARE ALL BROTHERS HERE. YOU HAVE NOTHING TO FEAR.
BATT
SIGNAL
EXCEPT, OF COURSE, IF YOU ARE AN INFIDEL INVADER...
...THEN, YOUR BLOOD MUST SPILL.
ETERNAL
G
VIGILANCE
10:14:12

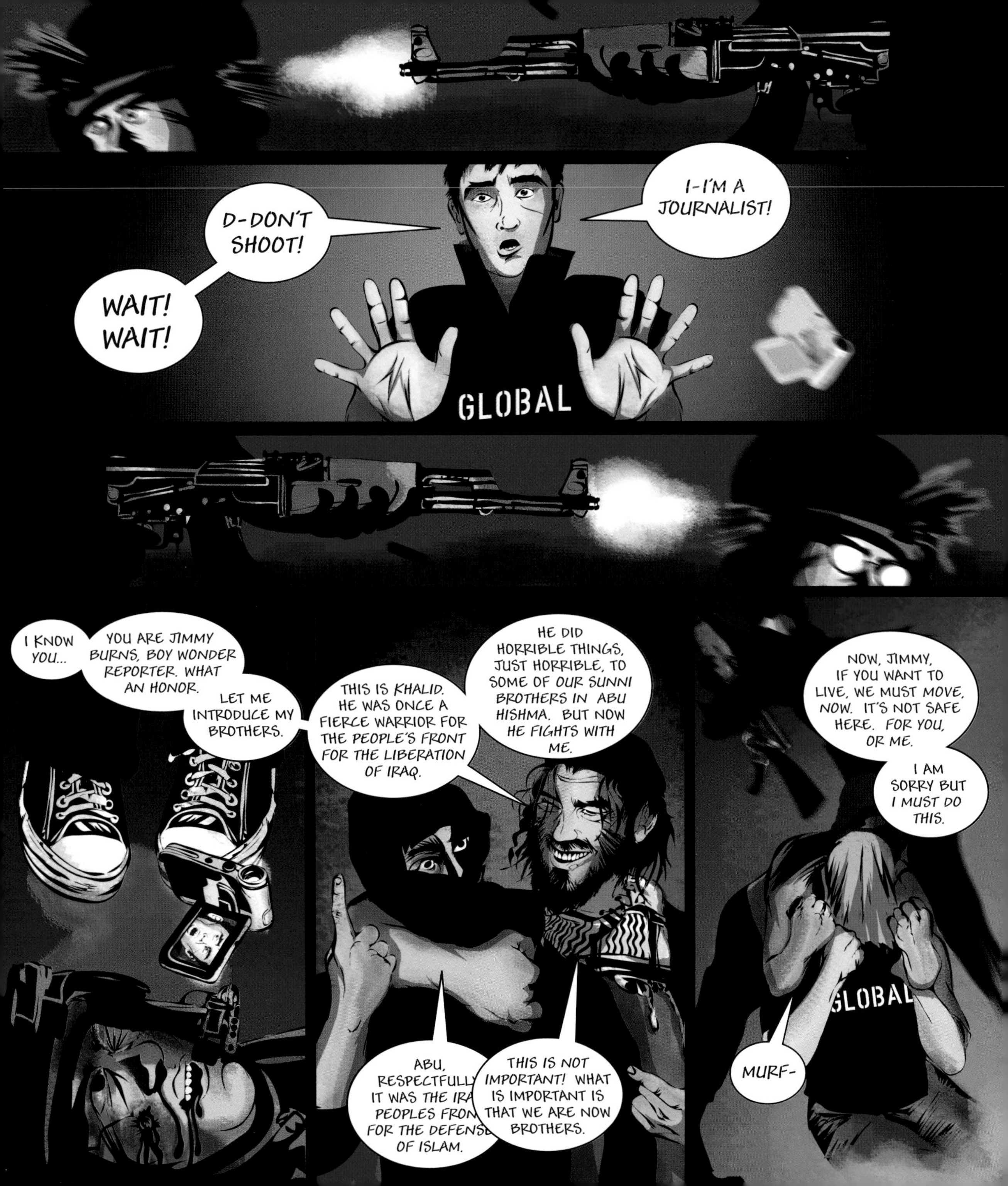
D-DON'T SHOOT!
I-I'M A JOURNALIST!
WAIT! WAIT!
GLOBAL
I KNOW YOU...
YOU ARE JIMMY BURNS, BOY WONDER REPORTER. WHAT AN HONOR.
LET ME INTRODUCE MY BROTHERS.
THIS IS KHALID. HE WAS ONCE A FIERCE WARRIOR FOR THE PEOPLE'S FRONT FOR THE LIBERATION OF IRAQ.
HE DID HORRIBLE THINGS, JUST HORRIBLE, TO SOME OF OUR SUNNI BROTHERS IN ABU HISHMA. BUT NOW HE FIGHTS WITH ME.
ABU, RESPECTFULLY IT WAS THE IRA PEOPLES FRON FOR THE DEFENSE OF ISLAM.
THIS IS NOT IMPORTANT! WHAT IS IMPORTANT IS THAT WE ARE NOW BROTHERS.
NOW, JIMMY, IF YOU WANT TO LIVE, WE MUST MOVE, NOW. IT'S NOT SAFE HERE. FOR YOU, OR ME.
I AM SORRY BUT I MUST DO THIS.
GLOBAL
MURF-

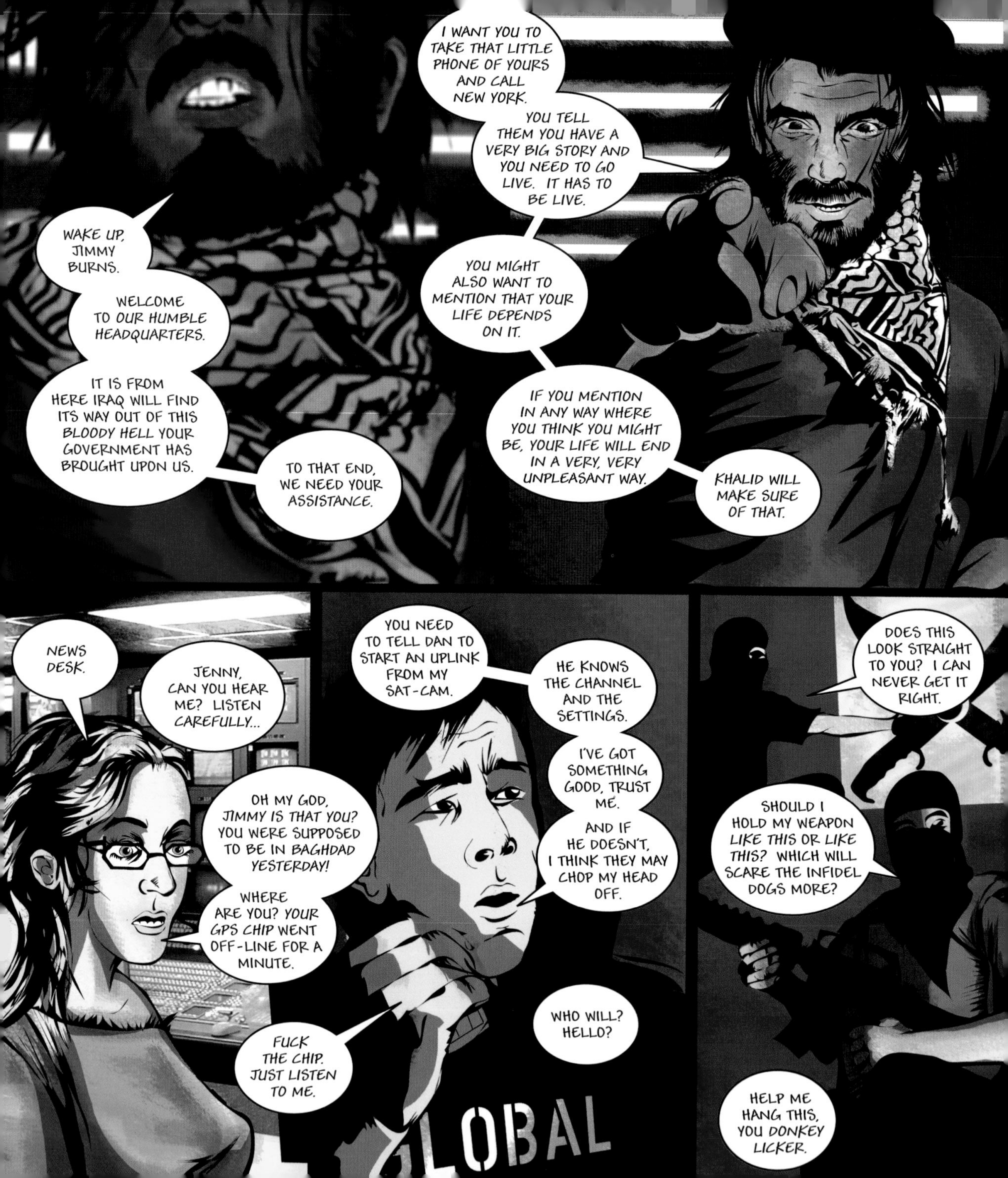
WAKE UP, JIMMY BURNS.
WELCOME TO OUR HUMBLE HEADQUARTERS.
IT IS FROM HERE IRAQ WILL FIND ITS WAY OUT OF THIS BLOODY HELL YOUR GOVERNMENT HAS BROUGHT UPON US.
TO THAT END, WE NEED YOUR ASSISTANCE.
I WANT YOU TO TAKE THAT LITTLE PHONE OF YOURS AND CALL NEW YORK.
YOU TELL THEM YOU HAVE A VERY BIG STORY AND YOU NEED TO GO LIVE. IT HAS TO BE LIVE.
YOU MIGHT ALSO WANT TO MENTION THAT YOUR LIFE DEPENDS ON IT.
IF YOU MENTION IN ANY WAY WHERE YOU THINK YOU MIGHT BE, YOUR LIFE WILL END IN A VERY, VERY UNPLEASANT WAY.
KHALID WILL MAKE SURE OF THAT.
NEWS DESK.
JENNY, CAN YOU HEAR ME? LISTEN CAREFULLY...
OH MY GOD, JIMMY IS THAT YOU? YOU WERE SUPPOSED TO BE IN BAGHDAD YESTERDAY!
WHERE ARE YOU? YOUR GPS CHIP WENT OFF-LINE FOR A MINUTE.
FUCK THE CHIP. JUST LISTEN TO ME.
YOU NEED TO TELL DAN TO START AN UPLINK FROM MY SAT-CAM.
HE KNOWS THE CHANNEL AND THE SETTINGS.
I'VE GOT SOMETHING GOOD, TRUST ME.
AND IF HE DOESN'T, I THINK THEY MAY CHOP MY HEAD OFF.
WHO WILL? HELLO?
GLOBAL
DOES THIS LOOK STRAIGHT TO YOU? I CAN NEVER GET IT RIGHT.
SHOULD I HOLD MY WEAPON LIKE THIS OR LIKE THIS? WHICH WILL SCARE THE INFIDEL DOGS MORE?
HELP ME HANG THIS, YOU DONKEY LICKER.

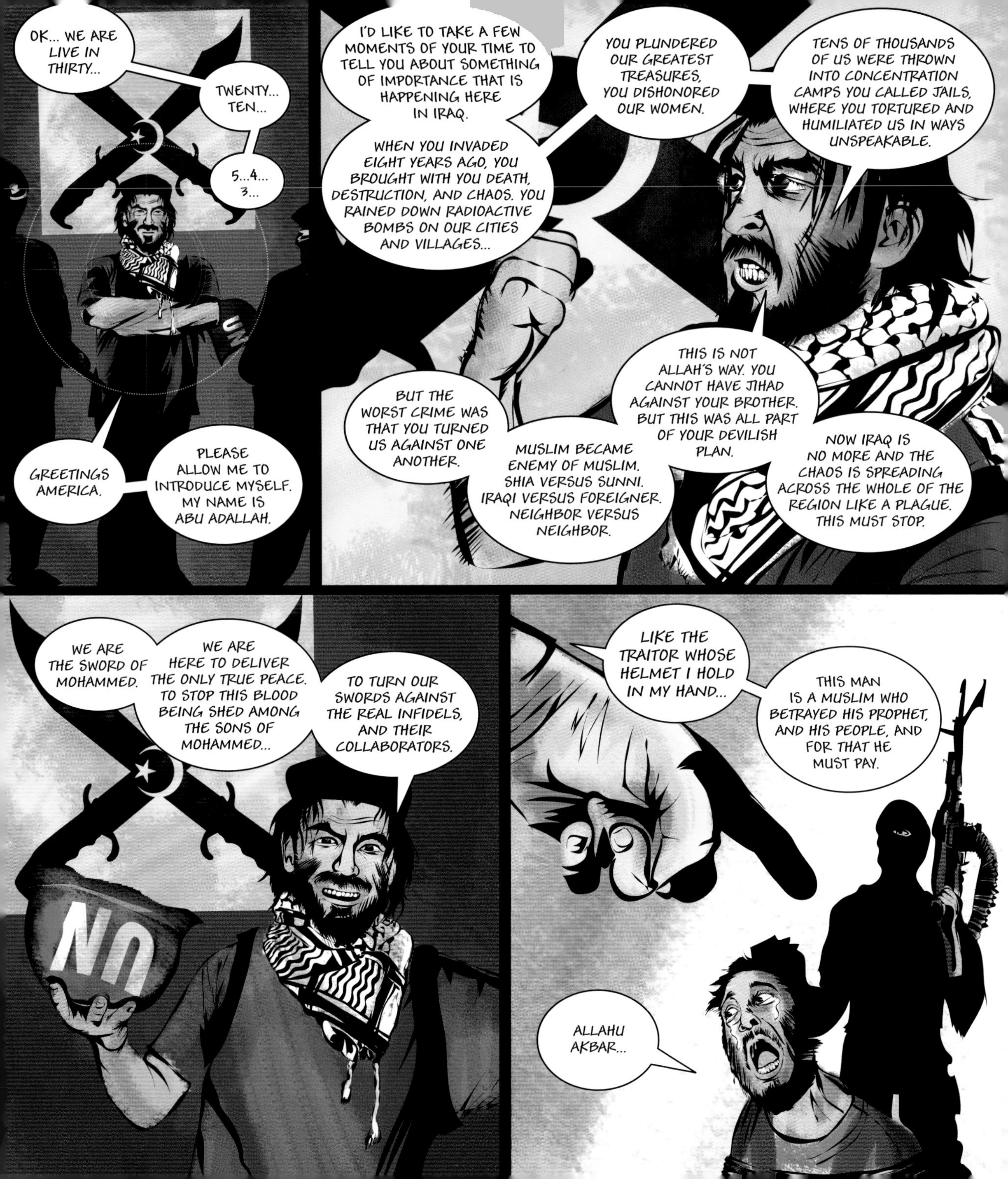
OK... WE ARE LIVE IN THIRTY...
TWENTY... TEN...
5...4... 3...
GREETINGS AMERICA.
PLEASE ALLOW ME TO INTRODUCE MYSELF. MY NAME IS ABU ADALLAH.
I'D LIKE TO TAKE A FEW MOMENTS OF YOUR TIME TO TELL YOU ABOUT SOMETHING OF IMPORTANCE THAT IS HAPPENING HERE IN IRAQ.
WHEN YOU INVADED EIGHT YEARS AGO, YOU BROUGHT WITH YOU DEATH, DESTRUCTION, AND CHAOS. YOU RAINED DOWN RADIOACTIVE BOMBS ON OUR CITIES AND VILLAGES...
YOU PLUNDERED OUR GREATEST TREASURES, YOU DISHONORED OUR WOMEN.
TENS OF THOUSANDS OF US WERE THROWN INTO CONCENTRATION CAMPS YOU CALLED JAILS, WHERE YOU TORTURED AND HUMILIATED US IN WAYS UNSPEAKABLE.
BUT THE WORST CRIME WAS THAT YOU TURNED US AGAINST ONE ANOTHER.
MUSLIM BECAME ENEMY OF MUSLIM. SHIA VERSUS SUNNI. IRAQI VERSUS FOREIGNER. NEIGHBOR VERSUS NEIGHBOR.
THIS IS NOT ALLAH'S WAY. YOU CANNOT HAVE JIHAD AGAINST YOUR BROTHER. BUT THIS WAS ALL PART OF YOUR DEVILISH PLAN.
NOW IRAQ IS NO MORE AND THE CHAOS IS SPREADING ACROSS THE WHOLE OF THE REGION LIKE A PLAGUE. THIS MUST STOP.
WE ARE THE SWORD OF MOHAMMED.
WE ARE HERE TO DELIVER THE ONLY TRUE PEACE. TO STOP THIS BLOOD BEING SHED AMONG THE SONS OF MOHAMMED...
TO TURN OUR SWORDS AGAINST THE REAL INFIDELS, AND THEIR COLLABORATORS.
UN
LIKE THE TRAITOR WHOSE HELMET I HOLD IN MY HAND...
THIS MAN IS A MUSLIM WHO BETRAYED HIS PROPHET, AND HIS PEOPLE, AND FOR THAT HE MUST PAY.
ALLAHU AKBAR...

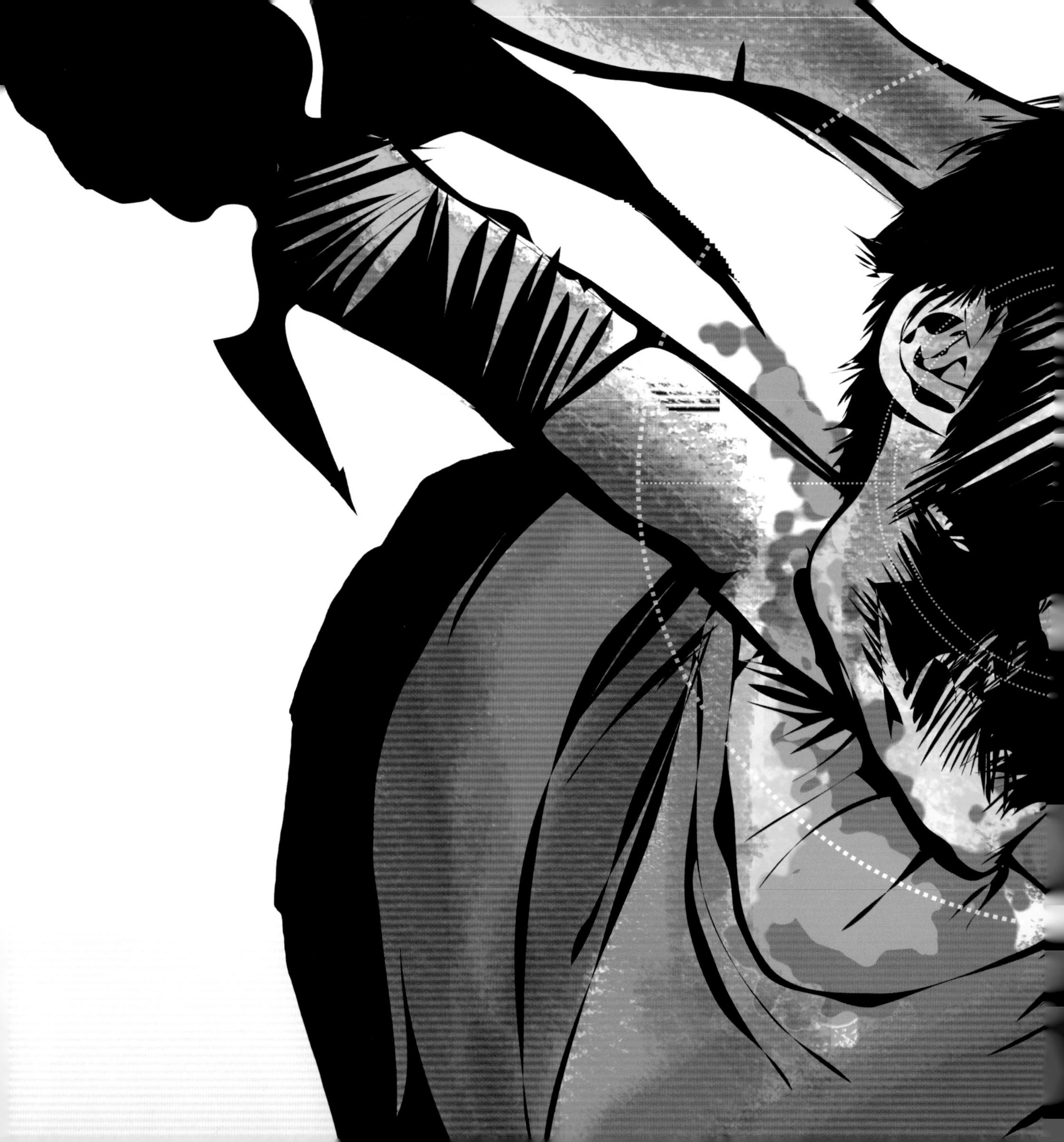

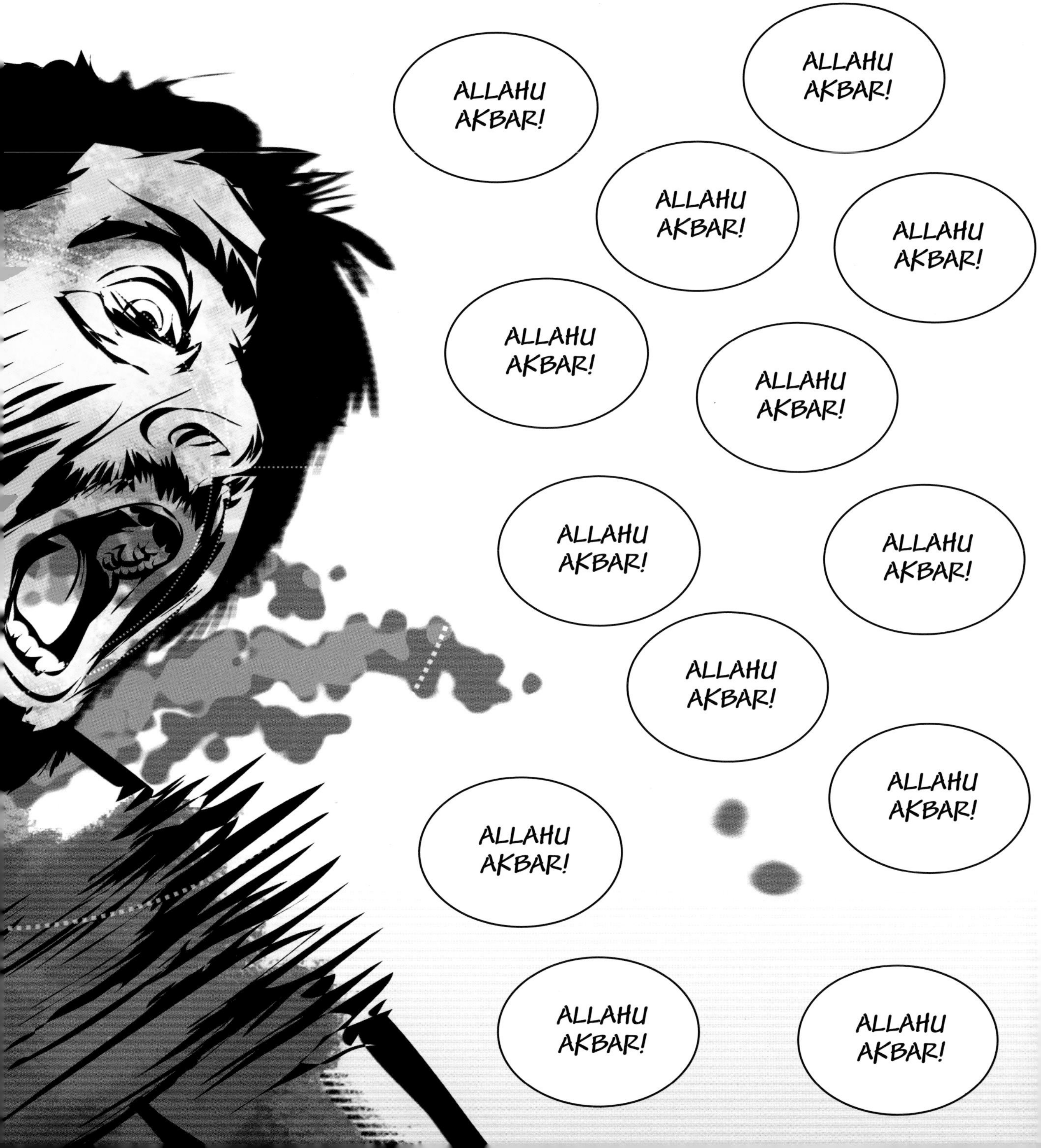
ALLAHU AKBAR!
ALLAHU AKBAR!
ALLAHU AKBAR!
ALLAHU AKBAR!
ALLAHU AKBAR!
ALLAHU AKBAR!
ALLAHU AKBAR!
ALLAHU AKBAR!
ALLAHU AKBAR!
ALLAHU AKBAR!
ALLAHU AKBAR!
ALLAHU AKBAR!
ALLAHU AKBAR!

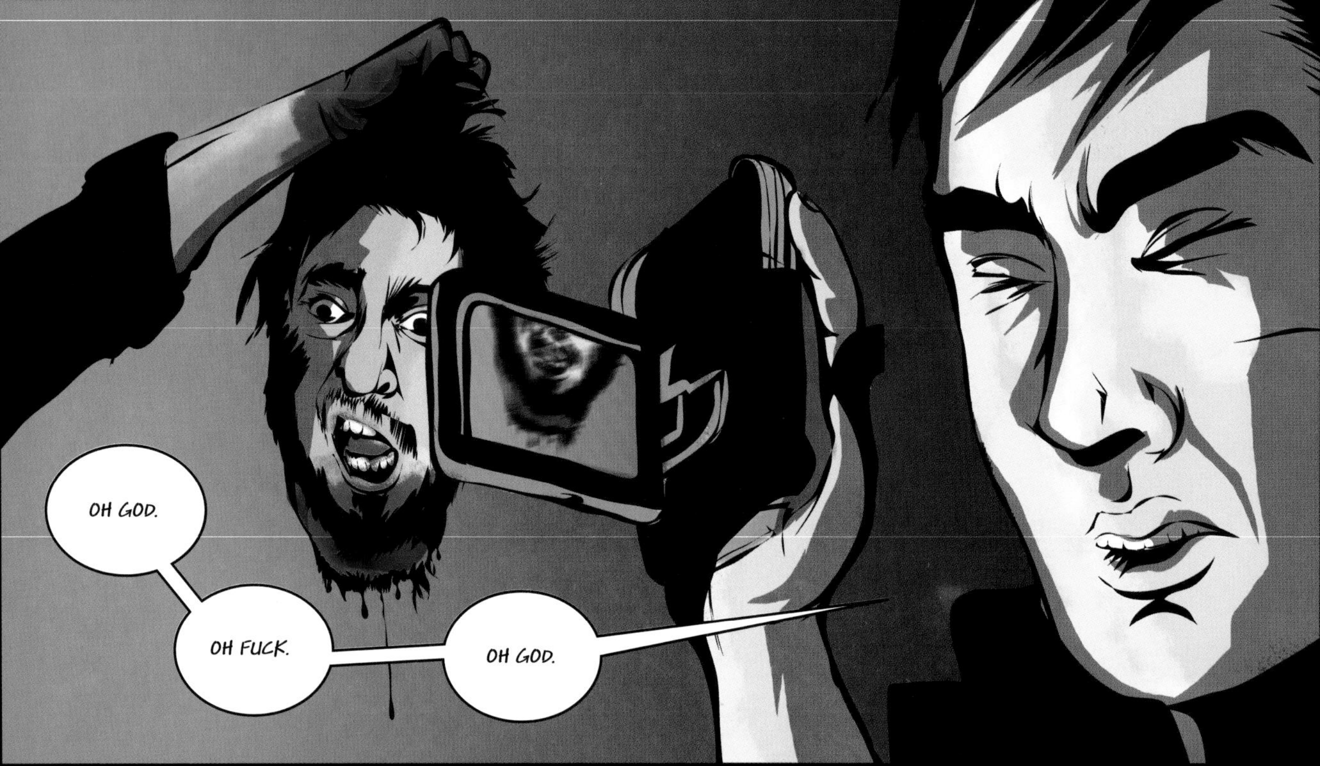
OH GOD.
OH FUCK.
OH GOD.
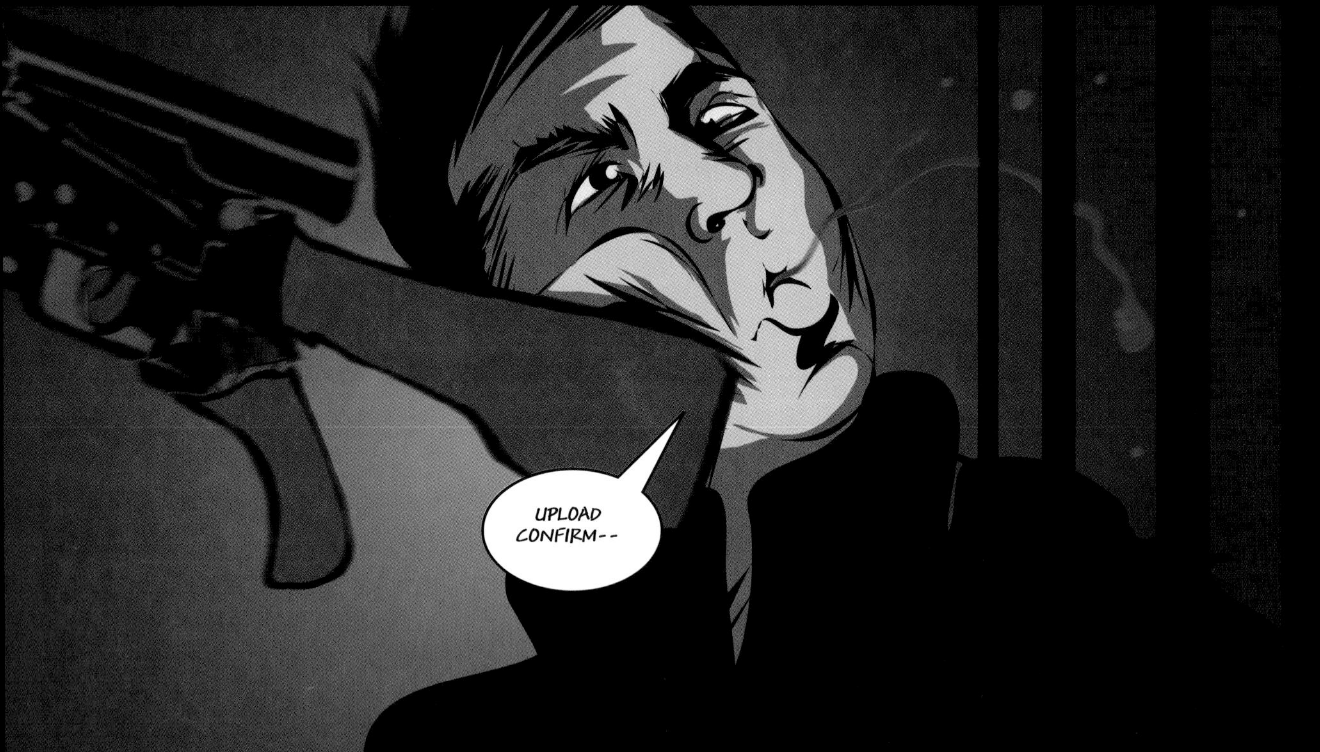
UPLOAD CONFIRM--

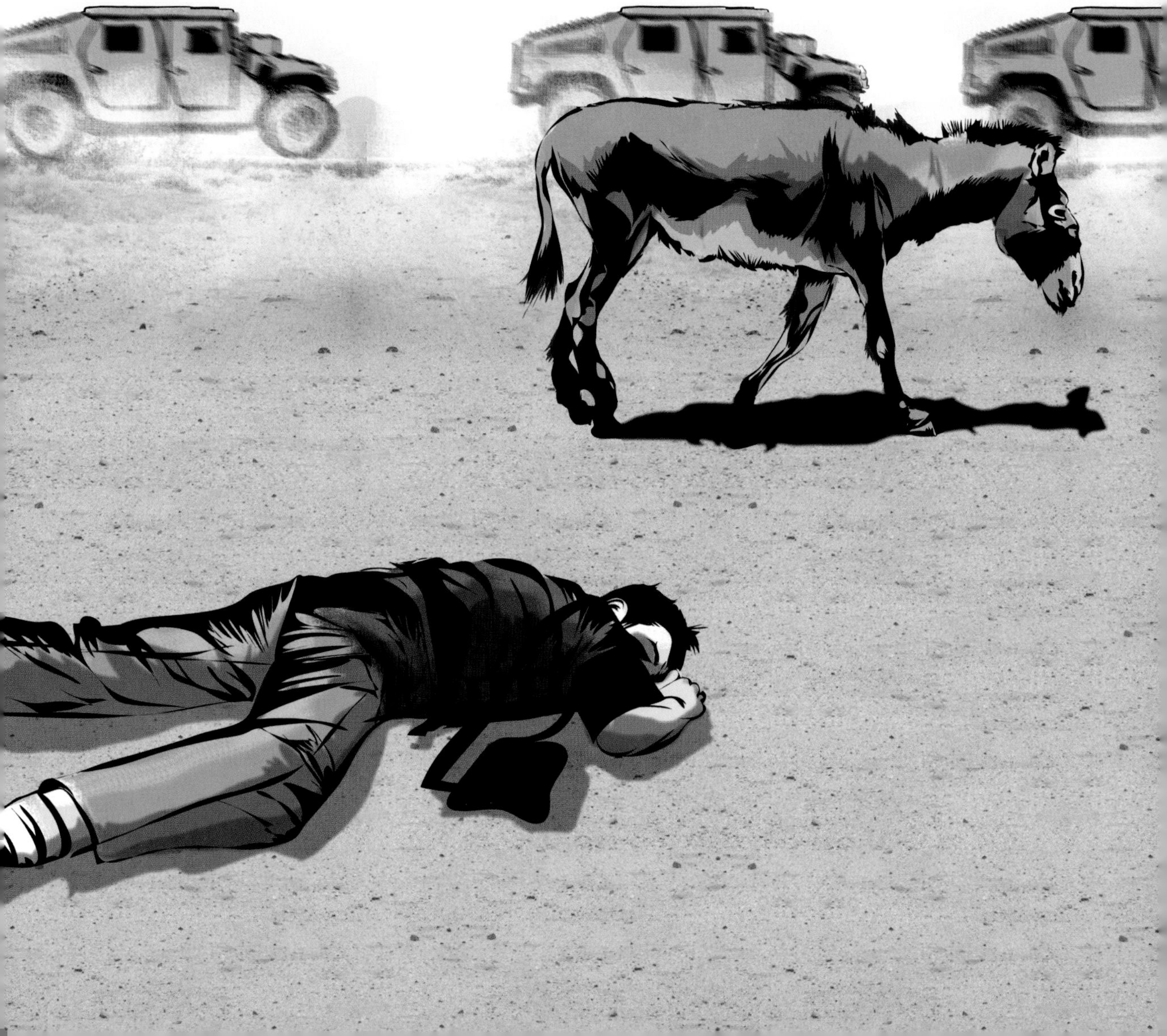

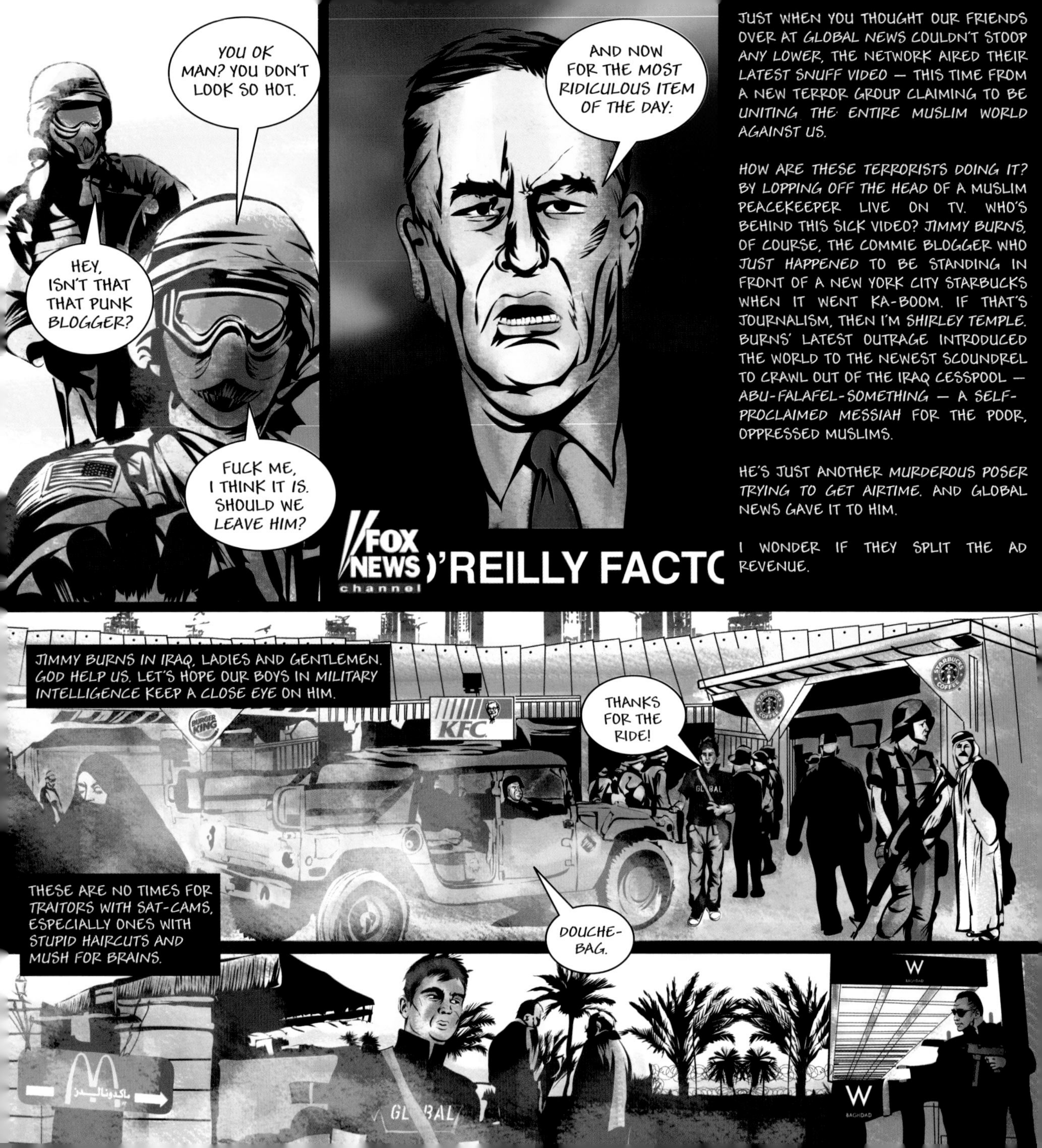
YOU OK MAN? YOU DON'T LOOK SO HOT.
HEY, ISN'T THAT THAT PUNK BLOGGER?
FUCK ME, I THINK IT IS. SHOULD WE LEAVE HIM?
AND NOW FOR THE MOST RIDICULOUS ITEM OF THE DAY:
FOX NEWS channel
'REILLY FACTO
JUST WHEN YOU THOUGHT OUR FRIENDS OVER AT GLOBAL NEWS COULDN'T STOOP ANY LOWER, THE NETWORK AIRED THEIR LATEST SNUFF VIDEO — THIS TIME FROM A NEW TERROR GROUP CLAIMING TO BE UNITING THE ENTIRE MUSLIM WORLD AGAINST US.
HOW ARE THESE TERRORISTS DOING IT? BY LOPPING OFF THE HEAD OF A MUSLIM PEACEKEEPER LIVE ON TV. WHO'S BEHIND THIS SICK VIDEO? JIMMY BURNS, OF COURSE, THE COMMIE BLOGGER WHO JUST HAPPENED TO BE STANDING IN FRONT OF A NEW YORK CITY STARBUCKS WHEN IT WENT KA-BOOM. IF THAT'S JOURNALISM, THEN I'M SHIRLEY TEMPLE. BURNS' LATEST OUTRAGE INTRODUCED THE WORLD TO THE NEWEST SCOUNDREL TO CRAWL OUT OF THE IRAQ CESSPOOL — ABU-FALAFEL-SOMETHING — A SELF-PROCLAIMED MESSIAH FOR THE POOR, OPPRESSED MUSLIMS.
HE'S JUST ANOTHER MURDEROUS POSER TRYING TO GET AIRTIME. AND GLOBAL NEWS GAVE IT TO HIM.
I WONDER IF THEY SPLIT THE AD REVENUE.
JIMMY BURNS IN IRAQ, LADIES AND GENTLEMEN. GOD HELP US. LET'S HOPE OUR BOYS IN MILITARY INTELLIGENCE KEEP A CLOSE EYE ON HIM.
BURGER KING
KFC
STARBUCKS COFFEE
THANKS FOR THE RIDE!
GLOBAL
THESE ARE NO TIMES FOR TRAITORS WITH SAT-CAMS, ESPECIALLY ONES WITH STUPID HAIRCUTS AND MUSH FOR BRAINS.
DOUCHE-BAG.
W BAGHDAD
ماكدونالدز
GLOBAL
W BAGHDAD

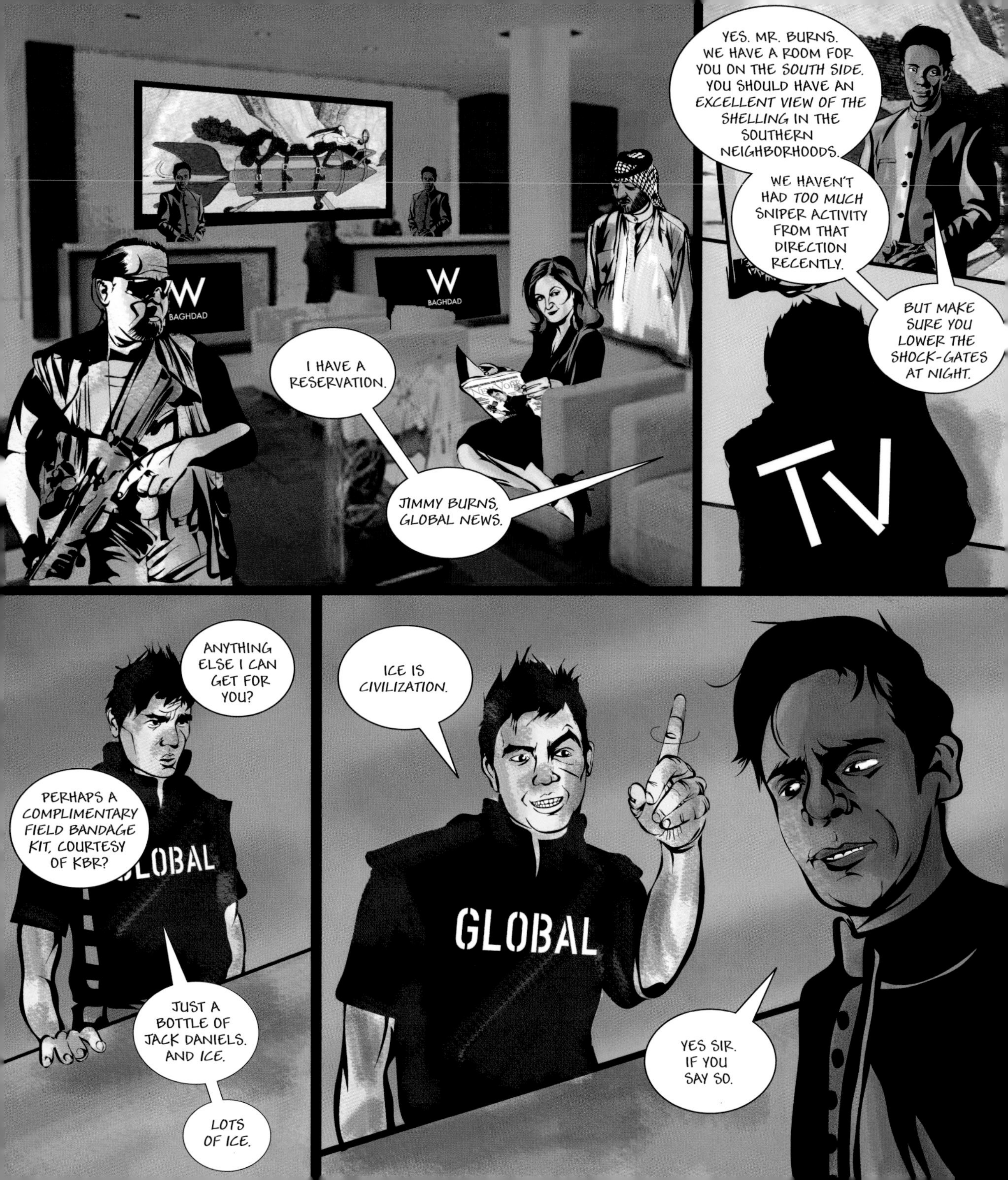
W BAGHDAD
W BAGHDAD
I HAVE A RESERVATION.
JIMMY BURNS, GLOBAL NEWS.
YES. MR. BURNS. WE HAVE A ROOM FOR YOU ON THE SOUTH SIDE. YOU SHOULD HAVE AN EXCELLENT VIEW OF THE SHELLING IN THE SOUTHERN NEIGHBORHOODS.
WE HAVEN'T HAD TOO MUCH SNIPER ACTIVITY FROM THAT DIRECTION RECENTLY.
BUT MAKE SURE YOU LOWER THE SHOCK-GATES AT NIGHT.
TV
ANYTHING ELSE I CAN GET FOR YOU?
PERHAPS A COMPLIMENTARY FIELD BANDAGE KIT, COURTESY OF KBR?
GLOBAL
JUST A BOTTLE OF JACK DANIELS. AND ICE.
LOTS OF ICE.
ICE IS CIVILIZATION.
GLOBAL
YES SIR. IF YOU SAY SO.

THE MOST DANGEROUS THING I EVER DID BACK IN NEW YORK WAS FUCK THAT TATTED-OUT CHICK I MET AT CHERRY TAVERN WITHOUT A DOME.

NOW EVERYWHERE I GO PEOPLE ARE DYING. THE TWO JOURNALISTS WHO DIED IN THE CRASH HAD COVERED 13 WARS BETWEEN THE TWO OF THEM. THE OLD DUDE TOLD ME HE AND HIS WIFE JUST HAD THEIR FIRST KID, AND HE WAS HOPING THIS WAS HIS LAST WAR. TWO HOURS LATER WE FACE PLANT INTO THE DESERT. AND I'M THE ONLY ONE TO COME OUT ALIVE.

THEN I GET SHANGHAIED INTO BEING THE PROPAGANDA BITCH FOR SOME MURDEROUS CHE WANNABE WHO ACTUALLY MADE SOME SOLID POLITICAL POINTS, BEFORE HIS BOY LOPPED SOME POOR FUCK'S HEAD OFF.

I DON'T THINK I'M *CUT OUT* FOR THIS SHIT..

I REALLY DON'T.

DEAD ZONE

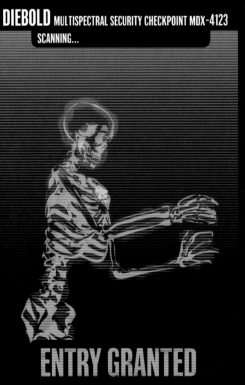

DIEBOLD MULTISPECTRAL SECURITY CHECKPOINT MDX-4123

SCANNING...

ENTRY GRANTED

NICE GIRL. CLEAN GIRL.

TEN U.S. DOLLARS. YOU WANT?

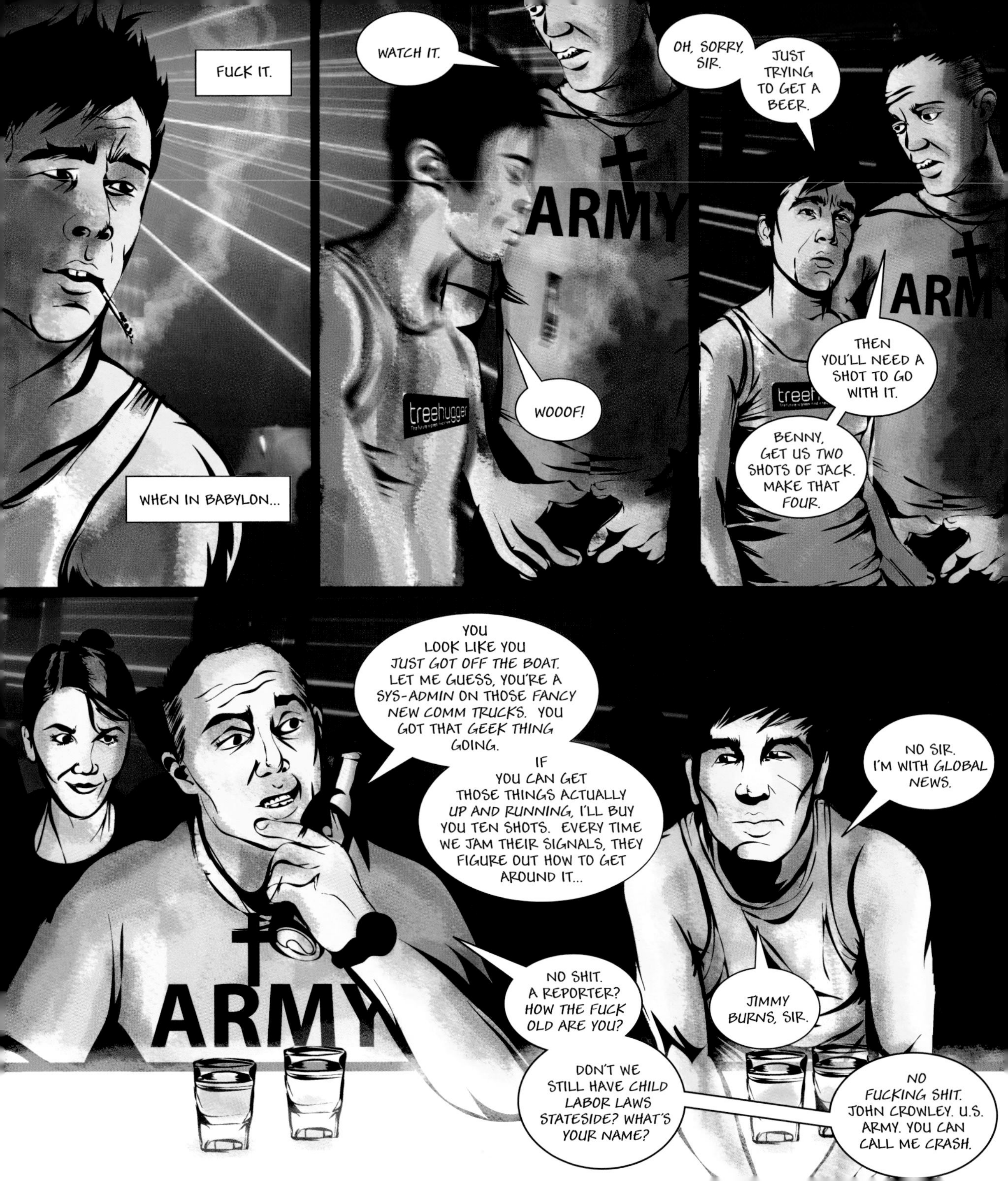
FUCK IT.
WHEN IN BABYLON...
WATCH IT.
treehugger
WOOOF!
ARMY
OH, SORRY, SIR.
JUST TRYING TO GET A BEER.
THEN YOU'LL NEED A SHOT TO GO WITH IT.
BENNY, GET US TWO SHOTS OF JACK. MAKE THAT FOUR.
YOU LOOK LIKE YOU JUST GOT OFF THE BOAT. LET ME GUESS, YOU'RE A SYS-ADMIN ON THOSE FANCY NEW COMM TRUCKS. YOU GOT THAT GEEK THING GOING.
IF YOU CAN GET THOSE THINGS ACTUALLY UP AND RUNNING, I'LL BUY YOU TEN SHOTS. EVERY TIME WE JAM THEIR SIGNALS, THEY FIGURE OUT HOW TO GET AROUND IT...
NO SIR. I'M WITH GLOBAL NEWS.
ARMY
NO SHIT. A REPORTER? HOW THE FUCK OLD ARE YOU?
DON'T WE STILL HAVE CHILD LABOR LAWS STATESIDE? WHAT'S YOUR NAME?
JIMMY BURNS, SIR.
NO FUCKING SHIT. JOHN CROWLEY. U.S. ARMY. YOU CAN CALL ME CRASH.

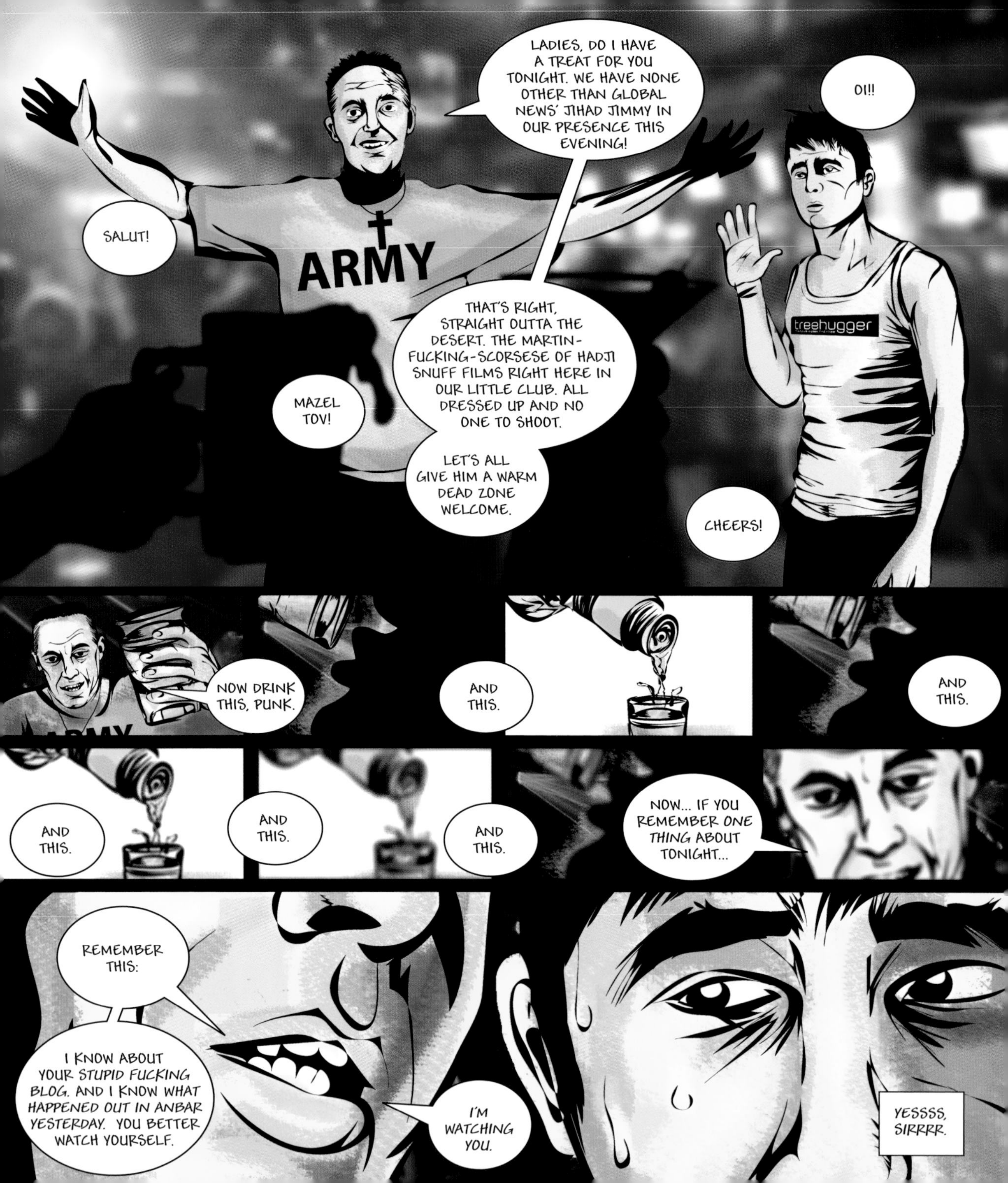
LADIES, DO I HAVE A TREAT FOR YOU TONIGHT. WE HAVE NONE OTHER THAN GLOBAL NEWS' JIHAD JIMMY IN OUR PRESENCE THIS EVENING!
OI!!
SALUT!
ARMY
THAT'S RIGHT, STRAIGHT OUTTA THE DESERT. THE MARTIN-FUCKING-SCORSESE OF HADJI SNUFF FILMS RIGHT HERE IN OUR LITTLE CLUB. ALL DRESSED UP AND NO ONE TO SHOOT.
treehugger
MAZEL TOV!
LET'S ALL GIVE HIM A WARM DEAD ZONE WELCOME.
CHEERS!
NOW DRINK THIS, PUNK.
AND THIS.
AND THIS.
AND THIS.
AND THIS.
AND THIS.
NOW... IF YOU REMEMBER ONE THING ABOUT TONIGHT...
REMEMBER THIS:
I KNOW ABOUT YOUR STUPID FUCKING BLOG. AND I KNOW WHAT HAPPENED OUT IN ANBAR YESTERDAY. YOU BETTER WATCH YOURSELF.
I'M WATCHING YOU.
YESSSS, SIRRRR.

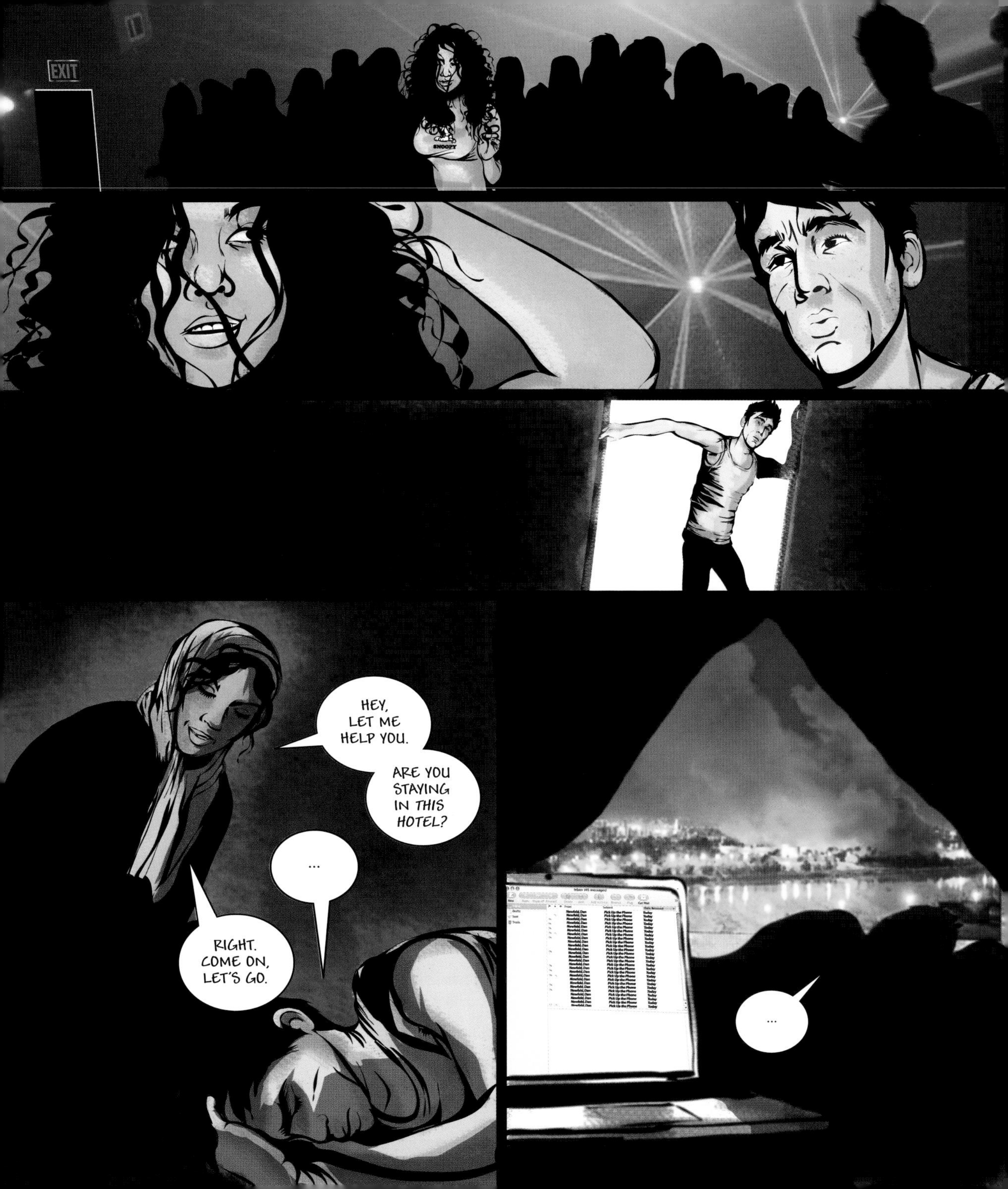
EXIT
SNOOPY
HEY, LET ME HELP YOU.
ARE YOU STAYING IN THIS HOTEL?
...
RIGHT. COME ON, LET'S GO.
...

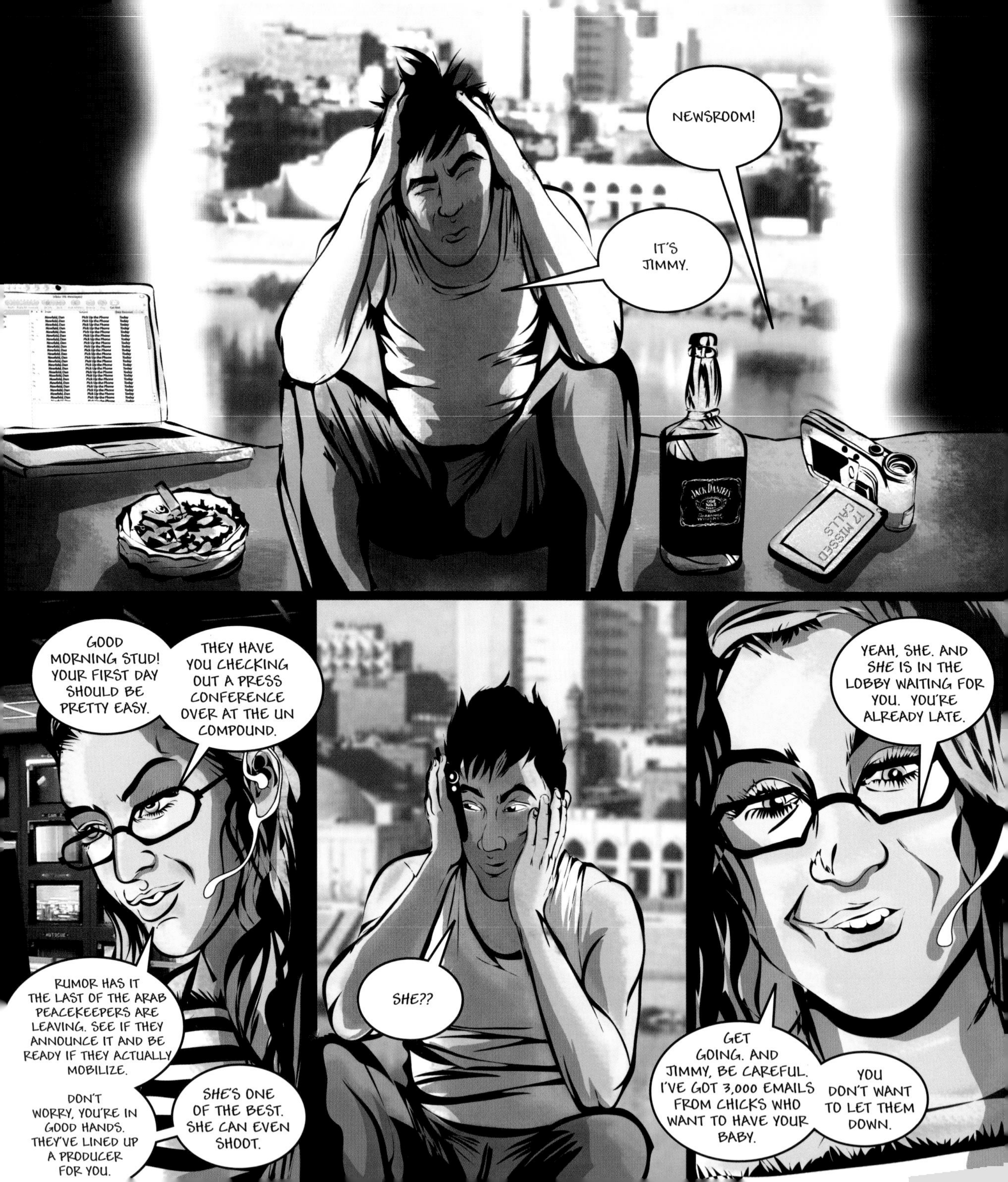
NEWSROOM!
IT'S JIMMY.
17 MISSED CALLS
GOOD MORNING STUD! YOUR FIRST DAY SHOULD BE PRETTY EASY.
THEY HAVE YOU CHECKING OUT A PRESS CONFERENCE OVER AT THE UN COMPOUND.
RUMOR HAS IT THE LAST OF THE ARAB PEACEKEEPERS ARE LEAVING. SEE IF THEY ANNOUNCE IT AND BE READY IF THEY ACTUALLY MOBILIZE.
DON'T WORRY, YOU'RE IN GOOD HANDS. THEY'VE LINED UP A PRODUCER FOR YOU.
SHE'S ONE OF THE BEST. SHE CAN EVEN SHOOT.
SHE??
YEAH, SHE. AND SHE IS IN THE LOBBY WAITING FOR YOU. YOU'RE ALREADY LATE.
GET GOING. AND JIMMY, BE CAREFUL. I'VE GOT 3,000 EMAILS FROM CHICKS WHO WANT TO HAVE YOUR BABY.
YOU DON'T WANT TO LET THEM DOWN.

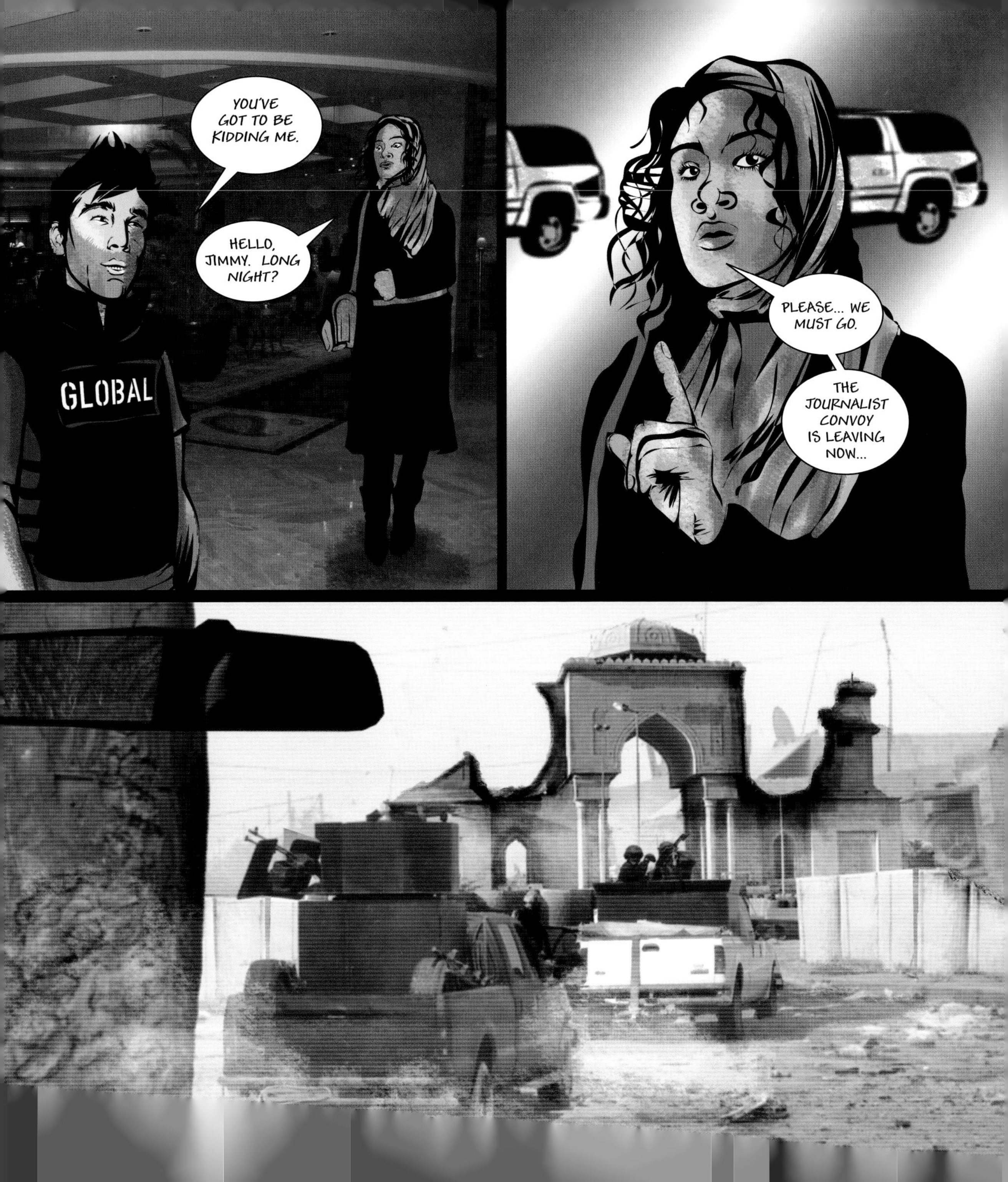
YOU'VE GOT TO BE KIDDING ME.
HELLO, JIMMY. LONG NIGHT?
GLOBAL
PLEASE... WE MUST GO.
THE JOURNALIST CONVOY IS LEAVING NOW...

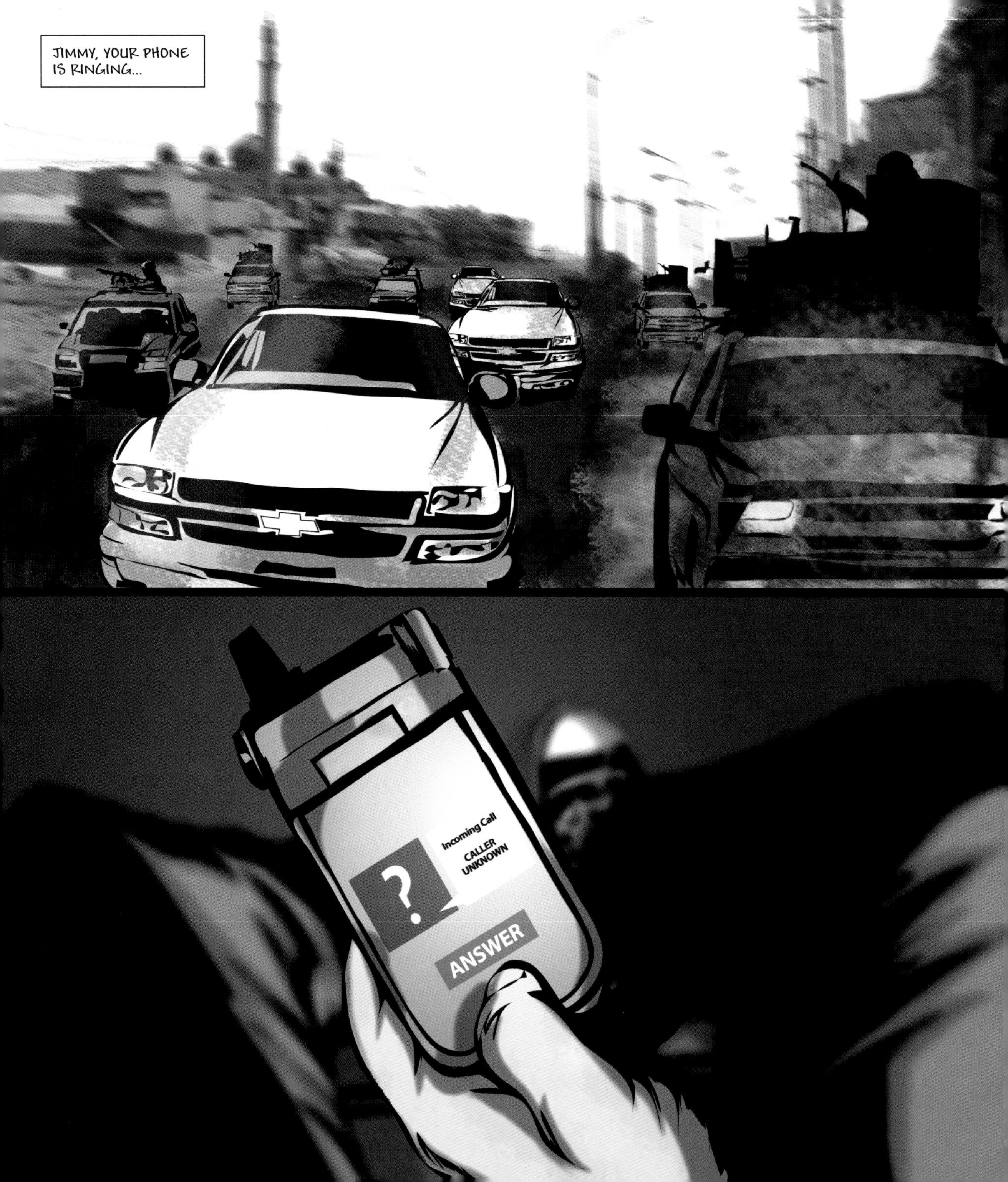
JIMMY, YOUR PHONE IS RINGING...
Incoming Call
CALLER UNKNOWN
?
ANSWER

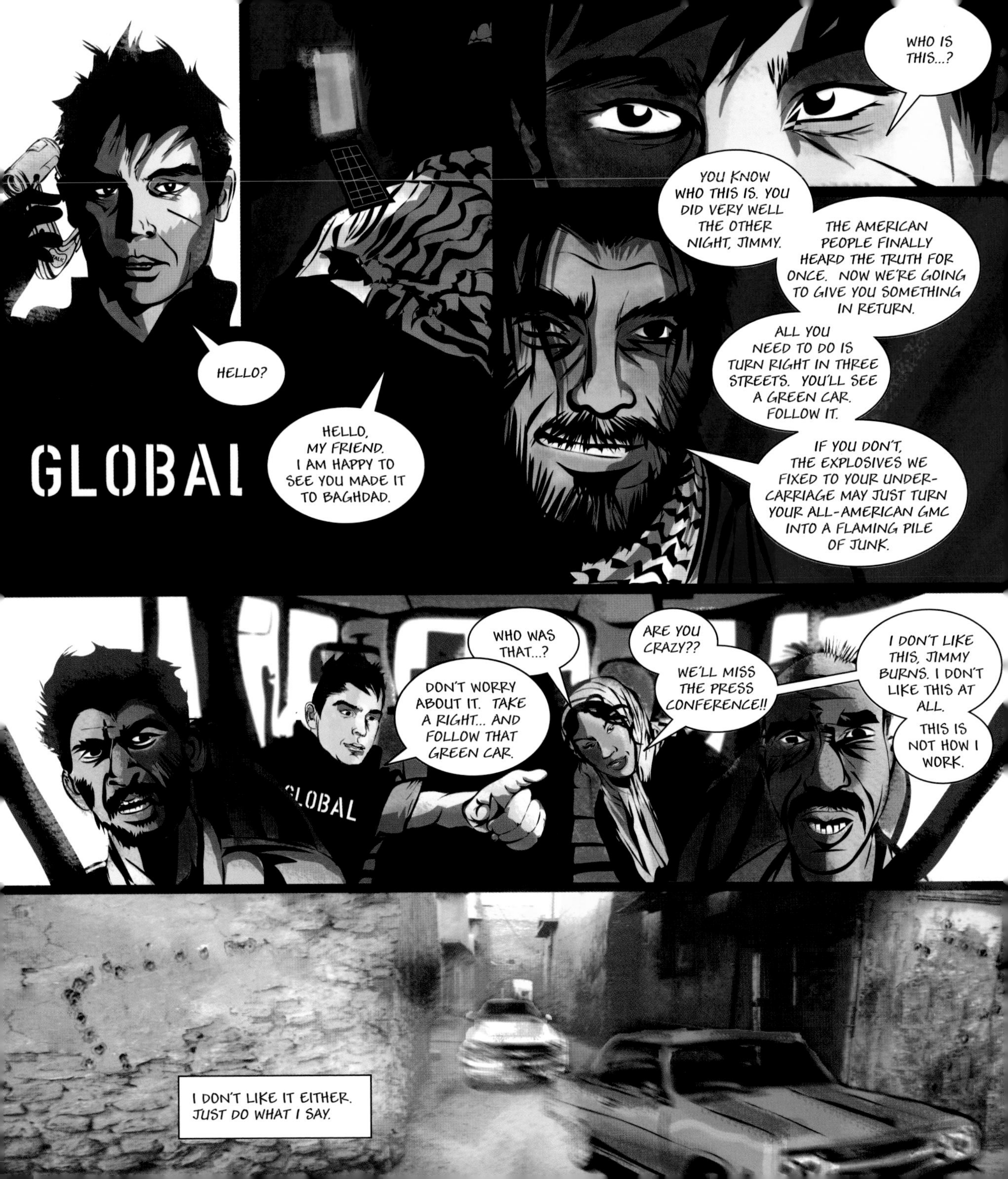
WHO IS THIS...?
HELLO?
GLOBAL
HELLO, MY FRIEND. I AM HAPPY TO SEE YOU MADE IT TO BAGHDAD.
YOU KNOW WHO THIS IS. YOU DID VERY WELL THE OTHER NIGHT, JIMMY.
THE AMERICAN PEOPLE FINALLY HEARD THE TRUTH FOR ONCE. NOW WE'RE GOING TO GIVE YOU SOMETHING IN RETURN.
ALL YOU NEED TO DO IS TURN RIGHT IN THREE STREETS. YOU'LL SEE A GREEN CAR. FOLLOW IT.
IF YOU DON'T, THE EXPLOSIVES WE FIXED TO YOUR UNDER-CARRIAGE MAY JUST TURN YOUR ALL-AMERICAN GMC INTO A FLAMING PILE OF JUNK.
WHO WAS THAT...?
DON'T WORRY ABOUT IT. TAKE A RIGHT... AND FOLLOW THAT GREEN CAR.
ARE YOU CRAZY??
WE'LL MISS THE PRESS CONFERENCE!!
I DON'T LIKE THIS, JIMMY BURNS. I DON'T LIKE THIS AT ALL.
THIS IS NOT HOW I WORK.
GLOBAL
I DON'T LIKE IT EITHER. JUST DO WHAT I SAY.

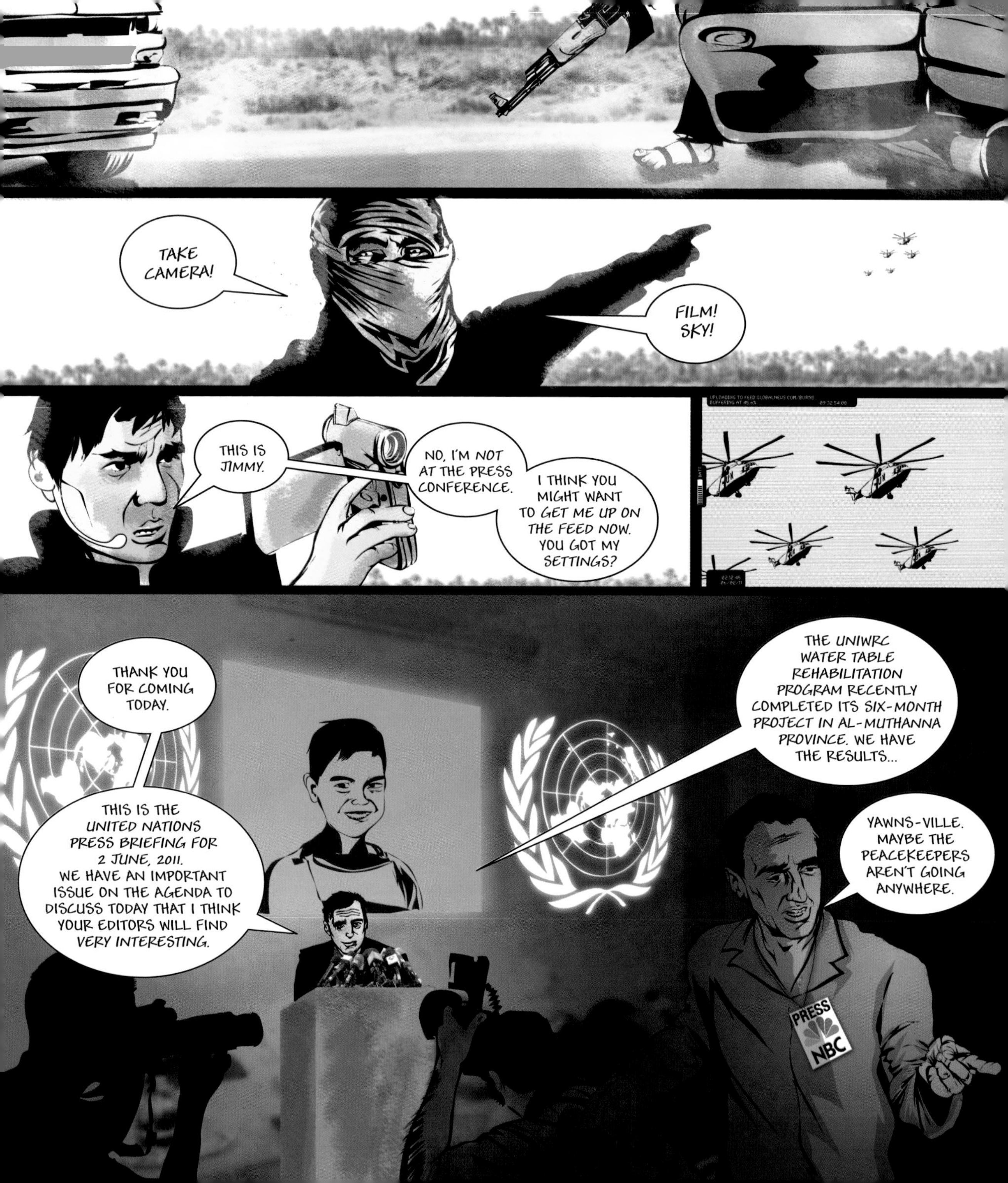
TAKE CAMERA!
FILM! SKY!
THIS IS JIMMY.
NO, I'M NOT AT THE PRESS CONFERENCE.
I THINK YOU MIGHT WANT TO GET ME UP ON THE FEED NOW. YOU GOT MY SETTINGS?
THANK YOU FOR COMING TODAY.
THIS IS THE UNITED NATIONS PRESS BRIEFING FOR 2 JUNE, 2011. WE HAVE AN IMPORTANT ISSUE ON THE AGENDA TO DISCUSS TODAY THAT I THINK YOUR EDITORS WILL FIND VERY INTERESTING.
THE UNIWRC WATER TABLE REHABILITATION PROGRAM RECENTLY COMPLETED ITS SIX-MONTH PROJECT IN AL-MUTHANNA PROVINCE. WE HAVE THE RESULTS...
YAWNS-VILLE. MAYBE THE PEACEKEEPERS AREN'T GOING ANYWHERE.
PRESS
NBC

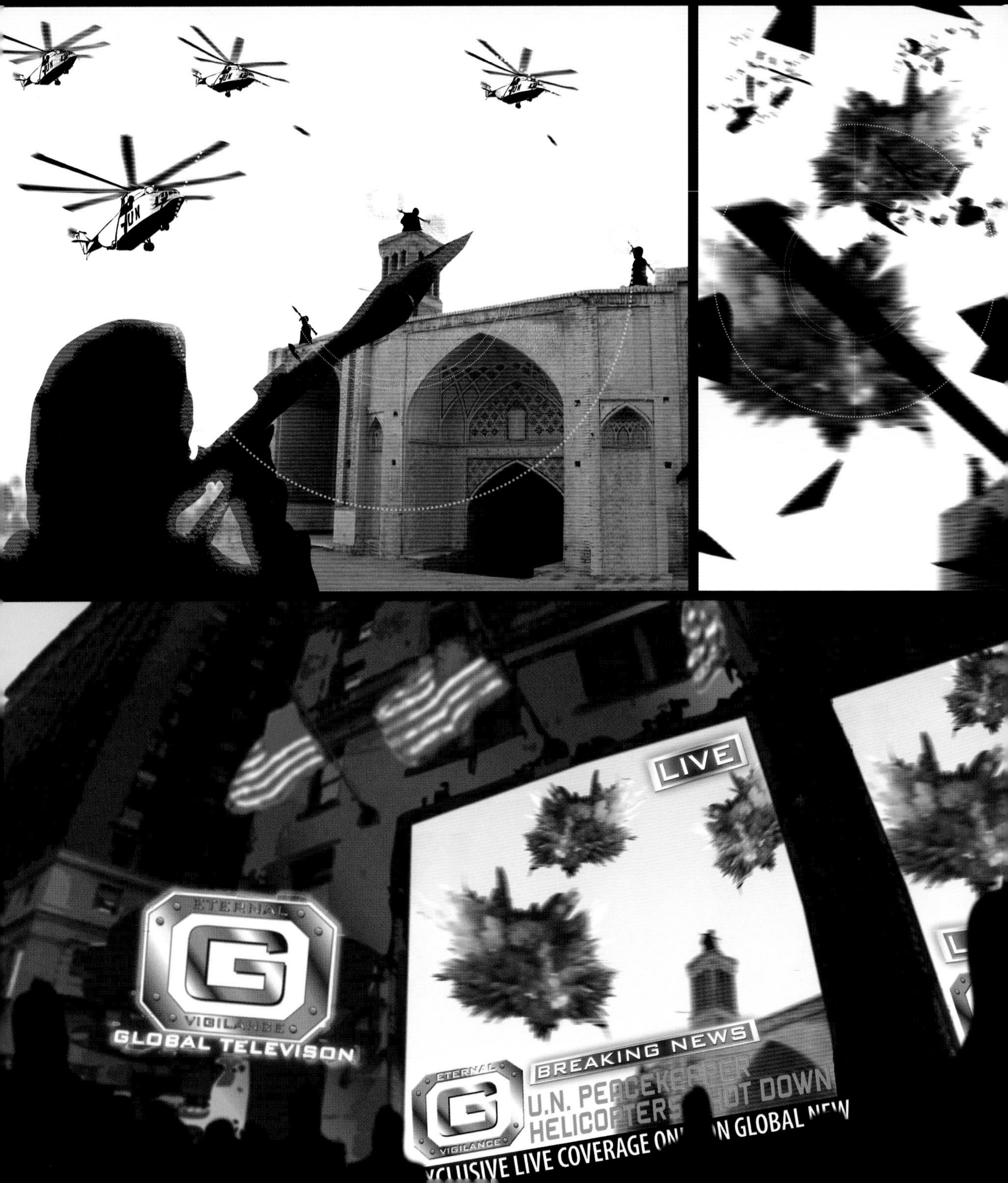

LIVE
ETERNAL
VIGILANCE
GLOBAL TELEVISON
BREAKING NEWS
ETERNAL
VIGILANCE
U.N. PEACEKEEPER
HELICOPTERS
OT DOWN
XCLUSIVE LIVE COVERAGE ON
N GLOBAL NEW

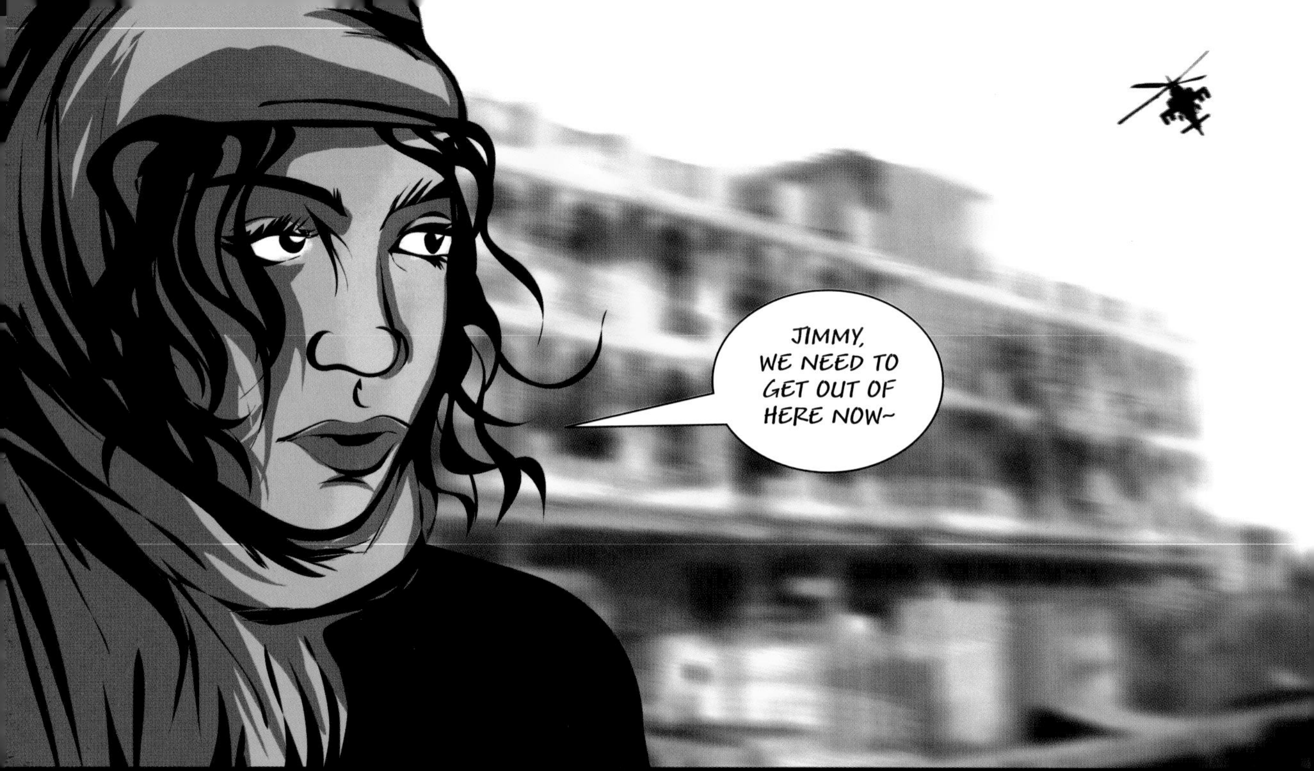
JIMMY, WE NEED TO GET OUT OF HERE NOW~

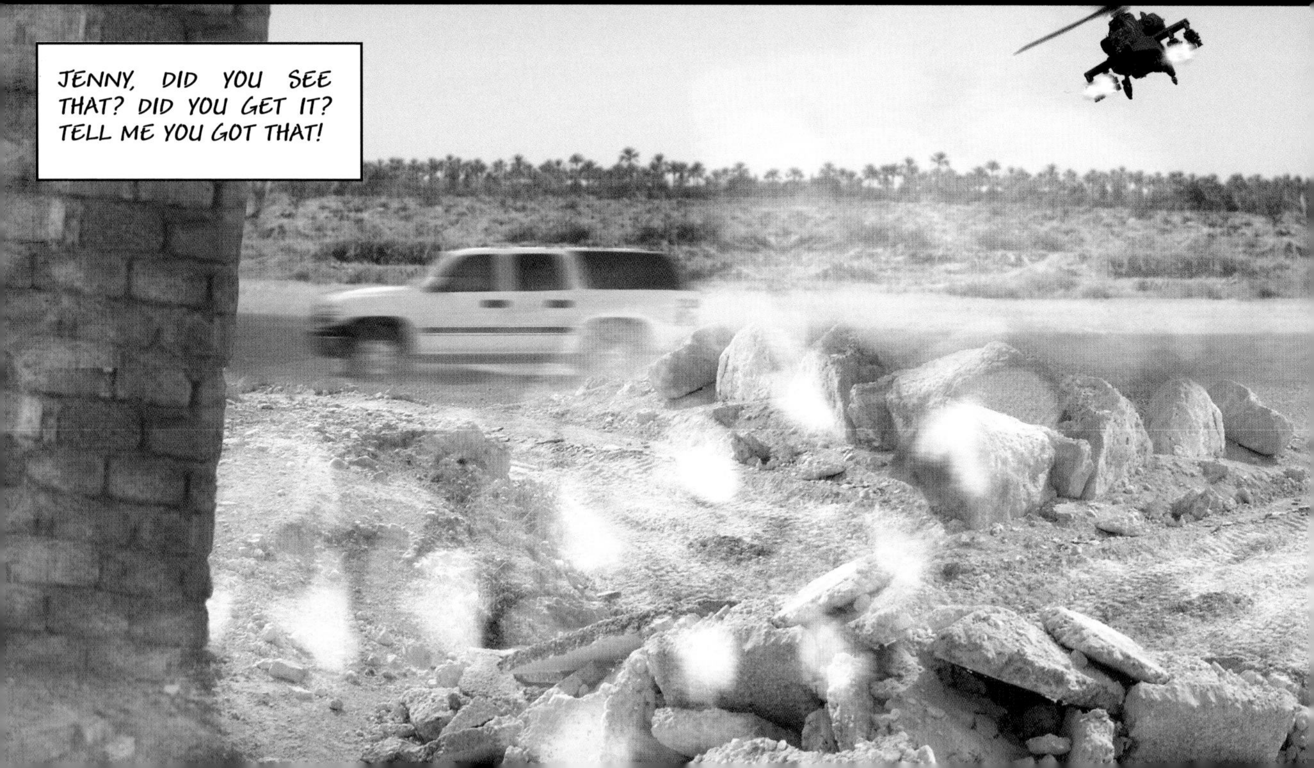
JENNY, DID YOU SEE THAT? DID YOU GET IT? TELL ME YOU GOT THAT!

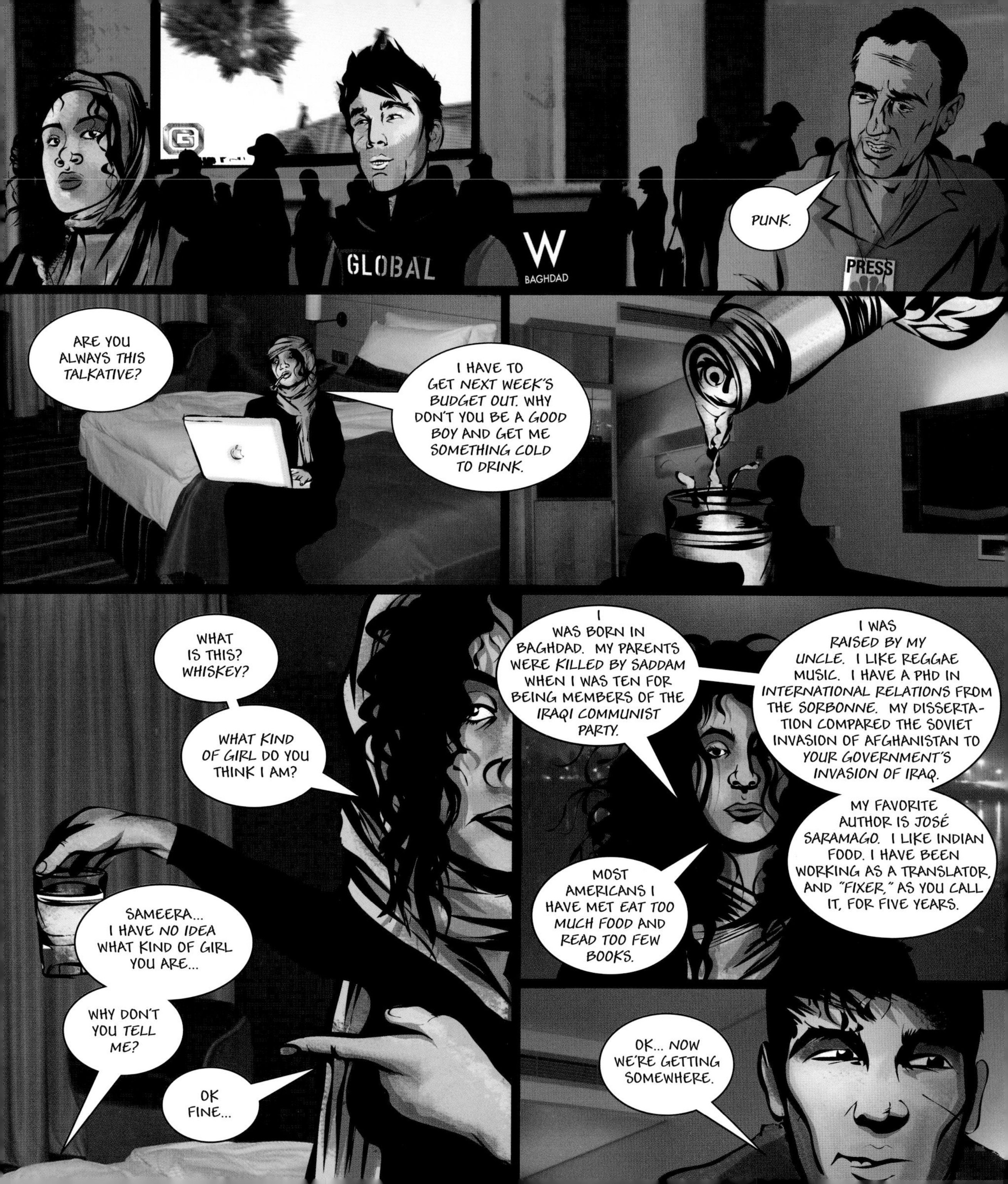
GLOBAL
W
BAGHDAD
PUNK.
PRESS
ARE YOU ALWAYS THIS TALKATIVE?
I HAVE TO GET NEXT WEEK'S BUDGET OUT. WHY DON'T YOU BE A GOOD BOY AND GET ME SOMETHING COLD TO DRINK.
WHAT IS THIS? WHISKEY?
WHAT KIND OF GIRL DO YOU THINK I AM?
SAMEERA... I HAVE NO IDEA WHAT KIND OF GIRL YOU ARE...
WHY DON'T YOU TELL ME?
OK FINE...
I WAS BORN IN BAGHDAD. MY PARENTS WERE KILLED BY SADDAM WHEN I WAS TEN FOR BEING MEMBERS OF THE IRAQI COMMUNIST PARTY.
I WAS RAISED BY MY UNCLE. I LIKE REGGAE MUSIC. I HAVE A PHD IN INTERNATIONAL RELATIONS FROM THE SORBONNE. MY DISSERTATION COMPARED THE SOVIET INVASION OF AFGHANISTAN TO YOUR GOVERNMENT'S INVASION OF IRAQ.
MY FAVORITE AUTHOR IS JOSÉ SARAMAGO. I LIKE INDIAN FOOD. I HAVE BEEN WORKING AS A TRANSLATOR, AND "FIXER," AS YOU CALL IT, FOR FIVE YEARS.
MOST AMERICANS I HAVE MET EAT TOO MUCH FOOD AND READ TOO FEW BOOKS.
OK... NOW WE'RE GETTING SOMEWHERE.

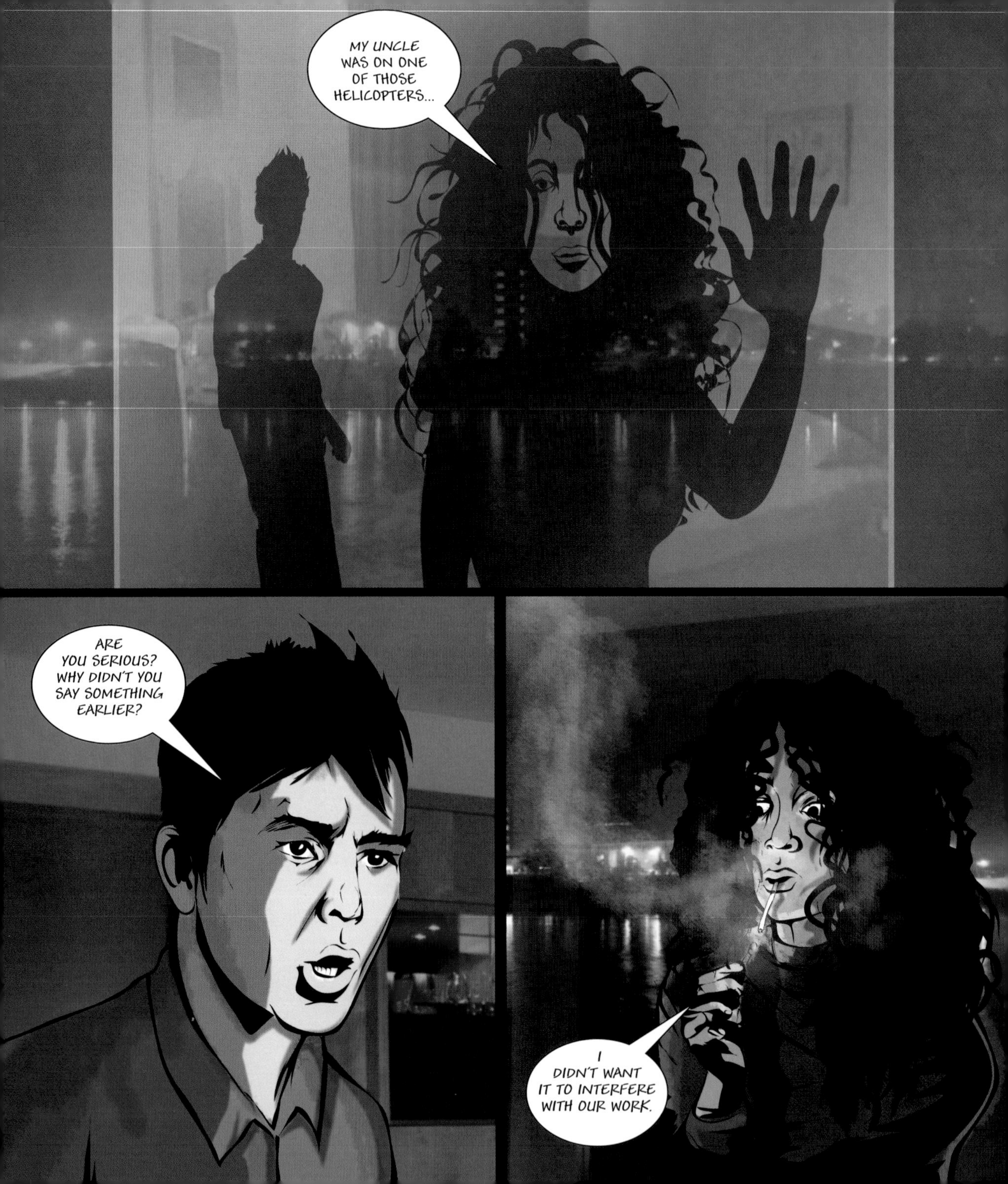
MY UNCLE WAS ON ONE OF THOSE HELICOPTERS...
ARE YOU SERIOUS? WHY DIDN'T YOU SAY SOMETHING EARLIER?
I DIDN'T WANT IT TO INTERFERE WITH OUR WORK.

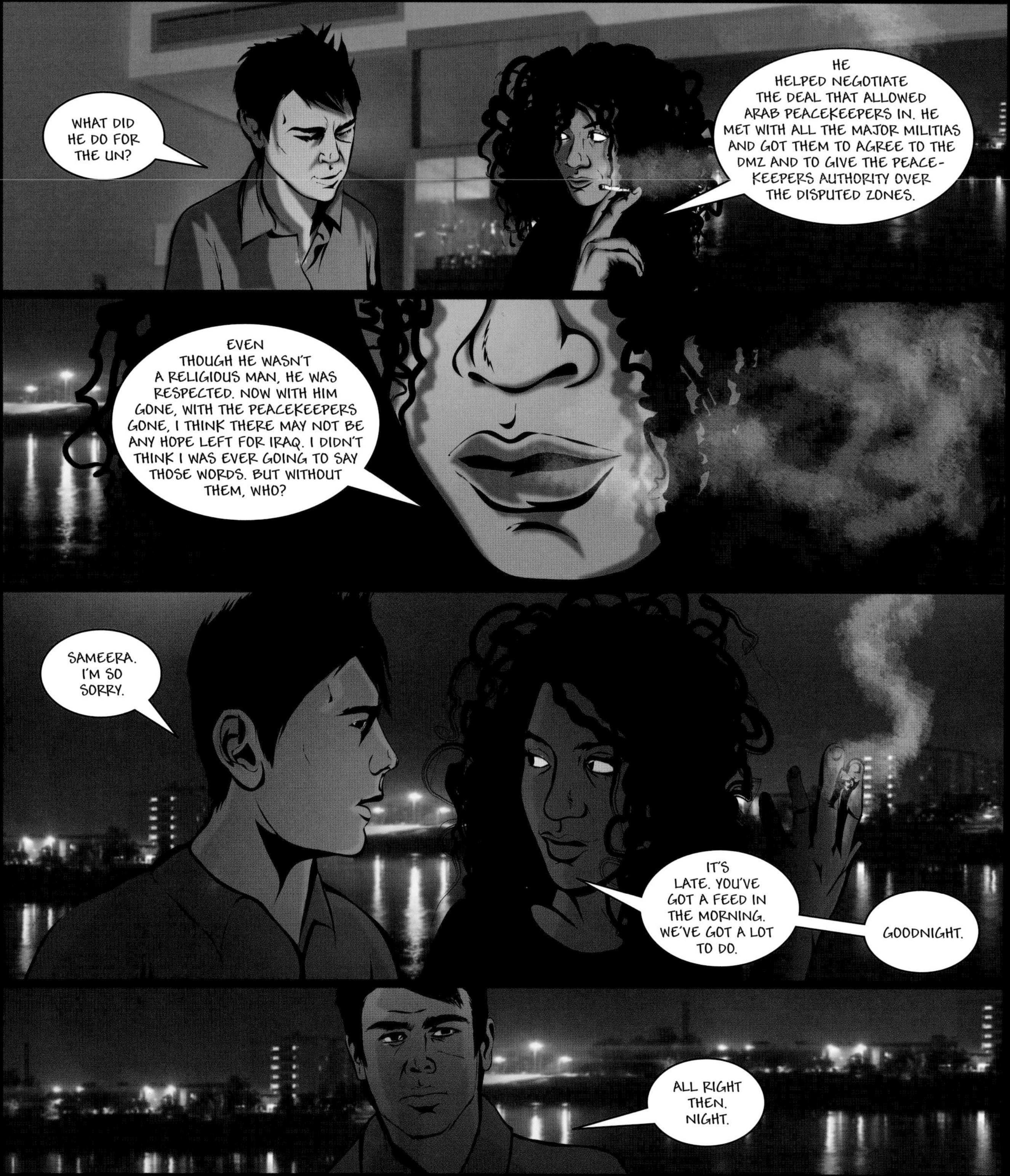
WHAT DID HE DO FOR THE UN?
HE HELPED NEGOTIATE THE DEAL THAT ALLOWED ARAB PEACEKEEPERS IN. HE MET WITH ALL THE MAJOR MILITIAS AND GOT THEM TO AGREE TO THE DMZ AND TO GIVE THE PEACE-KEEPERS AUTHORITY OVER THE DISPUTED ZONES.
EVEN THOUGH HE WASN'T A RELIGIOUS MAN, HE WAS RESPECTED. NOW WITH HIM GONE, WITH THE PEACEKEEPERS GONE, I THINK THERE MAY NOT BE ANY HOPE LEFT FOR IRAQ. I DIDN'T THINK I WAS EVER GOING TO SAY THOSE WORDS. BUT WITHOUT THEM, WHO?
SAMEERA. I'M SO SORRY.
IT'S LATE. YOU'VE GOT A FEED IN THE MORNING. WE'VE GOT A LOT TO DO.
GOODNIGHT.
ALL RIGHT THEN. NIGHT.

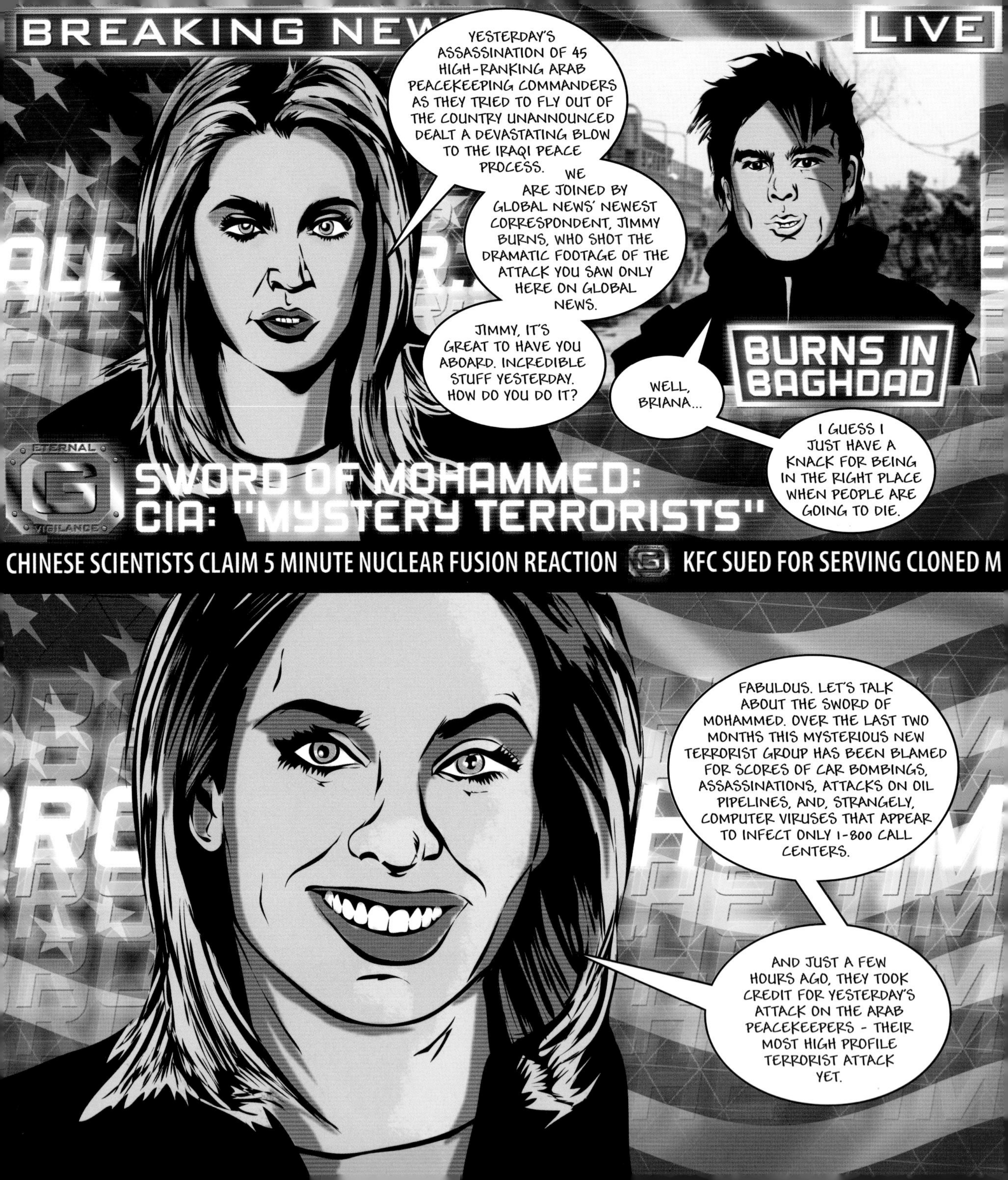

BREAKING NEWS
LIVE
YESTERDAY'S ASSASSINATION OF 45 HIGH-RANKING ARAB PEACEKEEPING COMMANDERS AS THEY TRIED TO FLY OUT OF THE COUNTRY UNANNOUNCED DEALT A DEVASTATING BLOW TO THE IRAQI PEACE PROCESS.
WE ARE JOINED BY GLOBAL NEWS' NEWEST CORRESPONDENT, JIMMY BURNS, WHO SHOT THE DRAMATIC FOOTAGE OF THE ATTACK YOU SAW ONLY HERE ON GLOBAL NEWS.
JIMMY, IT'S GREAT TO HAVE YOU ABOARD. INCREDIBLE STUFF YESTERDAY. HOW DO YOU DO IT?
BURNS IN BAGHDAD
WELL, BRIANA...
I GUESS I JUST HAVE A KNACK FOR BEING IN THE RIGHT PLACE WHEN PEOPLE ARE GOING TO DIE.
ETERNAL VIGILANCE
SWORD OF MOHAMMED:
CIA: "MYSTERY TERRORISTS"
CHINESE SCIENTISTS CLAIM 5 MINUTE NUCLEAR FUSION REACTION
KFC SUED FOR SERVING CLONED M
FABULOUS. LET'S TALK ABOUT THE SWORD OF MOHAMMED. OVER THE LAST TWO MONTHS THIS MYSTERIOUS NEW TERRORIST GROUP HAS BEEN BLAMED FOR SCORES OF CAR BOMBINGS, ASSASSINATIONS, ATTACKS ON OIL PIPELINES, AND, STRANGELY, COMPUTER VIRUSES THAT APPEAR TO INFECT ONLY 1-800 CALL CENTERS.
AND JUST A FEW HOURS AGO, THEY TOOK CREDIT FOR YESTERDAY'S ATTACK ON THE ARAB PEACEKEEPERS - THEIR MOST HIGH PROFILE TERRORIST ATTACK YET.

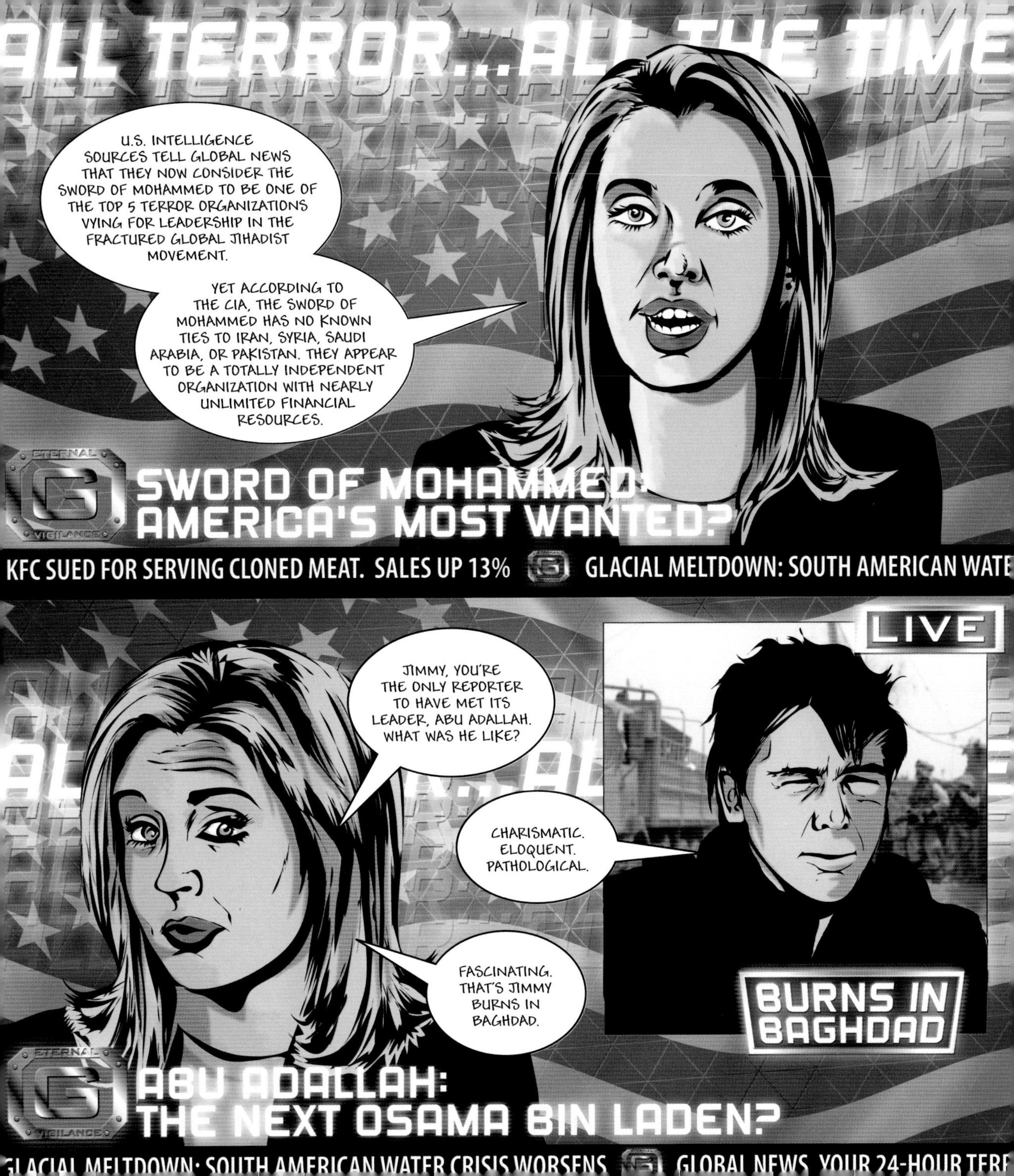
ALL TERROR...ALL THE TIME
U.S. INTELLIGENCE SOURCES TELL GLOBAL NEWS THAT THEY NOW CONSIDER THE SWORD OF MOHAMMED TO BE ONE OF THE TOP 5 TERROR ORGANIZATIONS VYING FOR LEADERSHIP IN THE FRACTURED GLOBAL JIHADIST MOVEMENT.
YET ACCORDING TO THE CIA, THE SWORD OF MOHAMMED HAS NO KNOWN TIES TO IRAN, SYRIA, SAUDI ARABIA, OR PAKISTAN. THEY APPEAR TO BE A TOTALLY INDEPENDENT ORGANIZATION WITH NEARLY UNLIMITED FINANCIAL RESOURCES.
ETERNAL G VIGILANCE
SWORD OF MOHAMMED: AMERICA'S MOST WANTED?
KFC SUED FOR SERVING CLONED MEAT. SALES UP 13%
GLACIAL MELTDOWN: SOUTH AMERICAN WATE
LIVE
JIMMY, YOU'RE THE ONLY REPORTER TO HAVE MET ITS LEADER, ABU ADALLAH. WHAT WAS HE LIKE?
CHARISMATIC. ELOQUENT. PATHOLOGICAL.
FASCINATING. THAT'S JIMMY BURNS IN BAGHDAD.
BURNS IN BAGHDAD
ETERNAL G VIGILANCE
ABU ADALLAH: THE NEXT OSAMA BIN LADEN?
GLACIAL MELTDOWN: SOUTH AMERICAN WATER CRISIS WORSENS
GLOBAL NEWS. YOUR 24-HOUR TERR

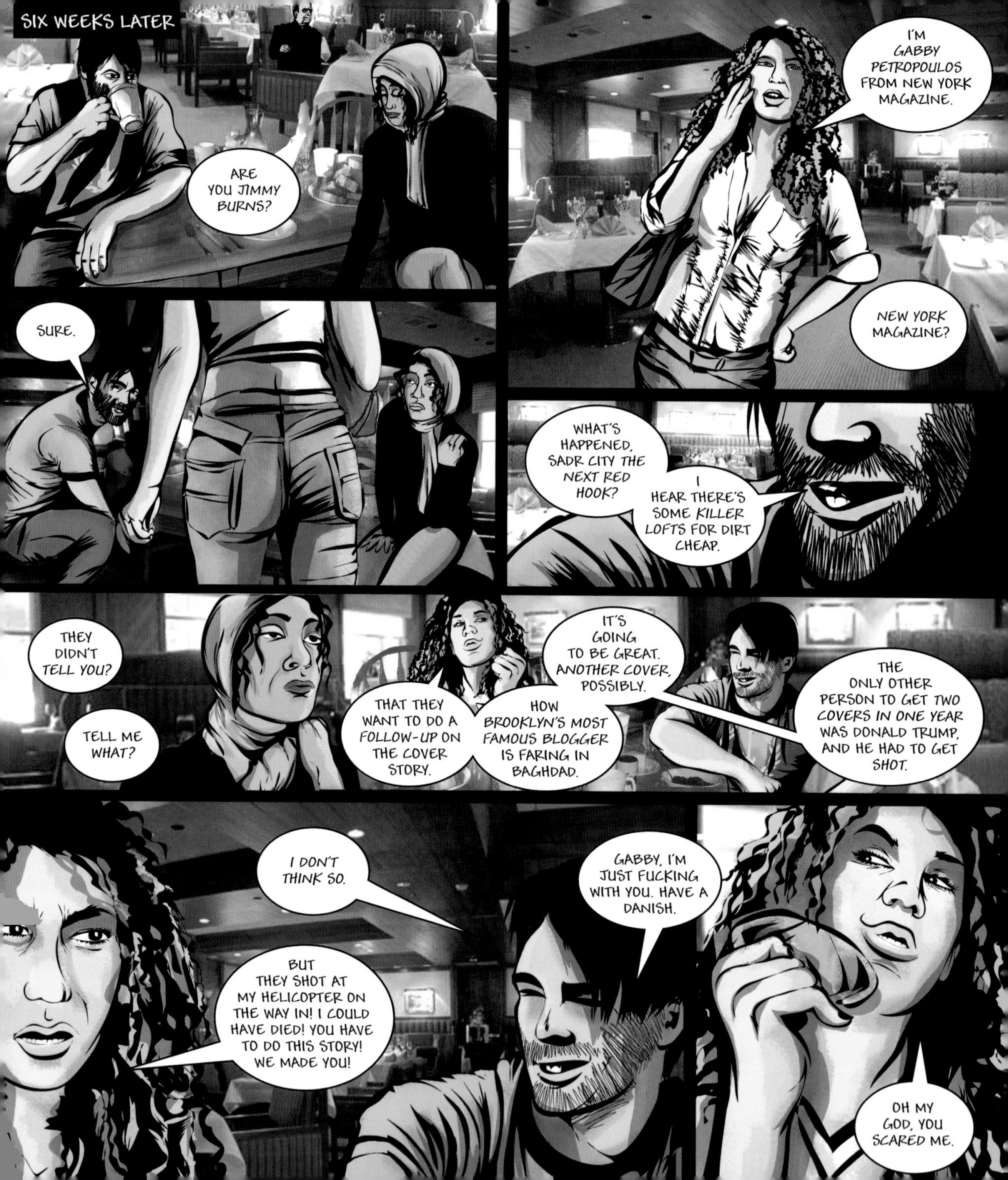
SIX WEEKS LATER
ARE YOU JIMMY BURNS?
I'M GABBY PETROPOULOS FROM NEW YORK MAGAZINE.
SURE.
NEW YORK MAGAZINE?
WHAT'S HAPPENED, SADR CITY THE NEXT RED HOOK?
I HEAR THERE'S SOME KILLER LOFTS FOR DIRT CHEAP.
THEY DIDN'T TELL YOU?
TELL ME WHAT?
THAT THEY WANT TO DO A FOLLOW-UP ON THE COVER STORY.
HOW BROOKLYN'S MOST FAMOUS BLOGGER IS FARING IN BAGHDAD.
IT'S GOING TO BE GREAT. ANOTHER COVER, POSSIBLY.
THE ONLY OTHER PERSON TO GET TWO COVERS IN ONE YEAR WAS DONALD TRUMP, AND HE HAD TO GET SHOT.
I DON'T THINK SO.
BUT THEY SHOT AT MY HELICOPTER ON THE WAY IN! I COULD HAVE DIED! YOU HAVE TO DO THIS STORY! WE MADE YOU!
GABBY, I'M JUST FUCKING WITH YOU. HAVE A DANISH.
OH MY GOD, YOU SCARED ME.

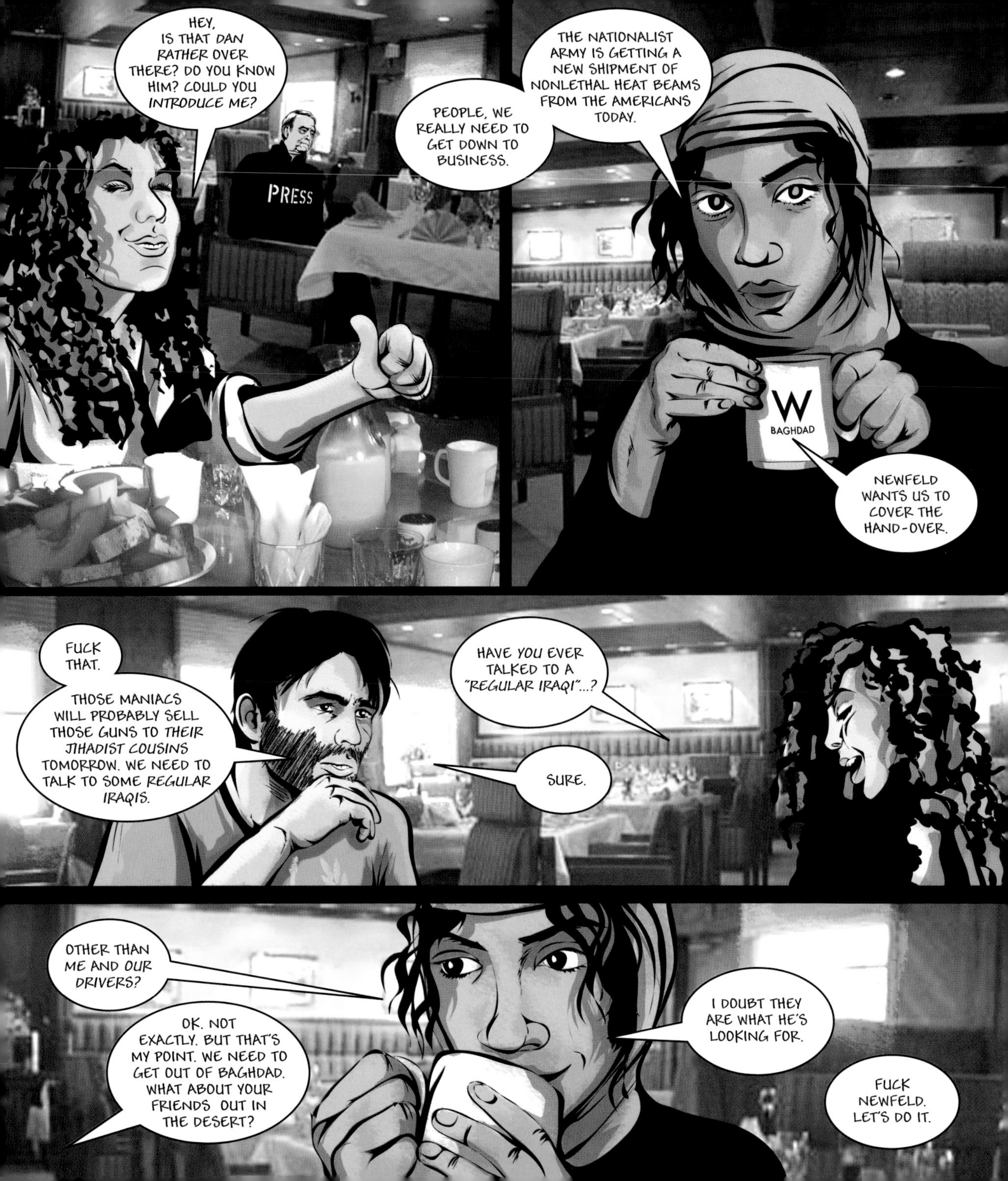
HEY, IS THAT DAN RATHER OVER THERE? DO YOU KNOW HIM? COULD YOU INTRODUCE ME?
PRESS
PEOPLE, WE REALLY NEED TO GET DOWN TO BUSINESS.
THE NATIONALIST ARMY IS GETTING A NEW SHIPMENT OF NONLETHAL HEAT BEAMS FROM THE AMERICANS TODAY.
W BAGHDAD
NEWFELD WANTS US TO COVER THE HAND-OVER.
FUCK THAT.
THOSE MANIACS WILL PROBABLY SELL THOSE GUNS TO THEIR JIHADIST COUSINS TOMORROW. WE NEED TO TALK TO SOME REGULAR IRAQIS.
HAVE YOU EVER TALKED TO A "REGULAR IRAQI"...?
SURE.
OTHER THAN ME AND OUR DRIVERS?
OK. NOT EXACTLY. BUT THAT'S MY POINT. WE NEED TO GET OUT OF BAGHDAD. WHAT ABOUT YOUR FRIENDS OUT IN THE DESERT?
I DOUBT THEY ARE WHAT HE'S LOOKING FOR.
FUCK NEWFELD. LET'S DO IT.

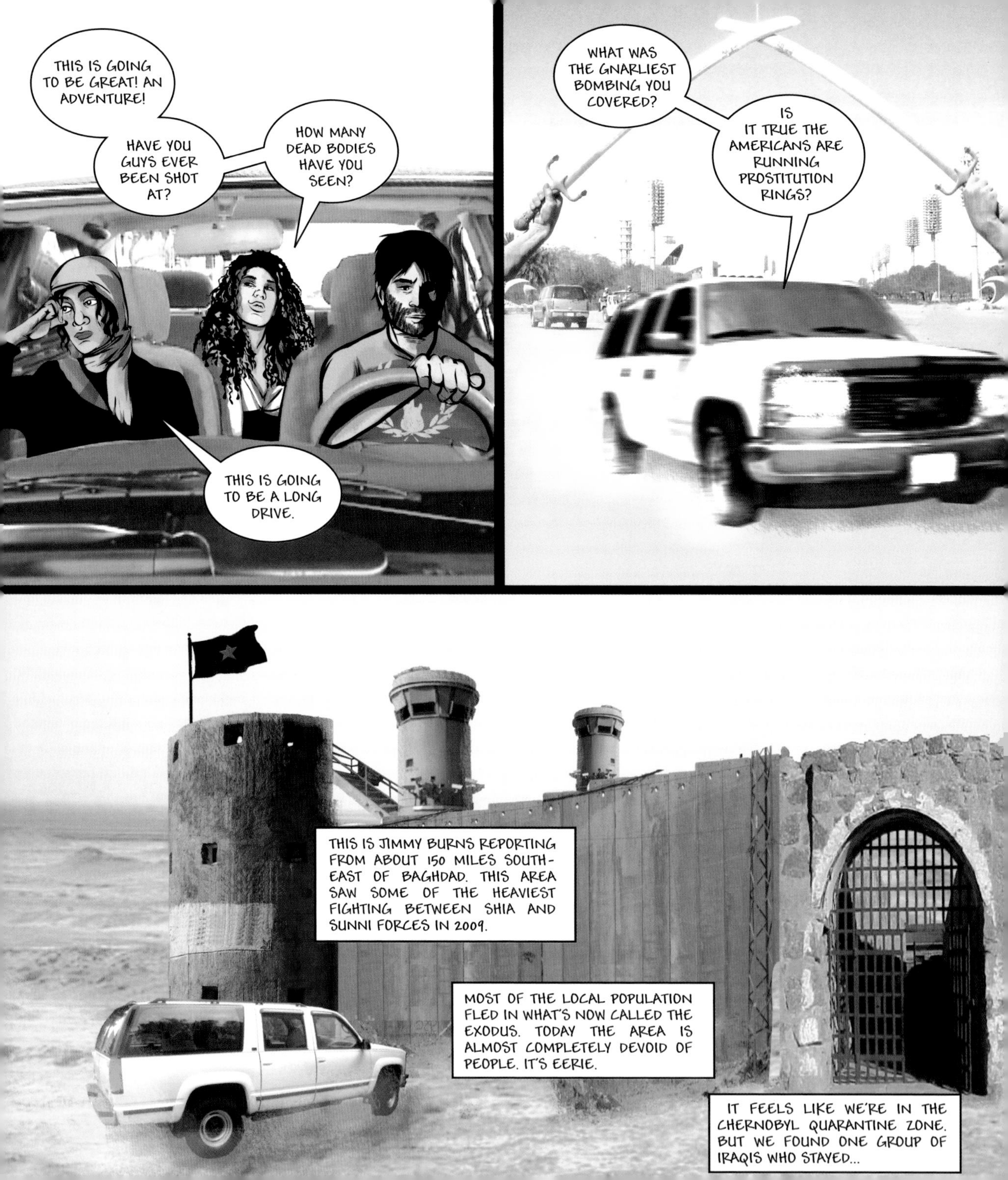
THIS IS GOING TO BE GREAT! AN ADVENTURE!
HAVE YOU GUYS EVER BEEN SHOT AT?
HOW MANY DEAD BODIES HAVE YOU SEEN?
THIS IS GOING TO BE A LONG DRIVE.
WHAT WAS THE GNARLIEST BOMBING YOU COVERED?
IS IT TRUE THE AMERICANS ARE RUNNING PROSTITUTION RINGS?
THIS IS JIMMY BURNS REPORTING FROM ABOUT 150 MILES SOUTH-EAST OF BAGHDAD. THIS AREA SAW SOME OF THE HEAVIEST FIGHTING BETWEEN SHIA AND SUNNI FORCES IN 2009.
MOST OF THE LOCAL POPULATION FLED IN WHAT'S NOW CALLED THE EXODUS. TODAY THE AREA IS ALMOST COMPLETELY DEVOID OF PEOPLE. IT'S EERIE.
IT FEELS LIKE WE'RE IN THE CHERNOBYL QUARANTINE ZONE. BUT WE FOUND ONE GROUP OF IRAQIS WHO STAYED...

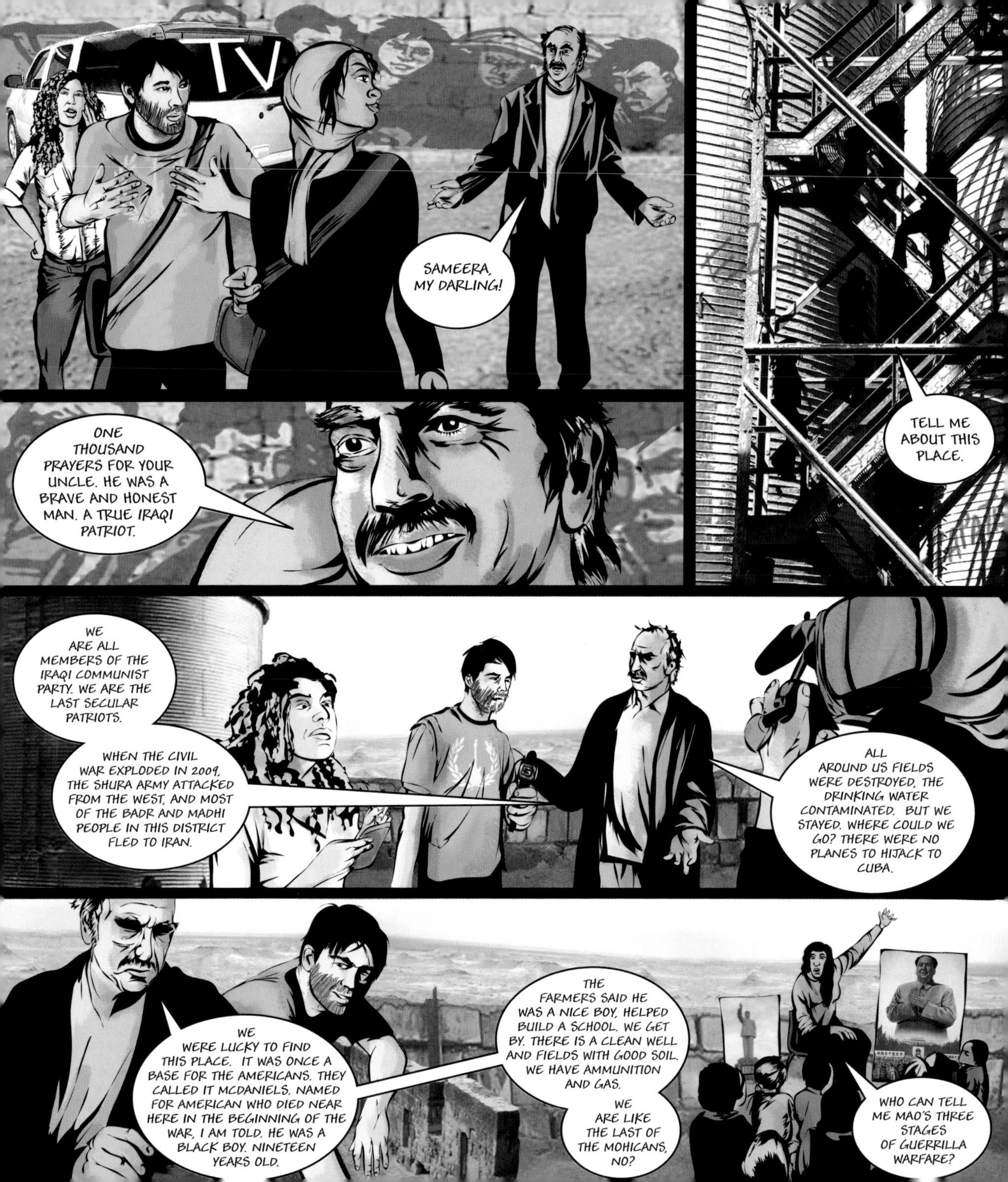
TV
SAMEERA, MY DARLING!
ONE THOUSAND PRAYERS FOR YOUR UNCLE. HE WAS A BRAVE AND HONEST MAN. A TRUE IRAQI PATRIOT.
TELL ME ABOUT THIS PLACE.
WE ARE ALL MEMBERS OF THE IRAQI COMMUNIST PARTY. WE ARE THE LAST SECULAR PATRIOTS.
WHEN THE CIVIL WAR EXPLODED IN 2009, THE SHURA ARMY ATTACKED FROM THE WEST, AND MOST OF THE BADR AND MADHI PEOPLE IN THIS DISTRICT FLED TO IRAN.
ALL AROUND US FIELDS WERE DESTROYED, THE DRINKING WATER CONTAMINATED. BUT WE STAYED. WHERE COULD WE GO? THERE WERE NO PLANES TO HIJACK TO CUBA.
WE WERE LUCKY TO FIND THIS PLACE. IT WAS ONCE A BASE FOR THE AMERICANS. THEY CALLED IT MCDANIELS. NAMED FOR AMERICAN WHO DIED NEAR HERE IN THE BEGINNING OF THE WAR, I AM TOLD. HE WAS A BLACK BOY. NINETEEN YEARS OLD.
THE FARMERS SAID HE WAS A NICE BOY, HELPED BUILD A SCHOOL. WE GET BY. THERE IS A CLEAN WELL AND FIELDS WITH GOOD SOIL. WE HAVE AMMUNITION AND GAS.
WE ARE LIKE THE LAST OF THE MOHICANS, NO?
WHO CAN TELL ME MAO'S THREE STAGES OF GUERRILLA WARFARE?

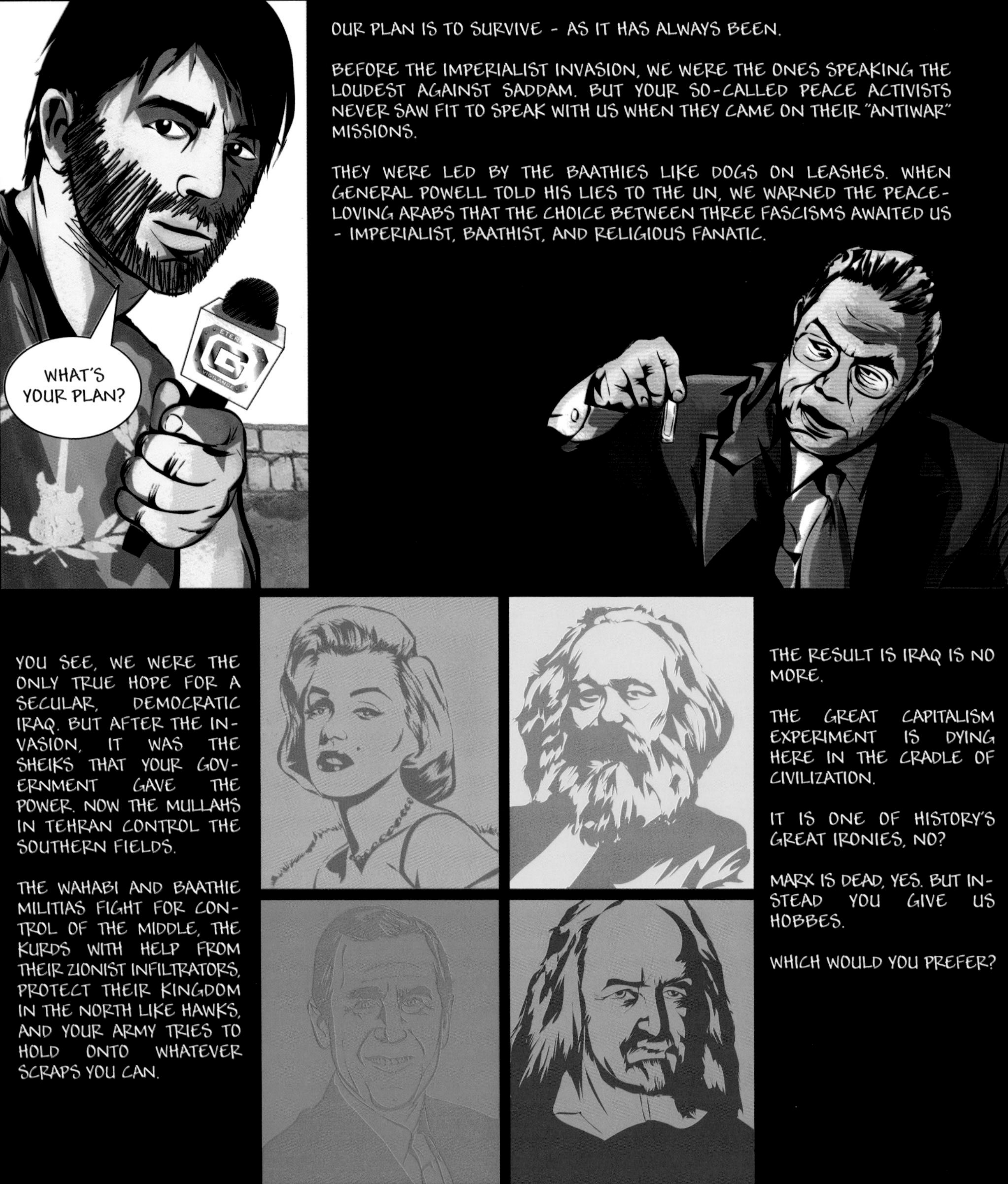
WHAT'S YOUR PLAN?
OUR PLAN IS TO SURVIVE - AS IT HAS ALWAYS BEEN.
BEFORE THE IMPERIALIST INVASION, WE WERE THE ONES SPEAKING THE LOUDEST AGAINST SADDAM. BUT YOUR SO-CALLED PEACE ACTIVISTS NEVER SAW FIT TO SPEAK WITH US WHEN THEY CAME ON THEIR "ANTIWAR" MISSIONS.
THEY WERE LED BY THE BAATHIES LIKE DOGS ON LEASHES. WHEN GENERAL POWELL TOLD HIS LIES TO THE UN, WE WARNED THE PEACE-LOVING ARABS THAT THE CHOICE BETWEEN THREE FASCISMS AWAITED US - IMPERIALIST, BAATHIST, AND RELIGIOUS FANATIC.
YOU SEE, WE WERE THE ONLY TRUE HOPE FOR A SECULAR, DEMOCRATIC IRAQ. BUT AFTER THE INVASION, IT WAS THE SHEIKS THAT YOUR GOVERNMENT GAVE THE POWER. NOW THE MULLAHS IN TEHRAN CONTROL THE SOUTHERN FIELDS.
THE WAHABI AND BAATHIE MILITIAS FIGHT FOR CONTROL OF THE MIDDLE, THE KURDS WITH HELP FROM THEIR ZIONIST INFILTRATORS, PROTECT THEIR KINGDOM IN THE NORTH LIKE HAWKS, AND YOUR ARMY TRIES TO HOLD ONTO WHATEVER SCRAPS YOU CAN.
THE RESULT IS IRAQ IS NO MORE.
THE GREAT CAPITALISM EXPERIMENT IS DYING HERE IN THE CRADLE OF CIVILIZATION.
IT IS ONE OF HISTORY'S GREAT IRONIES, NO?
MARX IS DEAD, YES. BUT INSTEAD YOU GIVE US HOBBES.
WHICH WOULD YOU PREFER?

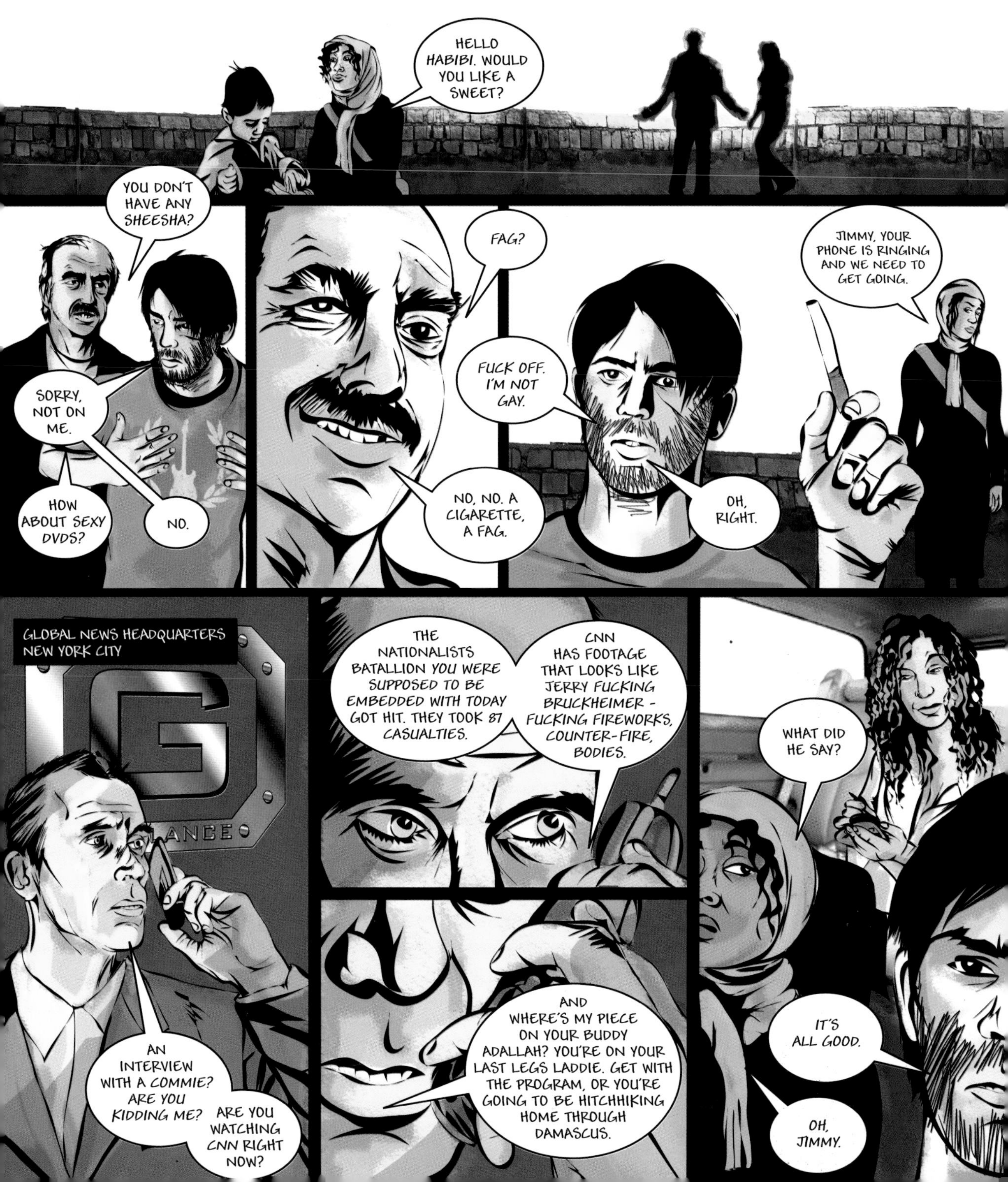

HELLO HABIBI. WOULD YOU LIKE A SWEET?
YOU DON'T HAVE ANY SHEESHA?
SORRY, NOT ON ME.
HOW ABOUT SEXY DVDS?
NO.
FAG?
NO, NO. A CIGARETTE, A FAG.
FUCK OFF. I'M NOT GAY.
OH, RIGHT.
JIMMY, YOUR PHONE IS RINGING AND WE NEED TO GET GOING.
GLOBAL NEWS HEADQUARTERS NEW YORK CITY
THE NATIONALISTS BATALLION YOU WERE SUPPOSED TO BE EMBEDDED WITH TODAY GOT HIT. THEY TOOK 87 CASUALTIES.
CNN HAS FOOTAGE THAT LOOKS LIKE JERRY FUCKING BRUCKHEIMER - FUCKING FIREWORKS, COUNTER-FIRE, BODIES.
AN INTERVIEW WITH A COMMIE? ARE YOU KIDDING ME?
ARE YOU WATCHING CNN RIGHT NOW?
AND WHERE'S MY PIECE ON YOUR BUDDY ADALLAH? YOU'RE ON YOUR LAST LEGS LADDIE. GET WITH THE PROGRAM, OR YOU'RE GOING TO BE HITCHHIKING HOME THROUGH DAMASCUS.
WHAT DID HE SAY?
IT'S ALL GOOD.
OH, JIMMY.

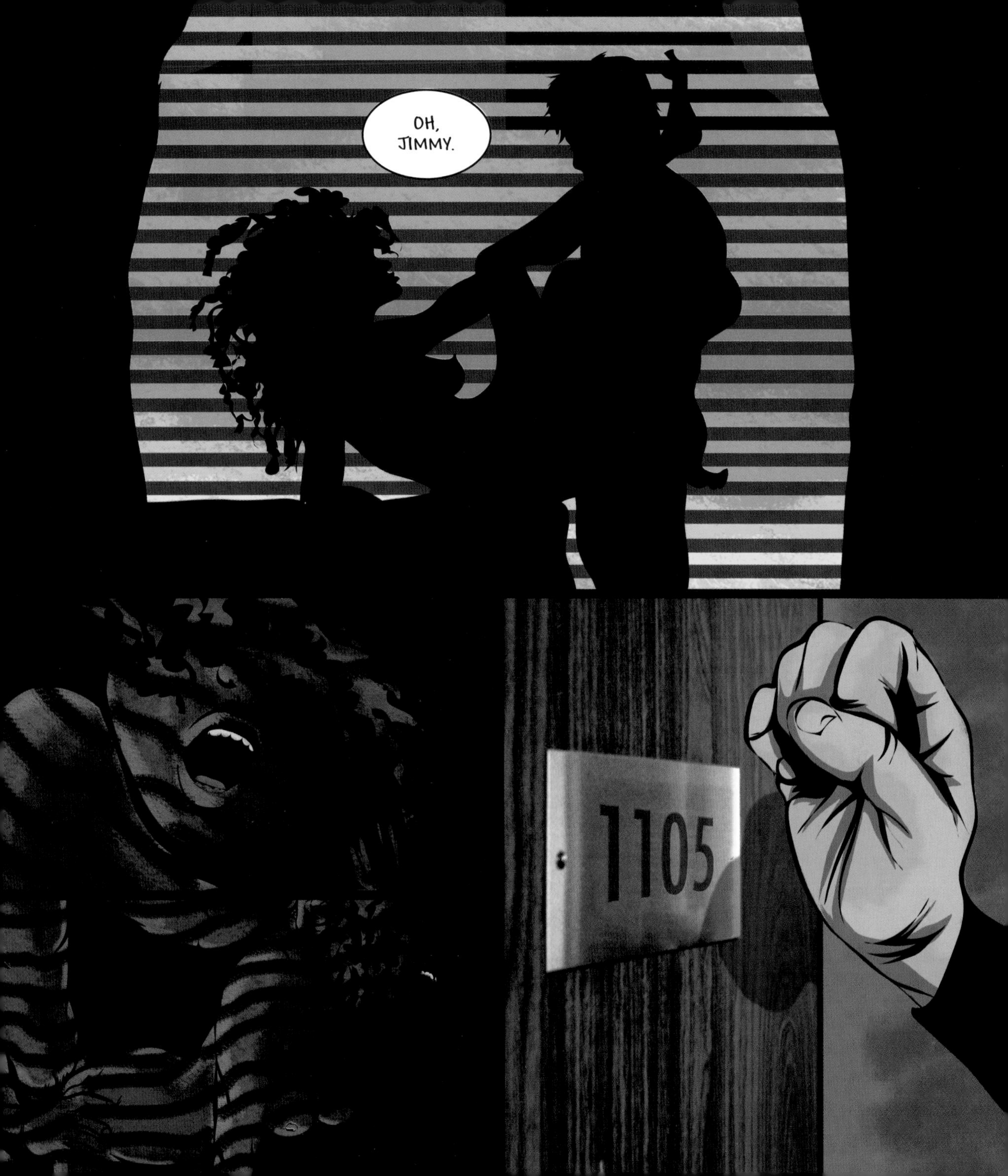
OH, JIMMY.
1105

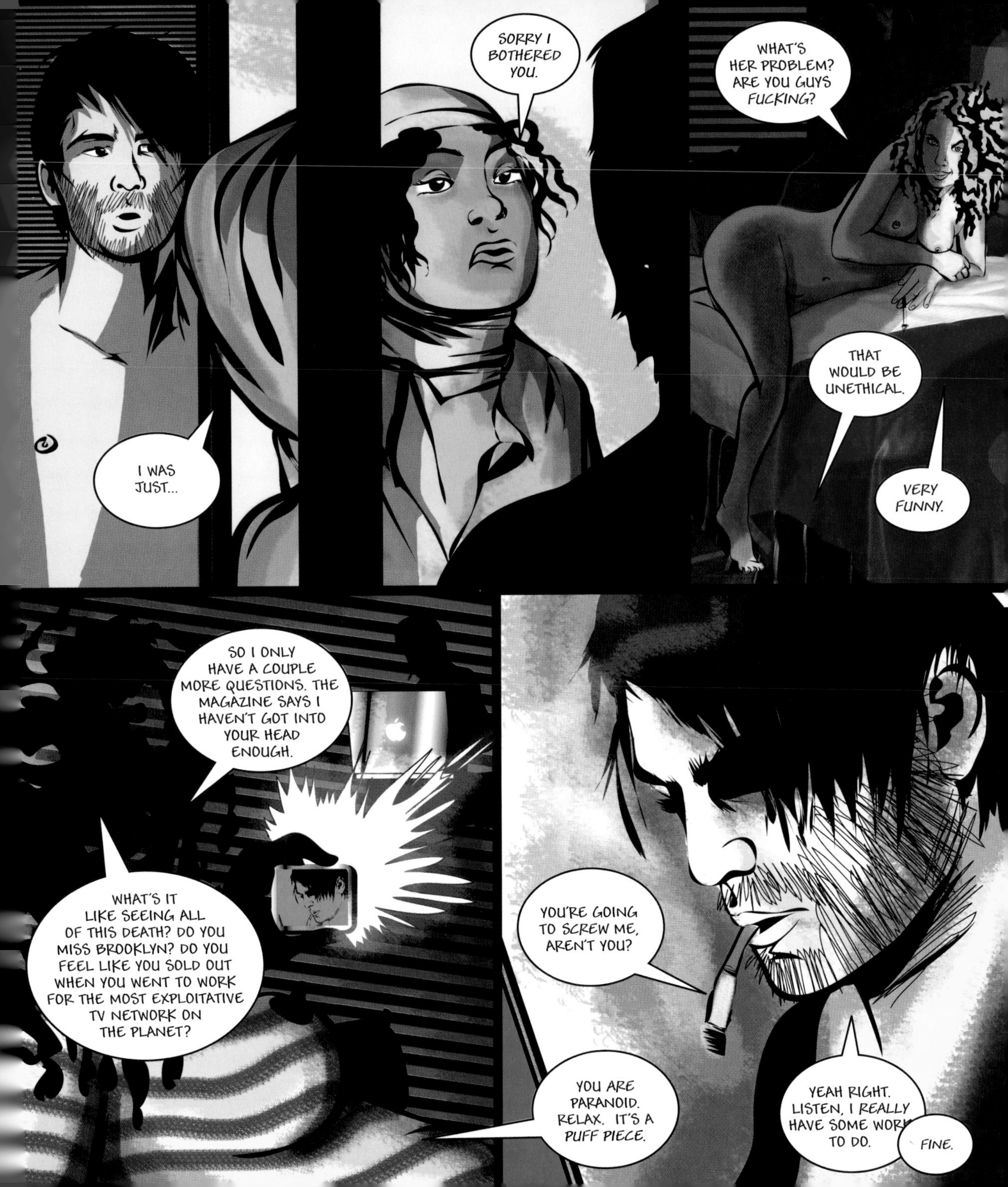
I WAS JUST...
SORRY I BOTHERED YOU.
WHAT'S HER PROBLEM? ARE YOU GUYS FUCKING?
THAT WOULD BE UNETHICAL.
VERY FUNNY.
SO I ONLY HAVE A COUPLE MORE QUESTIONS. THE MAGAZINE SAYS I HAVEN'T GOT INTO YOUR HEAD ENOUGH.
WHAT'S IT LIKE SEEING ALL OF THIS DEATH? DO YOU MISS BROOKLYN? DO YOU FEEL LIKE YOU SOLD OUT WHEN YOU WENT TO WORK FOR THE MOST EXPLOITATIVE TV NETWORK ON THE PLANET?
YOU'RE GOING TO SCREW ME, AREN'T YOU?
YOU ARE PARANOID. RELAX. IT'S A PUFF PIECE.
YEAH RIGHT. LISTEN, I REALLY HAVE SOME WOR TO DO.
FINE.

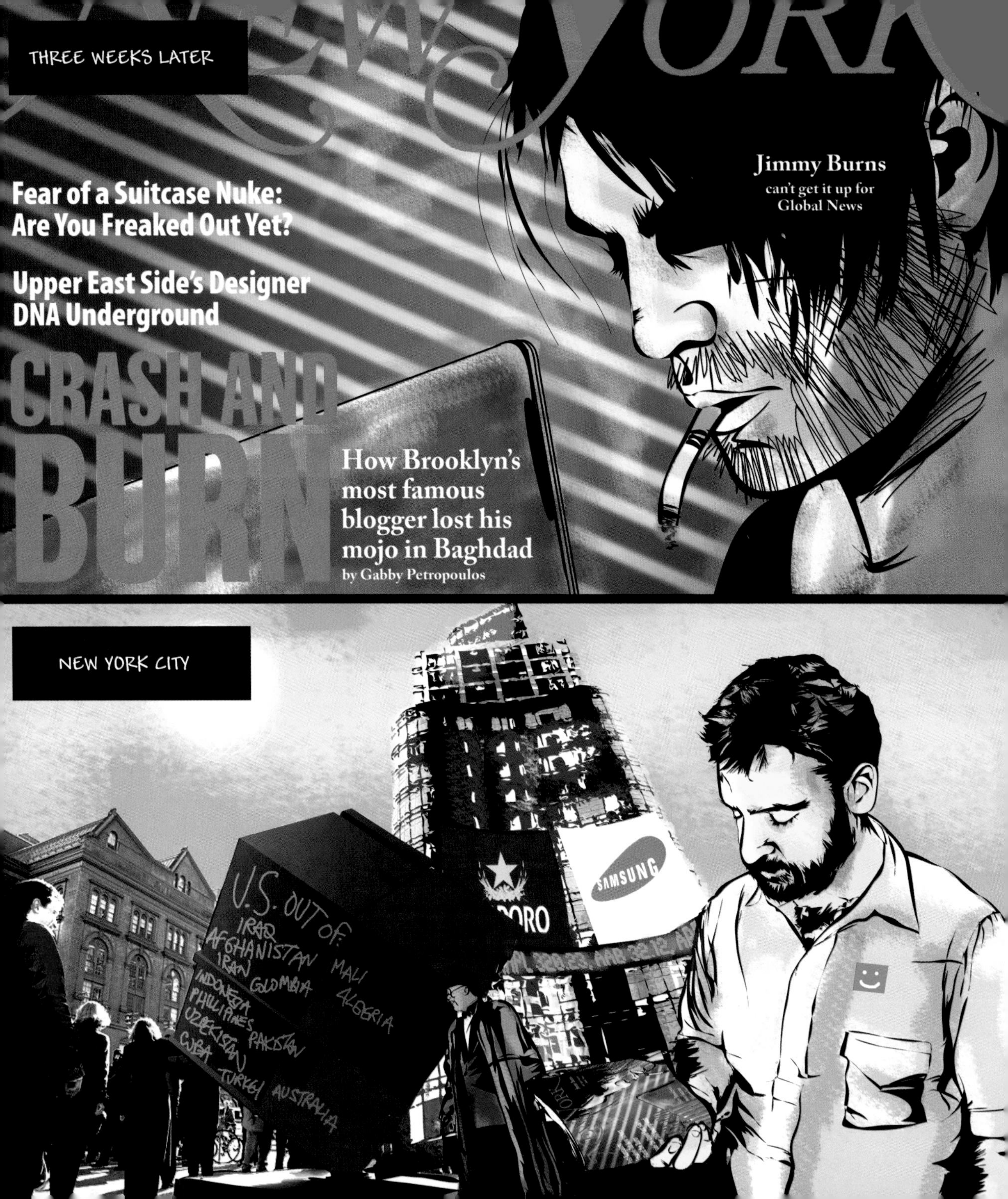
THREE WEEKS LATER
Jimmy Burns
can't get it up for Global News
Fear of a Suitcase Nuke: Are You Freaked Out Yet?
Upper East Side's Designer DNA Underground
CRASH AND BURN
How Brooklyn's most famous blogger lost his mojo in Baghdad
by Gabby Petropoulos
NEW YORK CITY
U.S. OUT OF:
IRAQ
AFGHANISTAN MALI
IRAN COLOMBIA ALGERIA
INDONESIA
PHILLIPINES PAKISTAN
UZBEKISTAN
CUBA TURKEY AUSTRALIA
SAMSUNG

NEW YORK
nymag.com

How Brooklyn's most famous blogger lost his mojo in Baghdad

Crash & Burn

by **Gabby Petropoulos**

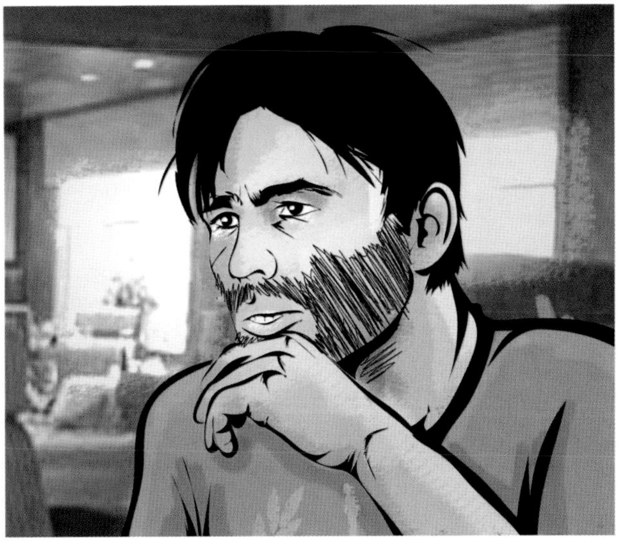

"Fuck New York"

It's 9:15 AM and the dingy restaurant of the W Hotel Baghdad is nearly empty.

Three South African mercenaries are barking death threats into a sat-phone at some unlucky soul who owes them money. Dan Rather is picking at his eggs like they are infected with ebola. A stylishly disheveled young American man and a plain but pretty Iraqi woman in a headscarf are huddled conspiratorially over coffee. It's blogger-turned-war correspondent Jimmy Burns and his producer, Sameera al Burkari. The day's assignment has just come in from their boss in New York, Global News' famously combative executive producer Dan Newfeld. But Burns isn't having any of it.

"Fuck New York," he announces. "And fuck Newfeld." — Burns has his own idea.

It is classic Burns — putting his own political agenda ahead of sound news judgment. And like most of what he's done since he arrived in Baghdad, the results are disastrous. Burns misses the day's headline, is scooped by CNN, and is nearly fired by an apoplectic Newfeld.

When Jimmy Burns literally burst into our living rooms this May he was a revelation, and for many, a savior. Younger, cuter, and more "real" than CNN's scion of a designer jean fortune, Burns personified outrage. He perfectly captured the anti-Big Media zeitgeist that swept the country last summer, killing off the broadcast networks' venerable evening newscasts, and nearly bankrupting several cable networks' news divisions. Burns appeared to be the antidote to a business that had long since embraced entertainment values over substance. It didn't hurt that Burns had impeccable populist street cred. He was the first blogger to make the jump from the obscurity of the web to fully-fledged war-on-terror correspondent. But it wasn't just the novelty of his career path. There was something about him that captured our imaginations, and our hearts. He was our blogger. Burns would redeem us.

Finally, there was a reporter who could explain what was really happening in that murky Mad Max cauldron of hate that was still taking the lives of our countrymen and women long after we'd all gone back to buying Blahniks and watching football (as if we ever stopped). But, alas, Burns has been a bust. His channel's ratings have sunk to their lowest ever and his Q rating, the closely guarded indicator of a television personality's familiarity and appeal, is allegedly scraping rock bottom. Burns' failures to perform under pressure in Baghdad has left many media insiders wondering whether Newfeld himself is one five-Foster lunch away from a red slip.

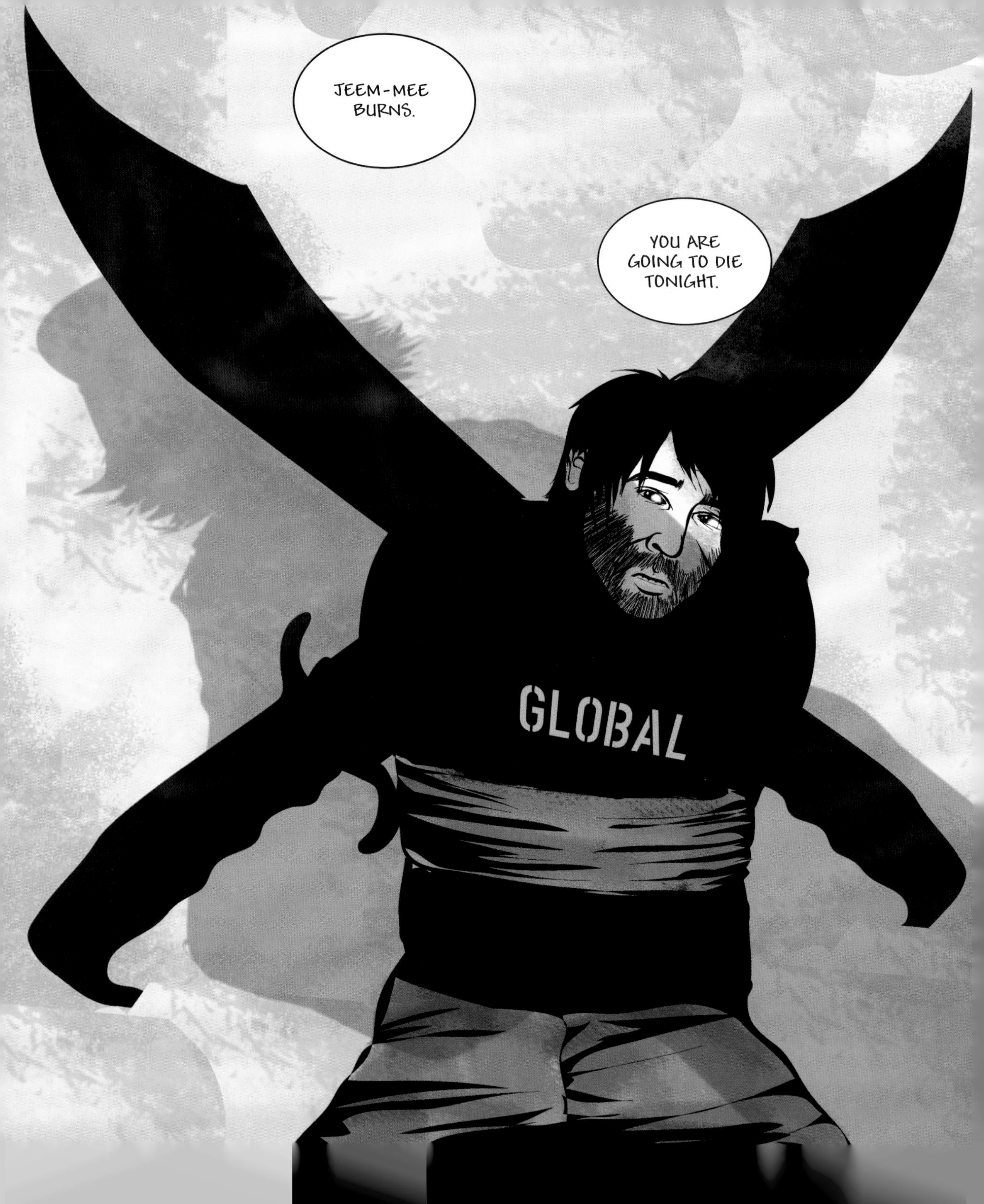
JEEM-MEE BURNS.
YOU ARE GOING TO DIE TONIGHT.
GLOBAL

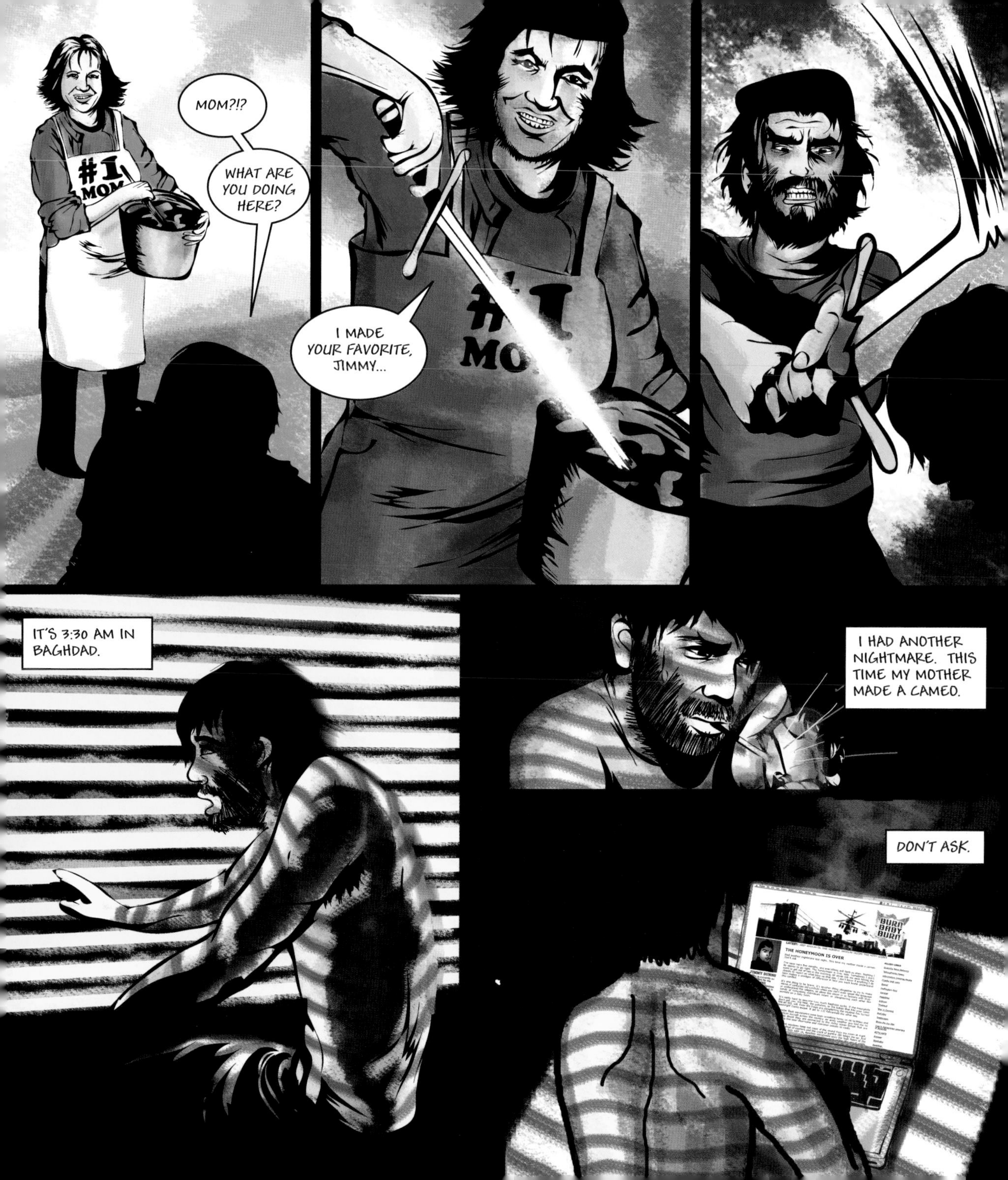
MOM?!?
WHAT ARE YOU DOING HERE?
#1 MOM
I MADE YOUR FAVORITE, JIMMY...
IT'S 3:30 AM IN BAGHDAD.
I HAD ANOTHER NIGHTMARE. THIS TIME MY MOTHER MADE A CAMEO.
DON'T ASK.
BURN BABY BURN
THE HONEYMOON IS OVER
JIMMY DUNNE

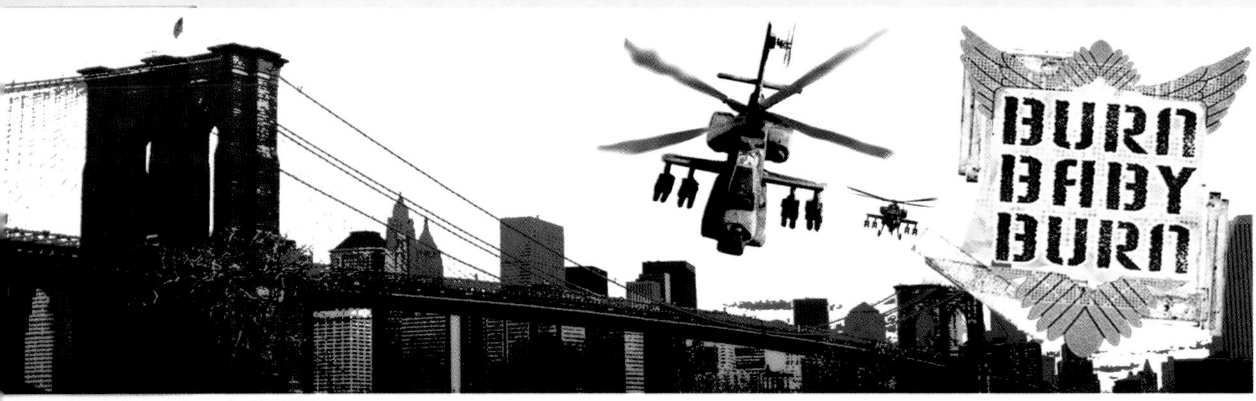
BURN BABY BURN

LATEST: WEST AFRICAN OIL WAR WORSENS. ANGOLAN TROOPS TAKE HEAVY LOSSES

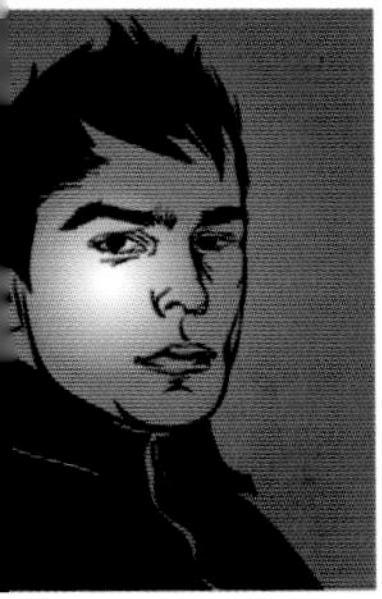

IMY BURNS

y is currently on
nment for the
BAL NEWS
ork as embedded
correspondent in
dad.

sat-cam feed here:
lobalnews.com/burns

ARCHIVE:

orate Takeover
merica series:

19: Eminent
ain Disasters

18: Your DNA,
$

17: ChoicePoint:
're back

THE HONEYMOON IS OVER

Had another nightmare last night. This time my mother made a cameo. Don't ask.

I've been here five months, and everything still feels so alien. Nothing I do seems to go right. The honeymoon is over, kids. Sometimes I don't want to get out of bed in the morning, let alone risk my neck hitting the streets to report on what blew up that day. I don't know if anything I do here makes a smidgen of difference in how you back home understand this conflict.

It's one thing to be brave. It's another thing altogether to try to make sense of centuries-old conflicts when you don't even speak the language or understand the religion, let alone the dozen or so factions with thousands of competing individuals intent on slaughtering each other like animals on a daily basis.

It's really hard to describe how much Baghdad sucks. If the insurgents don't get you, the heat, the pollution, or the kebab that hits your colon like an IED, will. Even the Iraqis are complaining the weather has turned downright Dante-esque. It got to 132 Fahrenheit the other day.

Monster flash sandstorms have been wreaking havoc on oil facilities and American aircraft across the country. An army weather guy told me he had no doubt they are connected to the rising ocean temps that are making this year's hurricane and monsoon season so nasty.

The blast windows keep out most of the sound from my room at night. But the thud of mortars and the crack of gunfire still keep me up. Just to fuck with us, Apaches sometimes buzz the high floors of the hotel in the ass crack of the morning. Your room rattles as if you're inside a giant vibrator.

I wish I could report the political situation is getting any better, but the new government (that's number 11 if you're counting) is AWOL. The PM hasn't left his bunker for weeks. No one has actually seen the Minister of the Interior — he won't allow his face to be photographed. Death squads continue to operate with impunity. As one journalist told me, "Iraq is Salvador without the surf." The problem is that trying to verify any of it is near impossible. Ever since the Pentagon got busted enlisting Pixar to create al-Zaraqwi's successor out of 0s and 1s, getting straight answers out of the military is like asking James Frey what he learned in prison.

And, no, I still have nothing on the Sword of Mohammed.

(MORE)

ALLIES LINKS

Guerrilla News Network
TalkingPoints Memo
Information Clearing H
Crooks and Liars
Sploid
Huffington Post
Gawker
Metafilter
Antiwar
Truthout
War in Context
DailyKos
Treehugger
Show Me the War
Iraq & Afghanistan Vete of America
ACT-I-VATE
Antiwar
Wonkette
Guardian
The Nation
Doc Searls
Village Voice
AlterNet
Entertainment Weekly
Independent Propagan
Rolling Stone

VLOG ARCHIVE:

Corporate Takeover of America series:

Part 19: Eminent Domain Disasters

Part 18: Your DNA, Their $

Part 17: ChoicePoint: They're back

Part 16: Net Neutrality: Moot?

SEE ALL >

Despite the fact Abu Adallah somehow considers me a soul brother. Scary, I know.

Lastly, thanks for your emails. Kiki77 in Laguna Beach writes: "My friends and I at the skate shop argue about you all the time. They say you're a sell out for working for Global News. I try to tell them you're just infiltrating the system. But I want to know what you say. Why did you take the job?"

Kiki & Co.: This gig is a chance to see things firsthand and to try and show all Americans what's going down in their name.

There's only four American correspondents left here, and one of them is Dan Rather. BTW, thanks for the Spring Break slideshow. It, um, sure helped pass the time between blackouts.

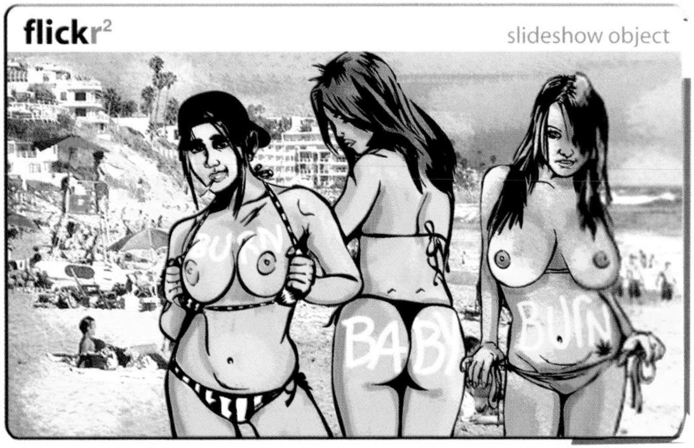
flickr²
slideshow object
BURN
BABY
BURN

The Nation

Doc Searls

Village Voic

AlterNet

Entertainme

Independen

Rolling Ston

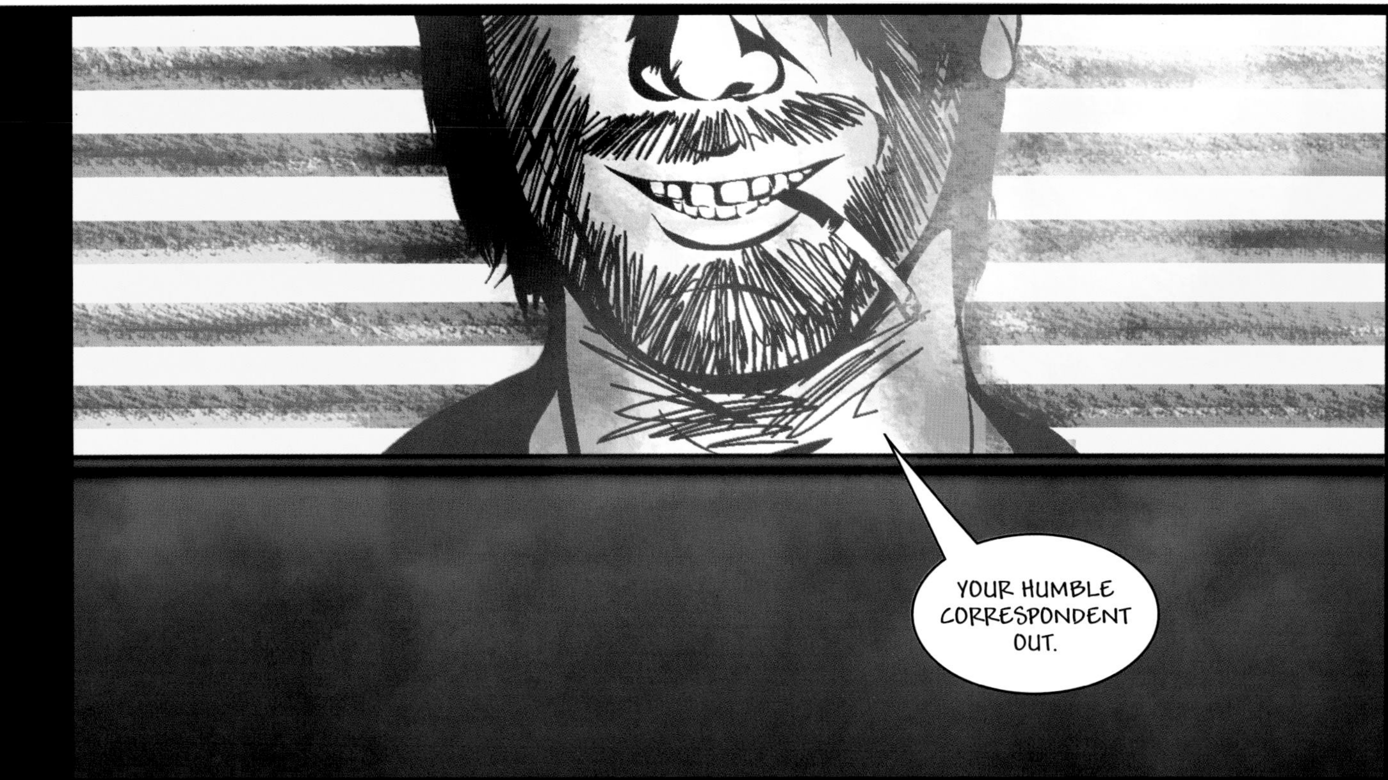
YOUR HUMBLE CORRESPONDENT OUT.

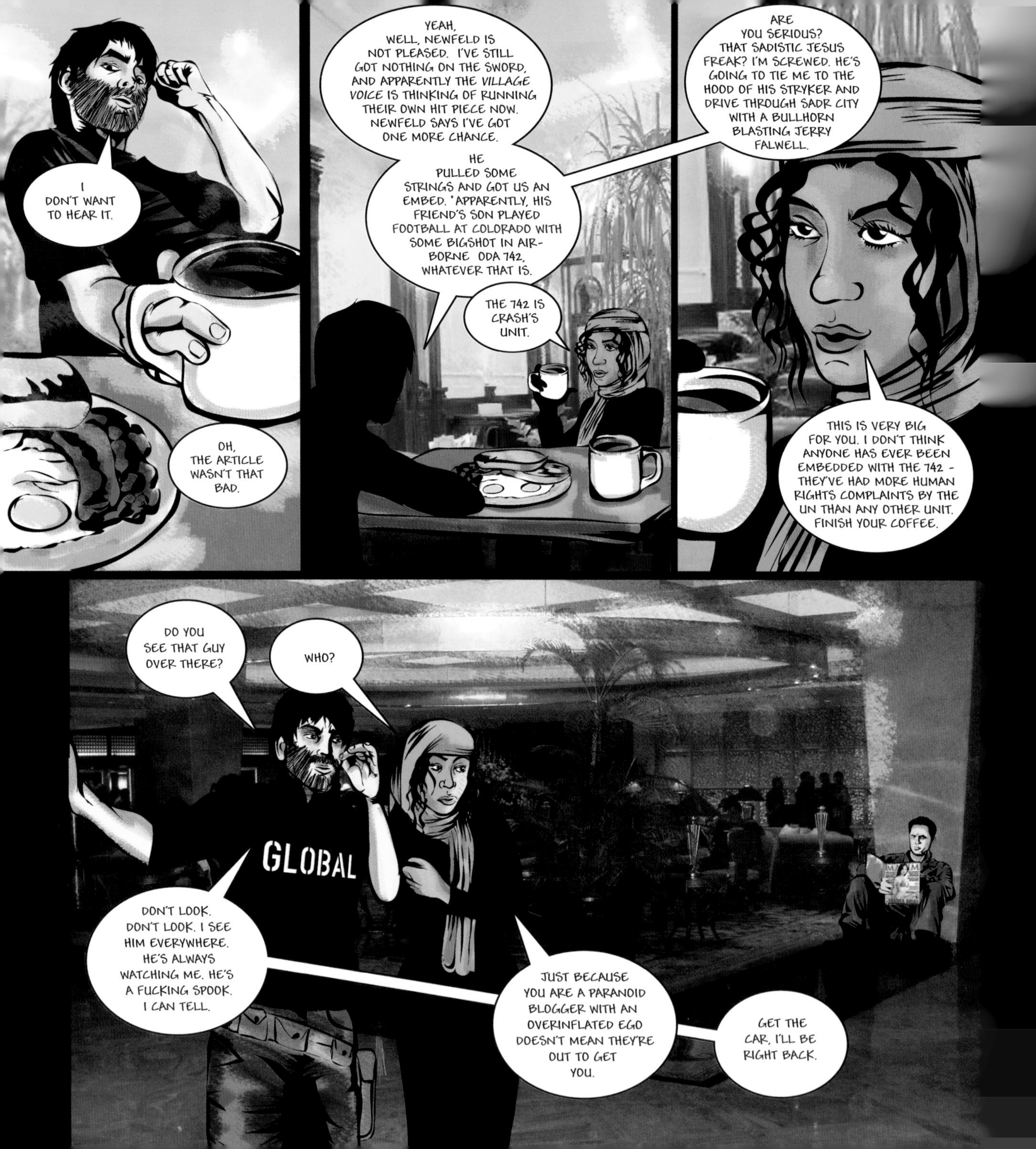
I DON'T WANT TO HEAR IT.
OH, THE ARTICLE WASN'T THAT BAD.
YEAH, WELL, NEWFELD IS NOT PLEASED. I'VE STILL GOT NOTHING ON THE SWORD, AND APPARENTLY THE VILLAGE VOICE IS THINKING OF RUNNING THEIR OWN HIT PIECE NOW. NEWFELD SAYS I'VE GOT ONE MORE CHANCE.
HE PULLED SOME STRINGS AND GOT US AN EMBED. *APPARENTLY, HIS FRIEND'S SON PLAYED FOOTBALL AT COLORADO WITH SOME BIGSHOT IN AIR-BORNE ODA 742, WHATEVER THAT IS.
THE 742 IS CRASH'S UNIT.
ARE YOU SERIOUS? THAT SADISTIC JESUS FREAK? I'M SCREWED. HE'S GOING TO TIE ME TO THE HOOD OF HIS STRYKER AND DRIVE THROUGH SADR CITY WITH A BULLHORN BLASTING JERRY FALWELL.
THIS IS VERY BIG FOR YOU. I DON'T THINK ANYONE HAS EVER BEEN EMBEDDED WITH THE 742 - THEY'VE HAD MORE HUMAN RIGHTS COMPLAINTS BY THE UN THAN ANY OTHER UNIT. FINISH YOUR COFFEE.
DO YOU SEE THAT GUY OVER THERE?
WHO?
GLOBAL
DON'T LOOK. DON'T LOOK. I SEE HIM EVERYWHERE. HE'S ALWAYS WATCHING ME. HE'S A FUCKING SPOOK. I CAN TELL.
JUST BECAUSE YOU ARE A PARANOID BLOGGER WITH AN OVERINFLATED EGO DOESN'T MEAN THEY'RE OUT TO GET YOU.
GET THE CAR, I'LL BE RIGHT BACK.

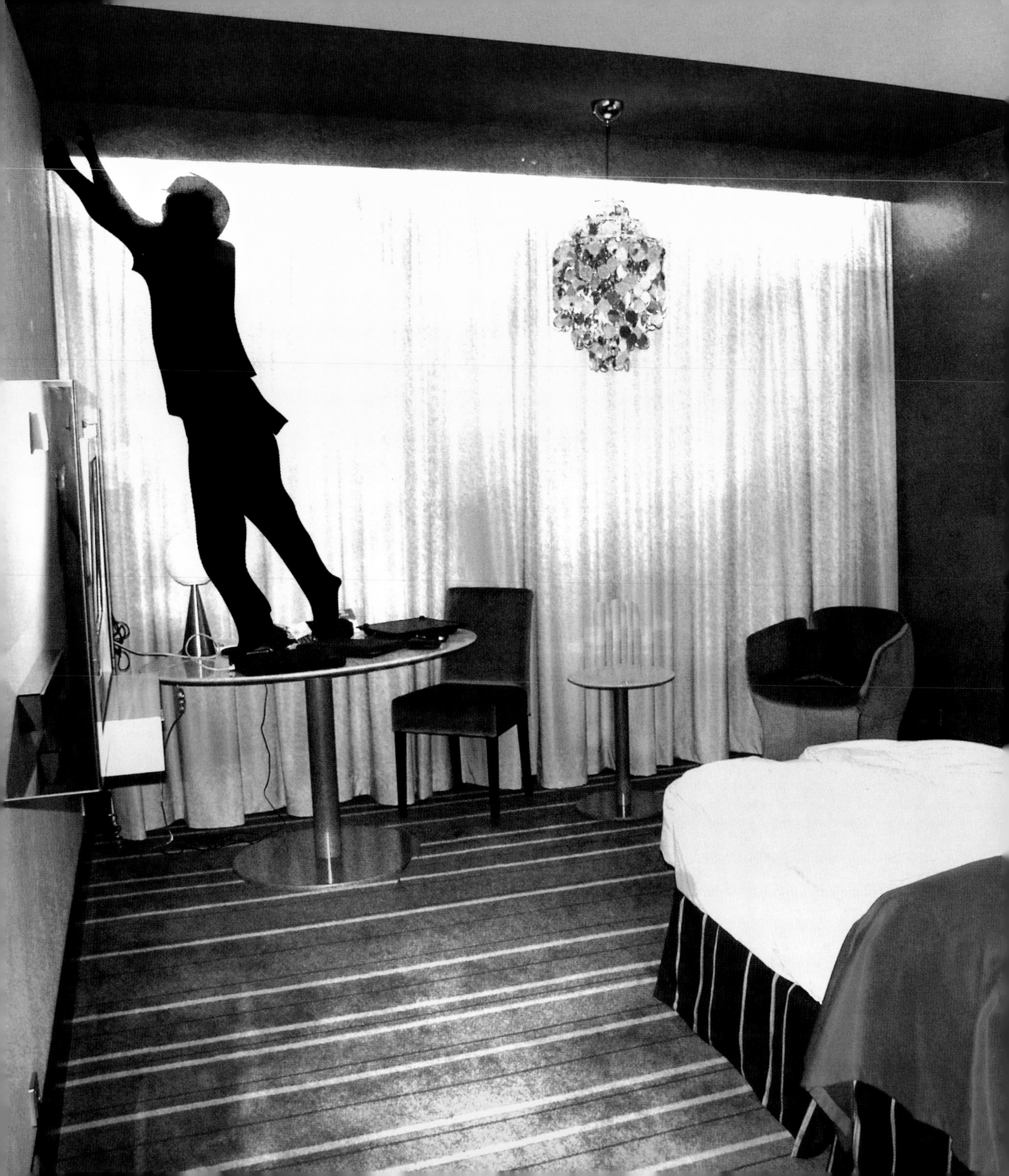

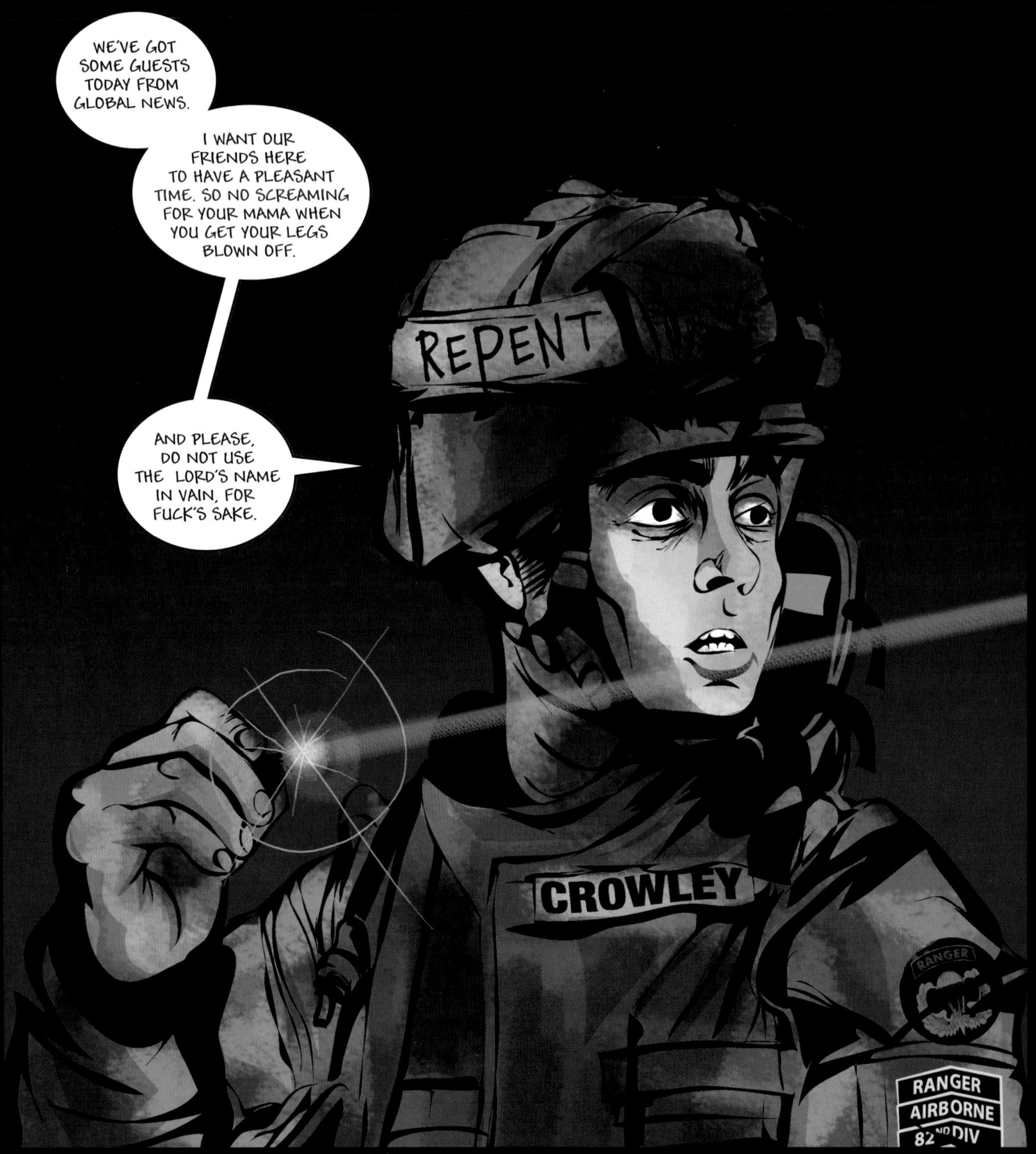
WE'VE GOT SOME GUESTS TODAY FROM GLOBAL NEWS.
I WANT OUR FRIENDS HERE TO HAVE A PLEASANT TIME. SO NO SCREAMING FOR YOUR MAMA WHEN YOU GET YOUR LEGS BLOWN OFF.
AND PLEASE, DO NOT USE THE LORD'S NAME IN VAIN, FOR FUCK'S SAKE.
REPENT
CROWLEY
RANGER
RANGER
AIRBORNE
82ND DIV

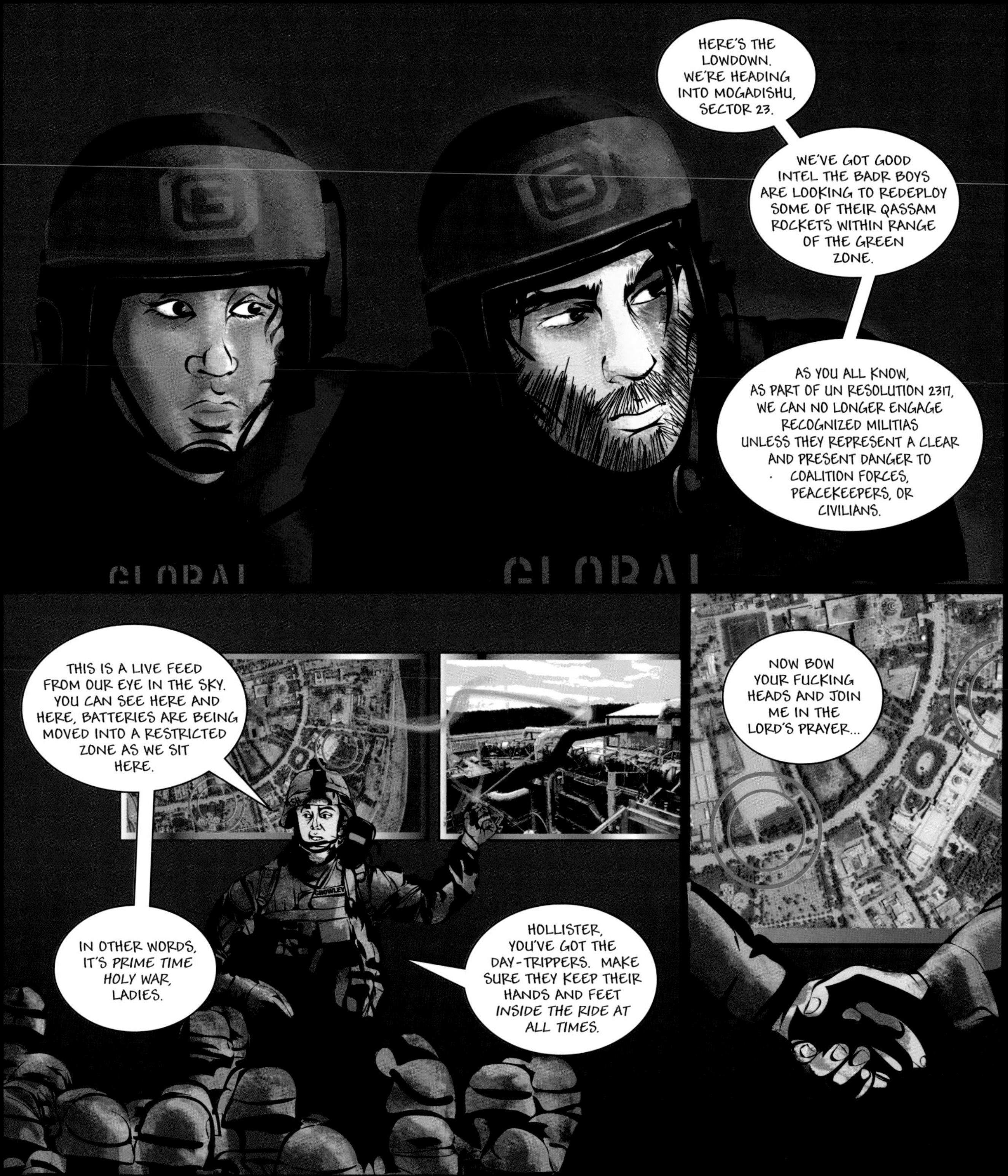
HERE'S THE LOWDOWN. WE'RE HEADING INTO MOGADISHU, SECTOR 23.
WE'VE GOT GOOD INTEL THE BADR BOYS ARE LOOKING TO REDEPLOY SOME OF THEIR QASSAM ROCKETS WITHIN RANGE OF THE GREEN ZONE.
AS YOU ALL KNOW, AS PART OF UN RESOLUTION 2317, WE CAN NO LONGER ENGAGE RECOGNIZED MILITIAS UNLESS THEY REPRESENT A CLEAR AND PRESENT DANGER TO COALITION FORCES, PEACEKEEPERS, OR CIVILIANS.
GLOBAL
GLOBAL
THIS IS A LIVE FEED FROM OUR EYE IN THE SKY. YOU CAN SEE HERE AND HERE, BATTERIES ARE BEING MOVED INTO A RESTRICTED ZONE AS WE SIT HERE.
CROWLEY
IN OTHER WORDS, IT'S PRIME TIME HOLY WAR, LADIES.
HOLLISTER, YOU'VE GOT THE DAY-TRIPPERS. MAKE SURE THEY KEEP THEIR HANDS AND FEET INSIDE THE RIDE AT ALL TIMES.
NOW BOW YOUR FUCKING HEADS AND JOIN ME IN THE LORD'S PRAYER...

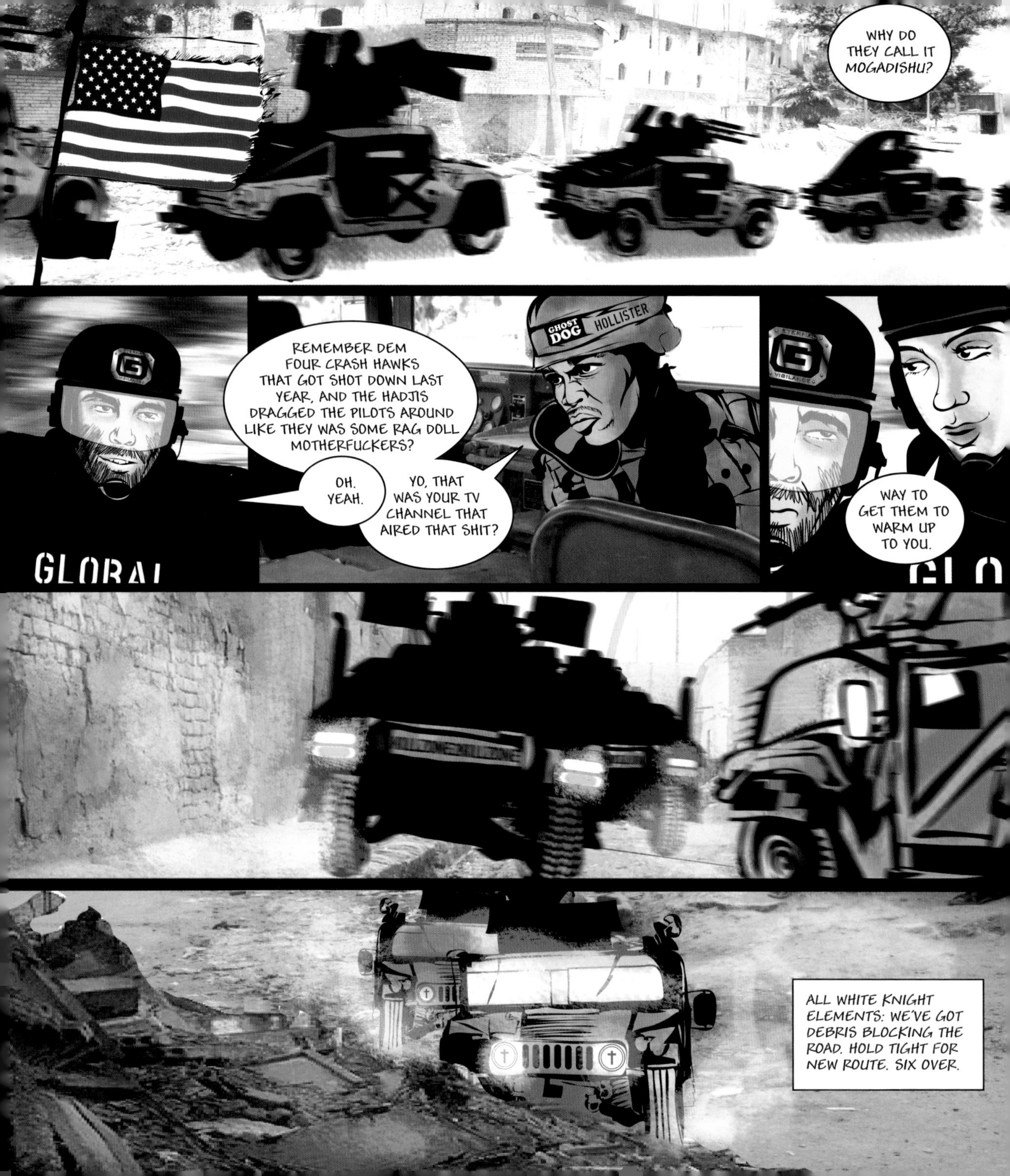
WHY DO THEY CALL IT MOGADISHU?
GHOST DOG HOLLISTER
REMEMBER DEM FOUR CRASH HAWKS THAT GOT SHOT DOWN LAST YEAR, AND THE HADJIS DRAGGED THE PILOTS AROUND LIKE THEY WAS SOME RAG DOLL MOTHERFUCKERS?
OH. YEAH.
YO, THAT WAS YOUR TV CHANNEL THAT AIRED THAT SHIT?
WAY TO GET THEM TO WARM UP TO YOU.
ALL WHITE KNIGHT ELEMENTS: WE'VE GOT DEBRIS BLOCKING THE ROAD. HOLD TIGHT FOR NEW ROUTE. SIX OVER.

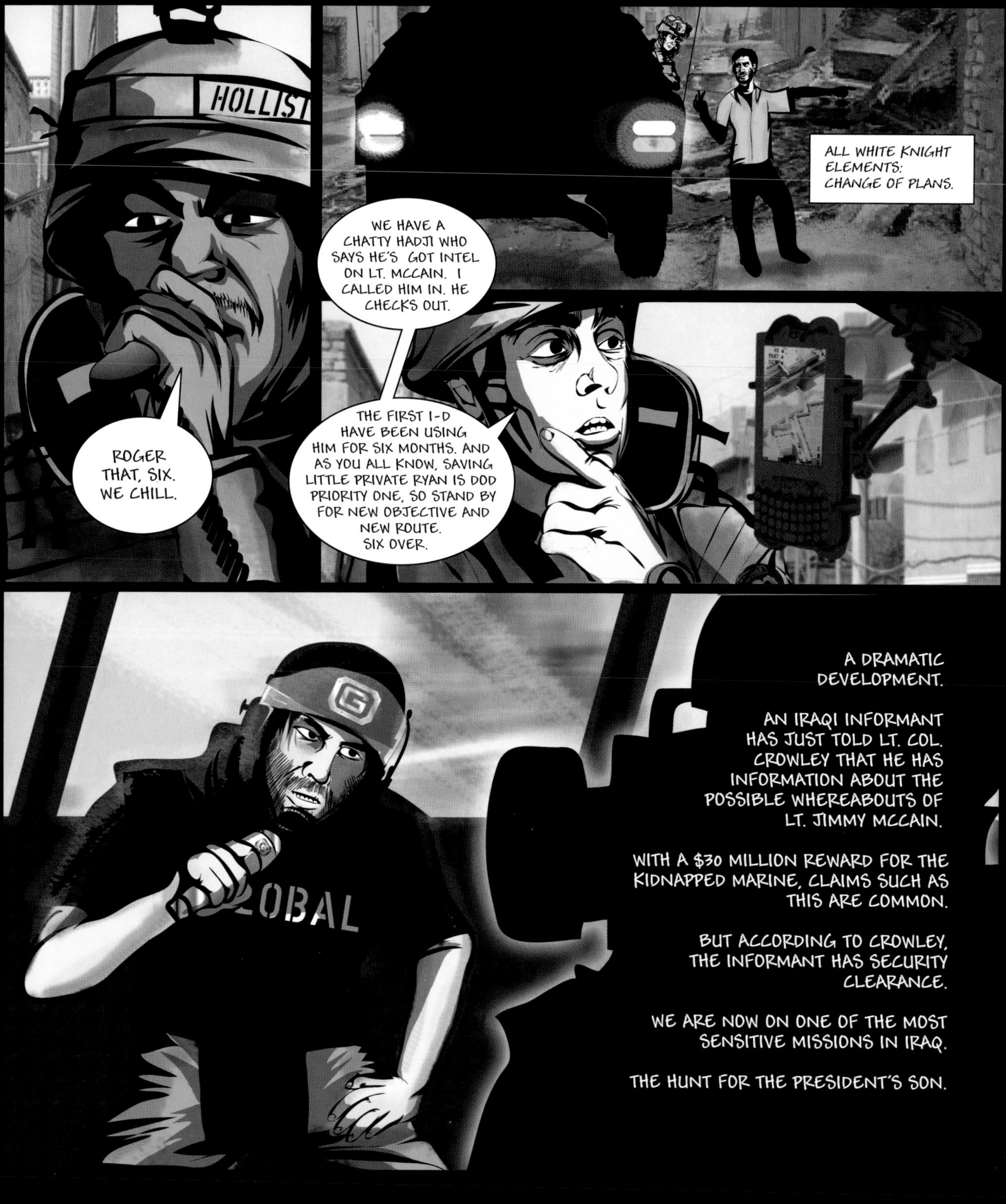
HOLLIST
ALL WHITE KNIGHT ELEMENTS: CHANGE OF PLANS.
WE HAVE A CHATTY HADJI WHO SAYS HE'S GOT INTEL ON LT. MCCAIN. I CALLED HIM IN. HE CHECKS OUT.
THE FIRST 1-D HAVE BEEN USING HIM FOR SIX MONTHS. AND AS YOU ALL KNOW, SAVING LITTLE PRIVATE RYAN IS DOD PRIORITY ONE, SO STAND BY FOR NEW OBJECTIVE AND NEW ROUTE. SIX OVER.
ROGER THAT, SIX. WE CHILL.
A DRAMATIC DEVELOPMENT.
AN IRAQI INFORMANT HAS JUST TOLD LT. COL. CROWLEY THAT HE HAS INFORMATION ABOUT THE POSSIBLE WHEREABOUTS OF LT. JIMMY MCCAIN.
WITH A $30 MILLION REWARD FOR THE KIDNAPPED MARINE, CLAIMS SUCH AS THIS ARE COMMON.
BUT ACCORDING TO CROWLEY, THE INFORMANT HAS SECURITY CLEARANCE.
WE ARE NOW ON ONE OF THE MOST SENSITIVE MISSIONS IN IRAQ.
THE HUNT FOR THE PRESIDENT'S SON.
LOBAL

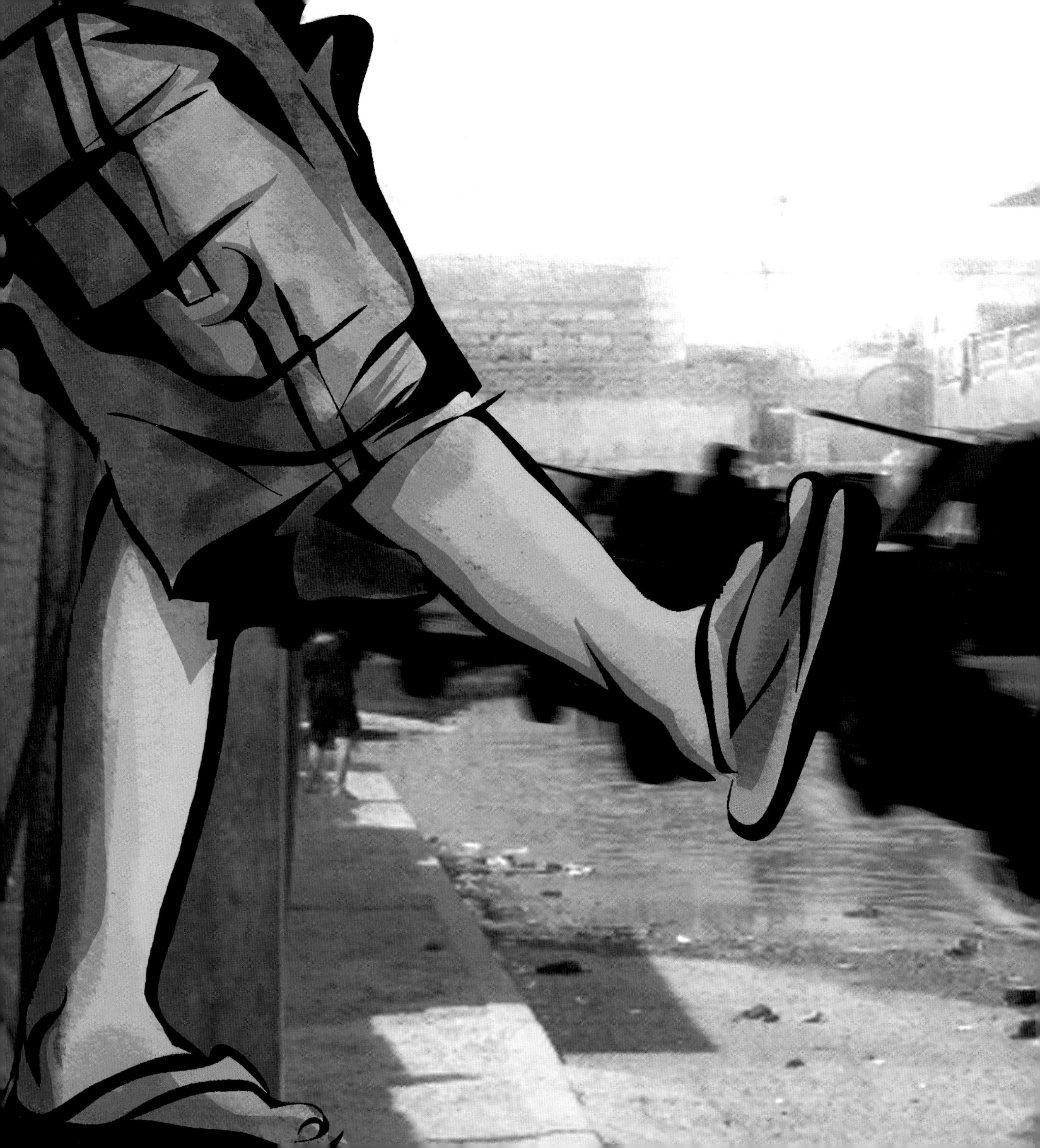

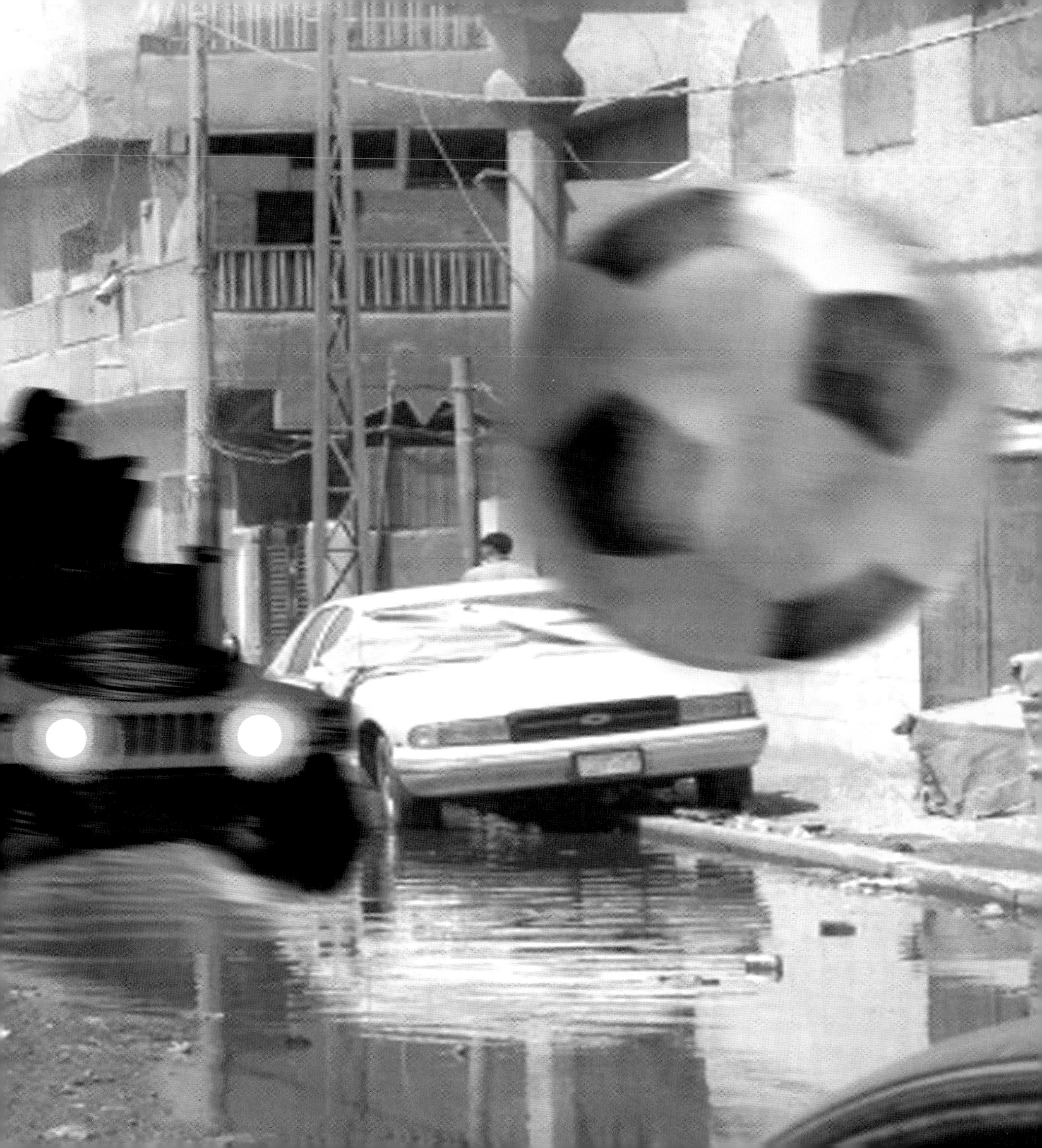

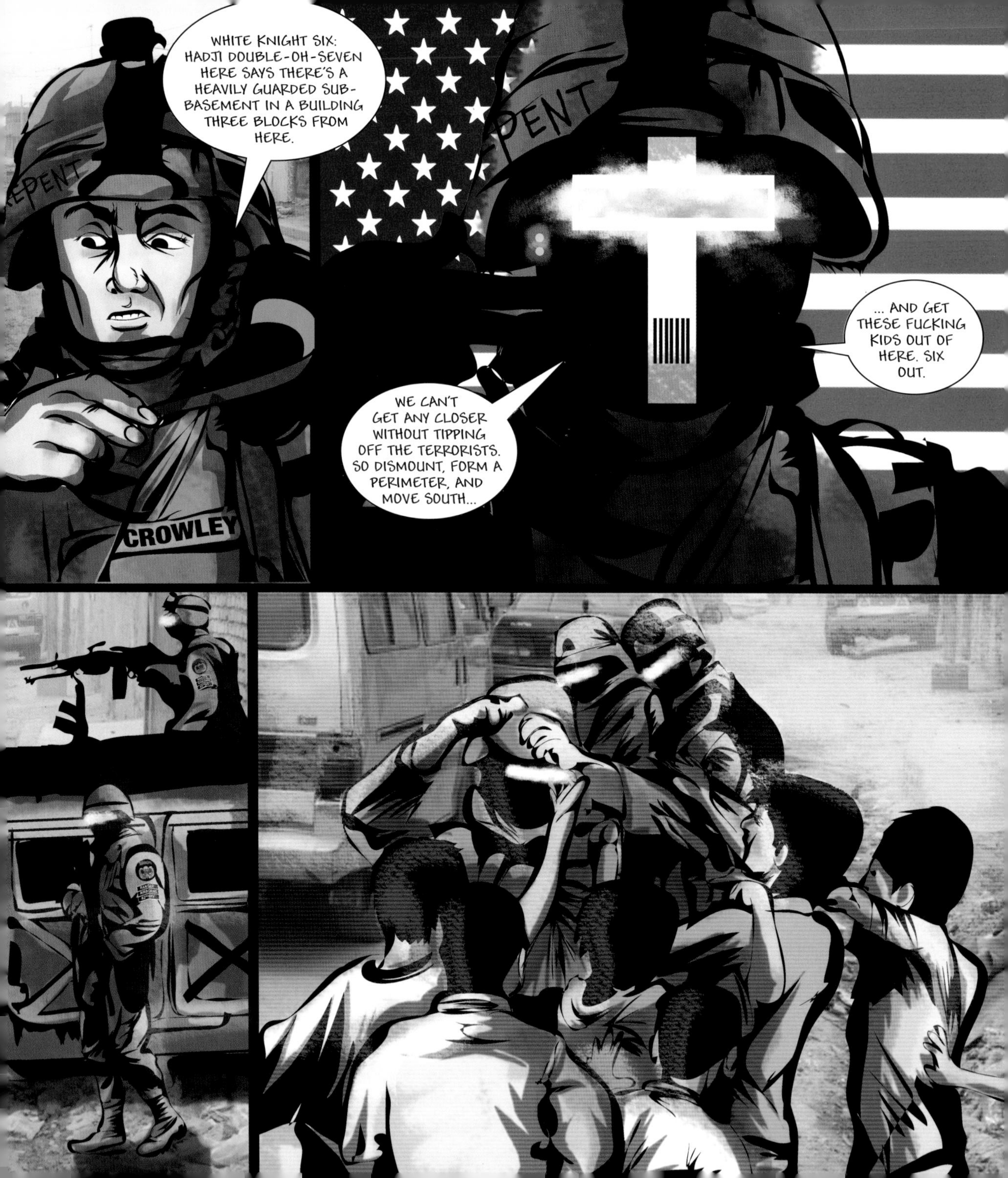
WHITE KNIGHT SIX: HADJI DOUBLE-OH-SEVEN HERE SAYS THERE'S A HEAVILY GUARDED SUB-BASEMENT IN A BUILDING THREE BLOCKS FROM HERE.
REPENT
CROWLEY
WE CAN'T GET ANY CLOSER WITHOUT TIPPING OFF THE TERRORISTS. SO DISMOUNT, FORM A PERIMETER, AND MOVE SOUTH...
... AND GET THESE FUCKING KIDS OUT OF HERE. SIX OUT.

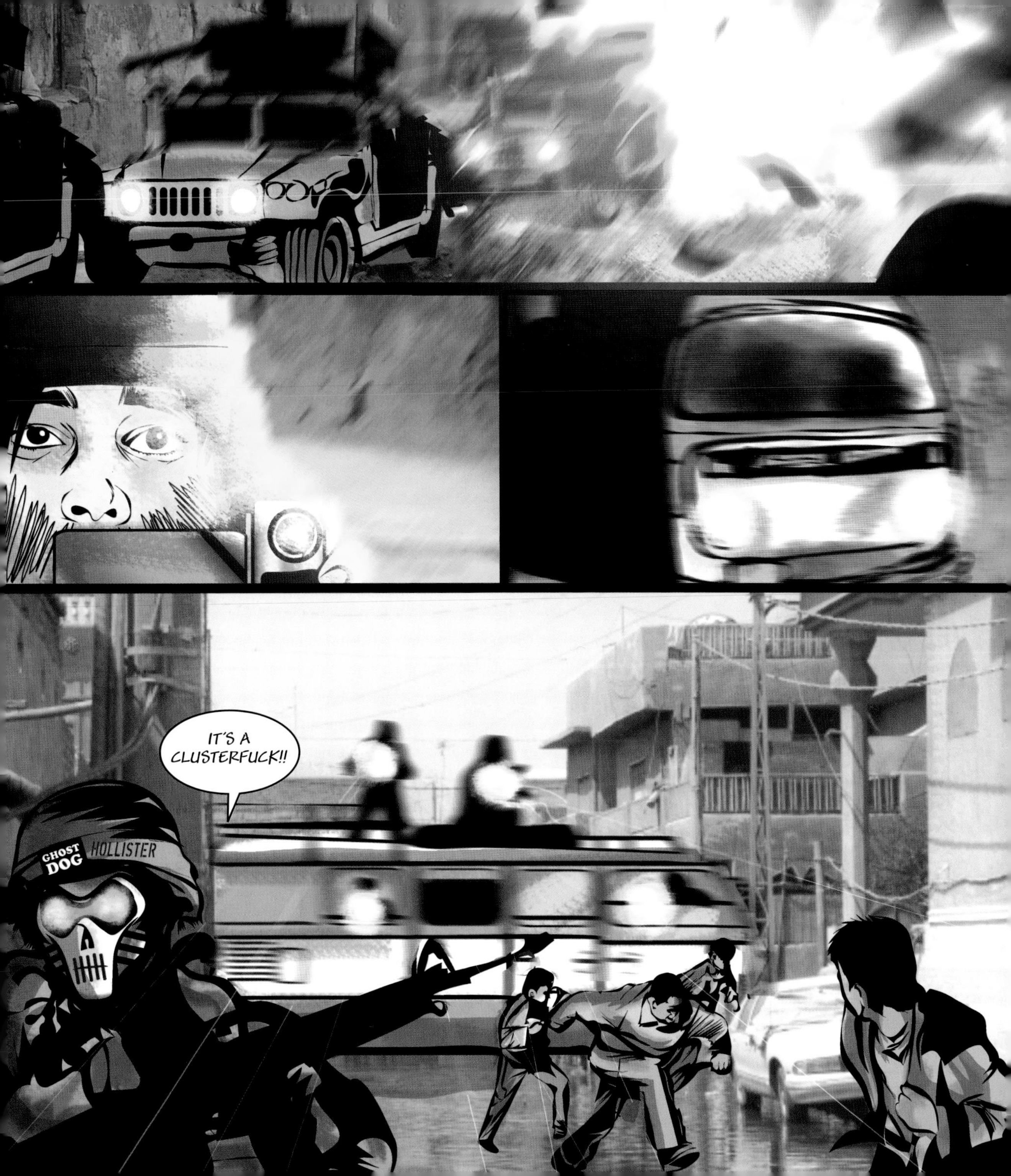
IT'S A CLUSTERFUCK!!
GHOST DOG
HOLLISTER

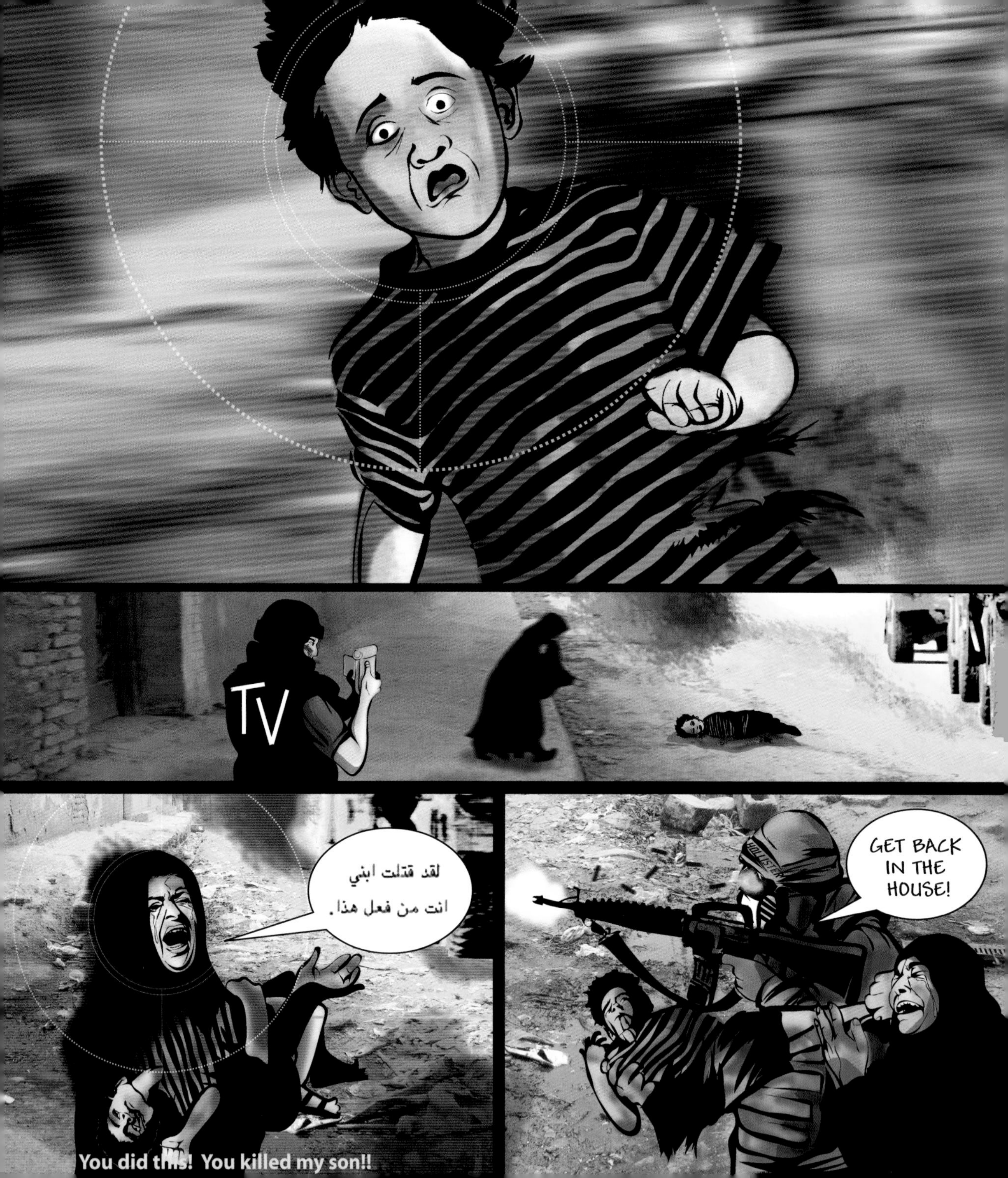
TV
لقد قتلت ابني
انت من فعل هذا.
You did this! You killed my son!!
GET BACK IN THE HOUSE!

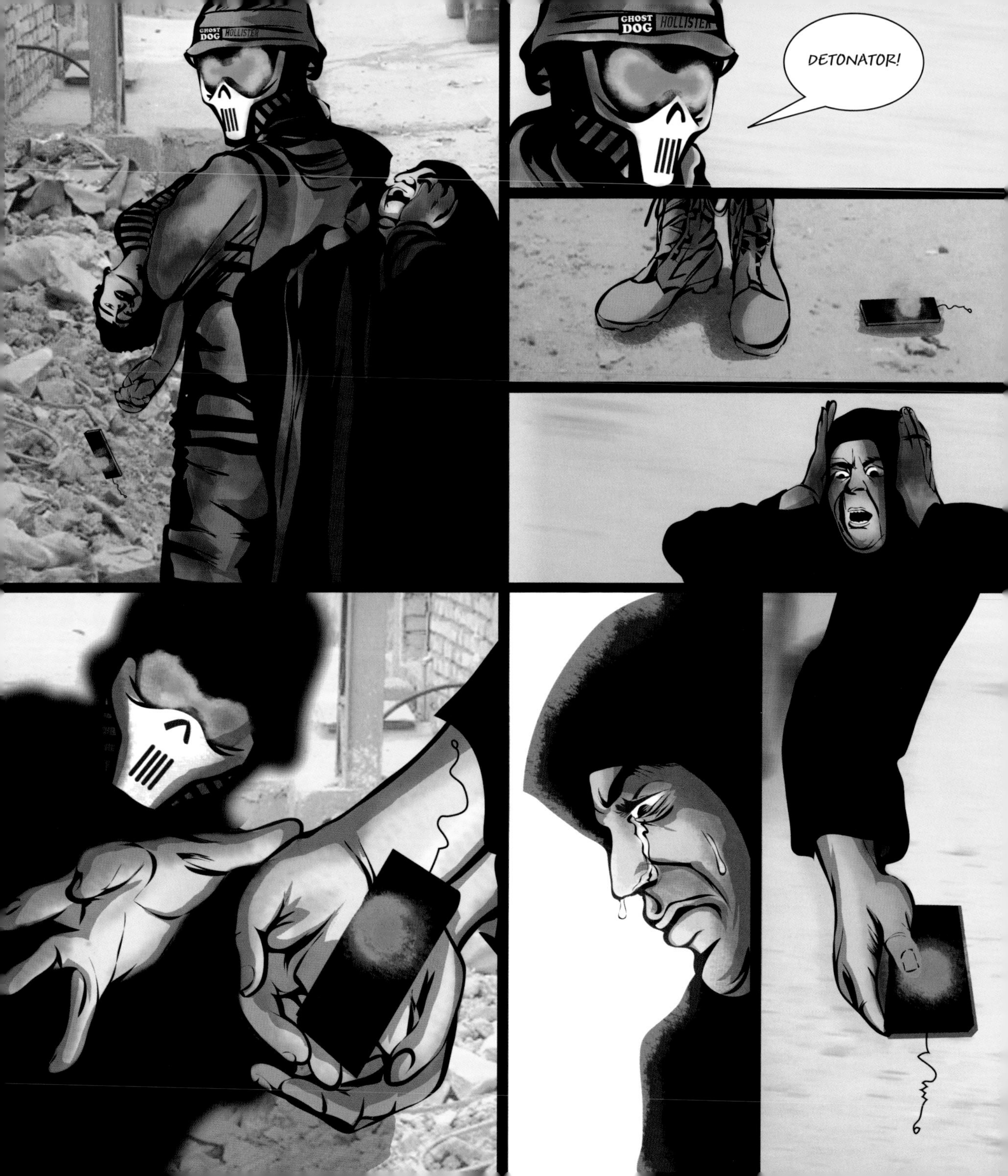
GHOST DOG HOLLISTER
DETONATOR!

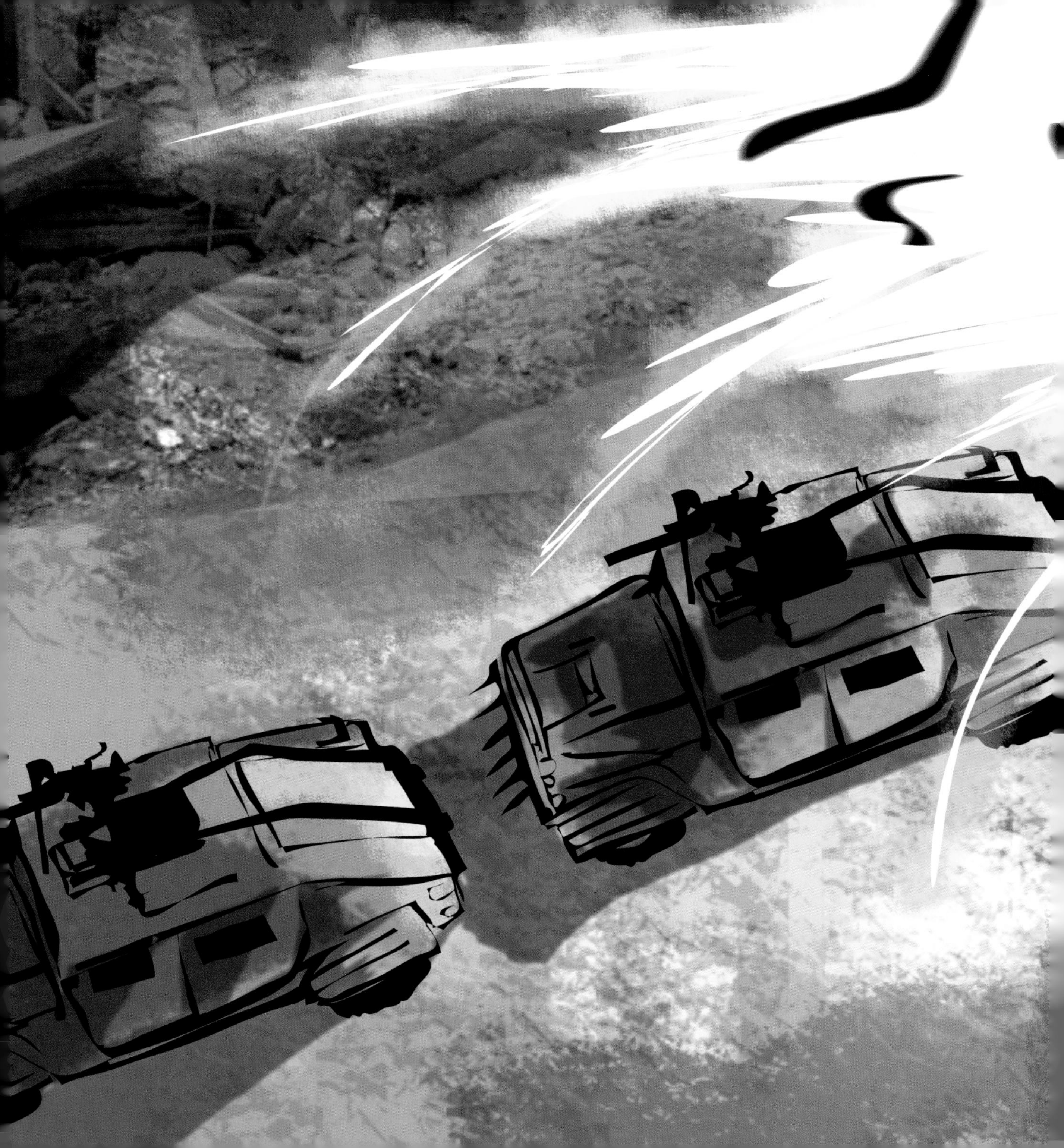

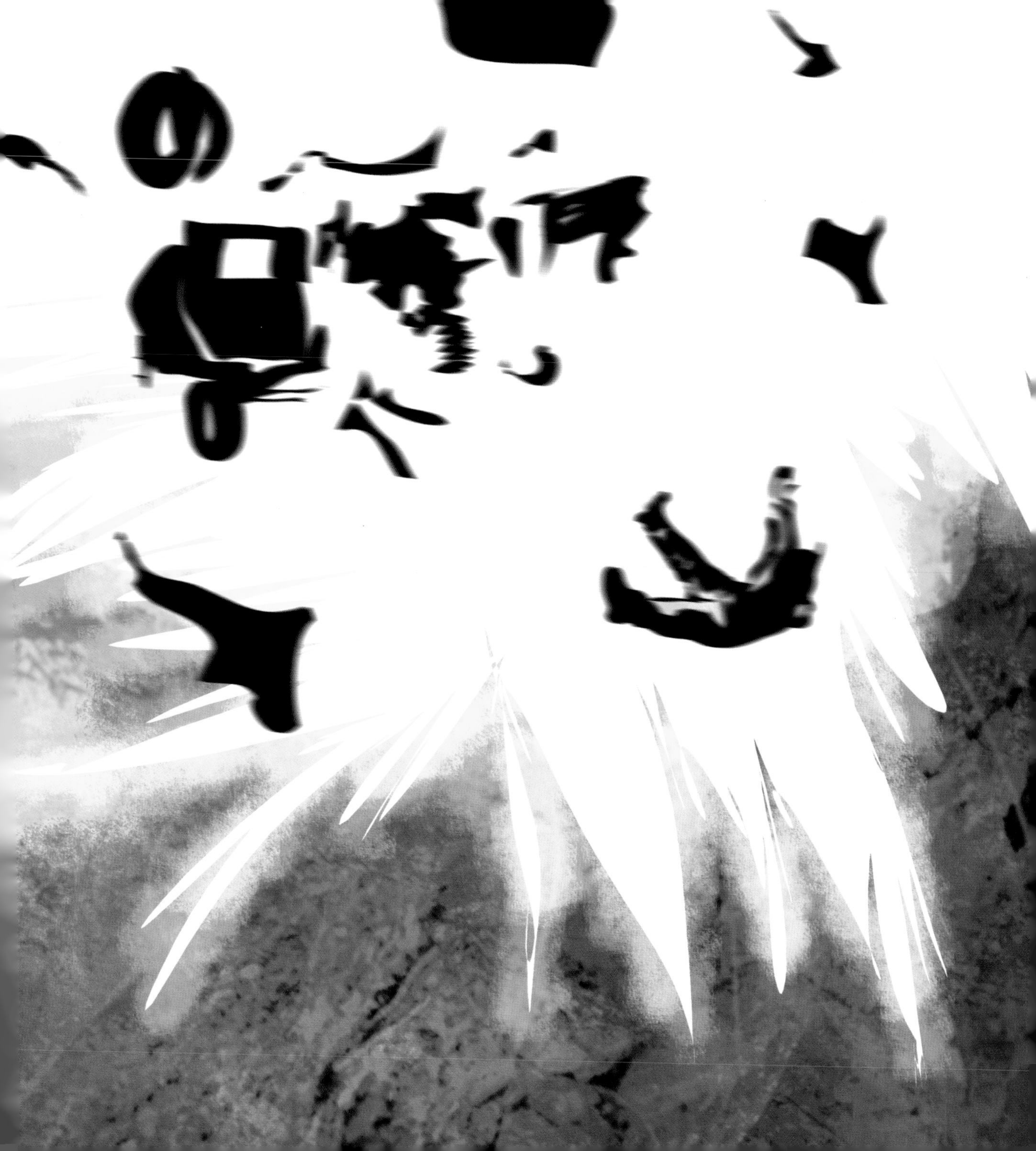

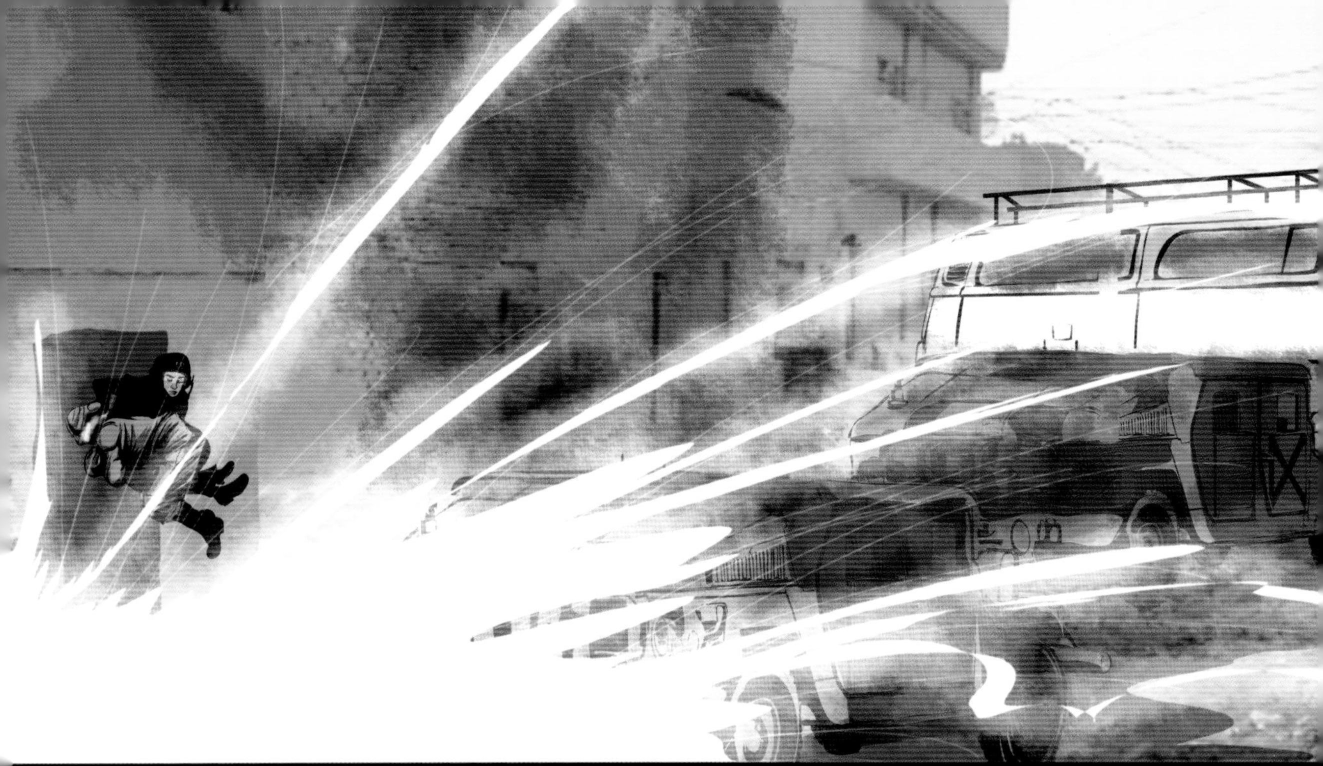

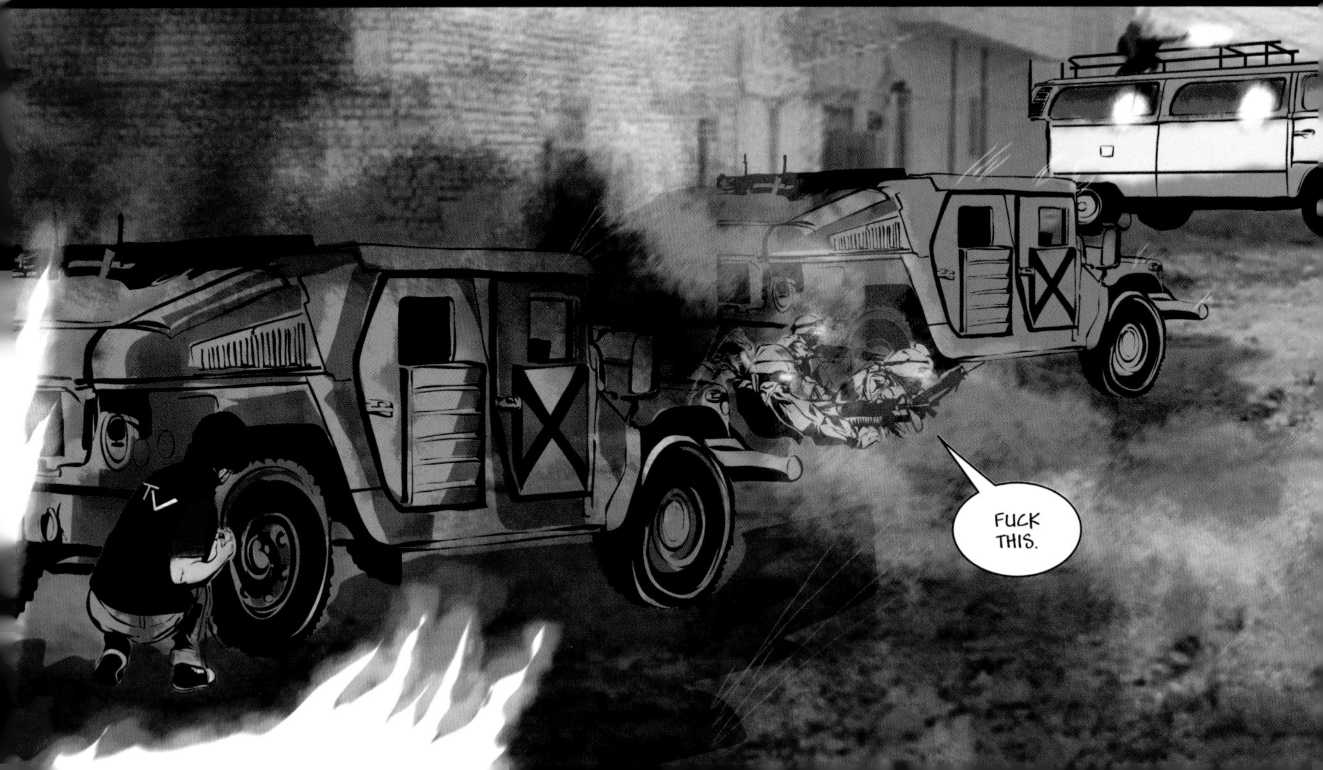
FUCK THIS.

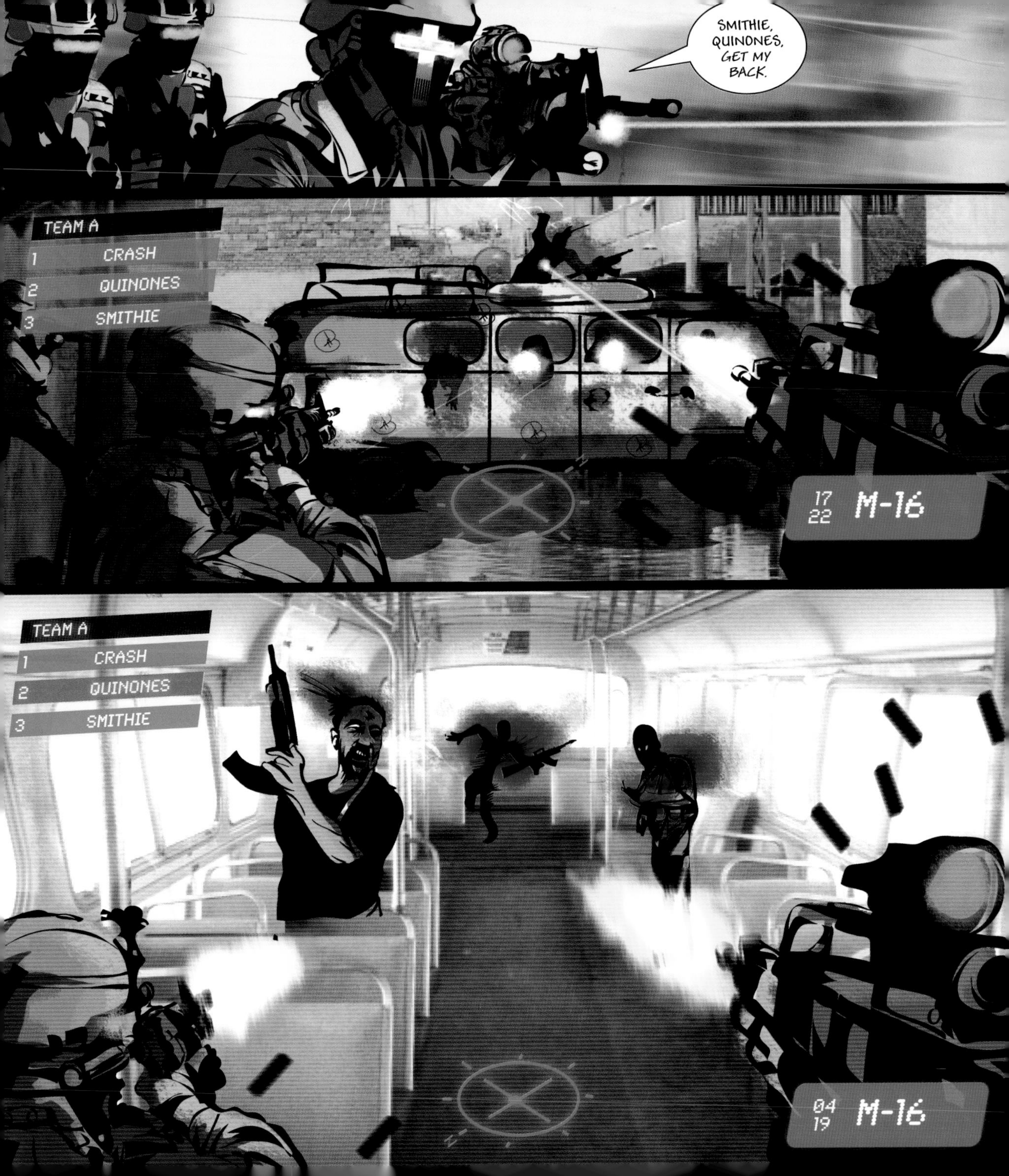
SMITHIE, QUINONES, GET MY BACK.
TEAM A
1 CRASH
2 QUINONES
3 SMITHIE
17
22
M-16
TEAM A
1 CRASH
2 QUINONES
3 SMITHIE
04
19
M-16

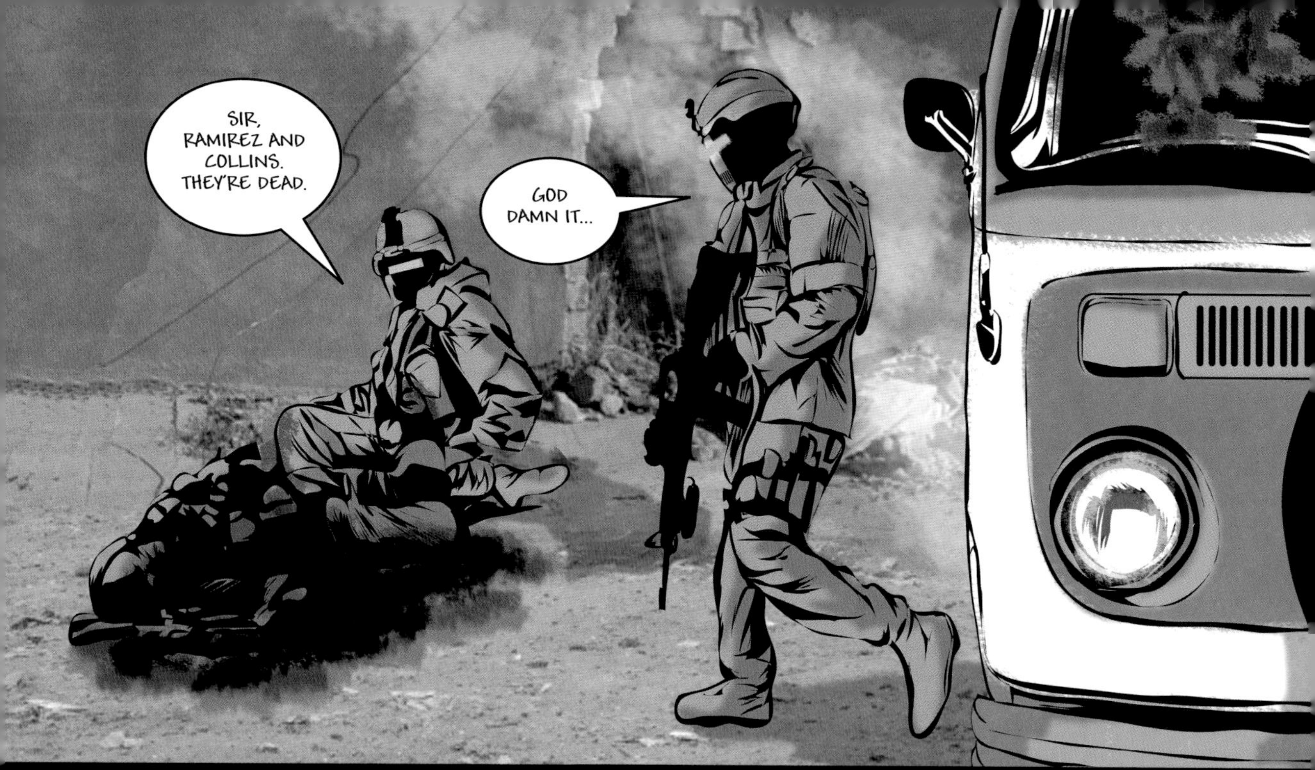
SIR, RAMIREZ AND COLLINS. THEY'RE DEAD.
GOD DAMN IT...
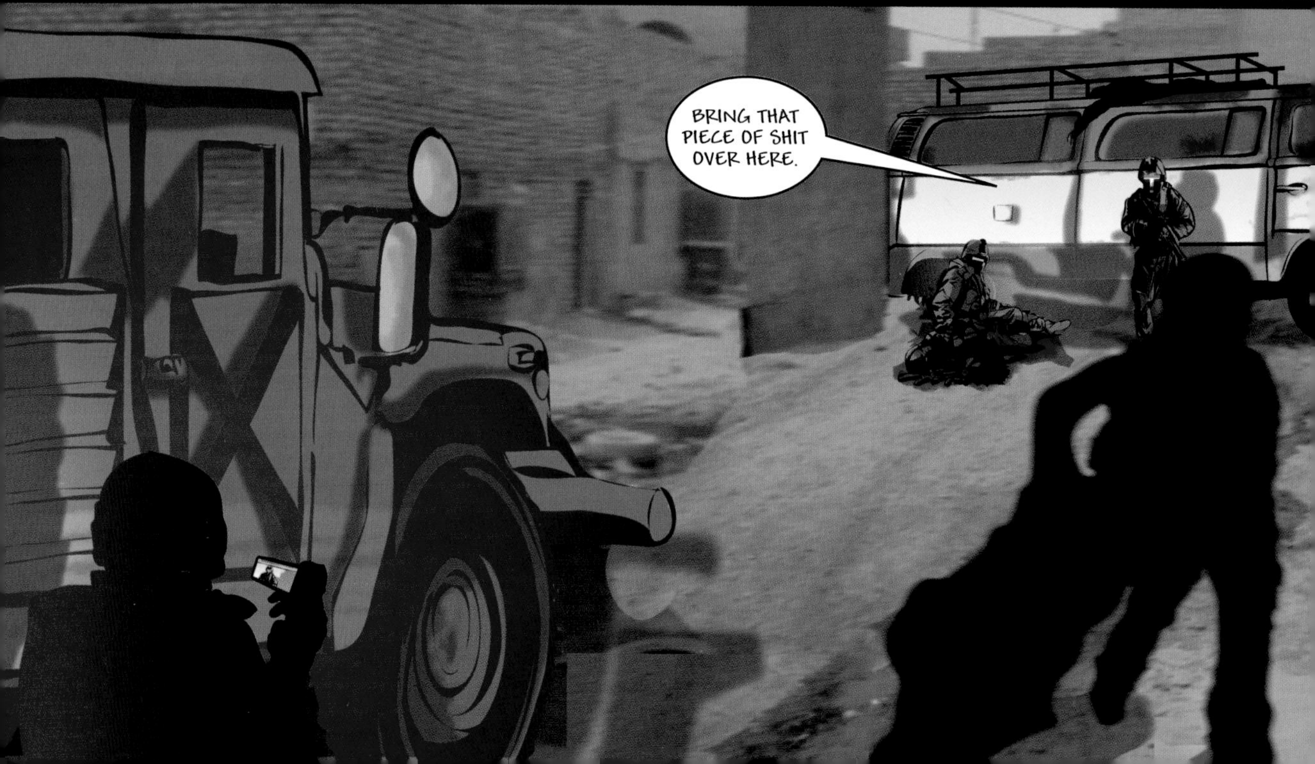
BRING THAT PIECE OF SHIT OVER HERE.

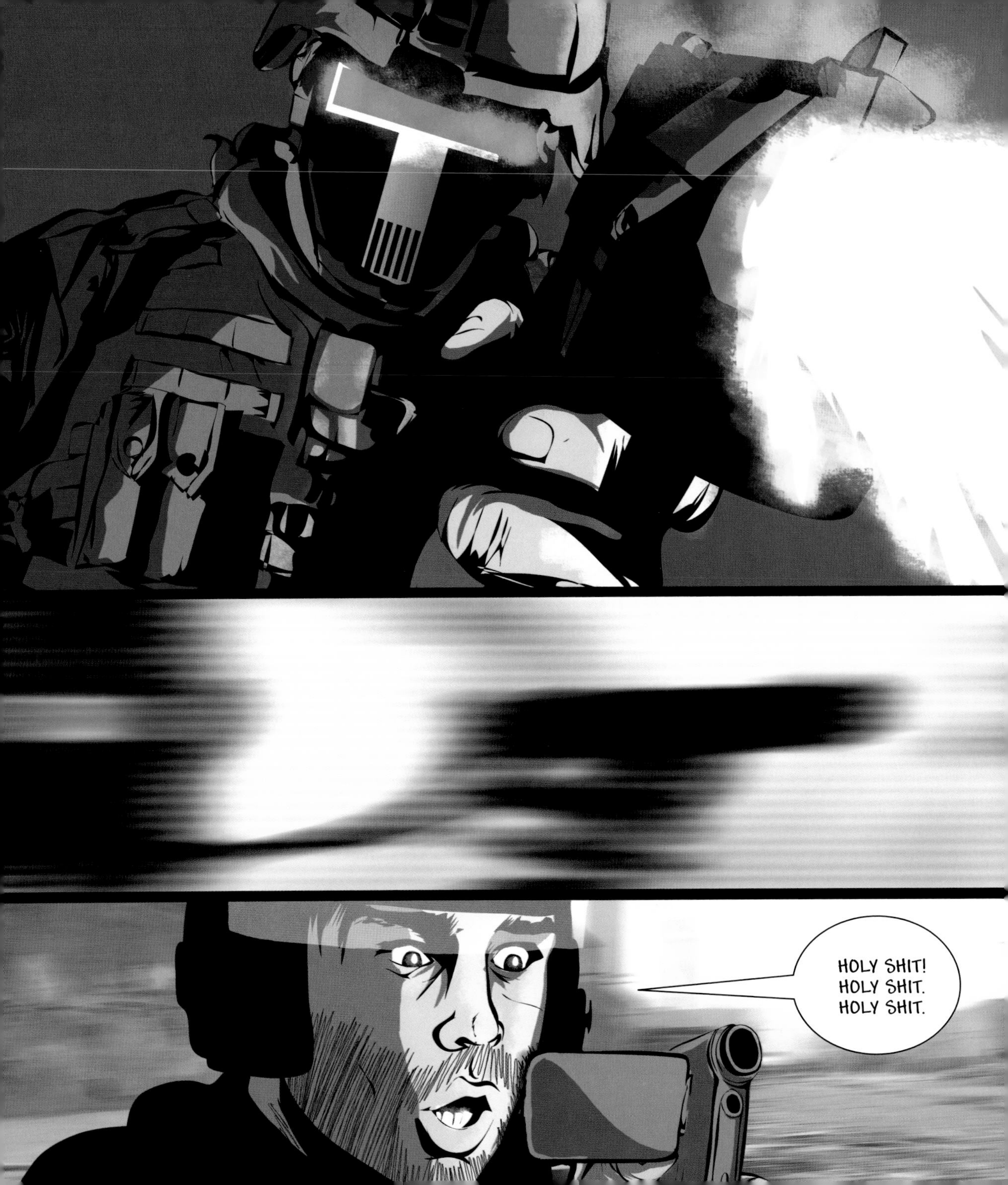
HOLY SHIT!
HOLY SHIT.
HOLY SHIT.

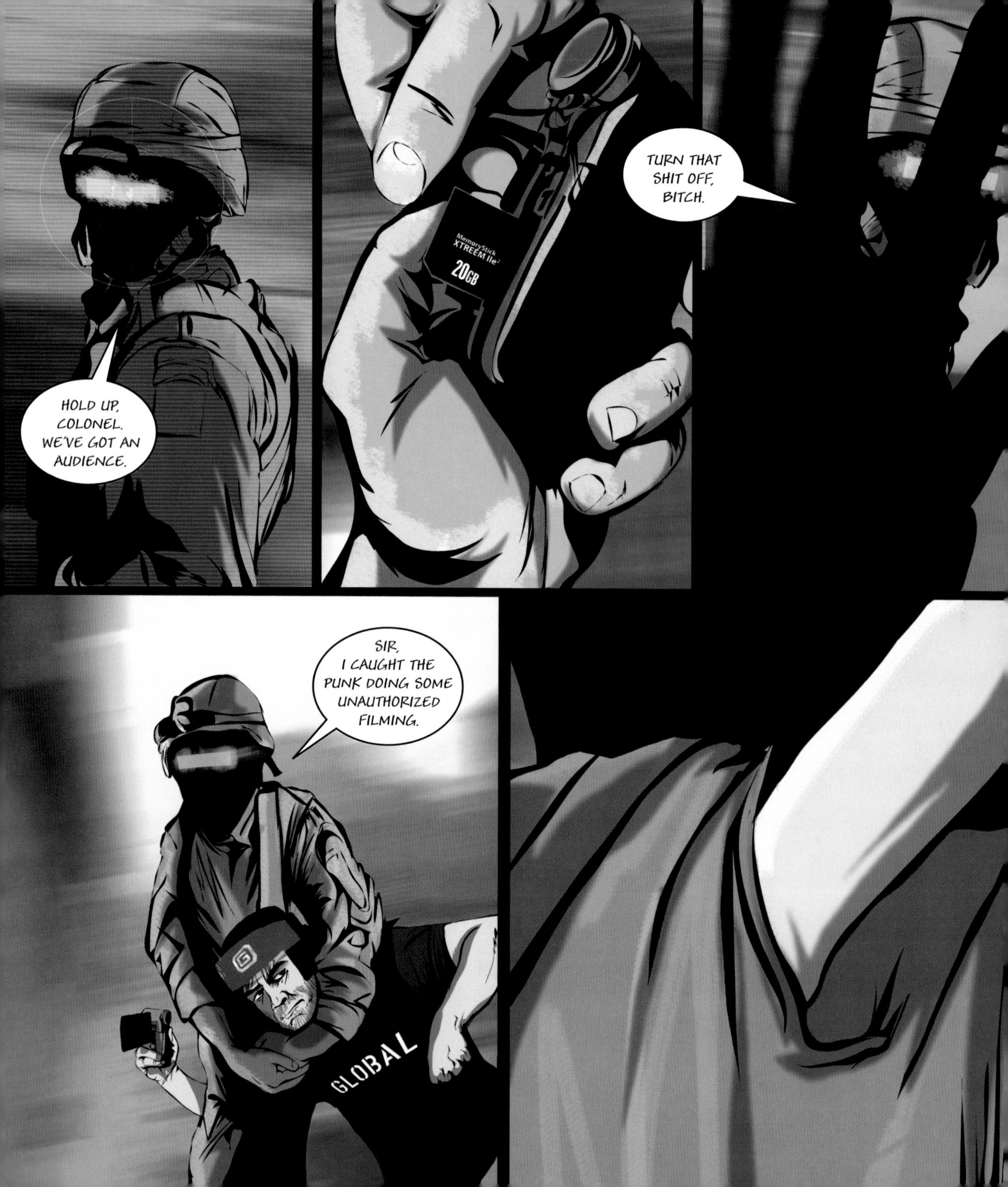
HOLD UP, COLONEL. WE'VE GOT AN AUDIENCE.
MemoryStick XTREEM IIe2 20GB
TURN THAT SHIT OFF, BITCH.
SIR, I CAUGHT THE PUNK DOING SOME UNAUTHORIZED FILMING.
GLOBAL

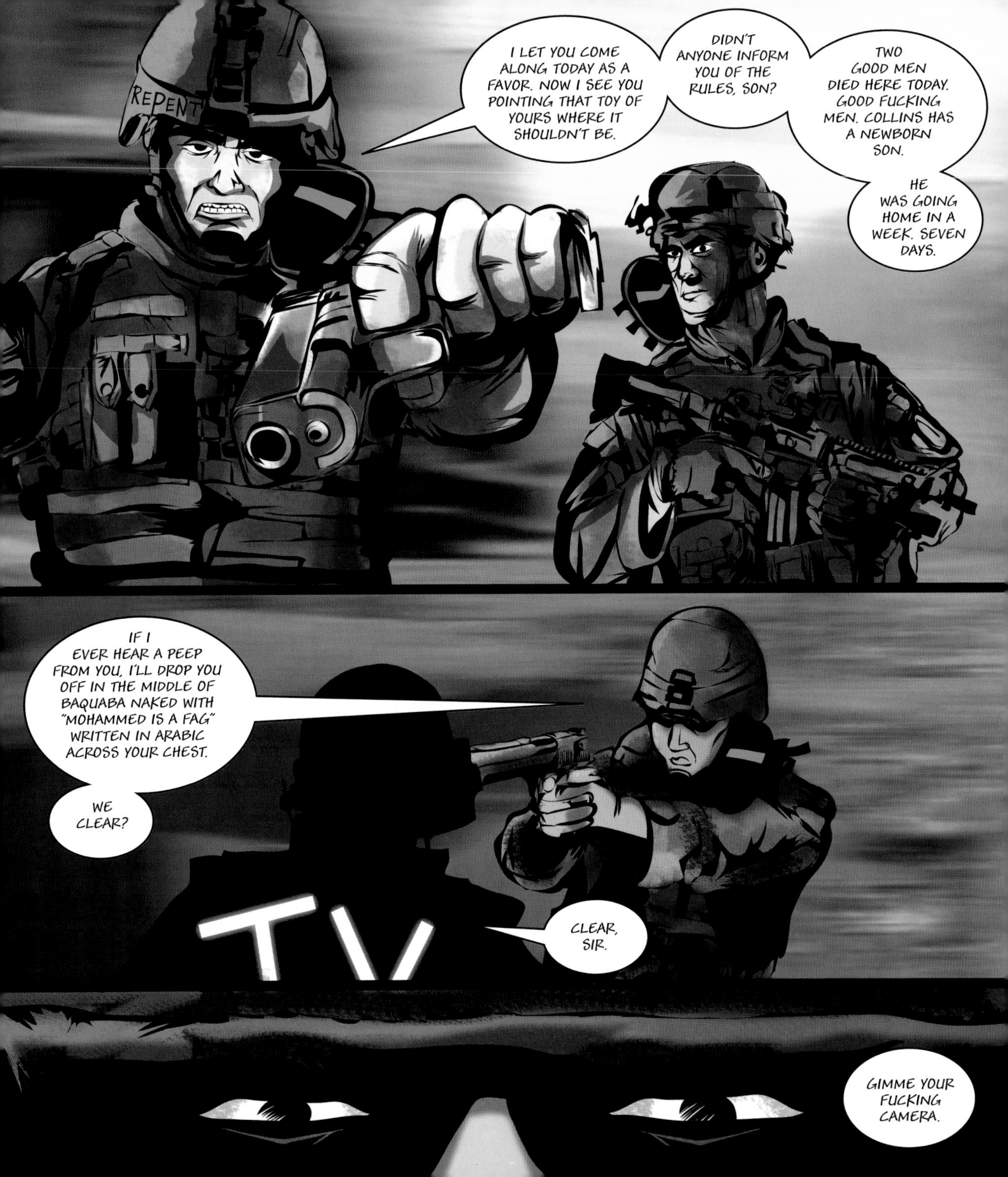
REPENT
I LET YOU COME ALONG TODAY AS A FAVOR. NOW I SEE YOU POINTING THAT TOY OF YOURS WHERE IT SHOULDN'T BE.
DIDN'T ANYONE INFORM YOU OF THE RULES, SON?
TWO GOOD MEN DIED HERE TODAY. GOOD FUCKING MEN. COLLINS HAS A NEWBORN SON.
HE WAS GOING HOME IN A WEEK. SEVEN DAYS.
IF I EVER HEAR A PEEP FROM YOU, I'LL DROP YOU OFF IN THE MIDDLE OF BAQUABA NAKED WITH "MOHAMMED IS A FAG" WRITTEN IN ARABIC ACROSS YOUR CHEST.
WE CLEAR?
TV
CLEAR, SIR.
GIMME YOUR FUCKING CAMERA.

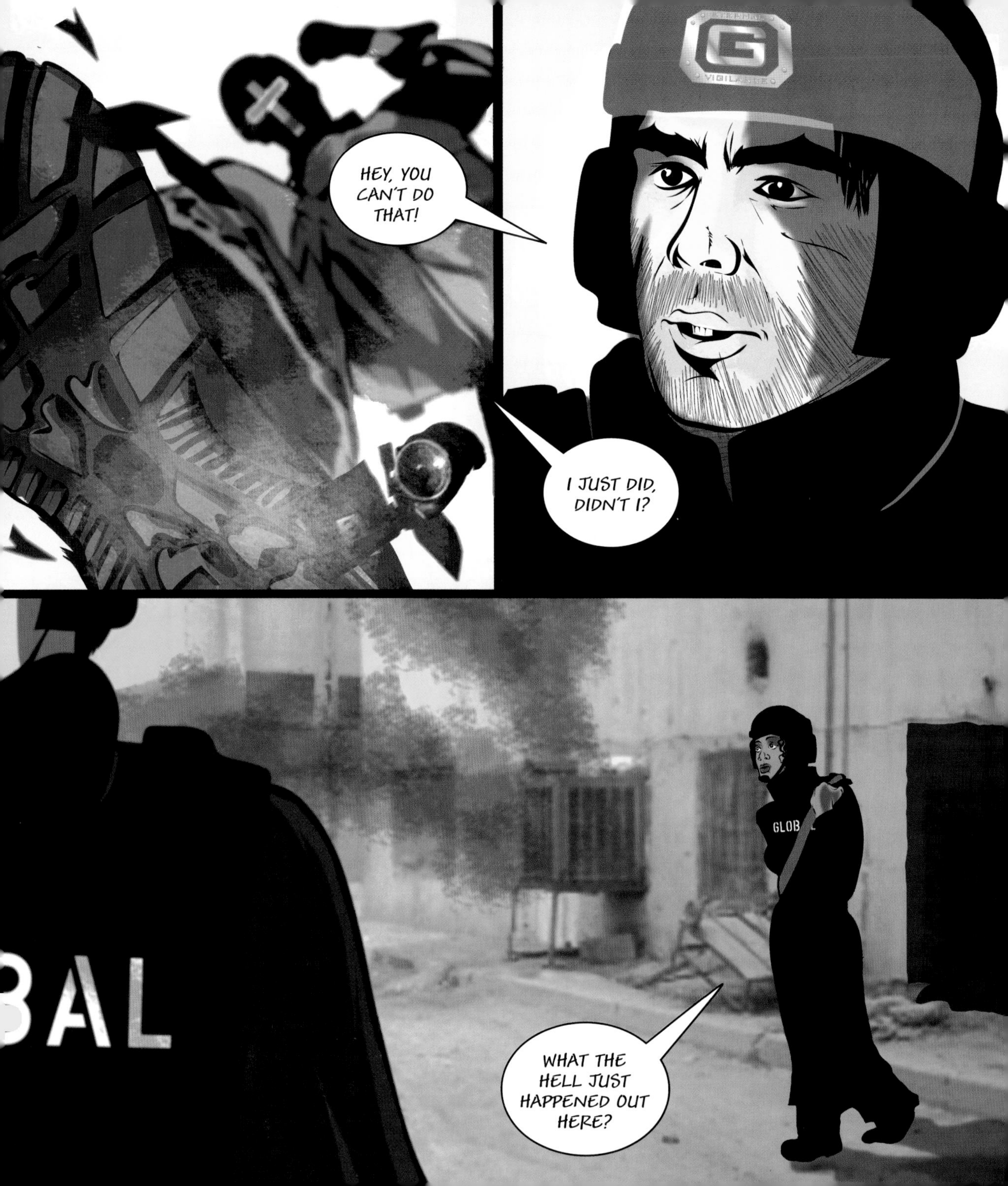
HEY, YOU CAN'T DO THAT!
I JUST DID, DIDN'T I?
BAL
WHAT THE HELL JUST HAPPENED OUT HERE?

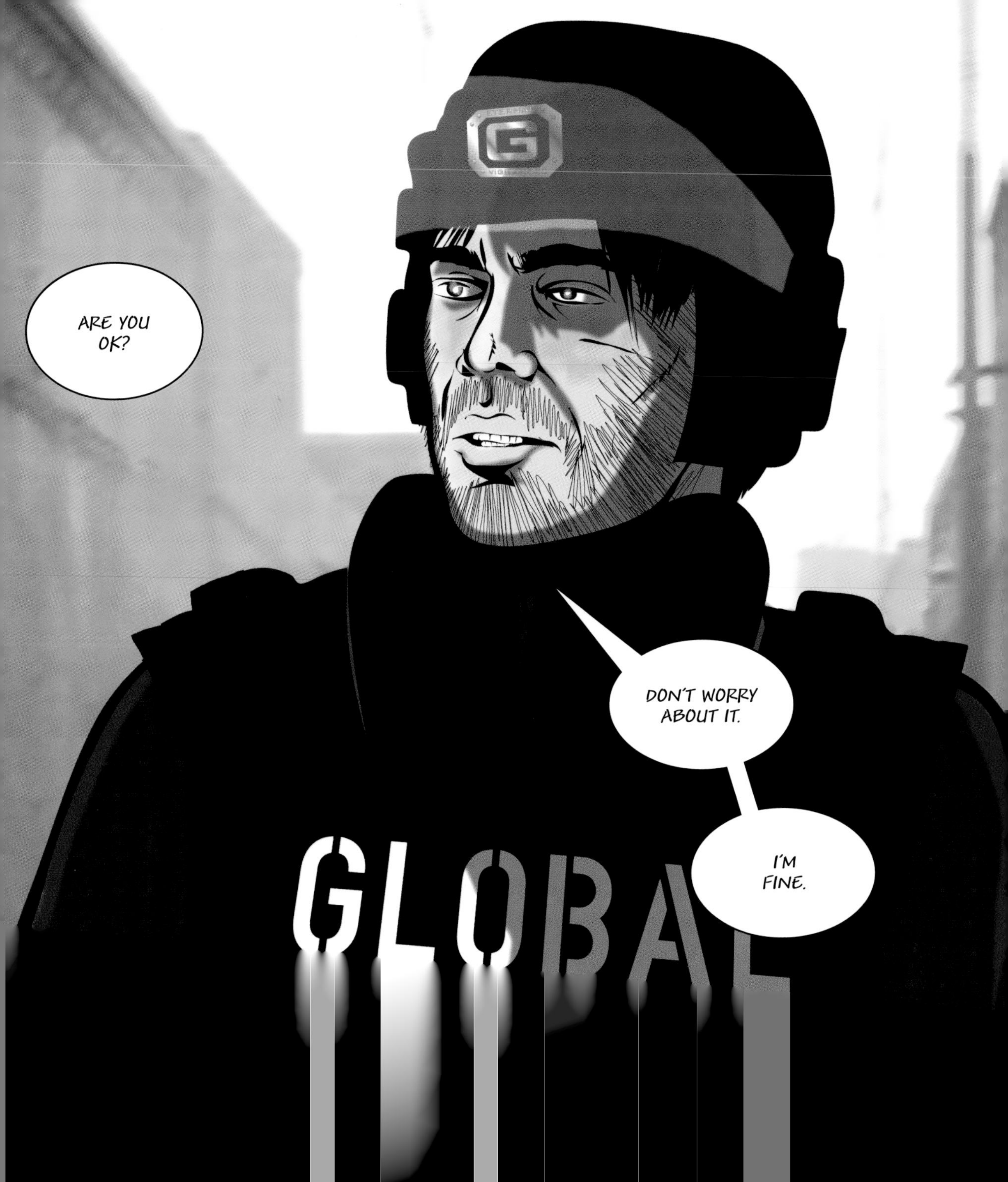
ARE YOU OK?
DON'T WORRY ABOUT IT.
I'M FINE.
GLOBAL

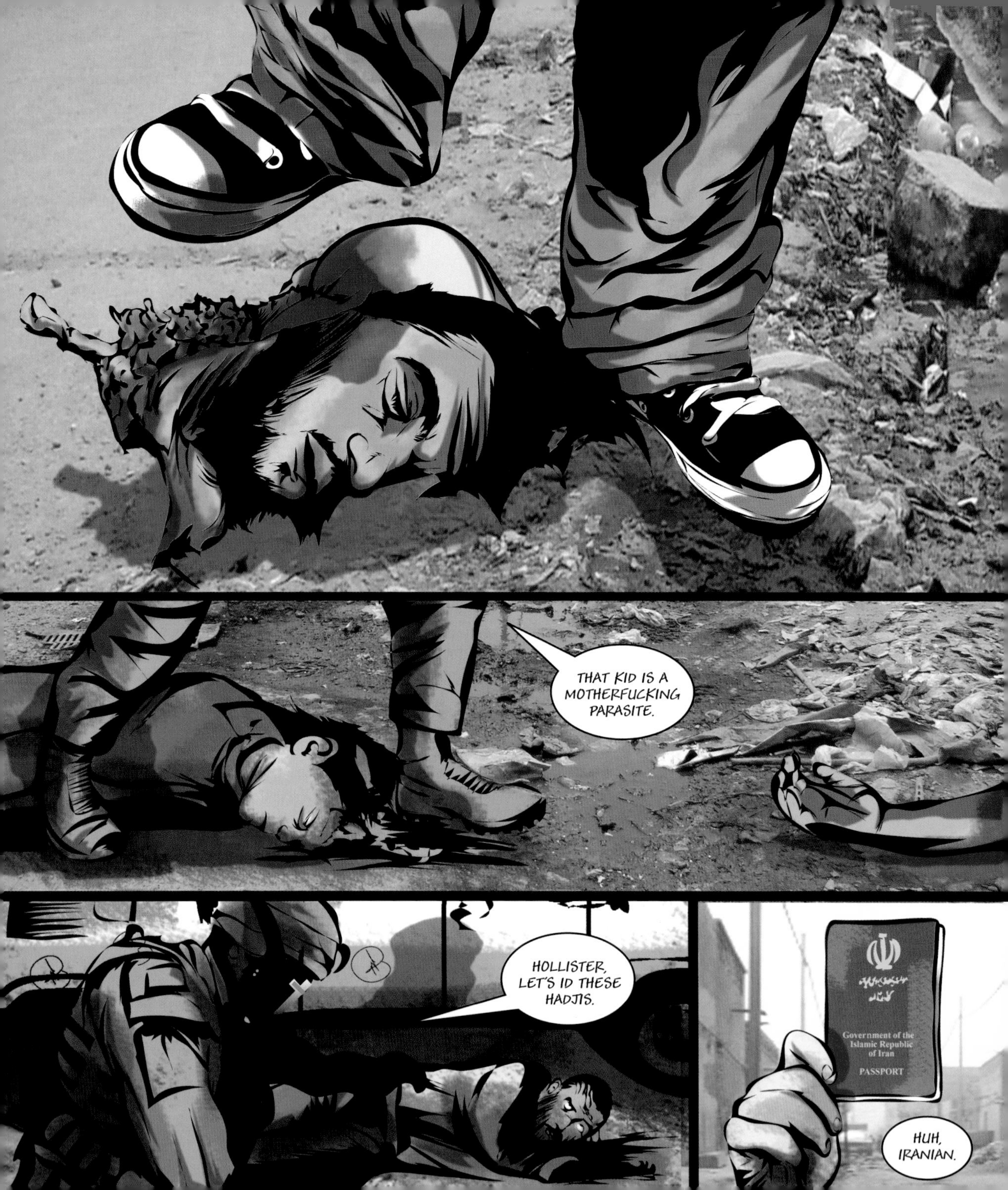
THAT KID IS A MOTHERFUCKING PARASITE.
HOLLISTER, LET'S ID THESE HADJIS.
Government of the Islamic Republic of Iran
PASSPORT
HUH, IRANIAN.

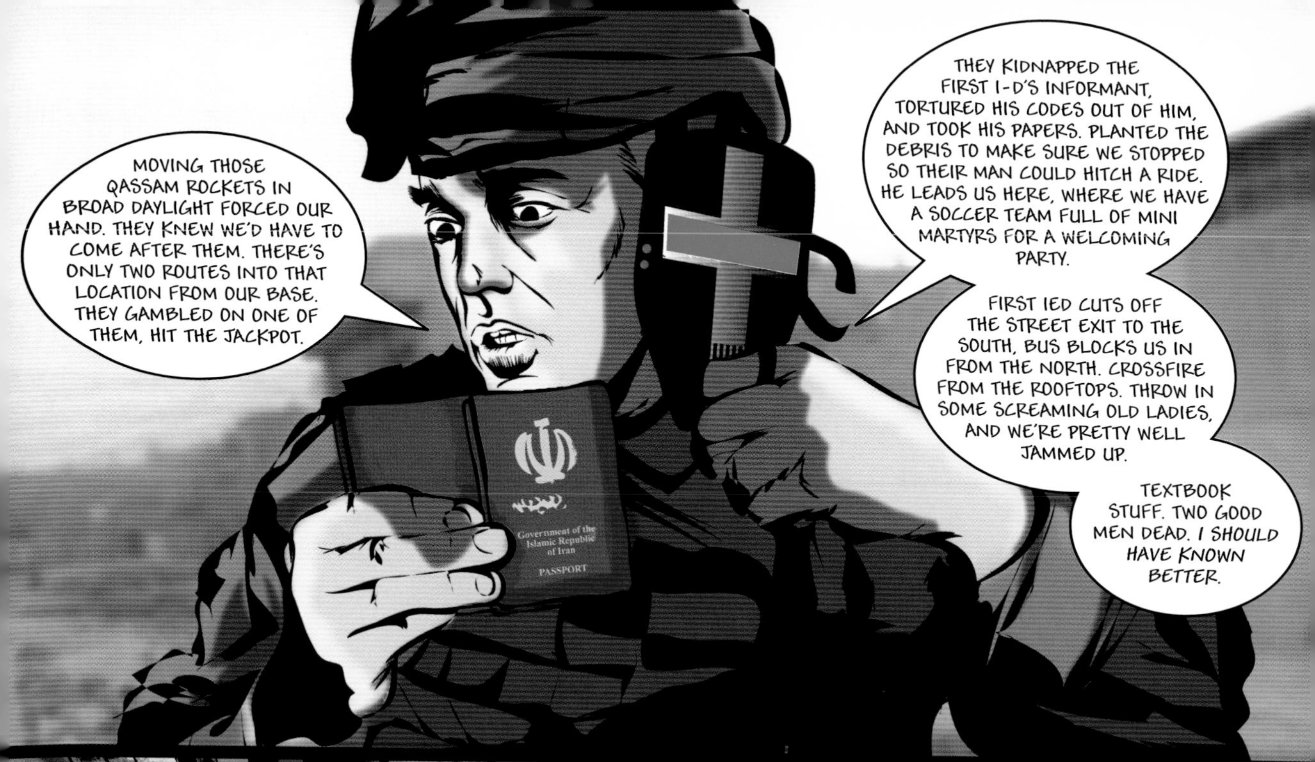
MOVING THOSE QASSAM ROCKETS IN BROAD DAYLIGHT FORCED OUR HAND. THEY KNEW WE'D HAVE TO COME AFTER THEM. THERE'S ONLY TWO ROUTES INTO THAT LOCATION FROM OUR BASE. THEY GAMBLED ON ONE OF THEM, HIT THE JACKPOT.
Government of the Islamic Republic of Iran
PASSPORT
THEY KIDNAPPED THE FIRST I-D'S INFORMANT, TORTURED HIS CODES OUT OF HIM, AND TOOK HIS PAPERS. PLANTED THE DEBRIS TO MAKE SURE WE STOPPED SO THEIR MAN COULD HITCH A RIDE. HE LEADS US HERE, WHERE WE HAVE A SOCCER TEAM FULL OF MINI MARTYRS FOR A WELCOMING PARTY.
FIRST IED CUTS OFF THE STREET EXIT TO THE SOUTH, BUS BLOCKS US IN FROM THE NORTH. CROSSFIRE FROM THE ROOFTOPS. THROW IN SOME SCREAMING OLD LADIES, AND WE'RE PRETTY WELL JAMMED UP.
TEXTBOOK STUFF. TWO GOOD MEN DEAD. I SHOULD HAVE KNOWN BETTER.

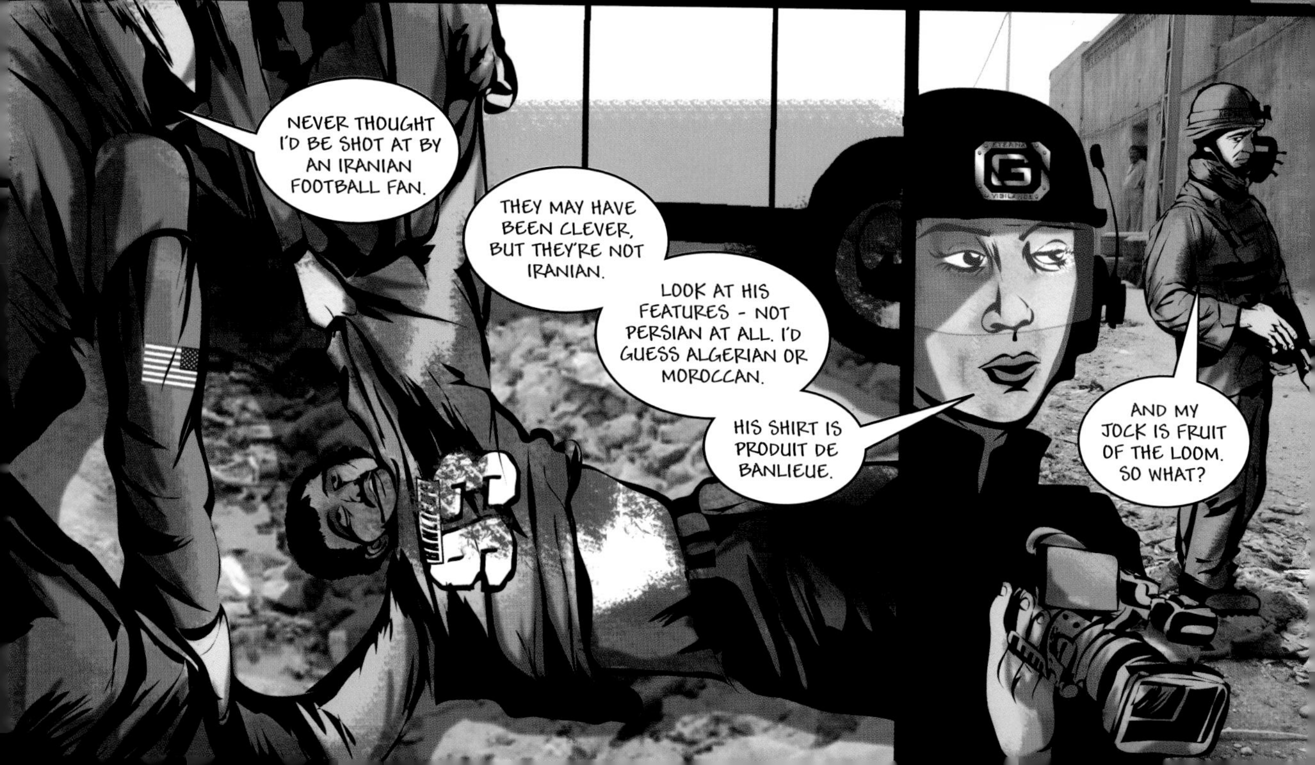
NEVER THOUGHT I'D BE SHOT AT BY AN IRANIAN FOOTBALL FAN.
THEY MAY HAVE BEEN CLEVER, BUT THEY'RE NOT IRANIAN.
LOOK AT HIS FEATURES - NOT PERSIAN AT ALL. I'D GUESS ALGERIAN OR MOROCCAN.
HIS SHIRT IS PRODUIT DE BANLIEUE.
AND MY JOCK IS FRUIT OF THE LOOM. SO WHAT?

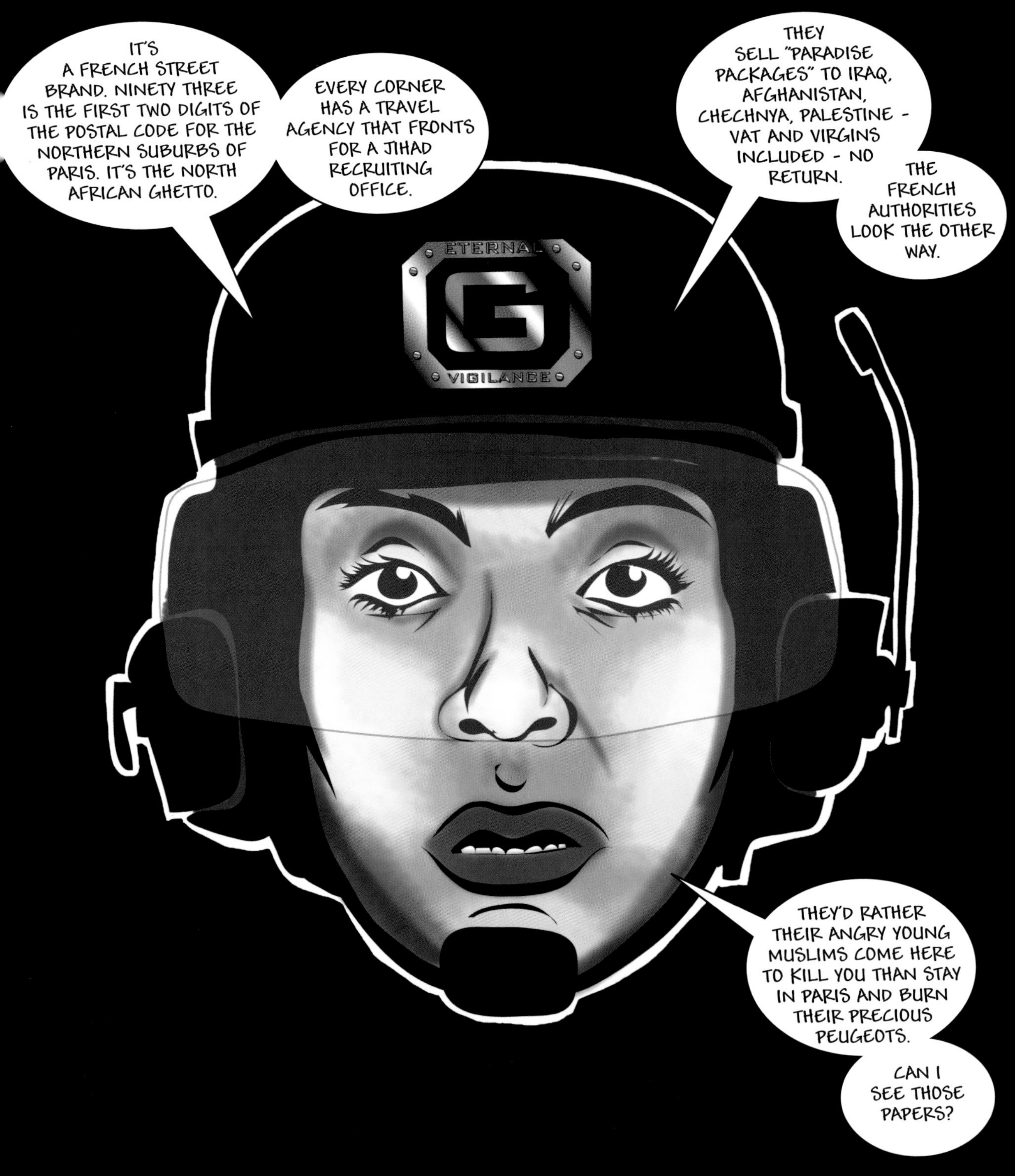
IT'S A FRENCH STREET BRAND. NINETY THREE IS THE FIRST TWO DIGITS OF THE POSTAL CODE FOR THE NORTHERN SUBURBS OF PARIS. IT'S THE NORTH AFRICAN GHETTO.
EVERY CORNER HAS A TRAVEL AGENCY THAT FRONTS FOR A JIHAD RECRUITING OFFICE.
THEY SELL "PARADISE PACKAGES" TO IRAQ, AFGHANISTAN, CHECHNYA, PALESTINE - VAT AND VIRGINS INCLUDED - NO RETURN.
THE FRENCH AUTHORITIES LOOK THE OTHER WAY.
ETERNAL
G
VIGILANCE
THEY'D RATHER THEIR ANGRY YOUNG MUSLIMS COME HERE TO KILL YOU THAN STAY IN PARIS AND BURN THEIR PRECIOUS PEUGEOTS.
CAN I SEE THOSE PAPERS?

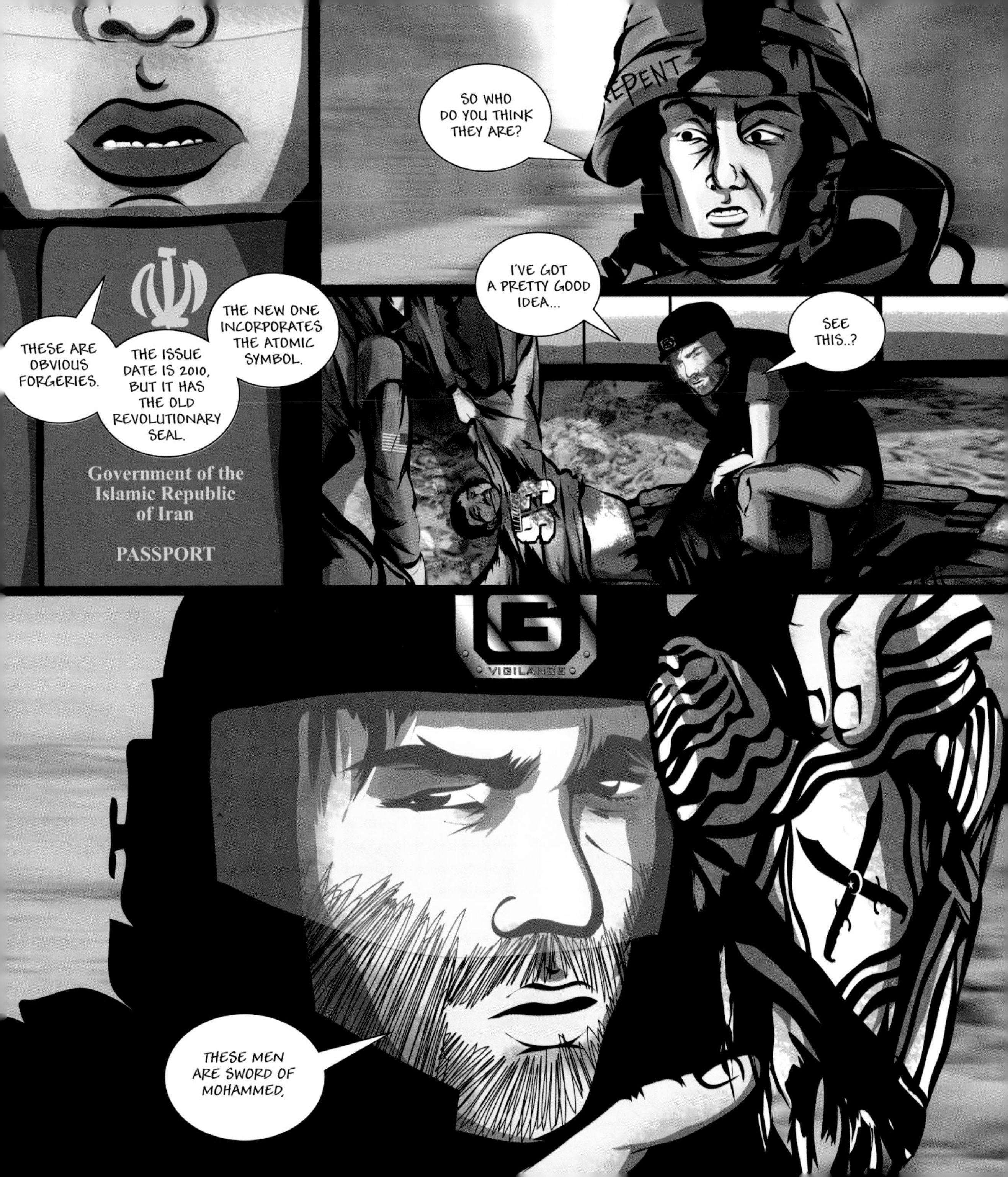
SO WHO DO YOU THINK THEY ARE?
REPENT
THESE ARE OBVIOUS FORGERIES.
THE ISSUE DATE IS 2010, BUT IT HAS THE OLD REVOLUTIONARY SEAL.
THE NEW ONE INCORPORATES THE ATOMIC SYMBOL.
Government of the Islamic Republic of Iran
PASSPORT
I'VE GOT A PRETTY GOOD IDEA...
SEE THIS..?
VIGILANCE
THESE MEN ARE SWORD OF MOHAMMED,

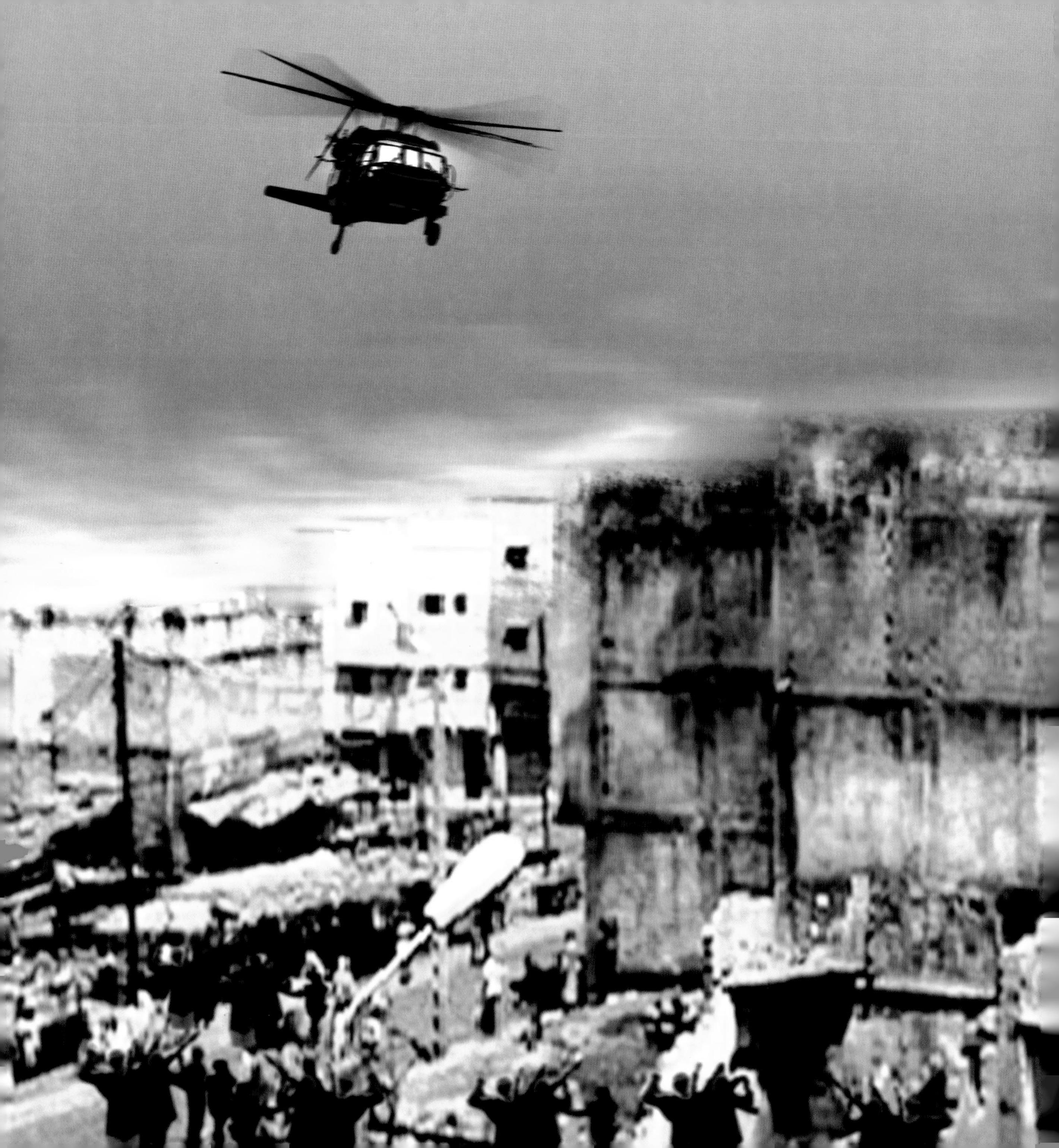

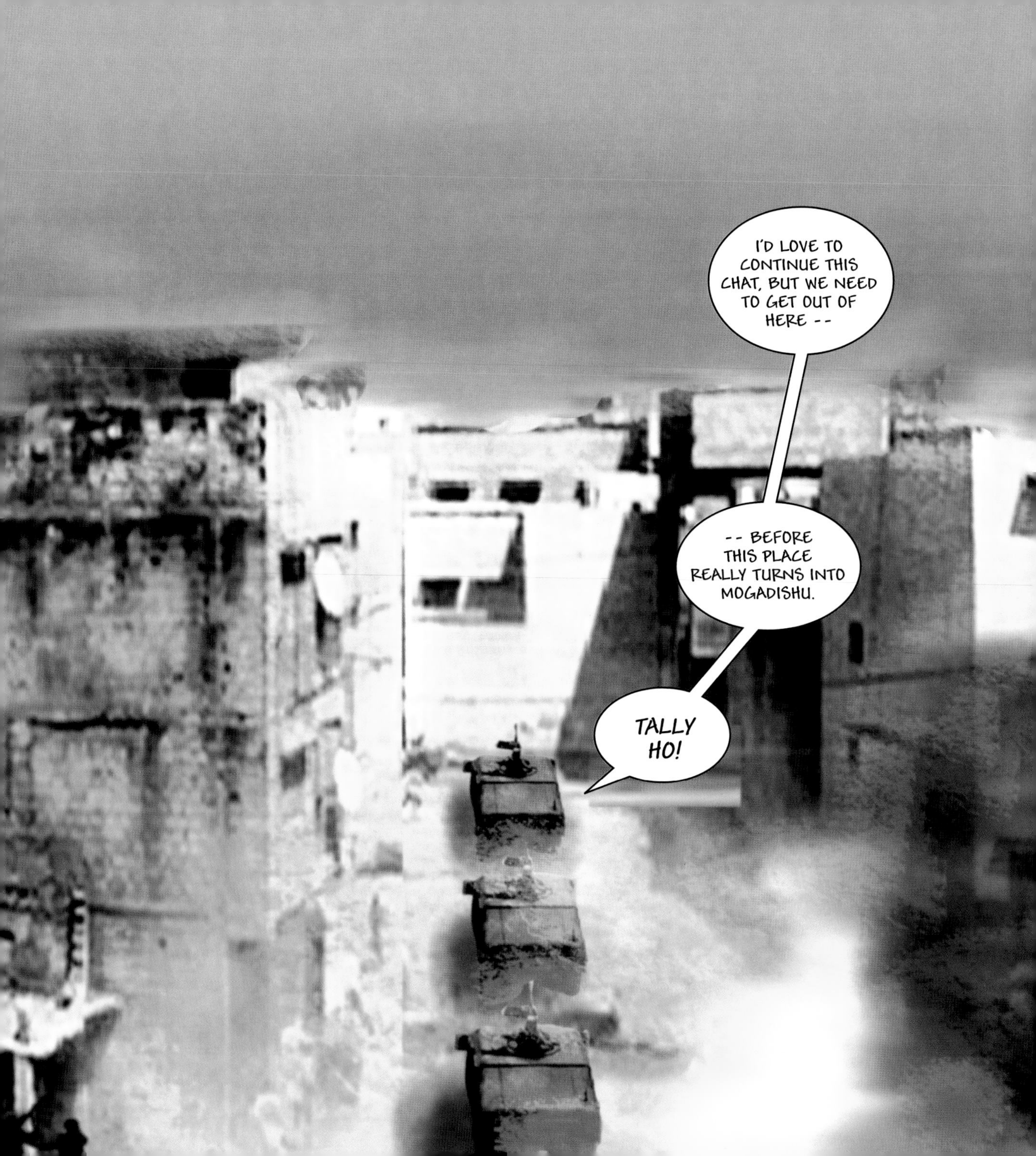
I'D LOVE TO CONTINUE THIS CHAT, BUT WE NEED TO GET OUT OF HERE --
-- BEFORE THIS PLACE REALLY TURNS INTO MOGADISHU.
TALLY HO!

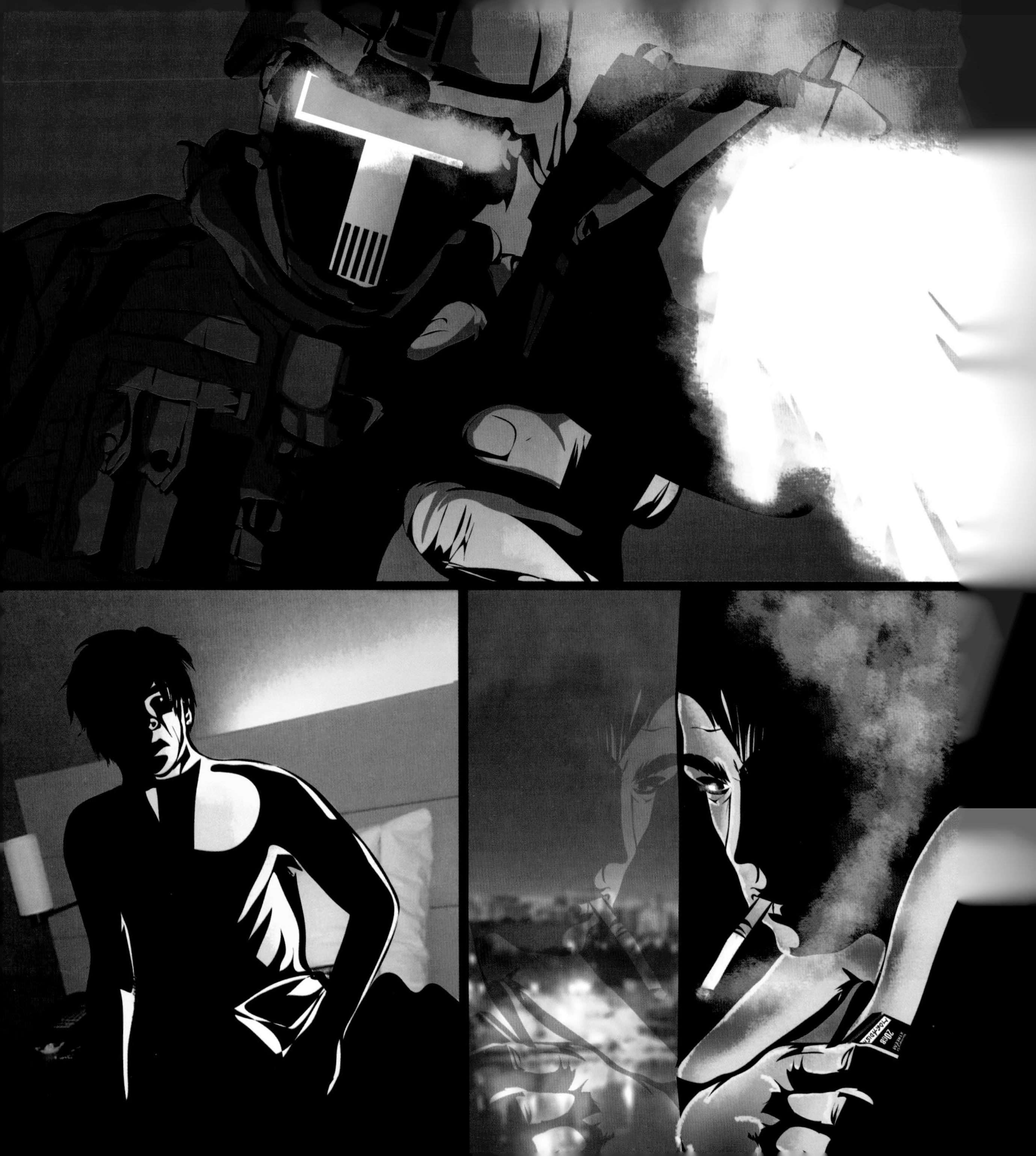

Burn Baby Burn

http://burnbabyburn.com

Google Images

BURN
BABY
BURN

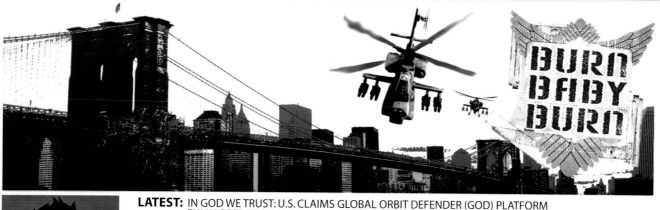

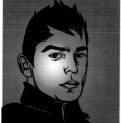

JIMMY BURNS

Jimmy is currently on assignment for the *GLOBAL NEWS* network as embedded vlog correspondent in Baghdad.

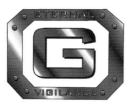

Live sat-cam feed here:
feed.globalnews.com/burns

VLOG ARCHIVE:

Corporate Takeover of America series:

Part 19: Eminent Domain Disasters

Part 18: Your DNA, Their $

Part 17: ChoicePoint: They're back

LATEST: IN GOD WE TRUST: U.S. CLAIMS GLOBAL ORBIT DEFENDER (GOD) PLATFORM FULLY OPERATIONAL BY 2012

DAMAGE

Being a war correspondent eats away at your soul. It happens slowly.

First, the guns, the bombs, and the explosions are exciting. Even the death is a rush. You dodged it. You've tricked the reaper. You must be special. You've never felt more alive. Then the blood finds its way into your dreams.

You find your mind wandering into the darkness at night as you lie in your bed. You replay the carnage over and over. The more you try to think about puppies and waterfalls and eating a slice of pizza on Bedford with your best friend Geno, the more your mind rebels and reminds you of the half a torso of a little boy you almost stepped on last Tuesday. Or the street full of kids you watched get gunned down in cold blood. Then the carnage bleeds all the way into your waking hours. You see it on the blank walls, in our food, in your reflection in the mirror. Doctors call it PTSD — post-traumatic stress disorder. I call it being human. If this shit doesn't fuck you up then you should see a doctor because you're a sociopath.

You cover it up, because you have to. You cover up a lot of things, because you have to — to survive.

Your humble correspondent out.

ALLIES LINKS

Guerrilla News Network

TalkingPoints Memo

Information Clearing House

Crooks and Liars

Sploid

Huffington Post

Gawker

Metafilter

Antiwar

Truthout

War in Context

DailyKos

Treehugger

Show Me the War

Iraq & Afghanistan Veterans of America

ACT-I-VATE

Antiwar

Wonkette

Guardian

The Nation

Doc Searls

Village Voice

AlterNet

Entertainment Weekly

Independent Propaganda

Rolling Stone

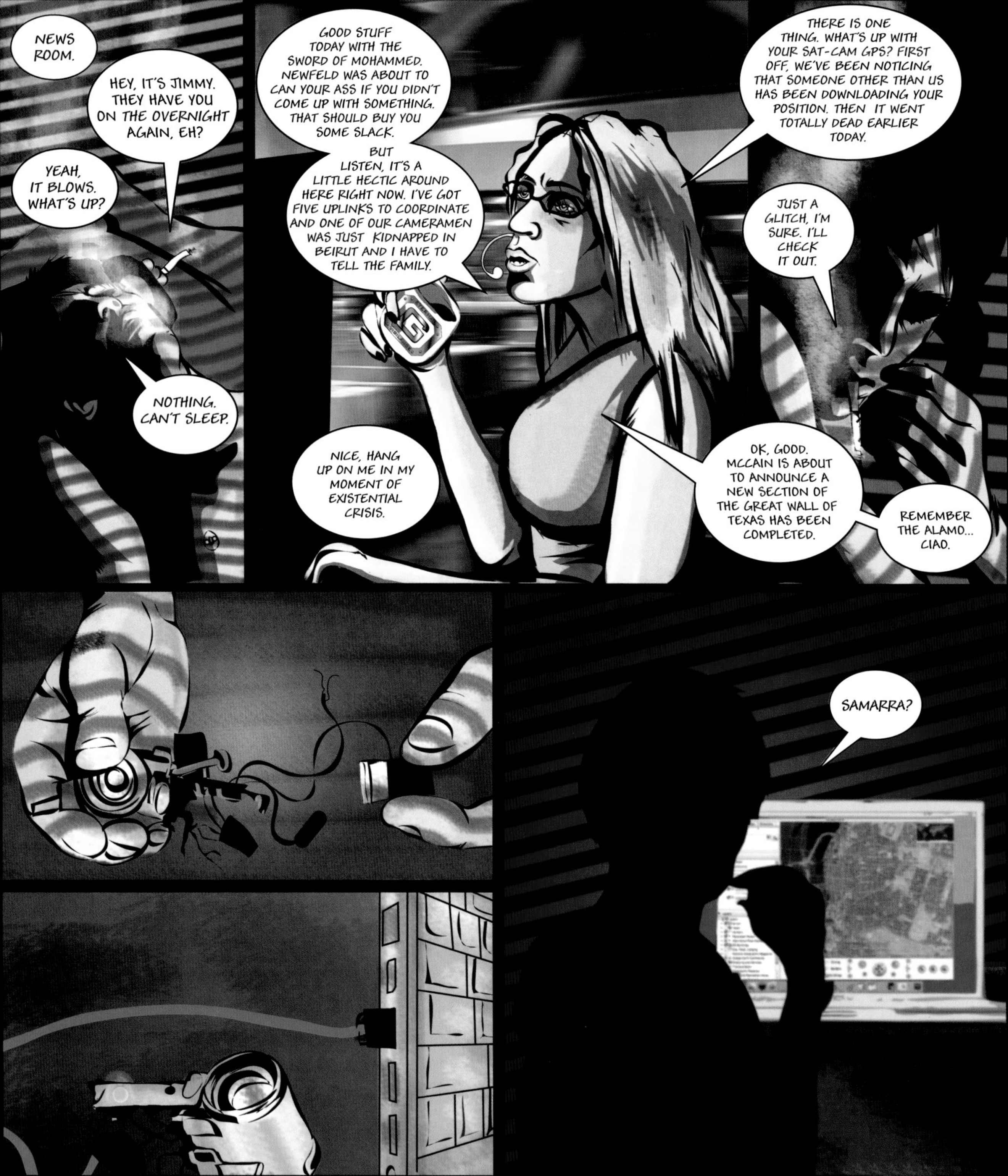
NEWS ROOM.
HEY, IT'S JIMMY. THEY HAVE YOU ON THE OVERNIGHT AGAIN, EH?
YEAH, IT BLOWS. WHAT'S UP?
NOTHING. CAN'T SLEEP.
GOOD STUFF TODAY WITH THE SWORD OF MOHAMMED. NEWFELD WAS ABOUT TO CAN YOUR ASS IF YOU DIDN'T COME UP WITH SOMETHING. THAT SHOULD BUY YOU SOME SLACK.
BUT LISTEN, IT'S A LITTLE HECTIC AROUND HERE RIGHT NOW. I'VE GOT FIVE UPLINKS TO COORDINATE AND ONE OF OUR CAMERAMEN WAS JUST KIDNAPPED IN BEIRUT AND I HAVE TO TELL THE FAMILY.
THERE IS ONE THING. WHAT'S UP WITH YOUR SAT-CAM GPS? FIRST OFF, WE'VE BEEN NOTICING THAT SOMEONE OTHER THAN US HAS BEEN DOWNLOADING YOUR POSITION. THEN IT WENT TOTALLY DEAD EARLIER TODAY.
JUST A GLITCH, I'M SURE. I'LL CHECK IT OUT.
OK, GOOD. MCCAIN IS ABOUT TO ANNOUNCE A NEW SECTION OF THE GREAT WALL OF TEXAS HAS BEEN COMPLETED.
REMEMBER THE ALAMO... CIAO.
NICE, HANG UP ON ME IN MY MOMENT OF EXISTENTIAL CRISIS.
SAMARRA?

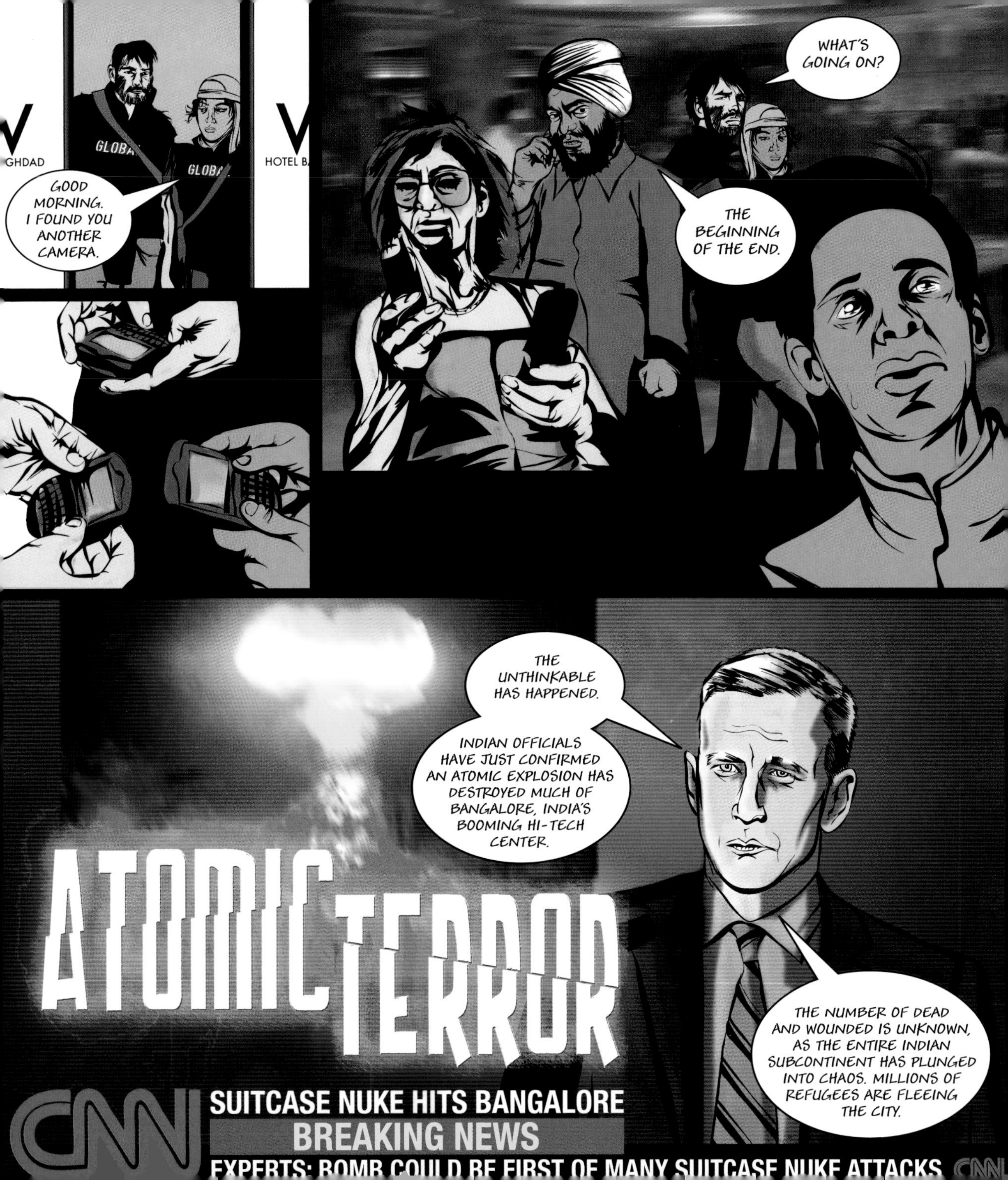
GHDAD
GLOBA
GLOBA
HOTEL BA
GOOD MORNING. I FOUND YOU ANOTHER CAMERA.
WHAT'S GOING ON?
THE BEGINNING OF THE END.
THE UNTHINKABLE HAS HAPPENED.
INDIAN OFFICIALS HAVE JUST CONFIRMED AN ATOMIC EXPLOSION HAS DESTROYED MUCH OF BANGALORE, INDIA'S BOOMING HI-TECH CENTER.
ATOMIC TERROR
THE NUMBER OF DEAD AND WOUNDED IS UNKNOWN, AS THE ENTIRE INDIAN SUBCONTINENT HAS PLUNGED INTO CHAOS. MILLIONS OF REFUGEES ARE FLEEING THE CITY.
CNN
SUITCASE NUKE HITS BANGALORE
BREAKING NEWS
EXPERTS: BOMB COULD BE FIRST OF MANY SUITCASE NUKE ATTACKS

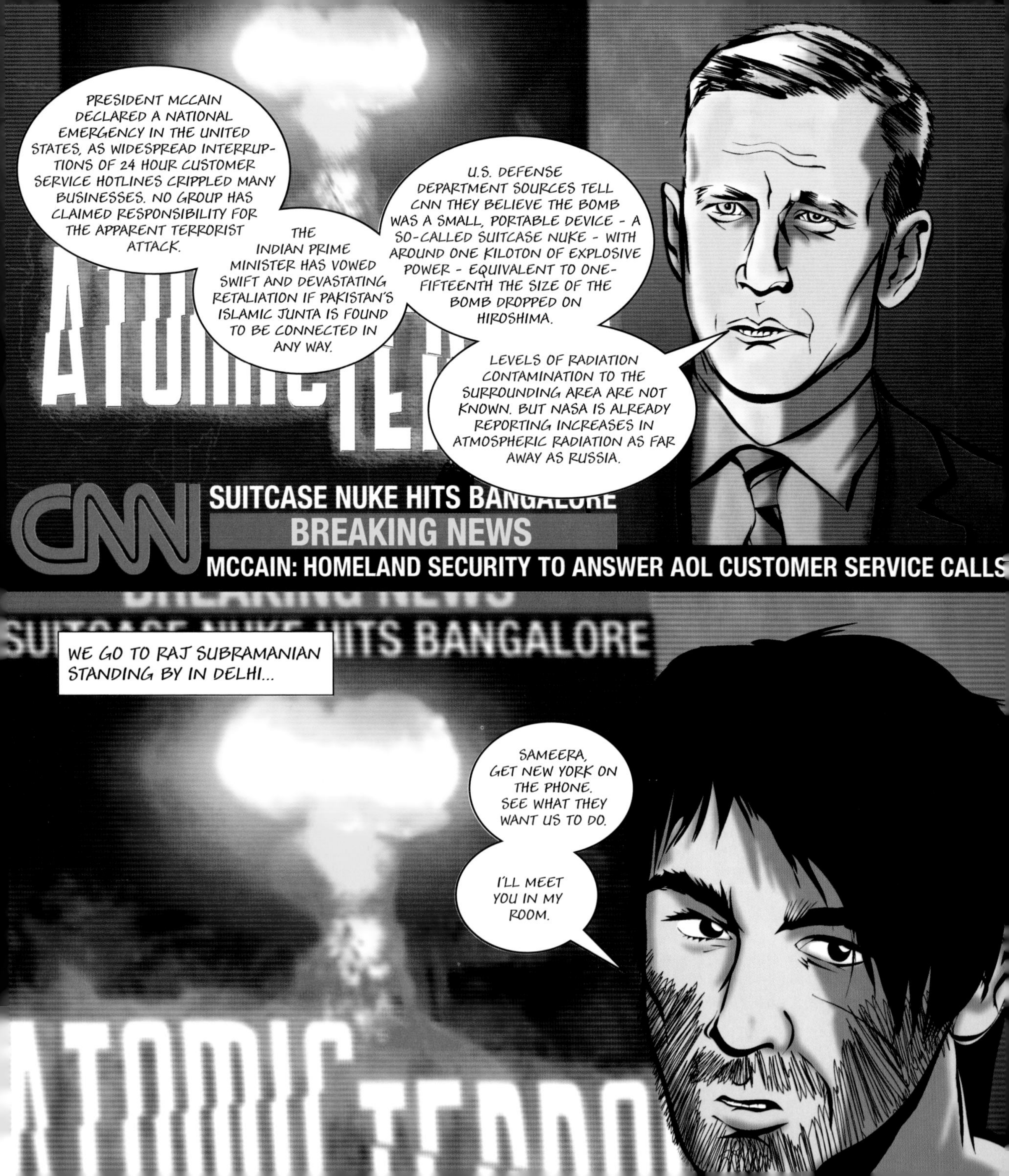

PRESIDENT MCCAIN DECLARED A NATIONAL EMERGENCY IN THE UNITED STATES, AS WIDESPREAD INTERRUPTIONS OF 24 HOUR CUSTOMER SERVICE HOTLINES CRIPPLED MANY BUSINESSES. NO GROUP HAS CLAIMED RESPONSIBILITY FOR THE APPARENT TERRORIST ATTACK.
THE INDIAN PRIME MINISTER HAS VOWED SWIFT AND DEVASTATING RETALIATION IF PAKISTAN'S ISLAMIC JUNTA IS FOUND TO BE CONNECTED IN ANY WAY.
U.S. DEFENSE DEPARTMENT SOURCES TELL CNN THEY BELIEVE THE BOMB WAS A SMALL, PORTABLE DEVICE - A SO-CALLED SUITCASE NUKE - WITH AROUND ONE KILOTON OF EXPLOSIVE POWER - EQUIVALENT TO ONE-FIFTEENTH THE SIZE OF THE BOMB DROPPED ON HIROSHIMA.
LEVELS OF RADIATION CONTAMINATION TO THE SURROUNDING AREA ARE NOT KNOWN. BUT NASA IS ALREADY REPORTING INCREASES IN ATMOSPHERIC RADIATION AS FAR AWAY AS RUSSIA.
CNN
SUITCASE NUKE HITS BANGALORE
BREAKING NEWS
MCCAIN: HOMELAND SECURITY TO ANSWER AOL CUSTOMER SERVICE CALLS
HITS BANGALORE
WE GO TO RAJ SUBRAMANIAN STANDING BY IN DELHI...
SAMEERA, GET NEW YORK ON THE PHONE. SEE WHAT THEY WANT US TO DO.
I'LL MEET YOU IN MY ROOM.

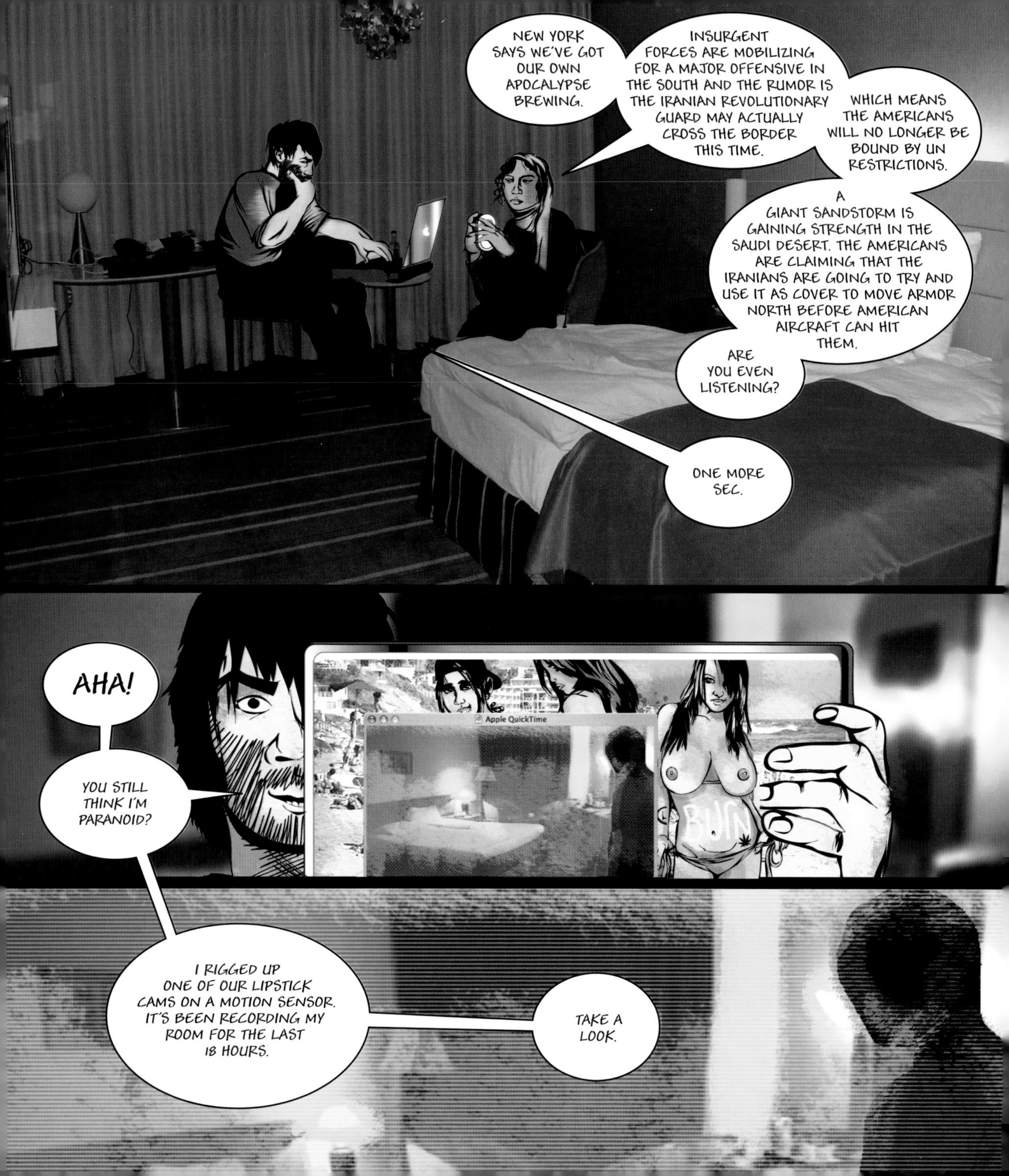

NEW YORK SAYS WE'VE GOT OUR OWN APOCALYPSE BREWING.
INSURGENT FORCES ARE MOBILIZING FOR A MAJOR OFFENSIVE IN THE SOUTH AND THE RUMOR IS THE IRANIAN REVOLUTIONARY GUARD MAY ACTUALLY CROSS THE BORDER THIS TIME.
WHICH MEANS THE AMERICANS WILL NO LONGER BE BOUND BY UN RESTRICTIONS.
A GIANT SANDSTORM IS GAINING STRENGTH IN THE SAUDI DESERT. THE AMERICANS ARE CLAIMING THAT THE IRANIANS ARE GOING TO TRY AND USE IT AS COVER TO MOVE ARMOR NORTH BEFORE AMERICAN AIRCRAFT CAN HIT THEM.
ARE YOU EVEN LISTENING?
ONE MORE SEC.
AHA!
Apple QuickTime
YOU STILL THINK I'M PARANOID?
I RIGGED UP ONE OF OUR LIPSTICK CAMS ON A MOTION SENSOR. IT'S BEEN RECORDING MY ROOM FOR THE LAST 18 HOURS.
TAKE A LOOK.

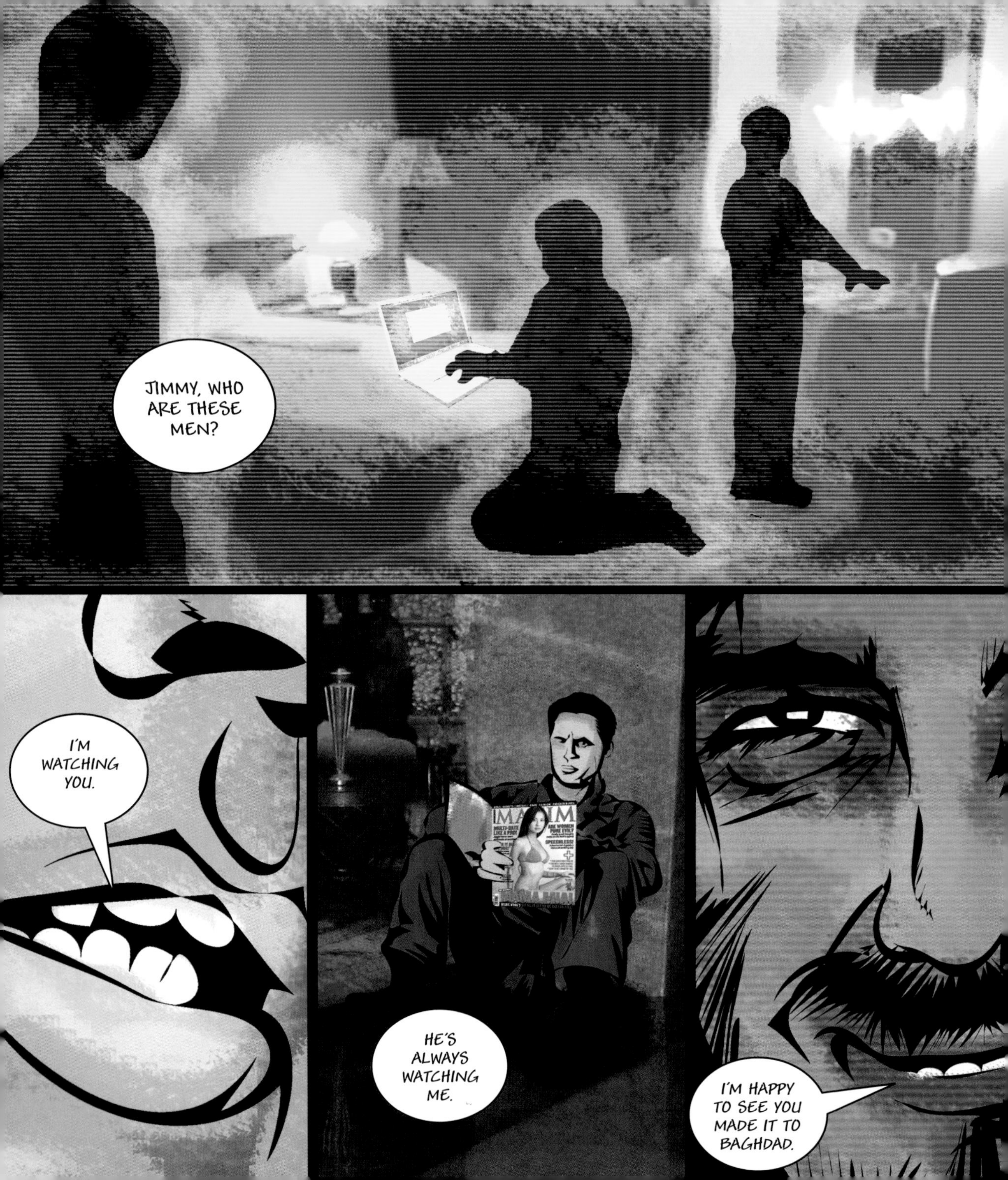
JIMMY, WHO ARE THESE MEN?
I'M WATCHING YOU.
HE'S ALWAYS WATCHING ME.
I'M HAPPY TO SEE YOU MADE IT TO BAGHDAD.

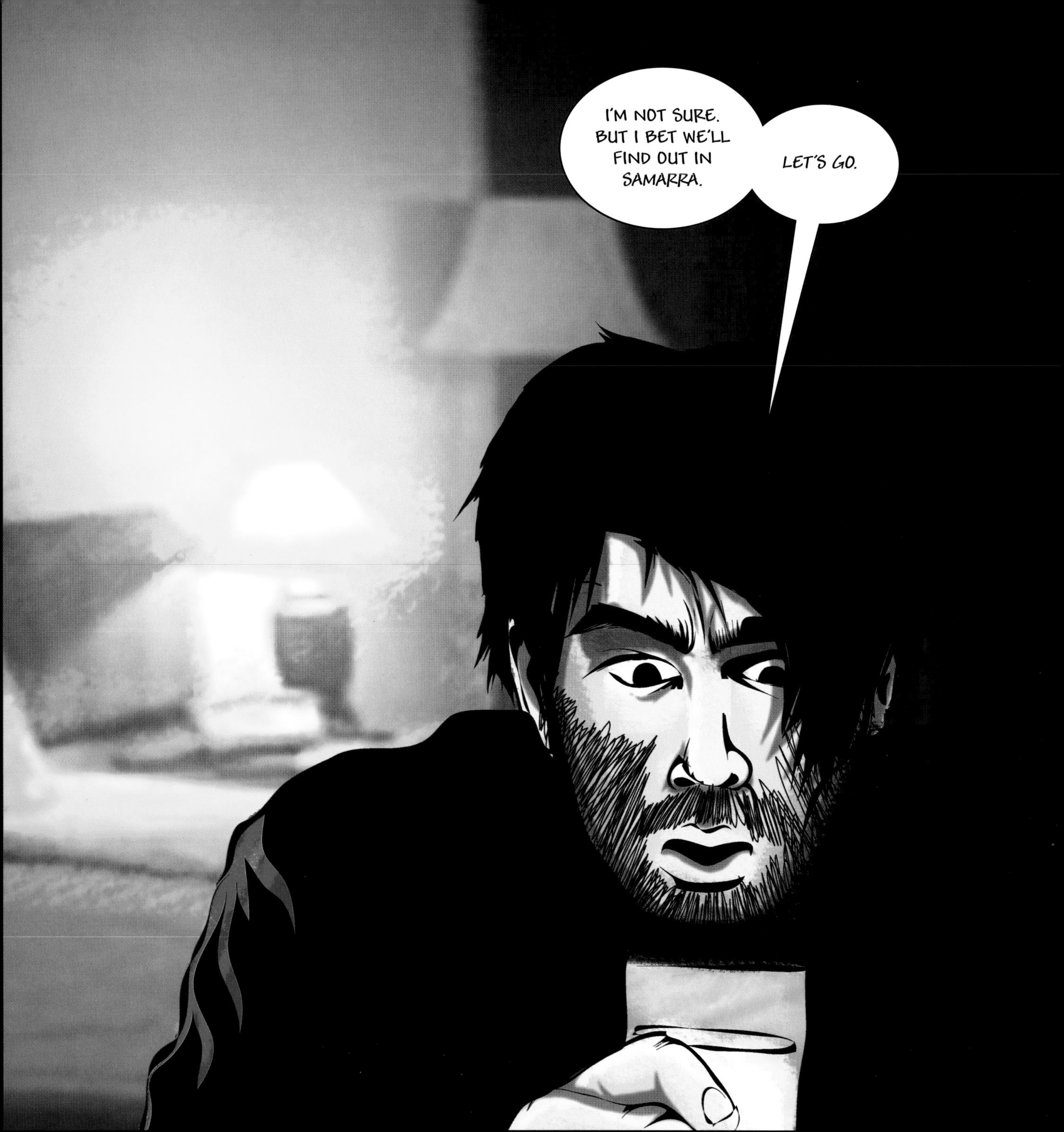
I'M NOT SURE. BUT I BET WE'LL FIND OUT IN SAMARRA.
LET'S GO.

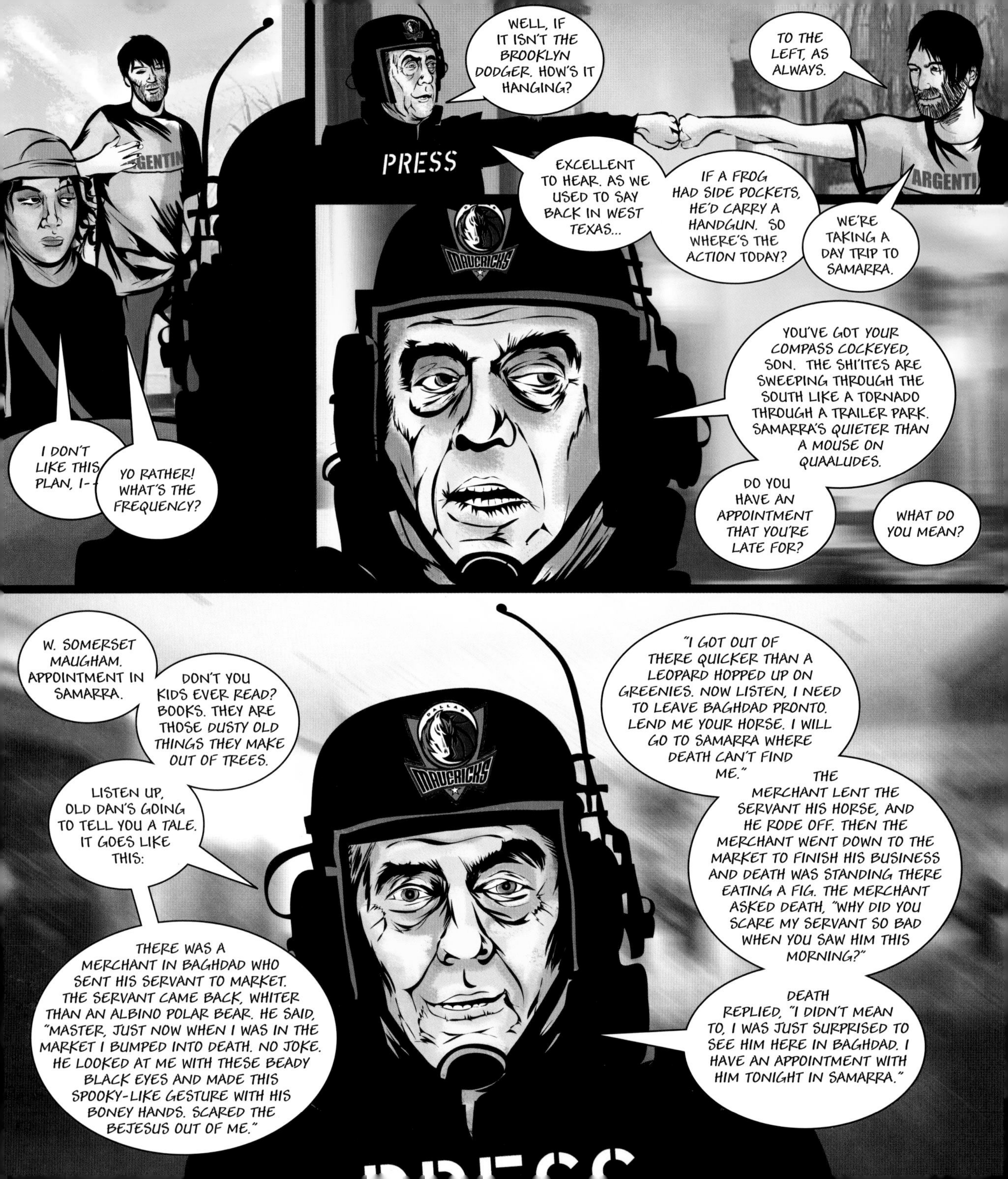
WELL, IF IT ISN'T THE BROOKLYN DODGER. HOW'S IT HANGING?
TO THE LEFT, AS ALWAYS.
PRESS
ARGENTI
EXCELLENT TO HEAR. AS WE USED TO SAY BACK IN WEST TEXAS...
IF A FROG HAD SIDE POCKETS, HE'D CARRY A HANDGUN. SO WHERE'S THE ACTION TODAY?
WE'RE TAKING A DAY TRIP TO SAMARRA.
MAVERICKS
YOU'VE GOT YOUR COMPASS COCKEYED, SON. THE SHI'ITES ARE SWEEPING THROUGH THE SOUTH LIKE A TORNADO THROUGH A TRAILER PARK. SAMARRA'S QUIETER THAN A MOUSE ON QUAALUDES.
I DON'T LIKE THIS PLAN, I--
YO RATHER! WHAT'S THE FREQUENCY?
DO YOU HAVE AN APPOINTMENT THAT YOU'RE LATE FOR?
WHAT DO YOU MEAN?
W. SOMERSET MAUGHAM. APPOINTMENT IN SAMARRA.
DON'T YOU KIDS EVER READ? BOOKS. THEY ARE THOSE DUSTY OLD THINGS THEY MAKE OUT OF TREES.
LISTEN UP, OLD DAN'S GOING TO TELL YOU A TALE. IT GOES LIKE THIS:
THERE WAS A MERCHANT IN BAGHDAD WHO SENT HIS SERVANT TO MARKET. THE SERVANT CAME BACK, WHITER THAN AN ALBINO POLAR BEAR. HE SAID, "MASTER, JUST NOW WHEN I WAS IN THE MARKET I BUMPED INTO DEATH. NO JOKE. HE LOOKED AT ME WITH THESE BEADY BLACK EYES AND MADE THIS SPOOKY-LIKE GESTURE WITH HIS BONEY HANDS. SCARED THE BEJESUS OUT OF ME."
"I GOT OUT OF THERE QUICKER THAN A LEOPARD HOPPED UP ON GREENIES. NOW LISTEN, I NEED TO LEAVE BAGHDAD PRONTO. LEND ME YOUR HORSE. I WILL GO TO SAMARRA WHERE DEATH CAN'T FIND ME."
THE MERCHANT LENT THE SERVANT HIS HORSE, AND HE RODE OFF. THEN THE MERCHANT WENT DOWN TO THE MARKET TO FINISH HIS BUSINESS AND DEATH WAS STANDING THERE EATING A FIG. THE MERCHANT ASKED DEATH, "WHY DID YOU SCARE MY SERVANT SO BAD WHEN YOU SAW HIM THIS MORNING?"
DEATH REPLIED, "I DIDN'T MEAN TO, I WAS JUST SURPRISED TO SEE HIM HERE IN BAGHDAD. I HAVE AN APPOINTMENT WITH HIM TONIGHT IN SAMARRA."

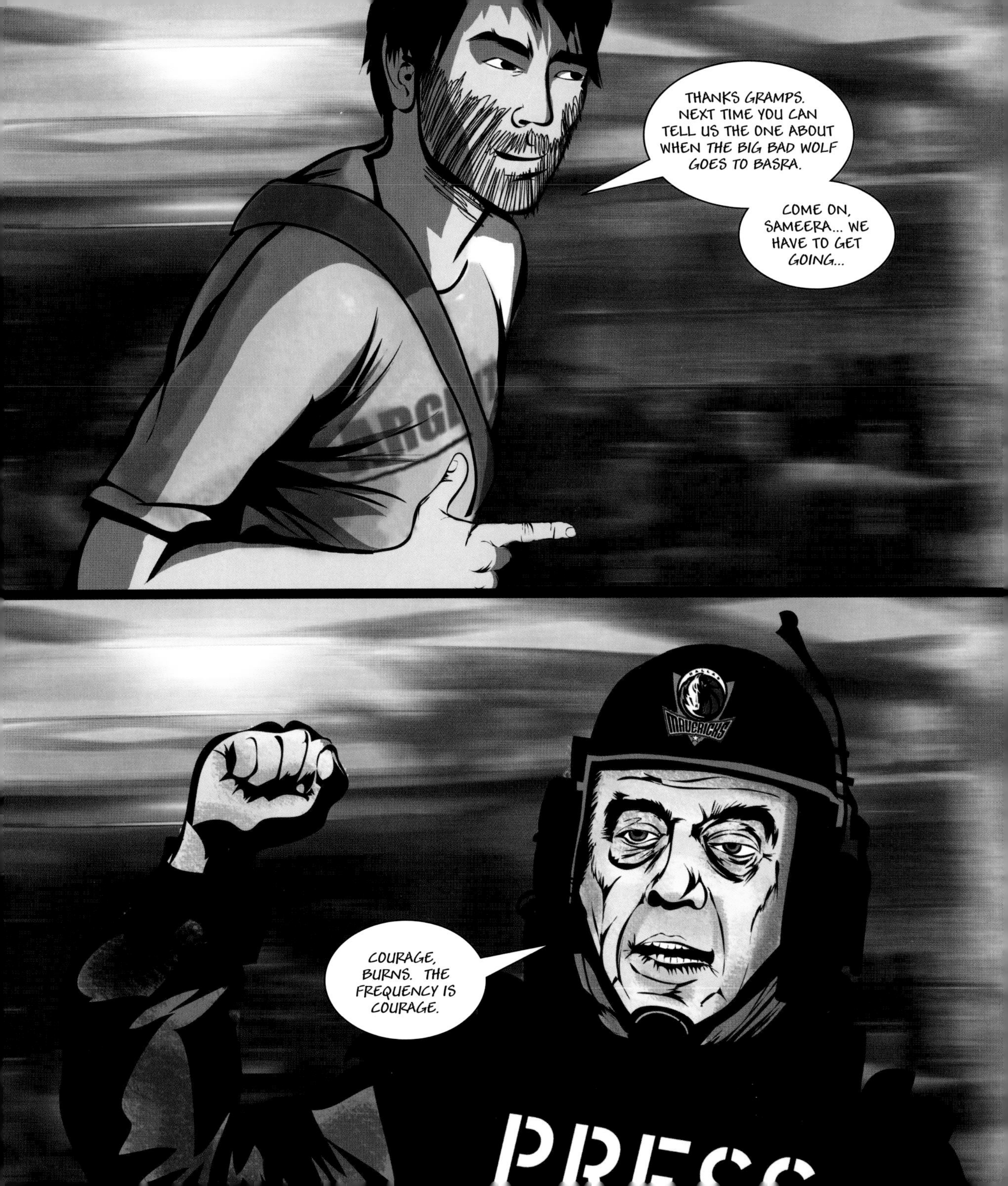
THANKS GRAMPS. NEXT TIME YOU CAN TELL US THE ONE ABOUT WHEN THE BIG BAD WOLF GOES TO BASRA.
COME ON, SAMEERA... WE HAVE TO GET GOING...
MAVERICKS
COURAGE, BURNS. THE FREQUENCY IS COURAGE.
PRESS

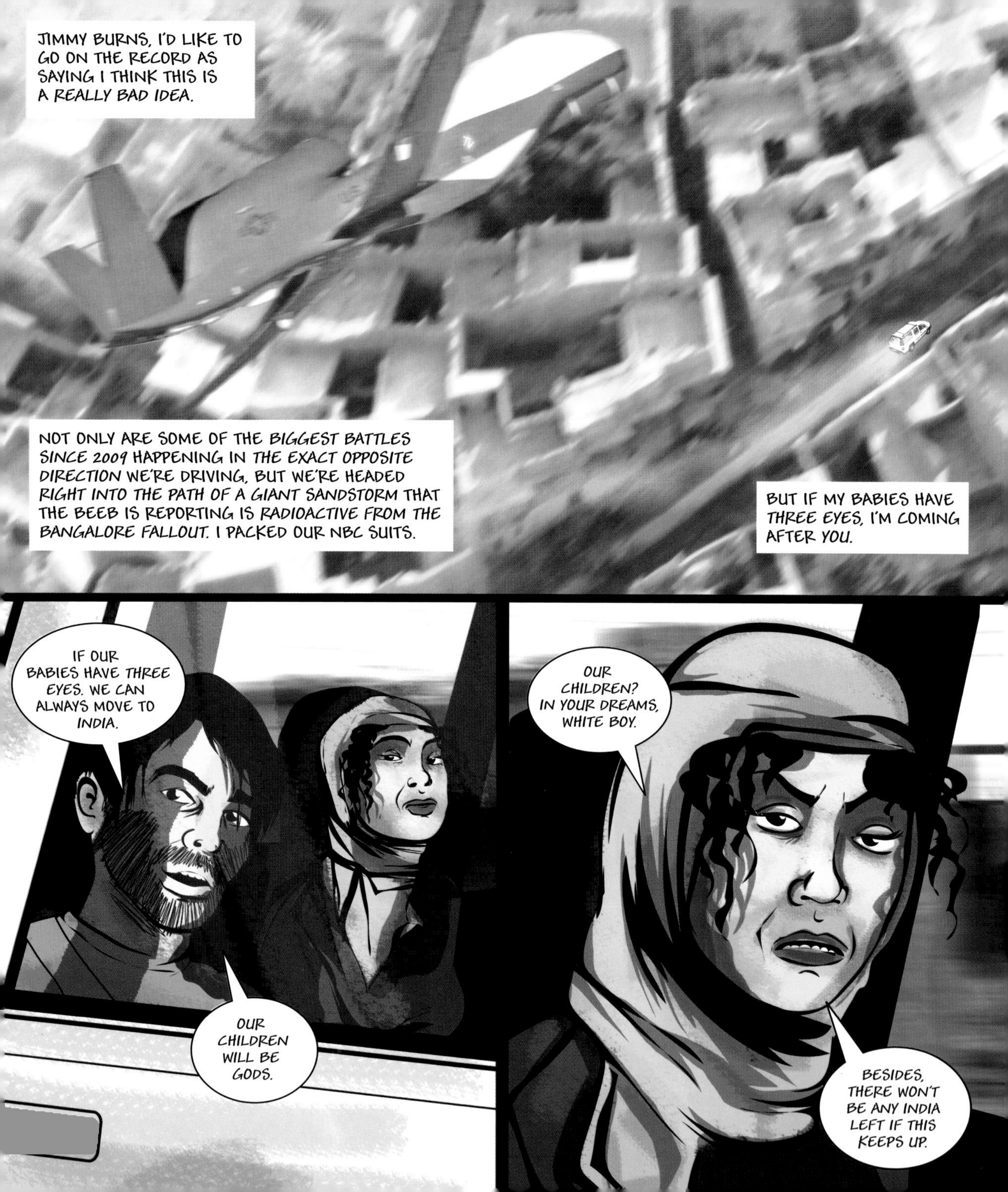
JIMMY BURNS, I'D LIKE TO GO ON THE RECORD AS SAYING I THINK THIS IS A REALLY BAD IDEA.
NOT ONLY ARE SOME OF THE BIGGEST BATTLES SINCE 2009 HAPPENING IN THE EXACT OPPOSITE DIRECTION WE'RE DRIVING, BUT WE'RE HEADED RIGHT INTO THE PATH OF A GIANT SANDSTORM THAT THE BEEB IS REPORTING IS RADIOACTIVE FROM THE BANGALORE FALLOUT. I PACKED OUR NBC SUITS.
BUT IF MY BABIES HAVE THREE EYES, I'M COMING AFTER YOU.
IF OUR BABIES HAVE THREE EYES. WE CAN ALWAYS MOVE TO INDIA.
OUR CHILDREN WILL BE GODS.
OUR CHILDREN? IN YOUR DREAMS, WHITE BOY.
BESIDES, THERE WON'T BE ANY INDIA LEFT IF THIS KEEPS UP.

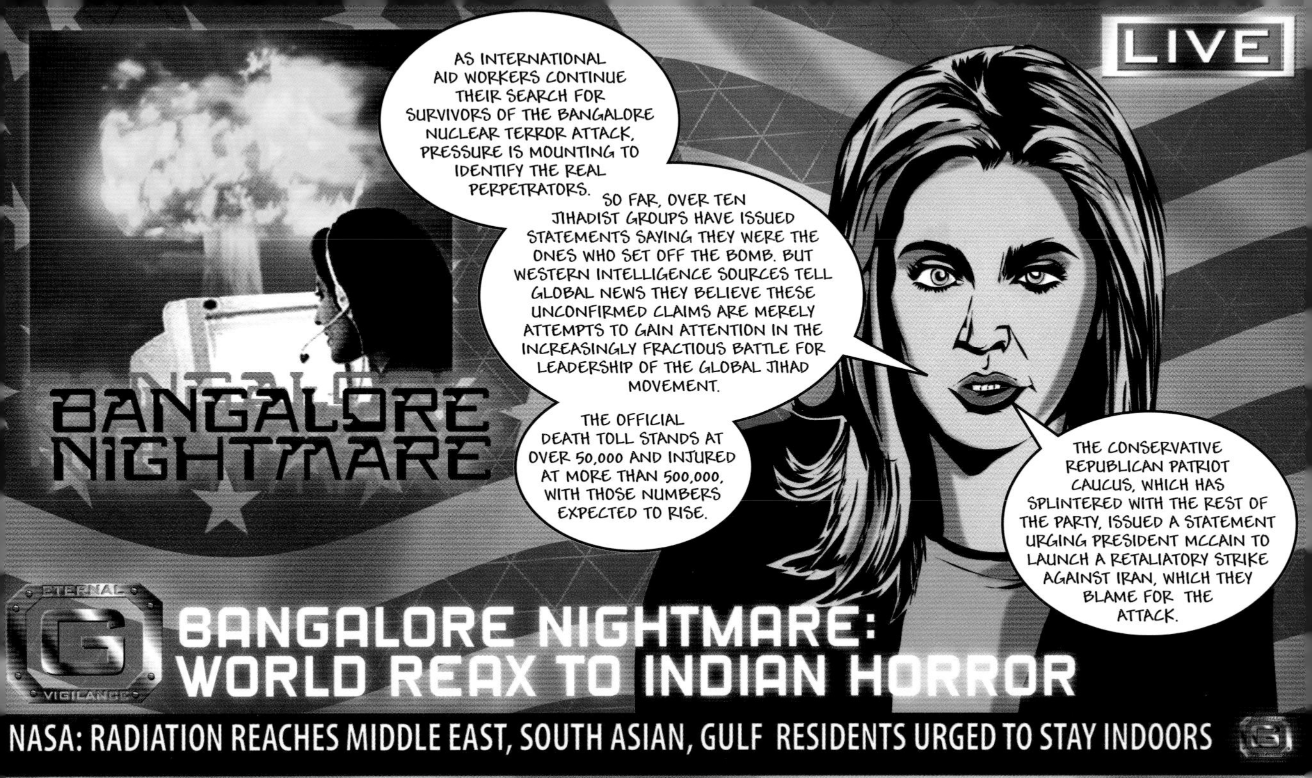
LIVE
AS INTERNATIONAL AID WORKERS CONTINUE THEIR SEARCH FOR SURVIVORS OF THE BANGALORE NUCLEAR TERROR ATTACK, PRESSURE IS MOUNTING TO IDENTIFY THE REAL PERPETRATORS.
SO FAR, OVER TEN JIHADIST GROUPS HAVE ISSUED STATEMENTS SAYING THEY WERE THE ONES WHO SET OFF THE BOMB. BUT WESTERN INTELLIGENCE SOURCES TELL GLOBAL NEWS THEY BELIEVE THESE UNCONFIRMED CLAIMS ARE MERELY ATTEMPTS TO GAIN ATTENTION IN THE INCREASINGLY FRACTIOUS BATTLE FOR LEADERSHIP OF THE GLOBAL JIHAD MOVEMENT.
THE OFFICIAL DEATH TOLL STANDS AT OVER 50,000 AND INJURED AT MORE THAN 500,000, WITH THOSE NUMBERS EXPECTED TO RISE.
THE CONSERVATIVE REPUBLICAN PATRIOT CAUCUS, WHICH HAS SPLINTERED WITH THE REST OF THE PARTY, ISSUED A STATEMENT URGING PRESIDENT MCCAIN TO LAUNCH A RETALIATORY STRIKE AGAINST IRAN, WHICH THEY BLAME FOR THE ATTACK.
BANGALORE NIGHTMARE
ETERNAL
VIGILANCE
BANGALORE NIGHTMARE:
WORLD REAX TO INDIAN HORROR
NASA: RADIATION REACHES MIDDLE EAST, SOUTH ASIAN, GULF RESIDENTS URGED TO STAY INDOORS

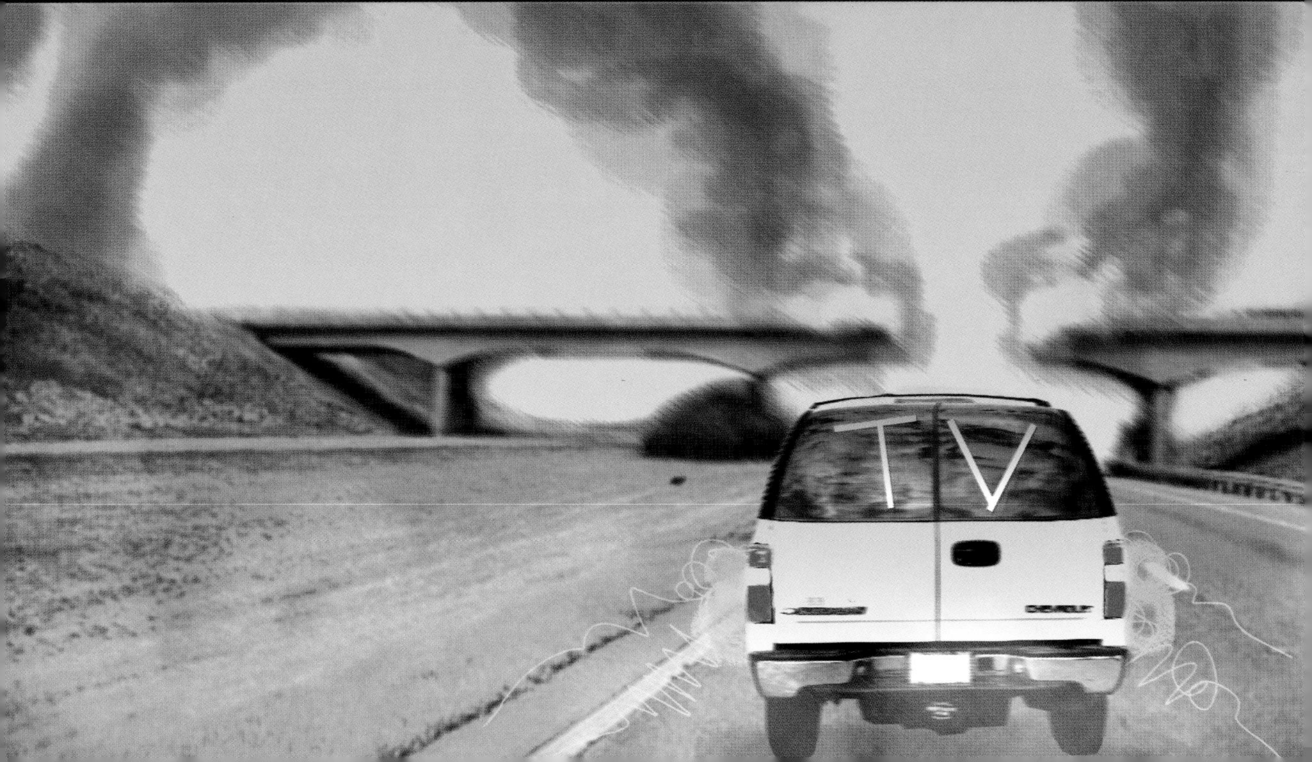
TV

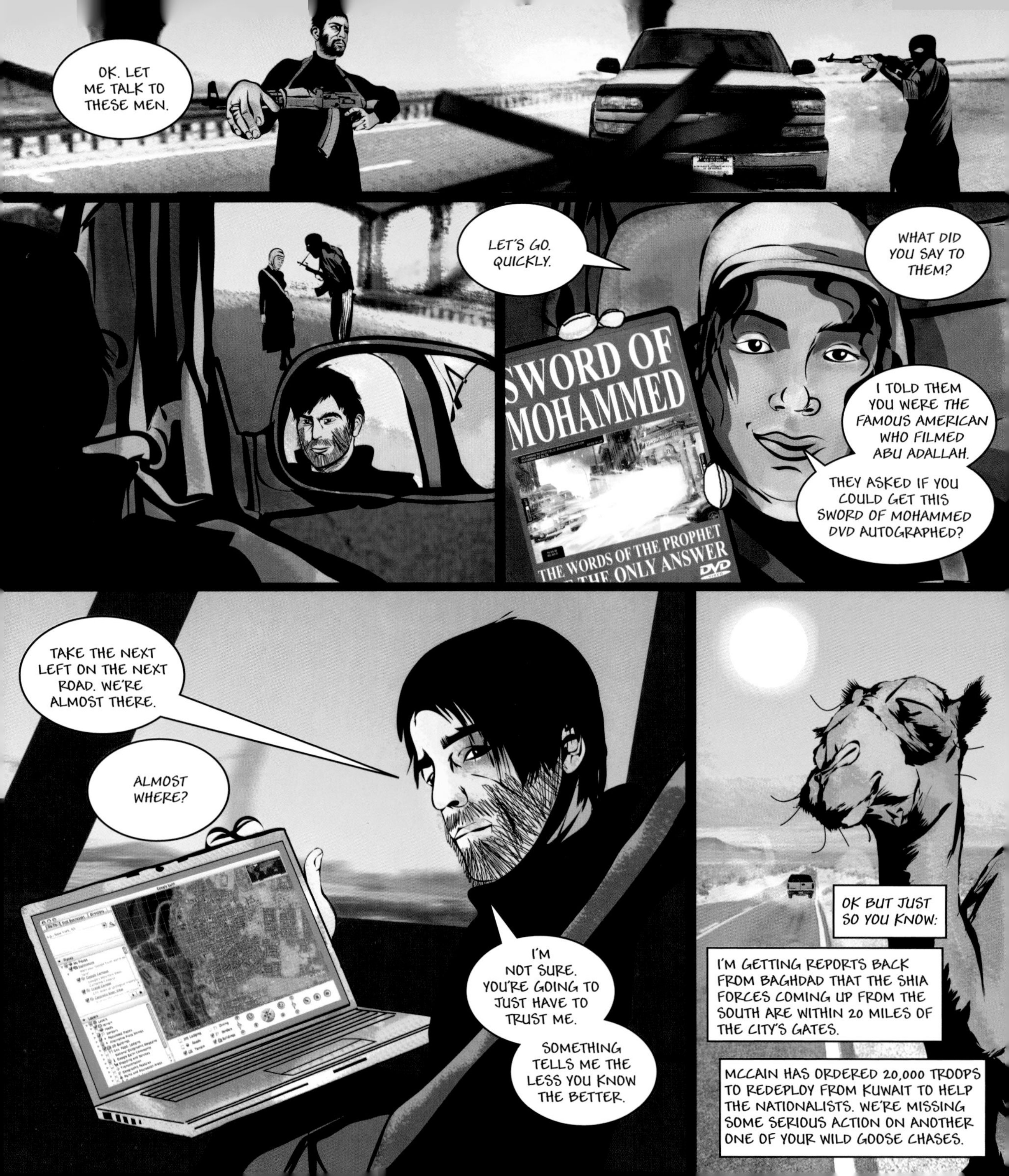

OK. LET ME TALK TO THESE MEN.
LET'S GO. QUICKLY.
WHAT DID YOU SAY TO THEM?
SWORD OF MOHAMMED
THE WORDS OF THE PROPHET
THE ONLY ANSWER
DVD
I TOLD THEM YOU WERE THE FAMOUS AMERICAN WHO FILMED ABU ADALLAH.
THEY ASKED IF YOU COULD GET THIS SWORD OF MOHAMMED DVD AUTOGRAPHED?
TAKE THE NEXT LEFT ON THE NEXT ROAD. WE'RE ALMOST THERE.
ALMOST WHERE?
I'M NOT SURE. YOU'RE GOING TO JUST HAVE TO TRUST ME.
SOMETHING TELLS ME THE LESS YOU KNOW THE BETTER.
OK BUT JUST SO YOU KNOW:
I'M GETTING REPORTS BACK FROM BAGHDAD THAT THE SHIA FORCES COMING UP FROM THE SOUTH ARE WITHIN 20 MILES OF THE CITY'S GATES.
MCCAIN HAS ORDERED 20,000 TROOPS TO REDEPLOY FROM KUWAIT TO HELP THE NATIONALISTS. WE'RE MISSING SOME SERIOUS ACTION ON ANOTHER ONE OF YOUR WILD GOOSE CHASES.

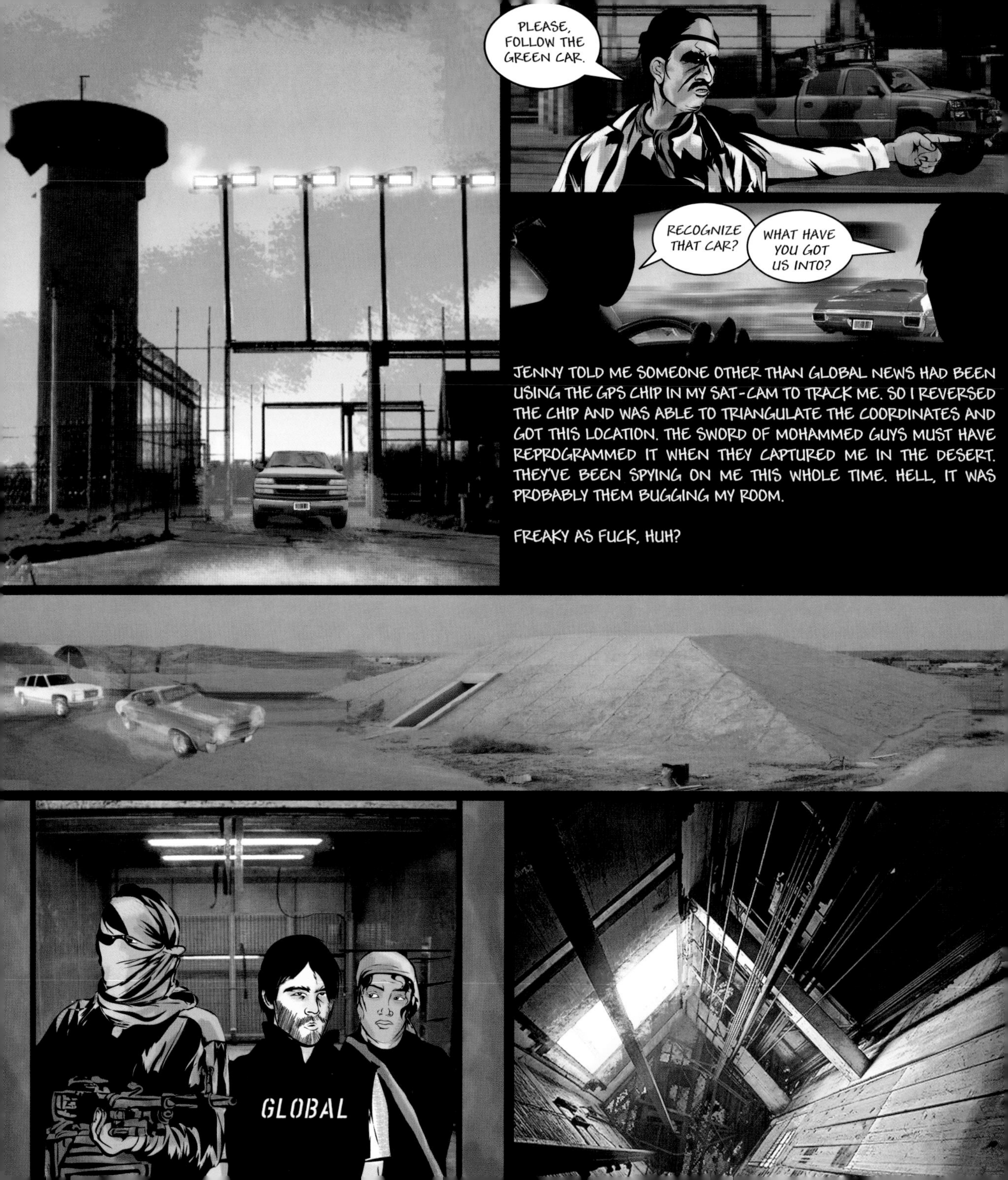
PLEASE, FOLLOW THE GREEN CAR.
RECOGNIZE THAT CAR?
WHAT HAVE YOU GOT US INTO?
JENNY TOLD ME SOMEONE OTHER THAN GLOBAL NEWS HAD BEEN USING THE GPS CHIP IN MY SAT-CAM TO TRACK ME. SO I REVERSED THE CHIP AND WAS ABLE TO TRIANGULATE THE COORDINATES AND GOT THIS LOCATION. THE SWORD OF MOHAMMED GUYS MUST HAVE REPROGRAMMED IT WHEN THEY CAPTURED ME IN THE DESERT. THEY'VE BEEN SPYING ON ME THIS WHOLE TIME. HELL, IT WAS PROBABLY THEM BUGGING MY ROOM.
FREAKY AS FUCK, HUH?
GLOBAL

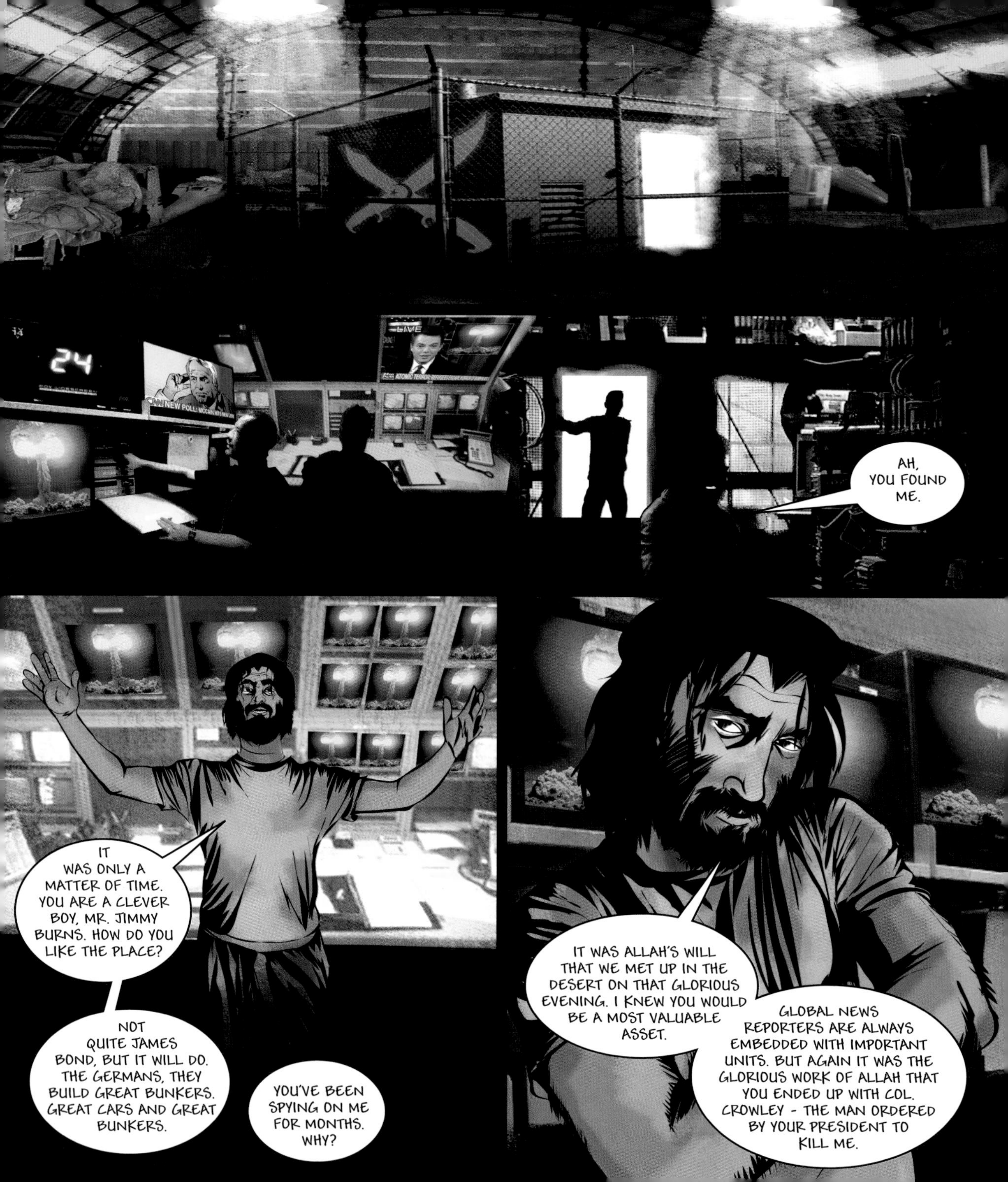
AH, YOU FOUND ME.
IT WAS ONLY A MATTER OF TIME. YOU ARE A CLEVER BOY, MR. JIMMY BURNS. HOW DO YOU LIKE THE PLACE?
NOT QUITE JAMES BOND, BUT IT WILL DO. THE GERMANS, THEY BUILD GREAT BUNKERS. GREAT CARS AND GREAT BUNKERS.
YOU'VE BEEN SPYING ON ME FOR MONTHS. WHY?
IT WAS ALLAH'S WILL THAT WE MET UP IN THE DESERT ON THAT GLORIOUS EVENING. I KNEW YOU WOULD BE A MOST VALUABLE ASSET.
GLOBAL NEWS REPORTERS ARE ALWAYS EMBEDDED WITH IMPORTANT UNITS. BUT AGAIN IT WAS THE GLORIOUS WORK OF ALLAH THAT YOU ENDED UP WITH COL. CROWLEY - THE MAN ORDERED BY YOUR PRESIDENT TO KILL ME.

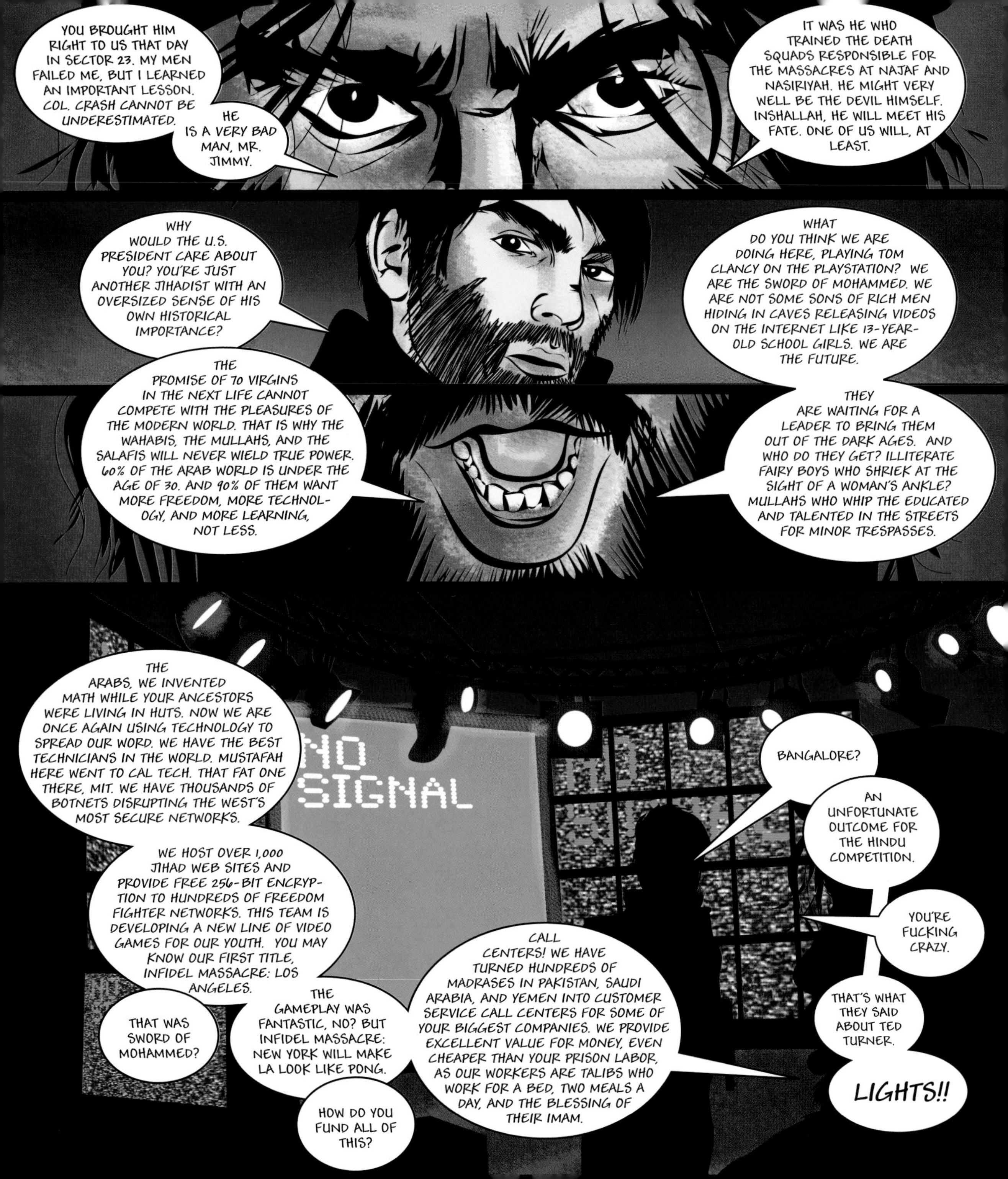

YOU BROUGHT HIM RIGHT TO US THAT DAY IN SECTOR 23. MY MEN FAILED ME, BUT I LEARNED AN IMPORTANT LESSON. COL. CRASH CANNOT BE UNDERESTIMATED.
HE IS A VERY BAD MAN, MR. JIMMY.
IT WAS HE WHO TRAINED THE DEATH SQUADS RESPONSIBLE FOR THE MASSACRES AT NAJAF AND NASIRIYAH. HE MIGHT VERY WELL BE THE DEVIL HIMSELF. INSHALLAH, HE WILL MEET HIS FATE. ONE OF US WILL, AT LEAST.
WHY WOULD THE U.S. PRESIDENT CARE ABOUT YOU? YOU'RE JUST ANOTHER JIHADIST WITH AN OVERSIZED SENSE OF HIS OWN HISTORICAL IMPORTANCE?
WHAT DO YOU THINK WE ARE DOING HERE, PLAYING TOM CLANCY ON THE PLAYSTATION? WE ARE THE SWORD OF MOHAMMED. WE ARE NOT SOME SONS OF RICH MEN HIDING IN CAVES RELEASING VIDEOS ON THE INTERNET LIKE 13-YEAR-OLD SCHOOL GIRLS. WE ARE THE FUTURE.
THE PROMISE OF 70 VIRGINS IN THE NEXT LIFE CANNOT COMPETE WITH THE PLEASURES OF THE MODERN WORLD. THAT IS WHY THE WAHABIS, THE MULLAHS, AND THE SALAFIS WILL NEVER WIELD TRUE POWER. 60% OF THE ARAB WORLD IS UNDER THE AGE OF 30. AND 90% OF THEM WANT MORE FREEDOM, MORE TECHNOLOGY, AND MORE LEARNING, NOT LESS.
THEY ARE WAITING FOR A LEADER TO BRING THEM OUT OF THE DARK AGES. AND WHO DO THEY GET? ILLITERATE FAIRY BOYS WHO SHRIEK AT THE SIGHT OF A WOMAN'S ANKLE? MULLAHS WHO WHIP THE EDUCATED AND TALENTED IN THE STREETS FOR MINOR TRESPASSES.
THE ARABS, WE INVENTED MATH WHILE YOUR ANCESTORS WERE LIVING IN HUTS. NOW WE ARE ONCE AGAIN USING TECHNOLOGY TO SPREAD OUR WORD. WE HAVE THE BEST TECHNICIANS IN THE WORLD. MUSTAFAH HERE WENT TO CAL TECH. THAT FAT ONE THERE, MIT. WE HAVE THOUSANDS OF BOTNETS DISRUPTING THE WEST'S MOST SECURE NETWORKS.
NO SIGNAL
BANGALORE?
AN UNFORTUNATE OUTCOME FOR THE HINDU COMPETITION.
WE HOST OVER 1,000 JIHAD WEB SITES AND PROVIDE FREE 256-BIT ENCRYPTION TO HUNDREDS OF FREEDOM FIGHTER NETWORKS. THIS TEAM IS DEVELOPING A NEW LINE OF VIDEO GAMES FOR OUR YOUTH. YOU MAY KNOW OUR FIRST TITLE, INFIDEL MASSACRE: LOS ANGELES.
THAT WAS SWORD OF MOHAMMED?
THE GAMEPLAY WAS FANTASTIC, NO? BUT INFIDEL MASSACRE: NEW YORK WILL MAKE LA LOOK LIKE PONG.
HOW DO YOU FUND ALL OF THIS?
CALL CENTERS! WE HAVE TURNED HUNDREDS OF MADRASES IN PAKISTAN, SAUDI ARABIA, AND YEMEN INTO CUSTOMER SERVICE CALL CENTERS FOR SOME OF YOUR BIGGEST COMPANIES. WE PROVIDE EXCELLENT VALUE FOR MONEY, EVEN CHEAPER THAN YOUR PRISON LABOR, AS OUR WORKERS ARE TALIBS WHO WORK FOR A BED, TWO MEALS A DAY, AND THE BLESSING OF THEIR IMAM.
YOU'RE FUCKING CRAZY.
THAT'S WHAT THEY SAID ABOUT TED TURNER.
LIGHTS!!

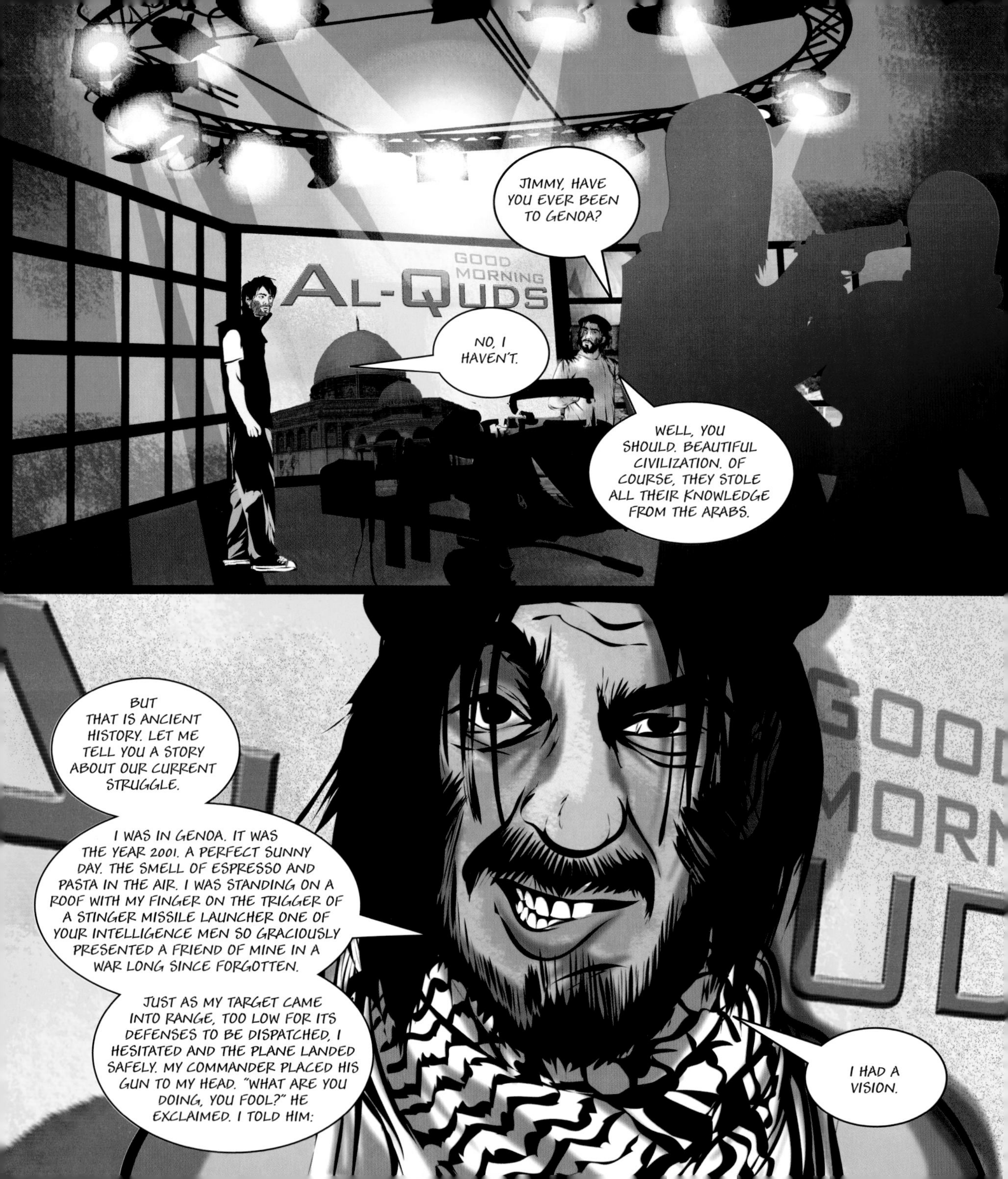
GOOD MORNING AL-QUDS
JIMMY, HAVE YOU EVER BEEN TO GENOA?
NO, I HAVEN'T.
WELL, YOU SHOULD. BEAUTIFUL CIVILIZATION. OF COURSE, THEY STOLE ALL THEIR KNOWLEDGE FROM THE ARABS.
BUT THAT IS ANCIENT HISTORY. LET ME TELL YOU A STORY ABOUT OUR CURRENT STRUGGLE.
I WAS IN GENOA. IT WAS THE YEAR 2001. A PERFECT SUNNY DAY. THE SMELL OF ESPRESSO AND PASTA IN THE AIR. I WAS STANDING ON A ROOF WITH MY FINGER ON THE TRIGGER OF A STINGER MISSILE LAUNCHER ONE OF YOUR INTELLIGENCE MEN SO GRACIOUSLY PRESENTED A FRIEND OF MINE IN A WAR LONG SINCE FORGOTTEN.
JUST AS MY TARGET CAME INTO RANGE, TOO LOW FOR ITS DEFENSES TO BE DISPATCHED, I HESITATED AND THE PLANE LANDED SAFELY. MY COMMANDER PLACED HIS GUN TO MY HEAD. "WHAT ARE YOU DOING, YOU FOOL?" HE EXCLAIMED. I TOLD HIM:
I HAD A VISION.

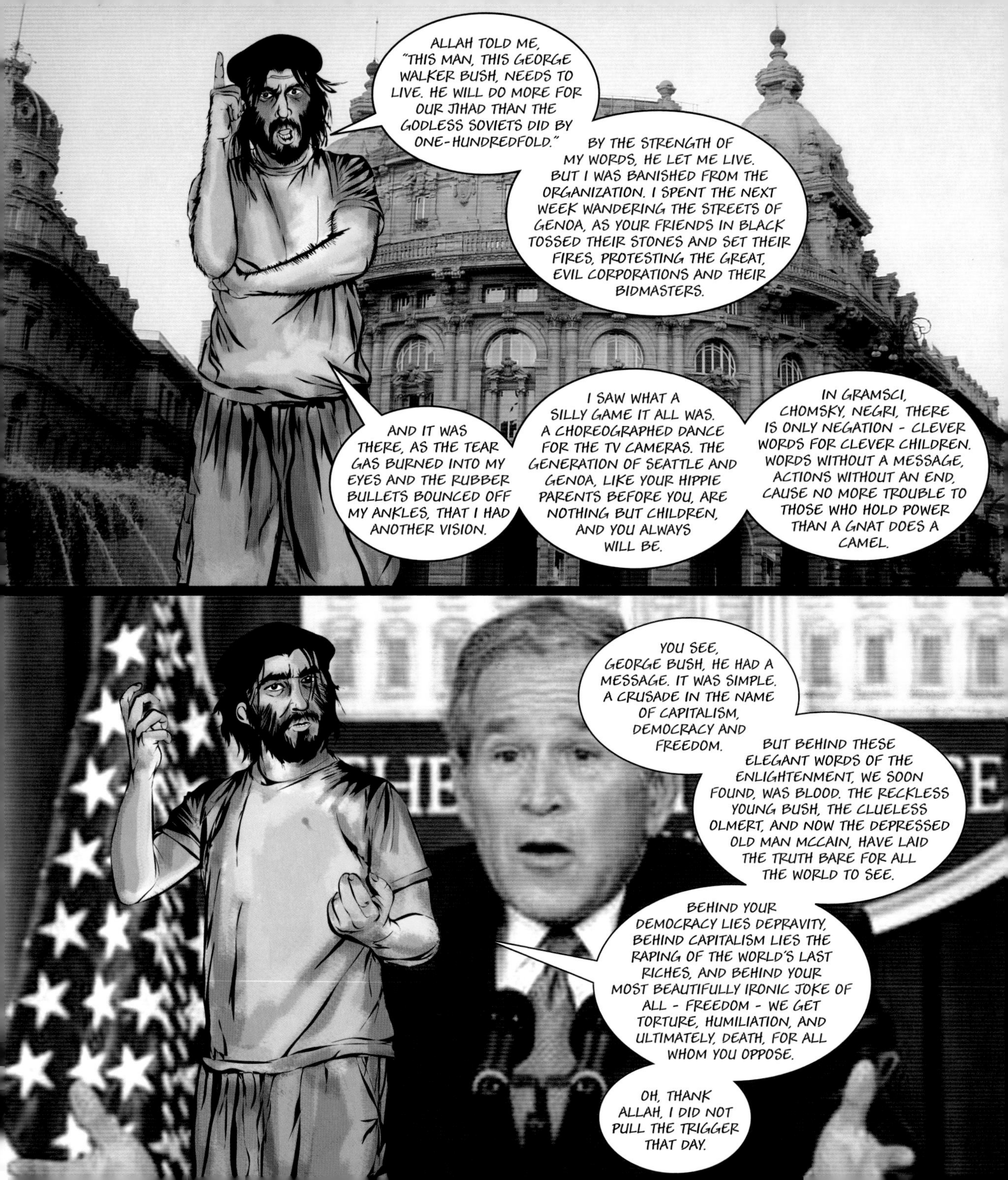
ALLAH TOLD ME, "THIS MAN, THIS GEORGE WALKER BUSH, NEEDS TO LIVE. HE WILL DO MORE FOR OUR JIHAD THAN THE GODLESS SOVIETS DID BY ONE-HUNDREDFOLD."
BY THE STRENGTH OF MY WORDS, HE LET ME LIVE. BUT I WAS BANISHED FROM THE ORGANIZATION. I SPENT THE NEXT WEEK WANDERING THE STREETS OF GENOA, AS YOUR FRIENDS IN BLACK TOSSED THEIR STONES AND SET THEIR FIRES, PROTESTING THE GREAT, EVIL CORPORATIONS AND THEIR BIDMASTERS.
AND IT WAS THERE, AS THE TEAR GAS BURNED INTO MY EYES AND THE RUBBER BULLETS BOUNCED OFF MY ANKLES, THAT I HAD ANOTHER VISION.
I SAW WHAT A SILLY GAME IT ALL WAS. A CHOREOGRAPHED DANCE FOR THE TV CAMERAS. THE GENERATION OF SEATTLE AND GENOA, LIKE YOUR HIPPIE PARENTS BEFORE YOU, ARE NOTHING BUT CHILDREN, AND YOU ALWAYS WILL BE.
IN GRAMSCI, CHOMSKY, NEGRI, THERE IS ONLY NEGATION - CLEVER WORDS FOR CLEVER CHILDREN. WORDS WITHOUT A MESSAGE, ACTIONS WITHOUT AN END, CAUSE NO MORE TROUBLE TO THOSE WHO HOLD POWER THAN A GNAT DOES A CAMEL.
YOU SEE, GEORGE BUSH, HE HAD A MESSAGE. IT WAS SIMPLE. A CRUSADE IN THE NAME OF CAPITALISM, DEMOCRACY AND FREEDOM.
BUT BEHIND THESE ELEGANT WORDS OF THE ENLIGHTENMENT, WE SOON FOUND, WAS BLOOD. THE RECKLESS YOUNG BUSH, THE CLUELESS OLMERT, AND NOW THE DEPRESSED OLD MAN MCCAIN, HAVE LAID THE TRUTH BARE FOR ALL THE WORLD TO SEE.
BEHIND YOUR DEMOCRACY LIES DEPRAVITY, BEHIND CAPITALISM LIES THE RAPING OF THE WORLD'S LAST RICHES, AND BEHIND YOUR MOST BEAUTIFULLY IRONIC JOKE OF ALL - FREEDOM - WE GET TORTURE, HUMILIATION, AND ULTIMATELY, DEATH, FOR ALL WHOM YOU OPPOSE.
OH, THANK ALLAH, I DID NOT PULL THE TRIGGER THAT DAY.

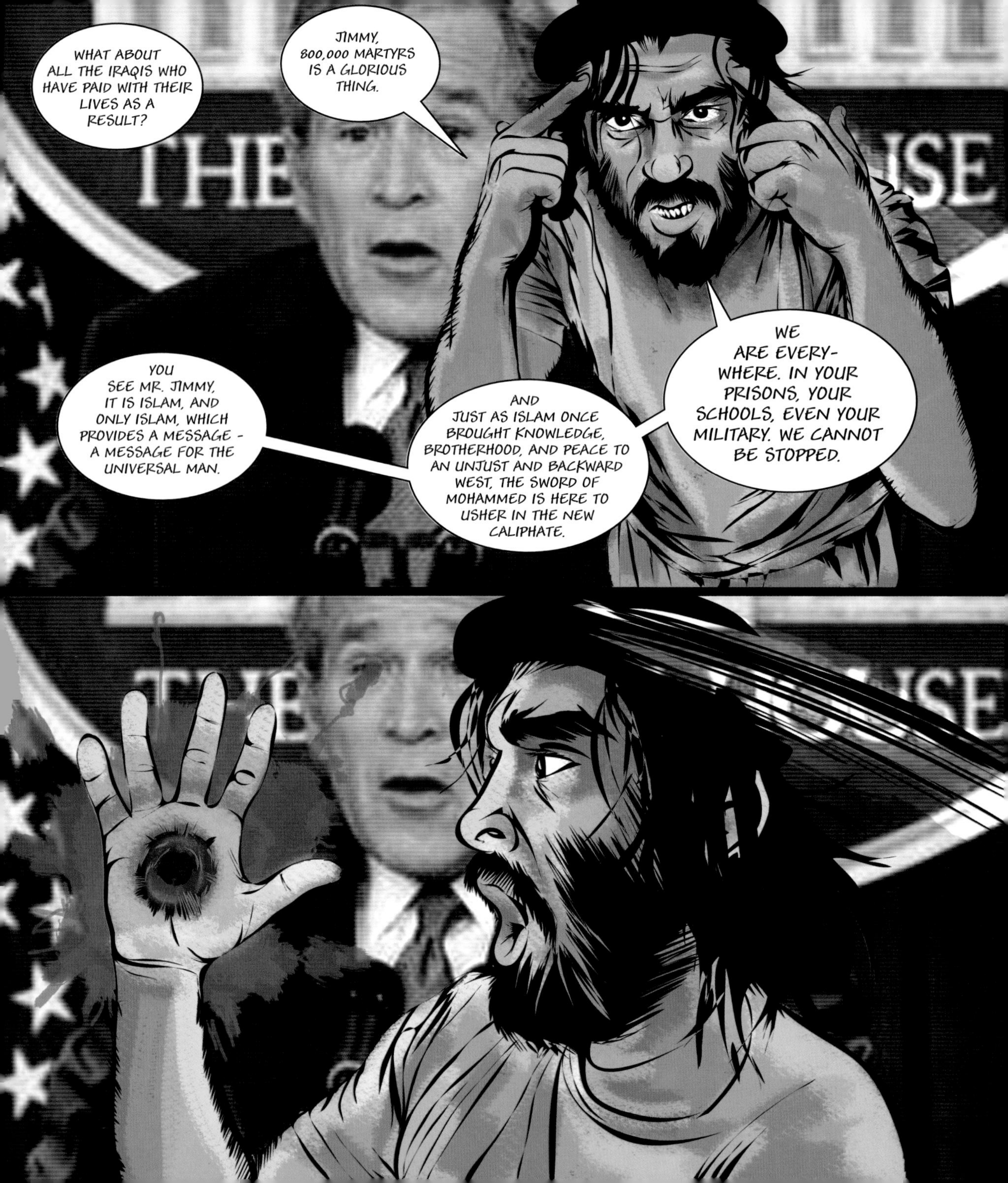
WHAT ABOUT ALL THE IRAQIS WHO HAVE PAID WITH THEIR LIVES AS A RESULT?
JIMMY, 800,000 MARTYRS IS A GLORIOUS THING.
WE ARE EVERY-WHERE. IN YOUR PRISONS, YOUR SCHOOLS, EVEN YOUR MILITARY. WE CANNOT BE STOPPED.
AND JUST AS ISLAM ONCE BROUGHT KNOWLEDGE, BROTHERHOOD, AND PEACE TO AN UNJUST AND BACKWARD WEST, THE SWORD OF MOHAMMED IS HERE TO USHER IN THE NEW CALIPHATE.
YOU SEE MR. JIMMY, IT IS ISLAM, AND ONLY ISLAM, WHICH PROVIDES A MESSAGE - A MESSAGE FOR THE UNIVERSAL MAN.

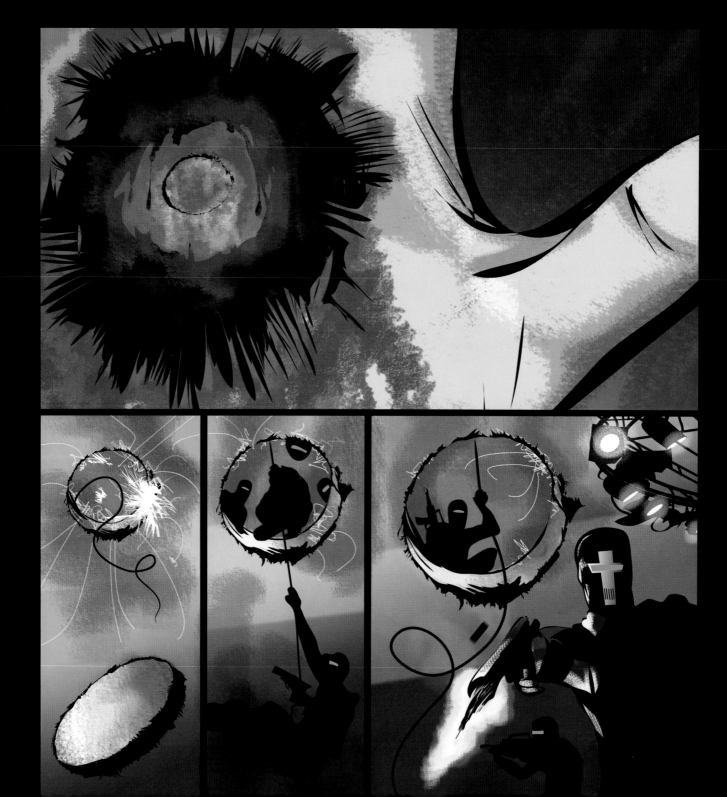

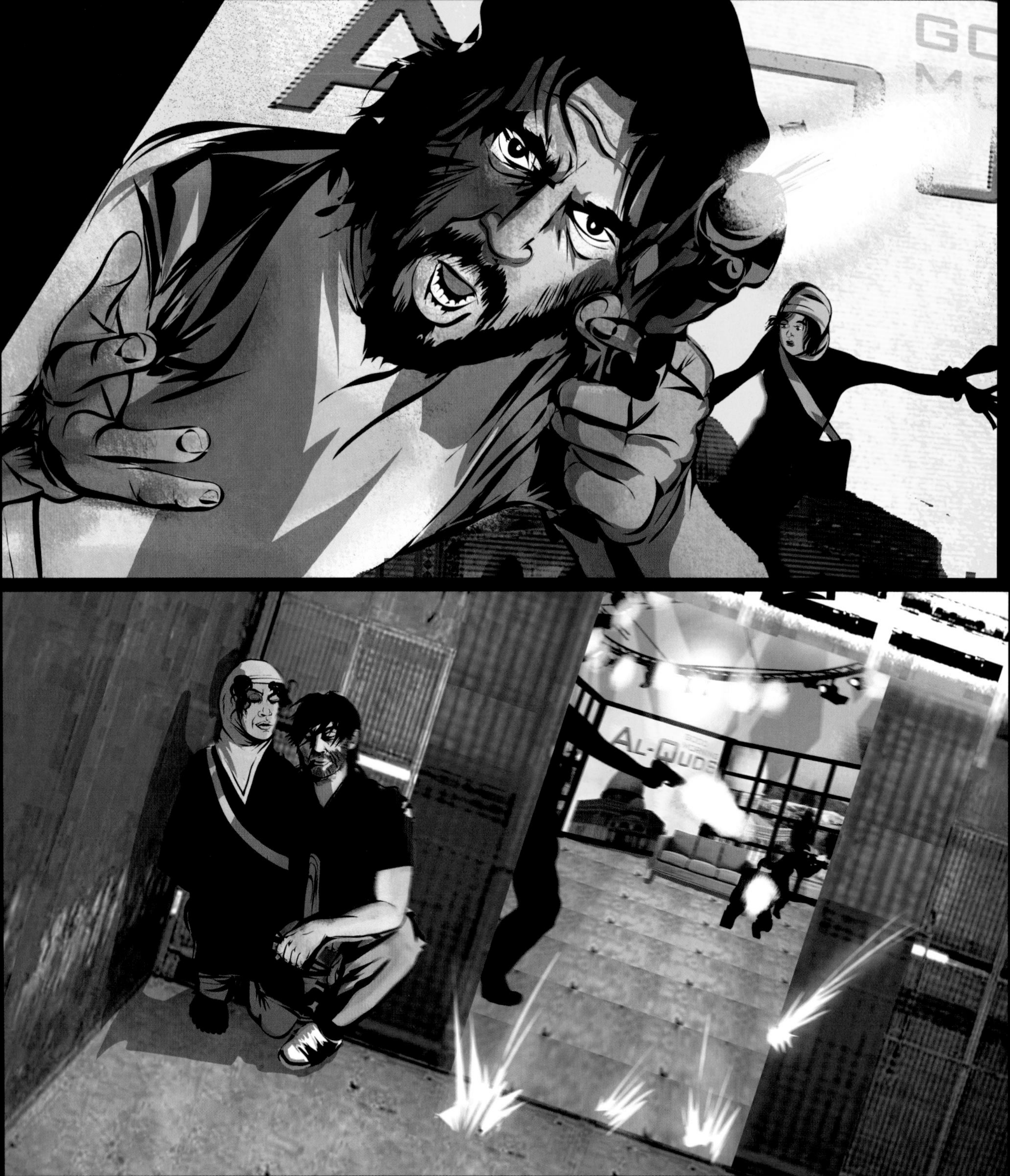

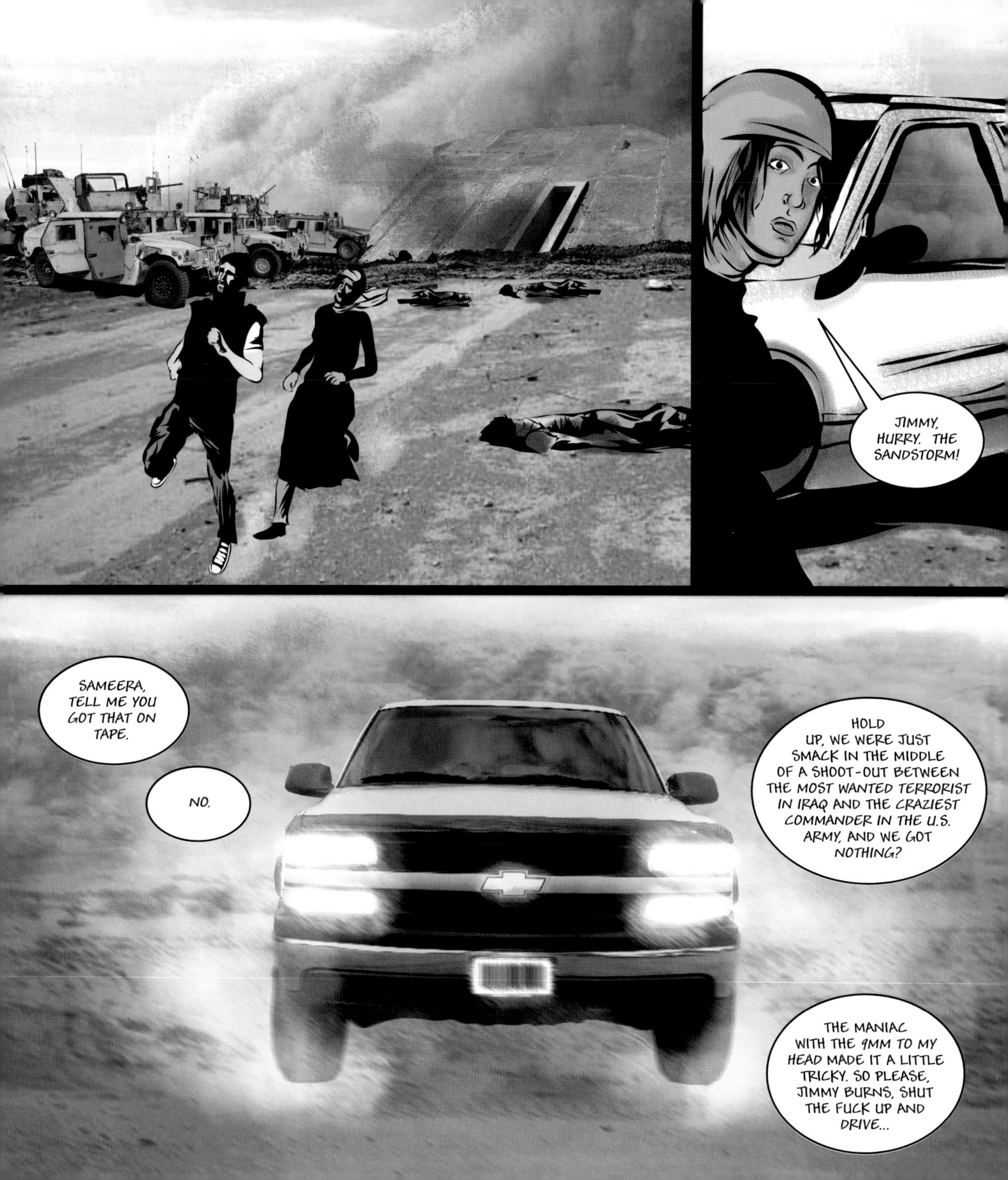
JIMMY, HURRY. THE SANDSTORM!
SAMEERA, TELL ME YOU GOT THAT ON TAPE.
NO.
HOLD UP, WE WERE JUST SMACK IN THE MIDDLE OF A SHOOT-OUT BETWEEN THE MOST WANTED TERRORIST IN IRAQ AND THE CRAZIEST COMMANDER IN THE U.S. ARMY, AND WE GOT NOTHING?
THE MANIAC WITH THE 9MM TO MY HEAD MADE IT A LITTLE TRICKY. SO PLEASE, JIMMY BURNS, SHUT THE FUCK UP AND DRIVE...

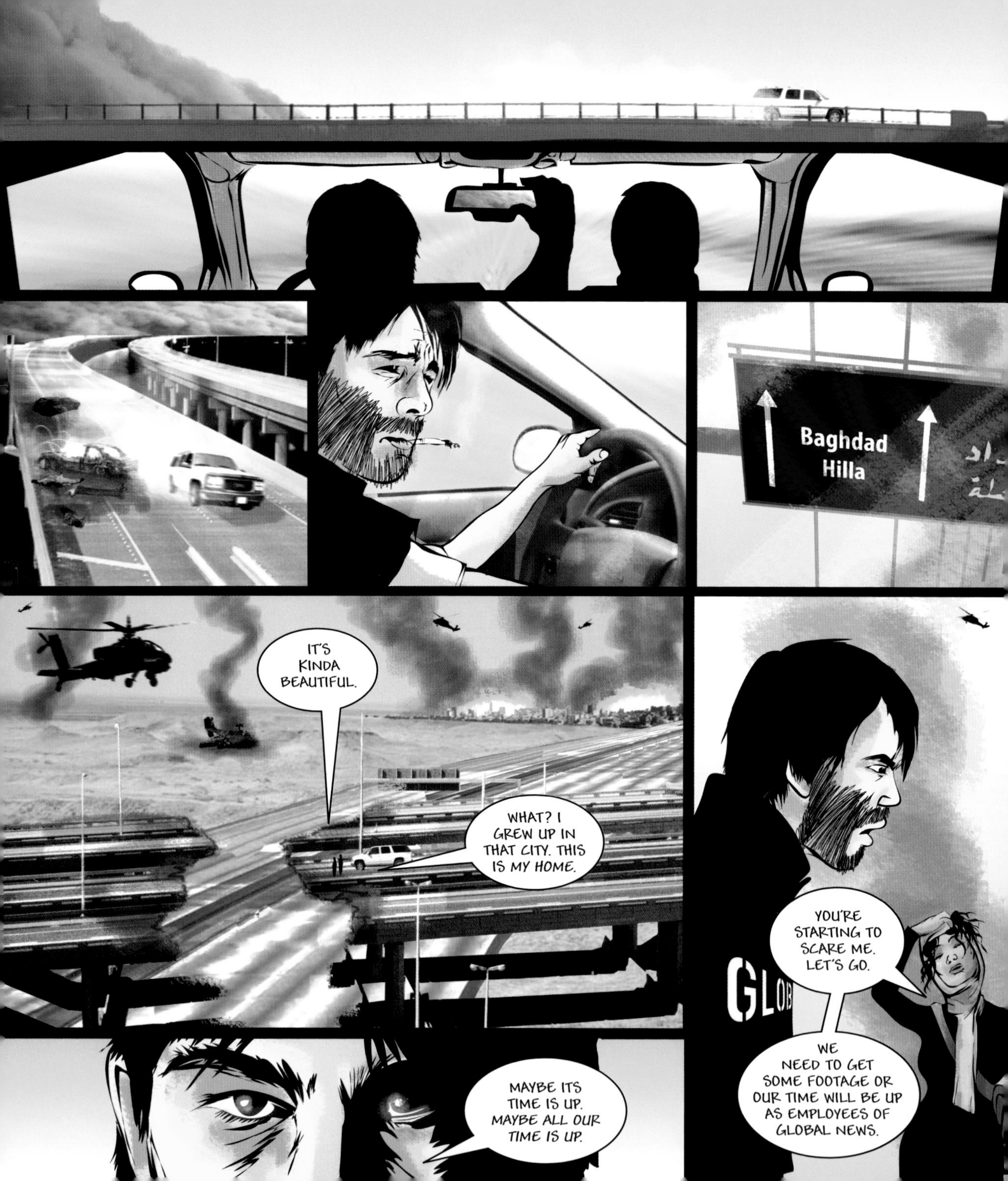
Baghdad
Hilla
IT'S KINDA BEAUTIFUL.
WHAT? I GREW UP IN THAT CITY. THIS IS MY HOME.
YOU'RE STARTING TO SCARE ME. LET'S GO.
MAYBE ITS TIME IS UP. MAYBE ALL OUR TIME IS UP.
WE NEED TO GET SOME FOOTAGE OR OUR TIME WILL BE UP AS EMPLOYEES OF GLOBAL NEWS.

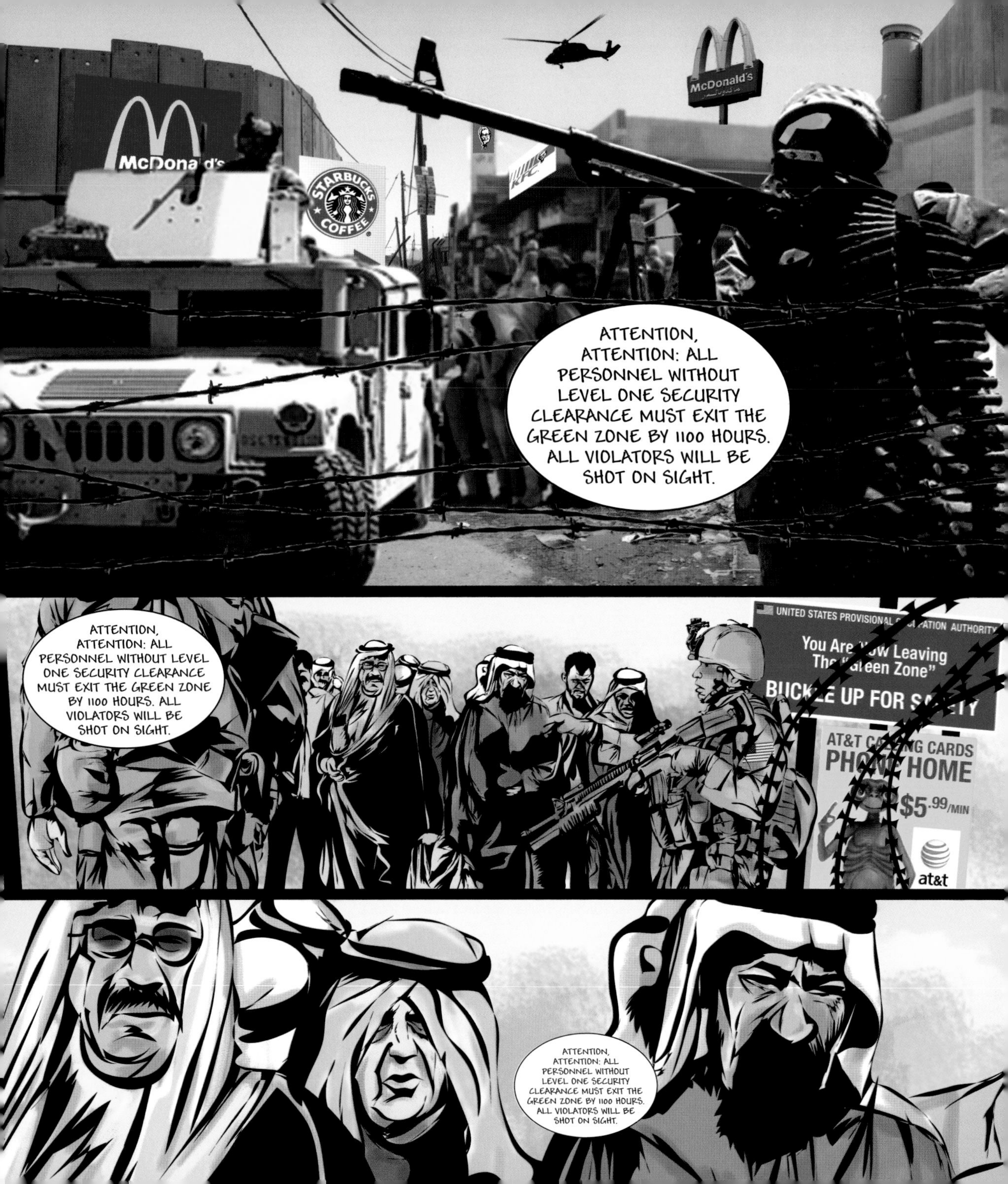
McDonald's
STARBUCKS COFFEE
KFC
McDonald's
ATTENTION, ATTENTION: ALL PERSONNEL WITHOUT LEVEL ONE SECURITY CLEARANCE MUST EXIT THE GREEN ZONE BY 1100 HOURS. ALL VIOLATORS WILL BE SHOT ON SIGHT.
ATTENTION, ATTENTION: ALL PERSONNEL WITHOUT LEVEL ONE SECURITY CLEARANCE MUST EXIT THE GREEN ZONE BY 1100 HOURS. ALL VIOLATORS WILL BE SHOT ON SIGHT.
UNITED STATES PROVISIONAL
AUTHORITY
$5.99/MIN
at&t
ATTENTION, ATTENTION: ALL PERSONNEL WITHOUT LEVEL ONE SECURITY CLEARANCE MUST EXIT THE GREEN ZONE BY 1100 HOURS. ALL VIOLATORS WILL BE SHOT ON SIGHT.

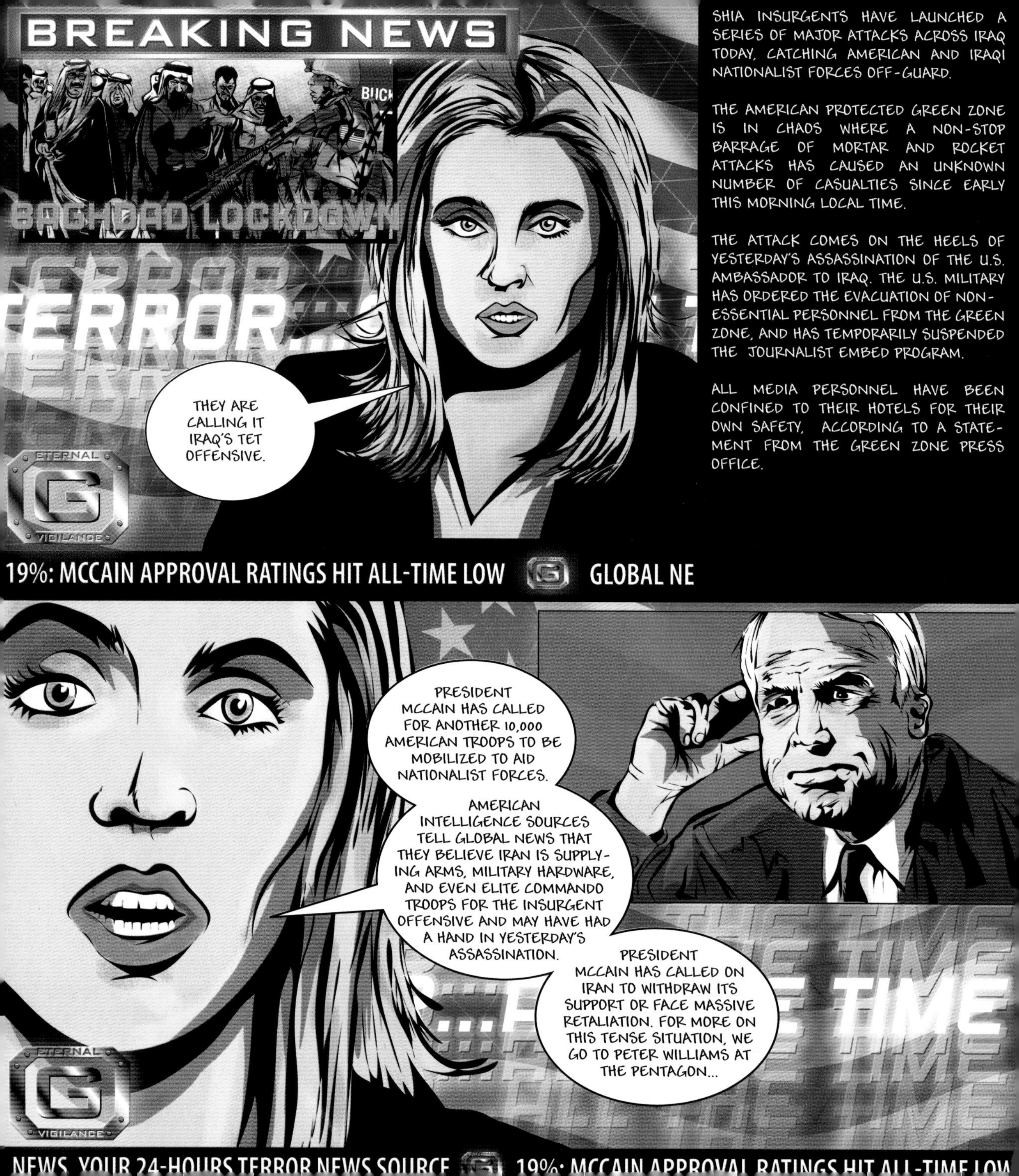
BREAKING NEWS
BAGHDAD LOCKDOWN
TERROR...
SHIA INSURGENTS HAVE LAUNCHED A SERIES OF MAJOR ATTACKS ACROSS IRAQ TODAY, CATCHING AMERICAN AND IRAQI NATIONALIST FORCES OFF-GUARD.
THE AMERICAN PROTECTED GREEN ZONE IS IN CHAOS WHERE A NON-STOP BARRAGE OF MORTAR AND ROCKET ATTACKS HAS CAUSED AN UNKNOWN NUMBER OF CASUALTIES SINCE EARLY THIS MORNING LOCAL TIME.
THE ATTACK COMES ON THE HEELS OF YESTERDAY'S ASSASSINATION OF THE U.S. AMBASSADOR TO IRAQ. THE U.S. MILITARY HAS ORDERED THE EVACUATION OF NON-ESSENTIAL PERSONNEL FROM THE GREEN ZONE, AND HAS TEMPORARILY SUSPENDED THE JOURNALIST EMBED PROGRAM.
ALL MEDIA PERSONNEL HAVE BEEN CONFINED TO THEIR HOTELS FOR THEIR OWN SAFETY, ACCORDING TO A STATEMENT FROM THE GREEN ZONE PRESS OFFICE.
THEY ARE CALLING IT IRAQ'S TET OFFENSIVE.
ETERNAL G VIGILANCE
19%: MCCAIN APPROVAL RATINGS HIT ALL-TIME LOW
GLOBAL NE
PRESIDENT MCCAIN HAS CALLED FOR ANOTHER 10,000 AMERICAN TROOPS TO BE MOBILIZED TO AID NATIONALIST FORCES.
AMERICAN INTELLIGENCE SOURCES TELL GLOBAL NEWS THAT THEY BELIEVE IRAN IS SUPPLYING ARMS, MILITARY HARDWARE, AND EVEN ELITE COMMANDO TROOPS FOR THE INSURGENT OFFENSIVE AND MAY HAVE HAD A HAND IN YESTERDAY'S ASSASSINATION.
PRESIDENT MCCAIN HAS CALLED ON IRAN TO WITHDRAW ITS SUPPORT OR FACE MASSIVE RETALIATION. FOR MORE ON THIS TENSE SITUATION, WE GO TO PETER WILLIAMS AT THE PENTAGON...
ETERNAL G VIGILANCE
NEWS, YOUR 24-HOURS TERROR NEWS SOURCE
19%: MCCAIN APPROVAL RATINGS HIT ALL-TIME LOW

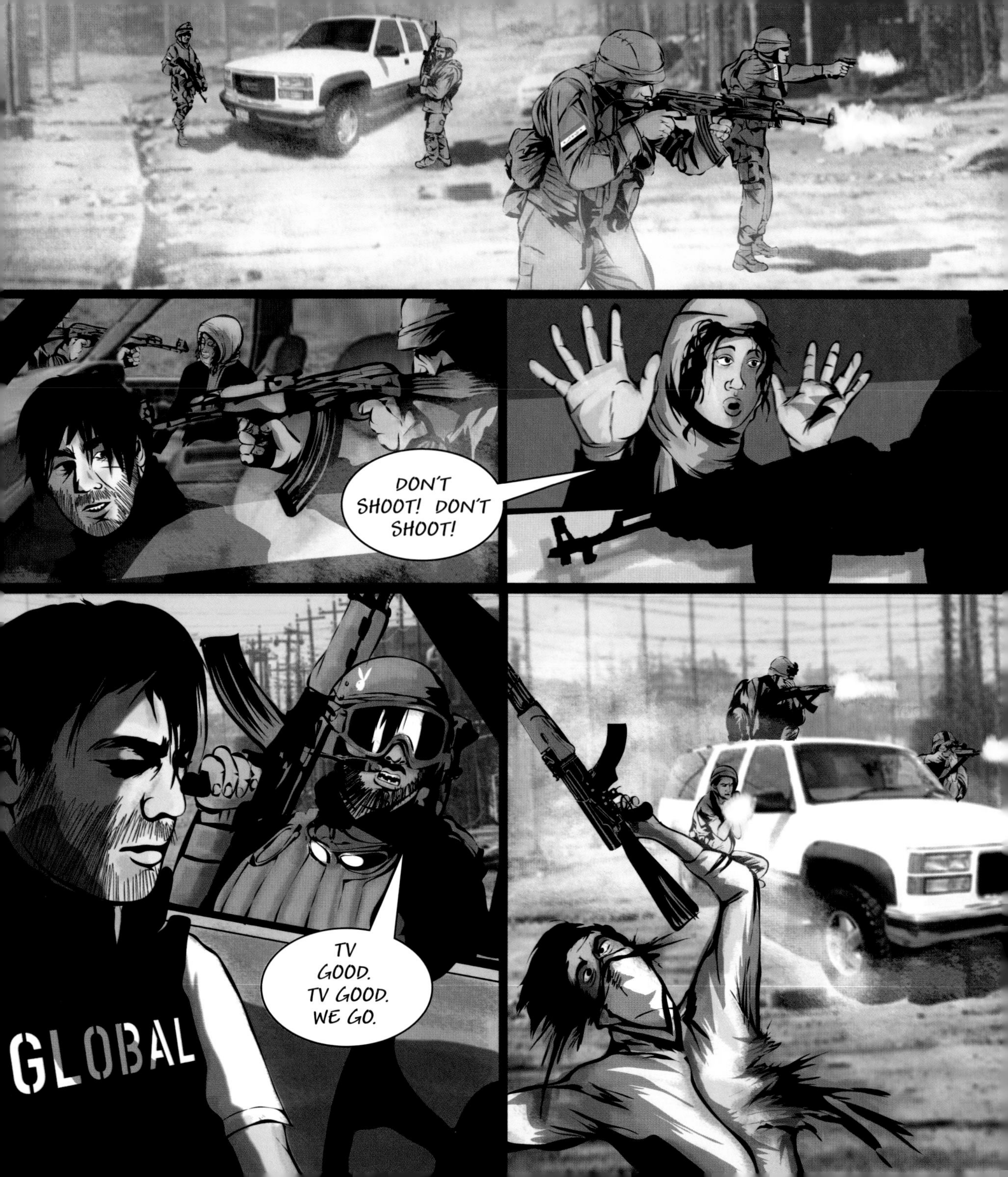
DON'T SHOOT! DON'T SHOOT!
TV GOOD. TV GOOD. WE GO.
GLOBAL

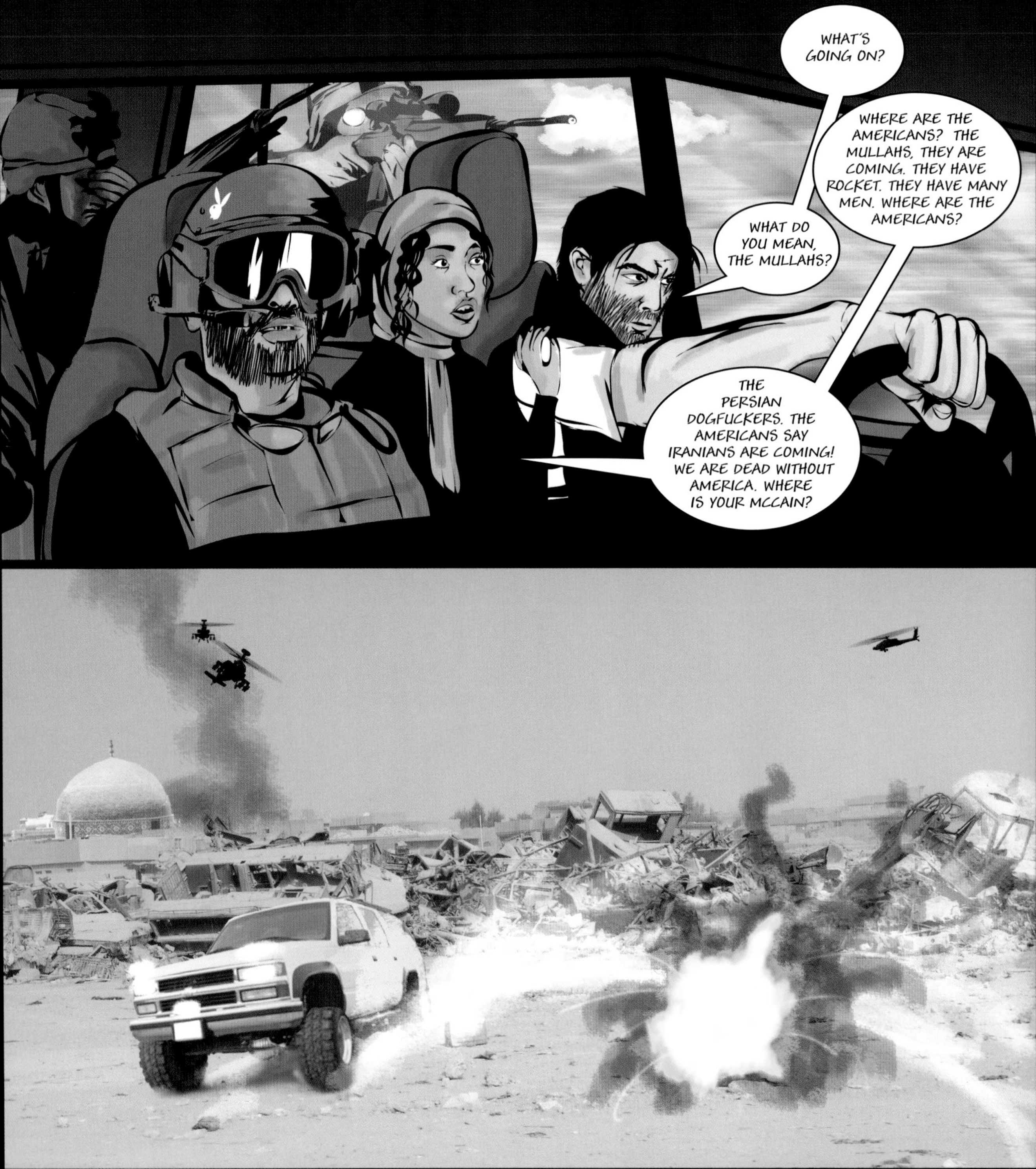
WHAT'S GOING ON?
WHERE ARE THE AMERICANS? THE MULLAHS, THEY ARE COMING. THEY HAVE ROCKET. THEY HAVE MANY MEN. WHERE ARE THE AMERICANS?
WHAT DO YOU MEAN, THE MULLAHS?
THE PERSIAN DOGFUCKERS. THE AMERICANS SAY IRANIANS ARE COMING! WE ARE DEAD WITHOUT AMERICA. WHERE IS YOUR MCCAIN?

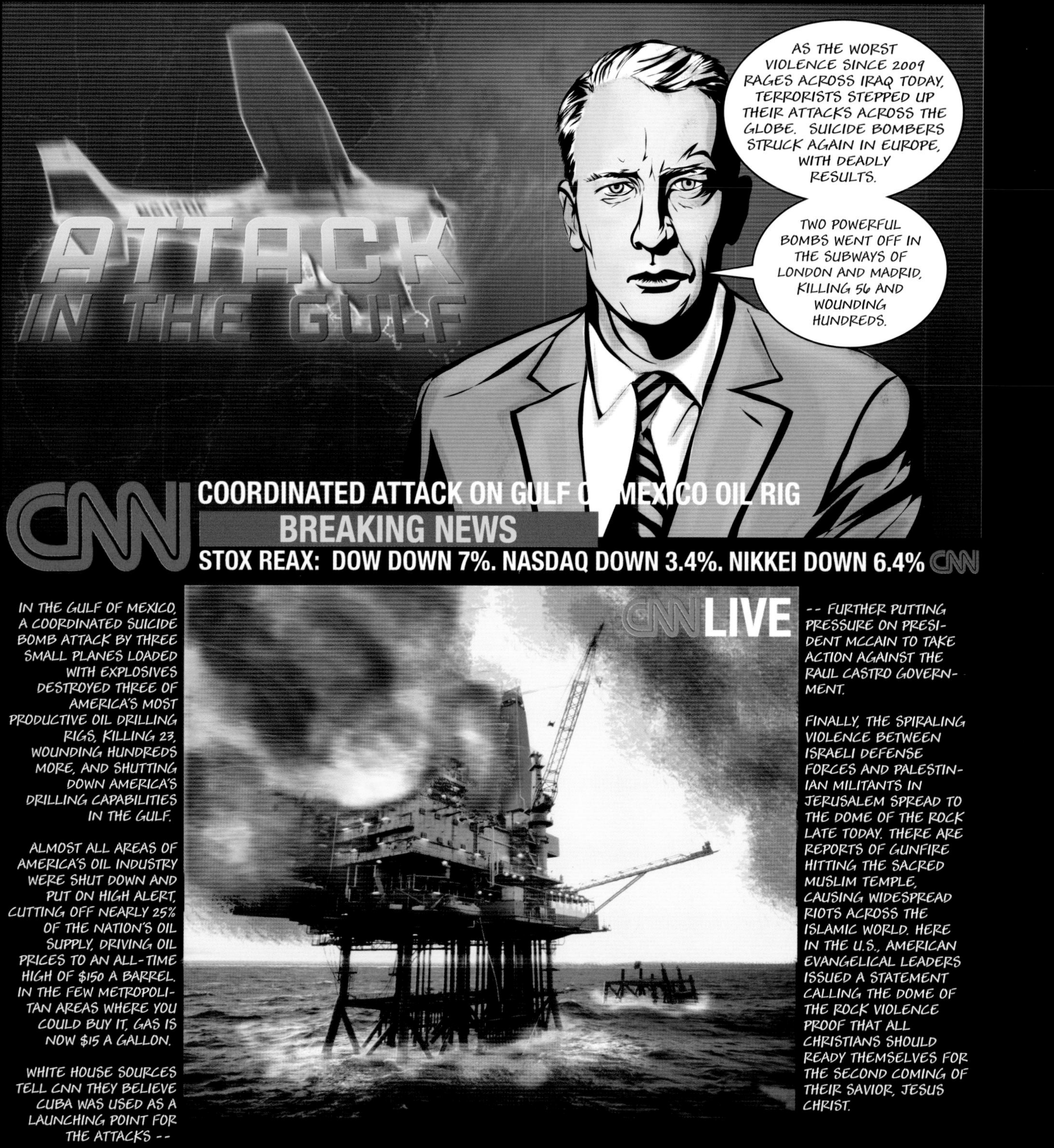
ATTACK IN THE GULF
AS THE WORST VIOLENCE SINCE 2009 RAGES ACROSS IRAQ TODAY, TERRORISTS STEPPED UP THEIR ATTACKS ACROSS THE GLOBE. SUICIDE BOMBERS STRUCK AGAIN IN EUROPE, WITH DEADLY RESULTS.
TWO POWERFUL BOMBS WENT OFF IN THE SUBWAYS OF LONDON AND MADRID, KILLING 56 AND WOUNDING HUNDREDS.
CNN
COORDINATED ATTACK ON GULF O MEXICO OIL RIG
BREAKING NEWS
STOX REAX: DOW DOWN 7%. NASDAQ DOWN 3.4%. NIKKEI DOWN 6.4%
CNN
IN THE GULF OF MEXICO, A COORDINATED SUICIDE BOMB ATTACK BY THREE SMALL PLANES LOADED WITH EXPLOSIVES DESTROYED THREE OF AMERICA'S MOST PRODUCTIVE OIL DRILLING RIGS, KILLING 23, WOUNDING HUNDREDS MORE, AND SHUTTING DOWN AMERICA'S DRILLING CAPABILITIES IN THE GULF.
ALMOST ALL AREAS OF AMERICA'S OIL INDUSTRY WERE SHUT DOWN AND PUT ON HIGH ALERT, CUTTING OFF NEARLY 25% OF THE NATION'S OIL SUPPLY, DRIVING OIL PRICES TO AN ALL-TIME HIGH OF $150 A BARREL. IN THE FEW METROPOLITAN AREAS WHERE YOU COULD BUY IT, GAS IS NOW $15 A GALLON.
WHITE HOUSE SOURCES TELL CNN THEY BELIEVE CUBA WAS USED AS A LAUNCHING POINT FOR THE ATTACKS --
CNN LIVE
-- FURTHER PUTTING PRESSURE ON PRESIDENT MCCAIN TO TAKE ACTION AGAINST THE RAUL CASTRO GOVERNMENT.
FINALLY, THE SPIRALING VIOLENCE BETWEEN ISRAELI DEFENSE FORCES AND PALESTINIAN MILITANTS IN JERUSALEM SPREAD TO THE DOME OF THE ROCK LATE TODAY. THERE ARE REPORTS OF GUNFIRE HITTING THE SACRED MUSLIM TEMPLE, CAUSING WIDESPREAD RIOTS ACROSS THE ISLAMIC WORLD. HERE IN THE U.S., AMERICAN EVANGELICAL LEADERS ISSUED A STATEMENT CALLING THE DOME OF THE ROCK VIOLENCE PROOF THAT ALL CHRISTIANS SHOULD READY THEMSELVES FOR THE SECOND COMING OF THEIR SAVIOR, JESUS CHRIST.

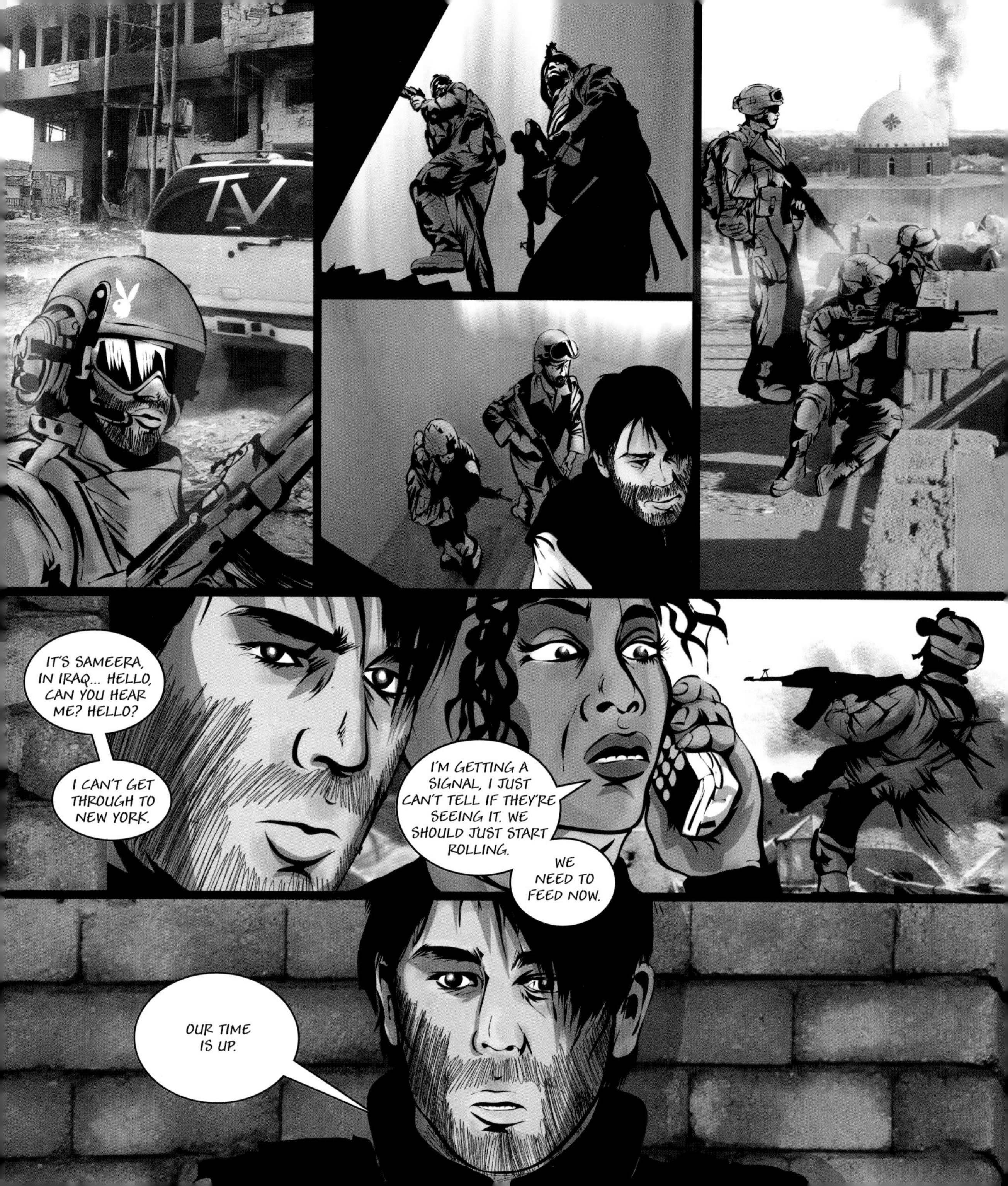
TV
IT'S SAMEERA, IN IRAQ... HELLO, CAN YOU HEAR ME? HELLO?
I CAN'T GET THROUGH TO NEW YORK.
I'M GETTING A SIGNAL, I JUST CAN'T TELL IF THEY'RE SEEING IT. WE SHOULD JUST START ROLLING.
WE NEED TO FEED NOW.
OUR TIME IS UP.

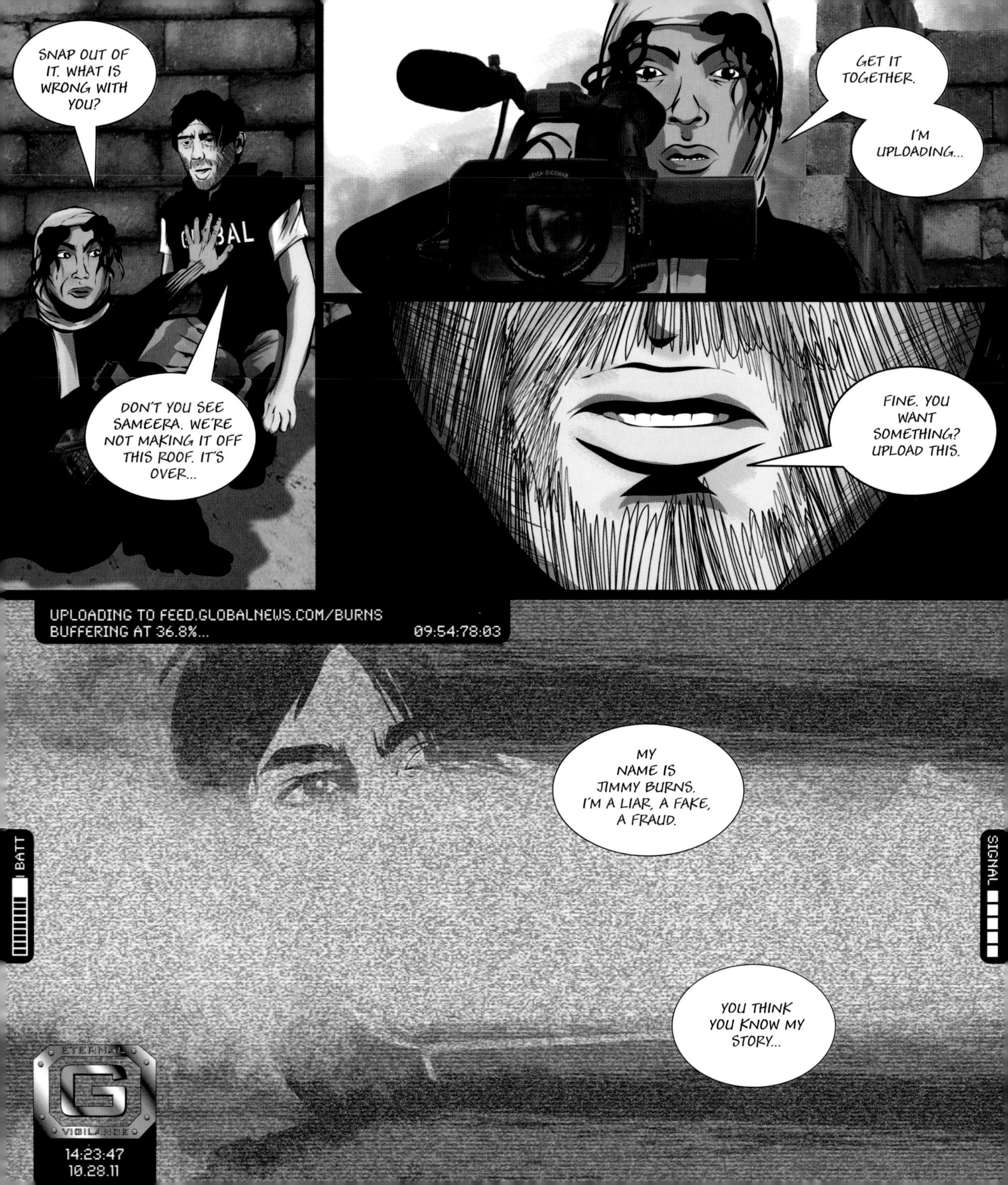

SNAP OUT OF IT. WHAT IS WRONG WITH YOU?
DON'T YOU SEE SAMEERA. WE'RE NOT MAKING IT OFF THIS ROOF. IT'S OVER...
GET IT TOGETHER.
I'M UPLOADING...
FINE. YOU WANT SOMETHING? UPLOAD THIS.
UPLOADING TO FEED.GLOBALNEWS.COM/BURNS
BUFFERING AT 36.8%...
09:54:78:03
MY NAME IS JIMMY BURNS. I'M A LIAR, A FAKE, A FRAUD.
YOU THINK YOU KNOW MY STORY...
BATT
SIGNAL
ETERNAL
VIGILANCE
14:23:47
10.28.11

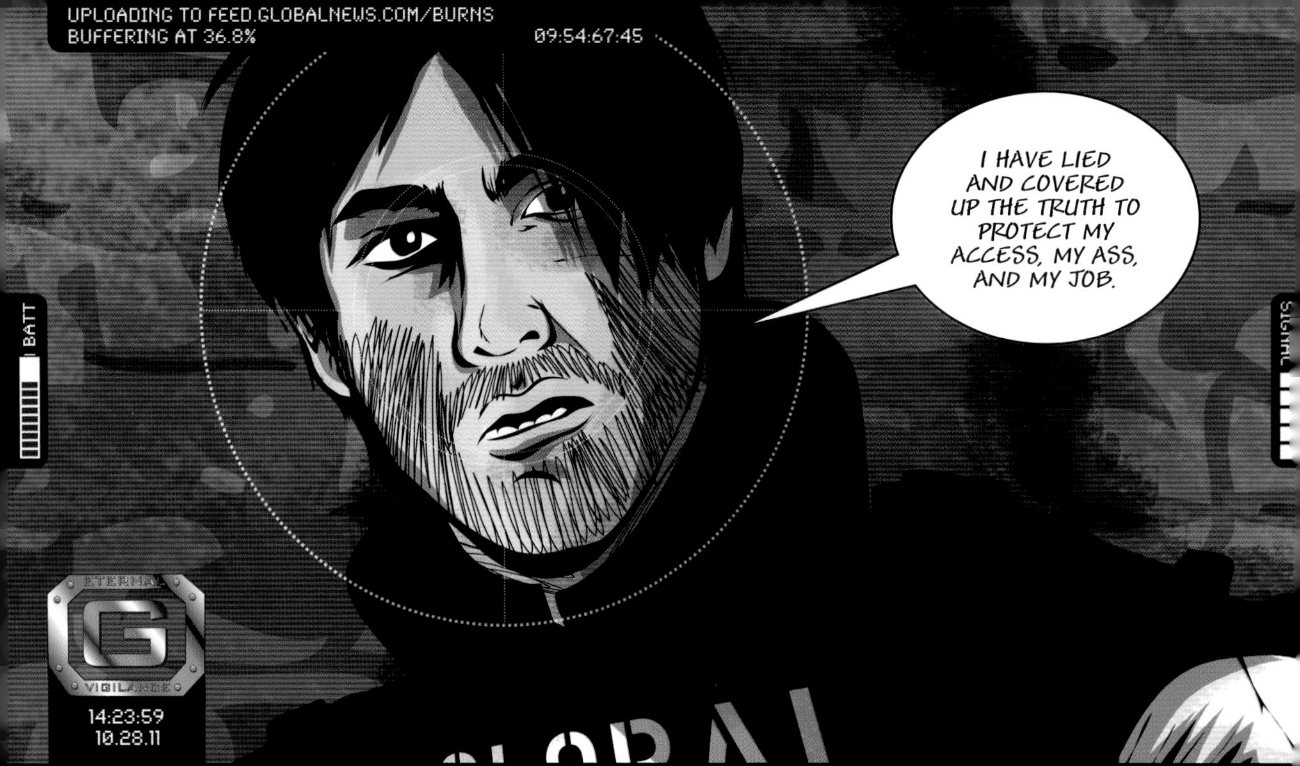
UPLOADING TO FEED.GLOBALNEWS.COM/BURNS
BUFFERING AT 36.8%
09:54:67:45
I HAVE LIED AND COVERED UP THE TRUTH TO PROTECT MY ACCESS, MY ASS, AND MY JOB.
BATT
SIGNAL
ETERNAL VIGILANCE
14:23:59
10.28.11

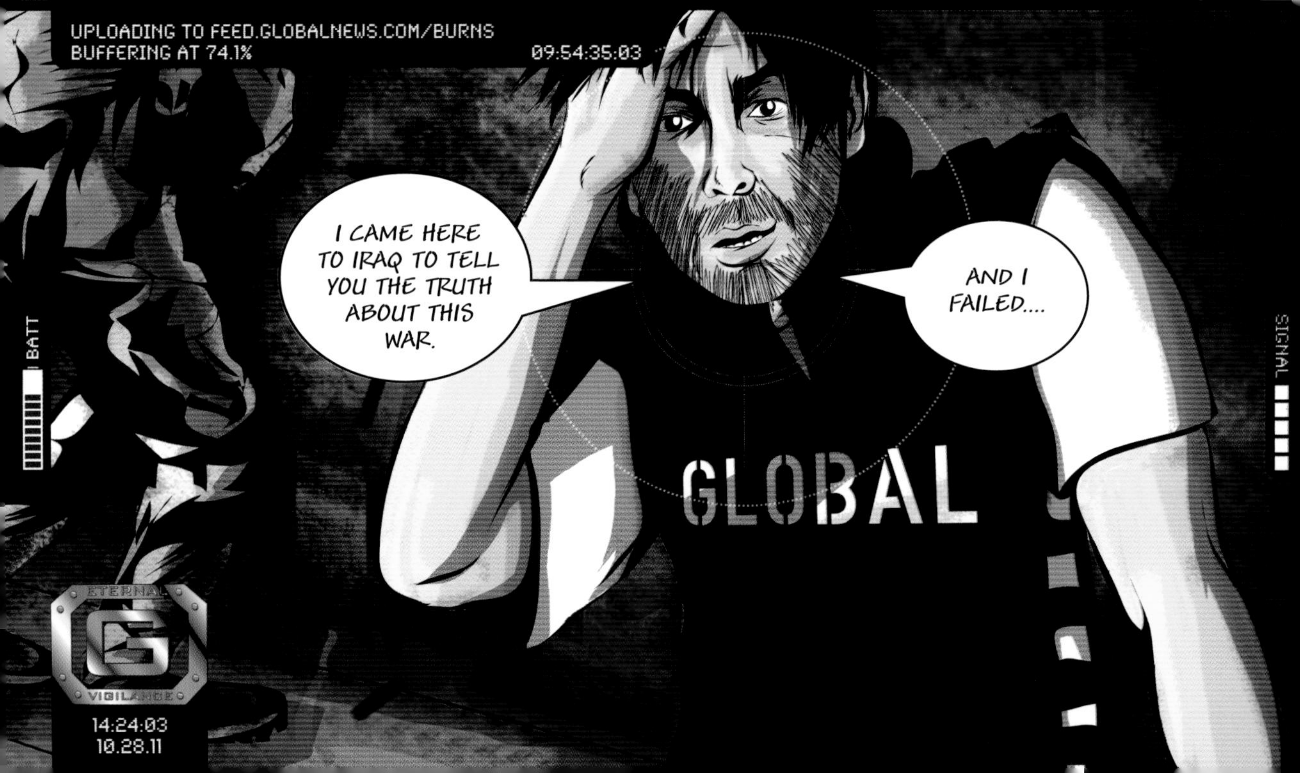
UPLOADING TO FEED.GLOBALNEWS.COM/BURNS
BUFFERING AT 74.1%
09:54:35:03
I CAME HERE TO IRAQ TO TELL YOU THE TRUTH ABOUT THIS WAR.
AND I FAILED....
BATT
SIGNAL
GLOBAL
ETERNAL VIGILANCE
14:24:03
10.28.11

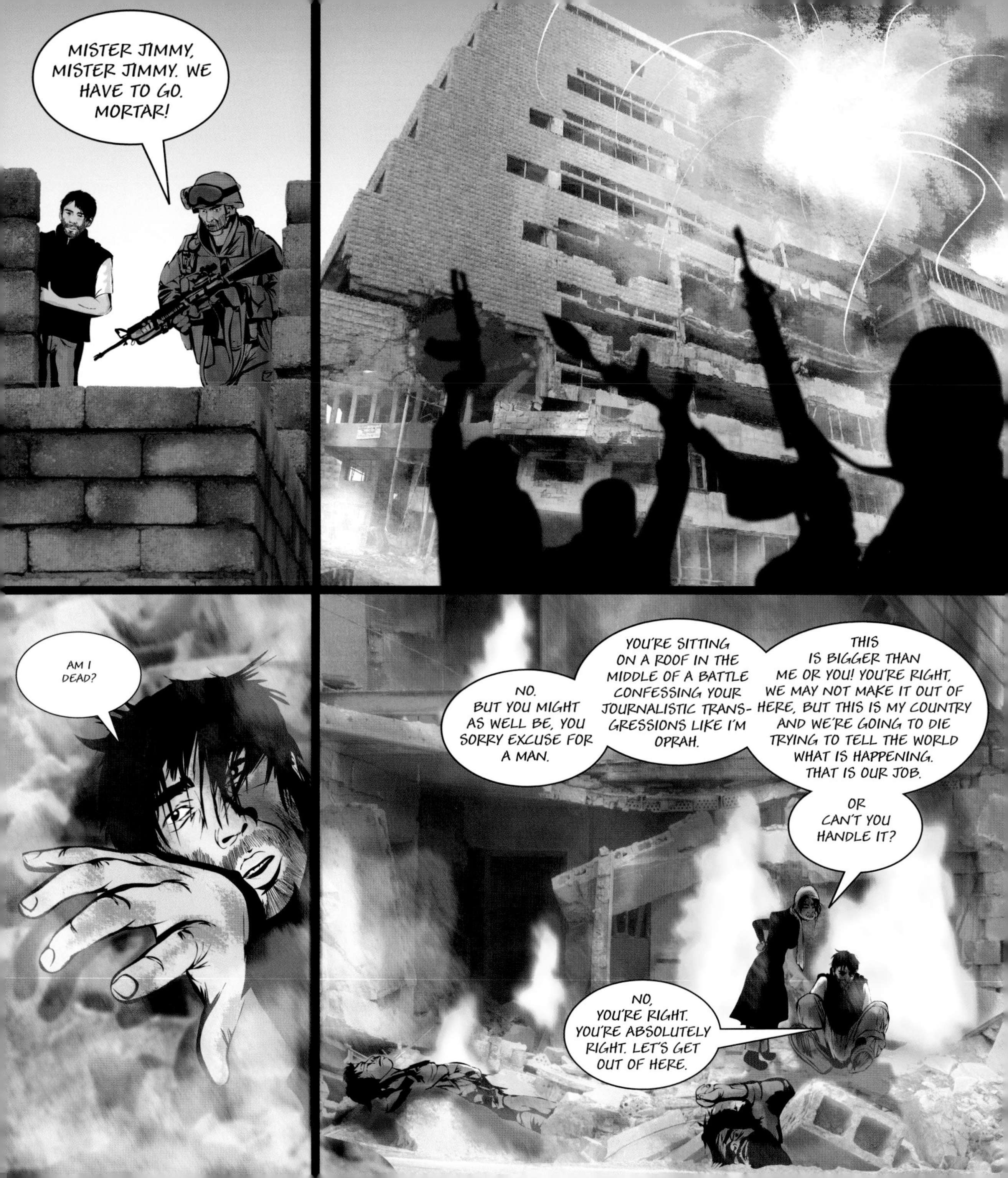

MISTER JIMMY, MISTER JIMMY. WE HAVE TO GO. MORTAR!
AM I DEAD?
NO. BUT YOU MIGHT AS WELL BE, YOU SORRY EXCUSE FOR A MAN.
YOU'RE SITTING ON A ROOF IN THE MIDDLE OF A BATTLE CONFESSING YOUR JOURNALISTIC TRANS-GRESSIONS LIKE I'M OPRAH.
THIS IS BIGGER THAN ME OR YOU! YOU'RE RIGHT, WE MAY NOT MAKE IT OUT OF HERE, BUT THIS IS MY COUNTRY AND WE'RE GOING TO DIE TRYING TO TELL THE WORLD WHAT IS HAPPENING. THAT IS OUR JOB.
OR CAN'T YOU HANDLE IT?
NO, YOU'RE RIGHT. YOU'RE ABSOLUTELY RIGHT. LET'S GET OUT OF HERE.

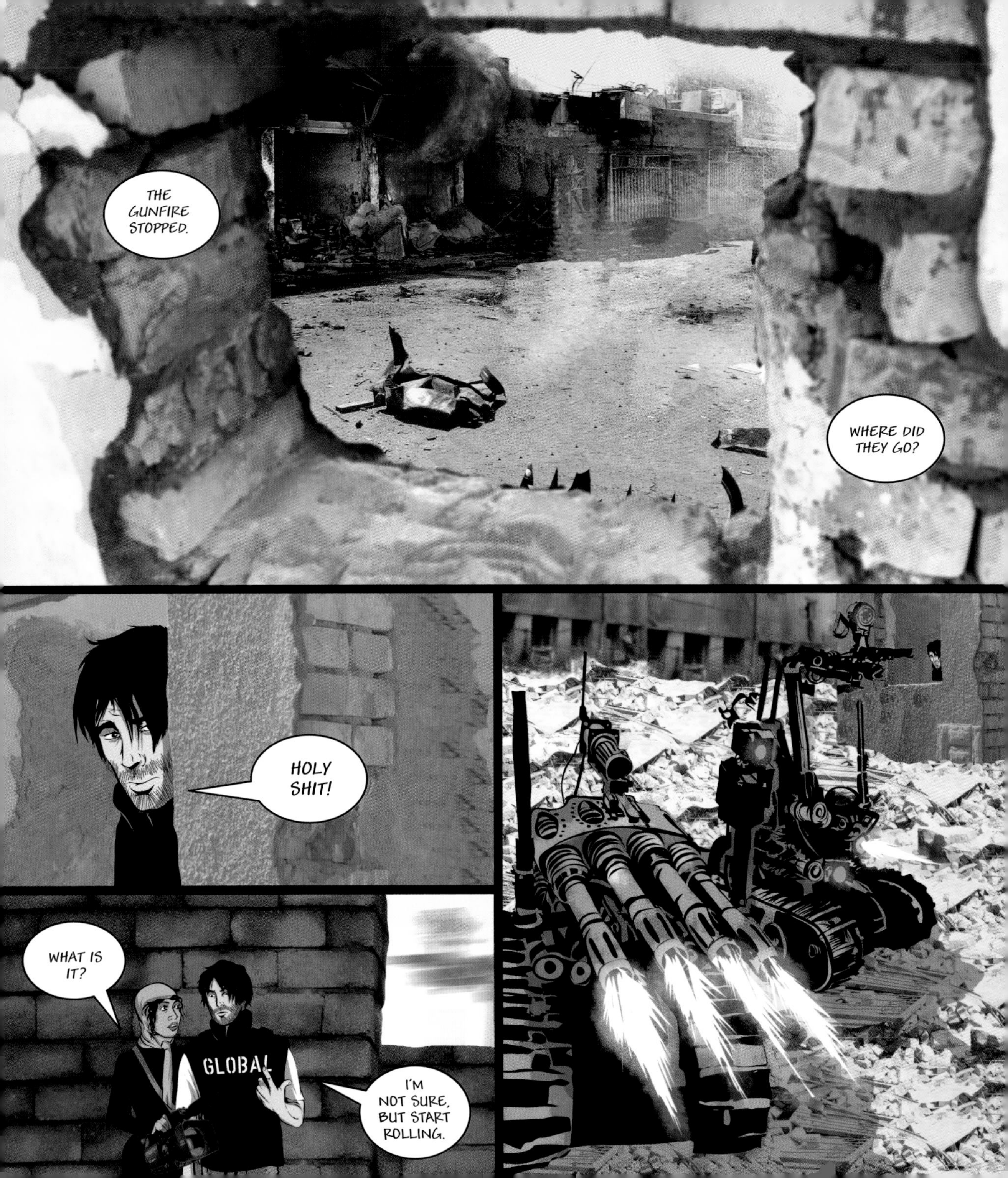
THE GUNFIRE STOPPED.
WHERE DID THEY GO?
HOLY SHIT!
WHAT IS IT?
GLOBAL
I'M NOT SURE, BUT START ROLLING.

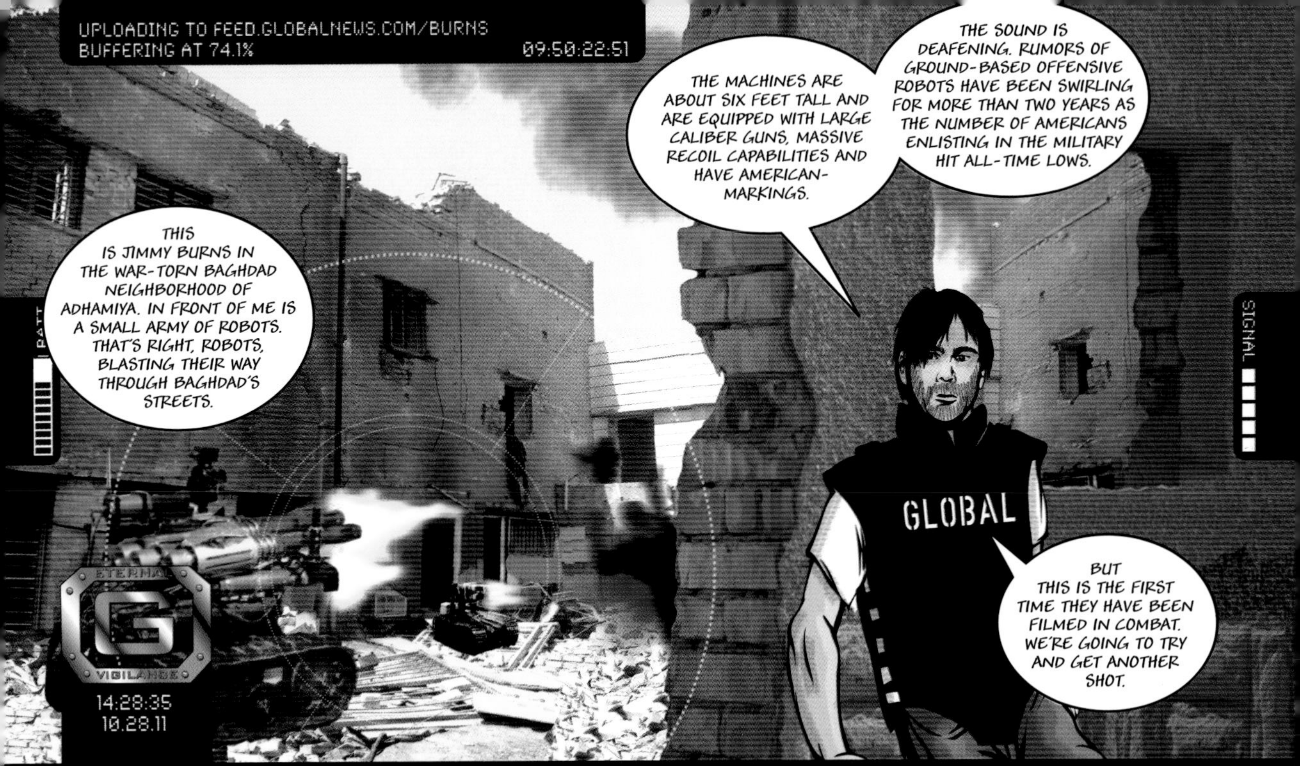
UPLOADING TO FEED.GLOBALNEWS.COM/BURNS
BUFFERING AT 74.1%
09:50:22:51
THIS IS JIMMY BURNS IN THE WAR-TORN BAGHDAD NEIGHBORHOOD OF ADHAMIYA. IN FRONT OF ME IS A SMALL ARMY OF ROBOTS. THAT'S RIGHT, ROBOTS, BLASTING THEIR WAY THROUGH BAGHDAD'S STREETS.
THE MACHINES ARE ABOUT SIX FEET TALL AND ARE EQUIPPED WITH LARGE CALIBER GUNS, MASSIVE RECOIL CAPABILITIES AND HAVE AMERICAN-MARKINGS.
THE SOUND IS DEAFENING. RUMORS OF GROUND-BASED OFFENSIVE ROBOTS HAVE BEEN SWIRLING FOR MORE THAN TWO YEARS AS THE NUMBER OF AMERICANS ENLISTING IN THE MILITARY HIT ALL-TIME LOWS.
BATT
SIGNAL
ETERNAL
VIGILANCE
14:28:35
10.28.11
GLOBAL
BUT THIS IS THE FIRST TIME THEY HAVE BEEN FILMED IN COMBAT. WE'RE GOING TO TRY AND GET ANOTHER SHOT.

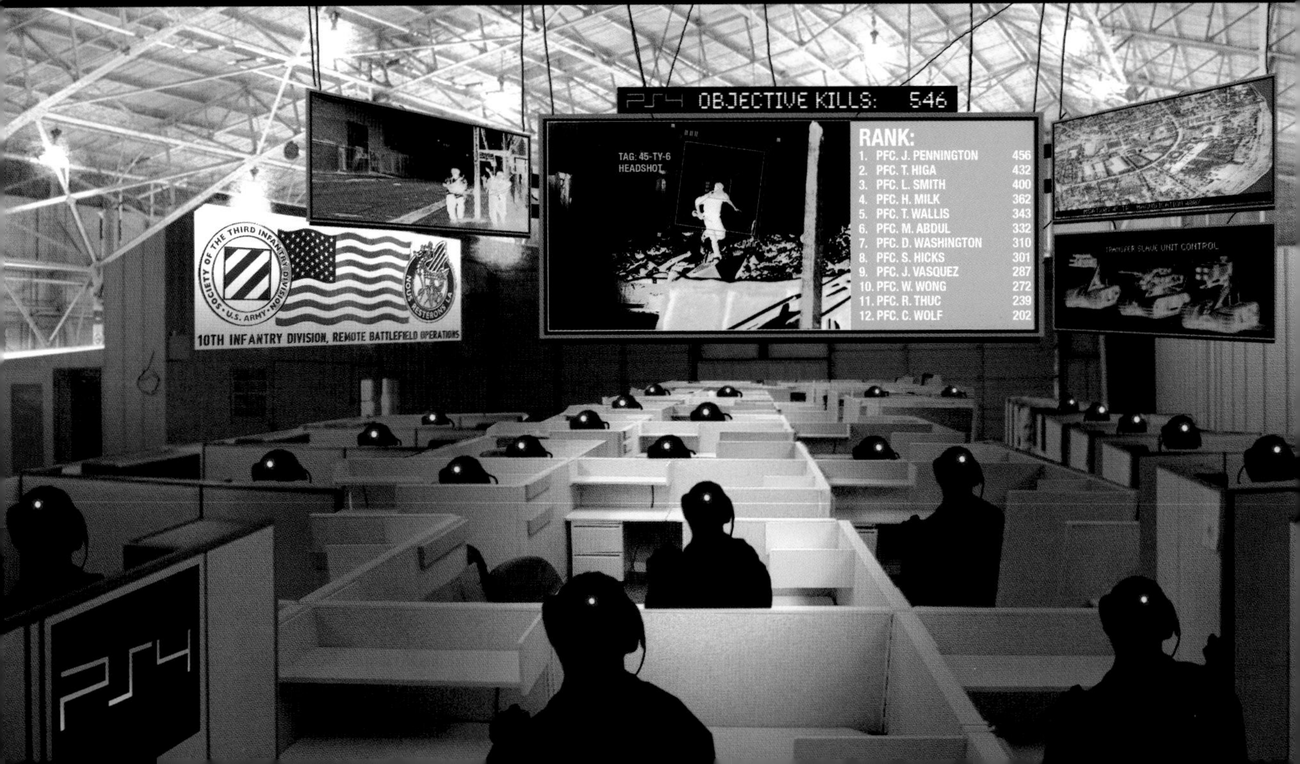
PS4 OBJECTIVE KILLS: 546
TAG: 45-TY-6
HEADSHOT
RANK:
1. PFC. J. PENNINGTON 456
2. PFC. T. HIGA 432
3. PFC. L. SMITH 400
4. PFC. H. MILK 362
5. PFC. T. WALLIS 343
6. PFC. M. ABDUL 332
7. PFC. D. WASHINGTON 310
8. PFC. S. HICKS 301
9. PFC. J. VASQUEZ 287
10. PFC. W. WONG 272
11. PFC. R. THUC 239
12. PFC. C. WOLF 202
SOCIETY OF THE THIRD INFANTRY DIVISION • U.S. ARMY •
10TH INFANTRY DIVISION, REMOTE BATTLEFIELD OPERATIONS
PS4

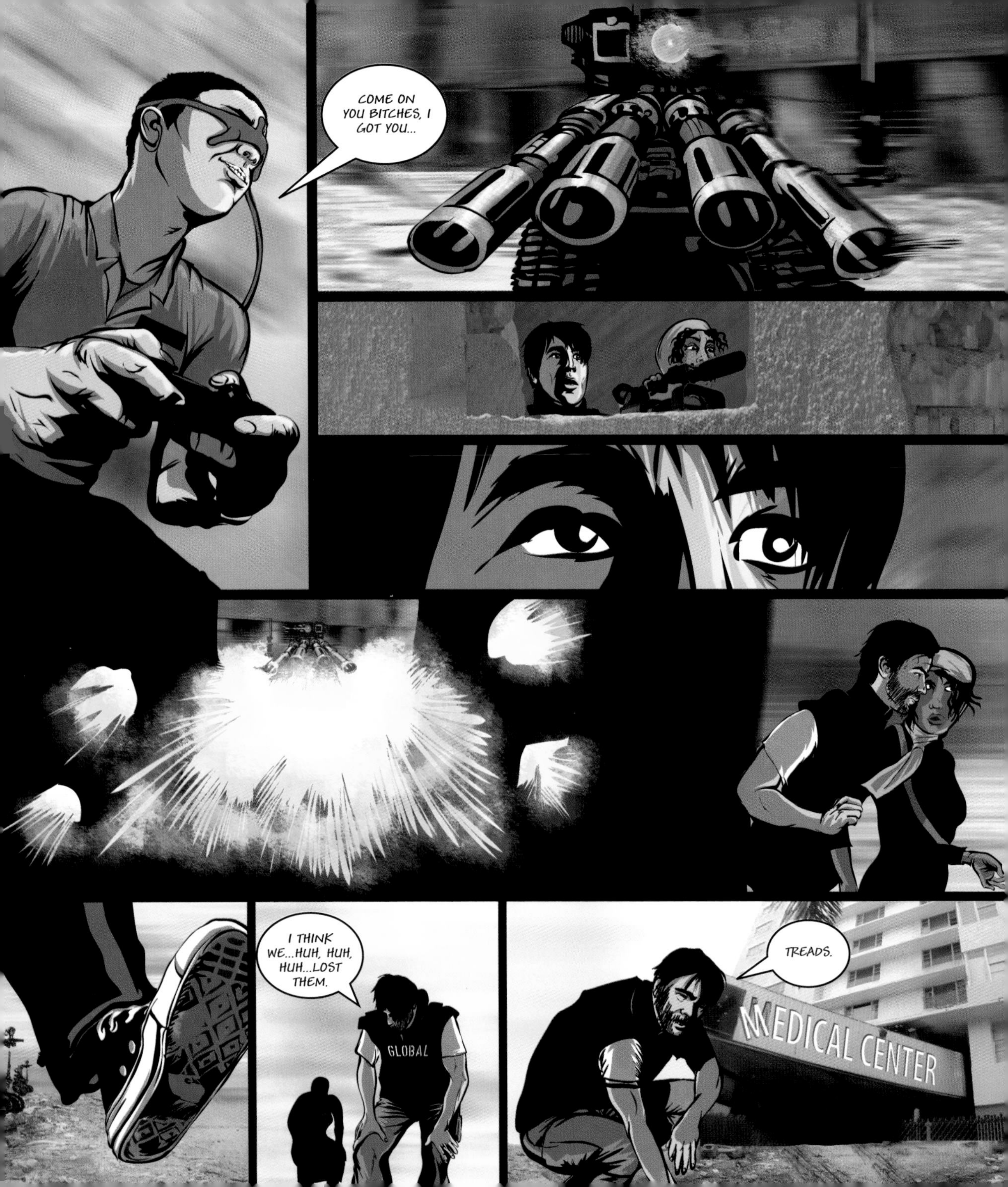
COME ON YOU BITCHES, I GOT YOU...
I THINK WE...HUH, HUH, HUH...LOST THEM.
GLOBAL
TREADS.
MEDICAL CENTER

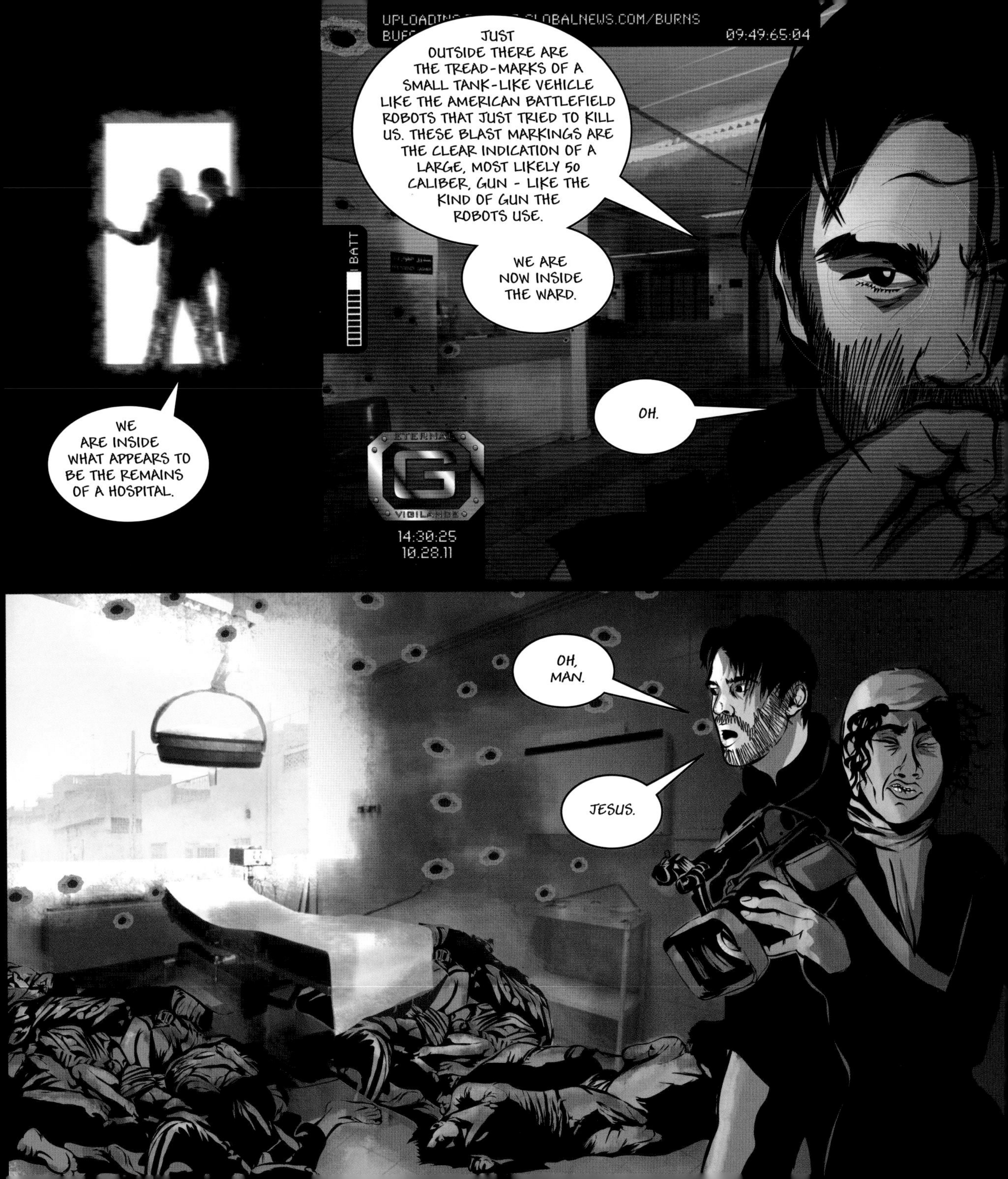
WE ARE INSIDE WHAT APPEARS TO BE THE REMAINS OF A HOSPITAL.
GLOBALNEWS.COM/BURNS
09:49:65:04
JUST OUTSIDE THERE ARE THE TREAD-MARKS OF A SMALL TANK-LIKE VEHICLE LIKE THE AMERICAN BATTLEFIELD ROBOTS THAT JUST TRIED TO KILL US. THESE BLAST MARKINGS ARE THE CLEAR INDICATION OF A LARGE, MOST LIKELY 50 CALIBER, GUN - LIKE THE KIND OF GUN THE ROBOTS USE.
WE ARE NOW INSIDE THE WARD.
BATT
OH.
14:30:25
10.28.11
OH, MAN.
JESUS.

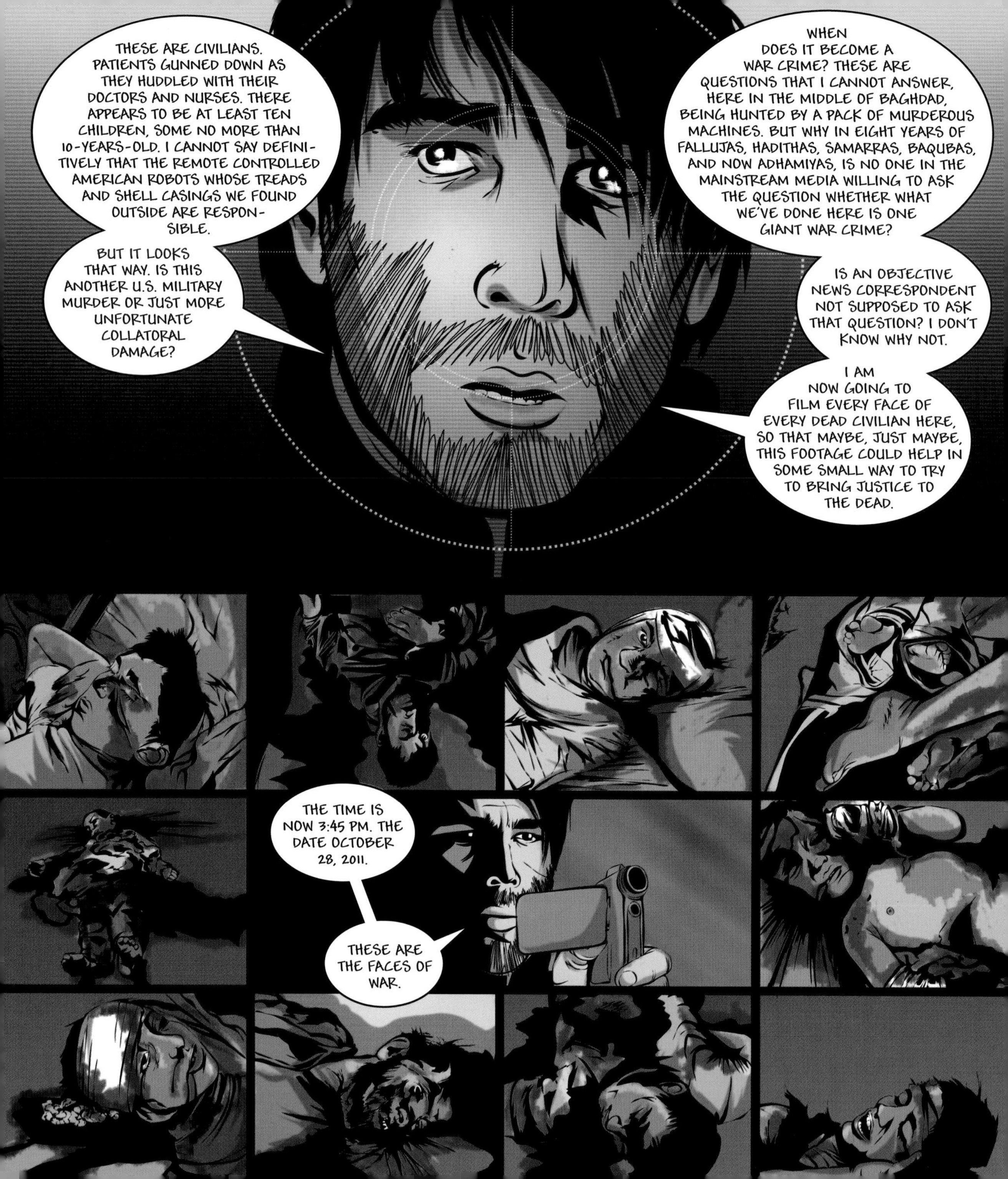
THESE ARE CIVILIANS. PATIENTS GUNNED DOWN AS THEY HUDDLED WITH THEIR DOCTORS AND NURSES. THERE APPEARS TO BE AT LEAST TEN CHILDREN, SOME NO MORE THAN 10-YEARS-OLD. I CANNOT SAY DEFINITIVELY THAT THE REMOTE CONTROLLED AMERICAN ROBOTS WHOSE TREADS AND SHELL CASINGS WE FOUND OUTSIDE ARE RESPONSIBLE.
BUT IT LOOKS THAT WAY. IS THIS ANOTHER U.S. MILITARY MURDER OR JUST MORE UNFORTUNATE COLLATORAL DAMAGE?
WHEN DOES IT BECOME A WAR CRIME? THESE ARE QUESTIONS THAT I CANNOT ANSWER, HERE IN THE MIDDLE OF BAGHDAD, BEING HUNTED BY A PACK OF MURDEROUS MACHINES. BUT WHY IN EIGHT YEARS OF FALLUJAS, HADITHAS, SAMARRAS, BAQUBAS, AND NOW ADHAMIYAS, IS NO ONE IN THE MAINSTREAM MEDIA WILLING TO ASK THE QUESTION WHETHER WHAT WE'VE DONE HERE IS ONE GIANT WAR CRIME?
IS AN OBJECTIVE NEWS CORRESPONDENT NOT SUPPOSED TO ASK THAT QUESTION? I DON'T KNOW WHY NOT.
I AM NOW GOING TO FILM EVERY FACE OF EVERY DEAD CIVILIAN HERE, SO THAT MAYBE, JUST MAYBE, THIS FOOTAGE COULD HELP IN SOME SMALL WAY TO TRY TO BRING JUSTICE TO THE DEAD.
THE TIME IS NOW 3:45 PM. THE DATE OCTOBER 28, 2011.
THESE ARE THE FACES OF WAR.

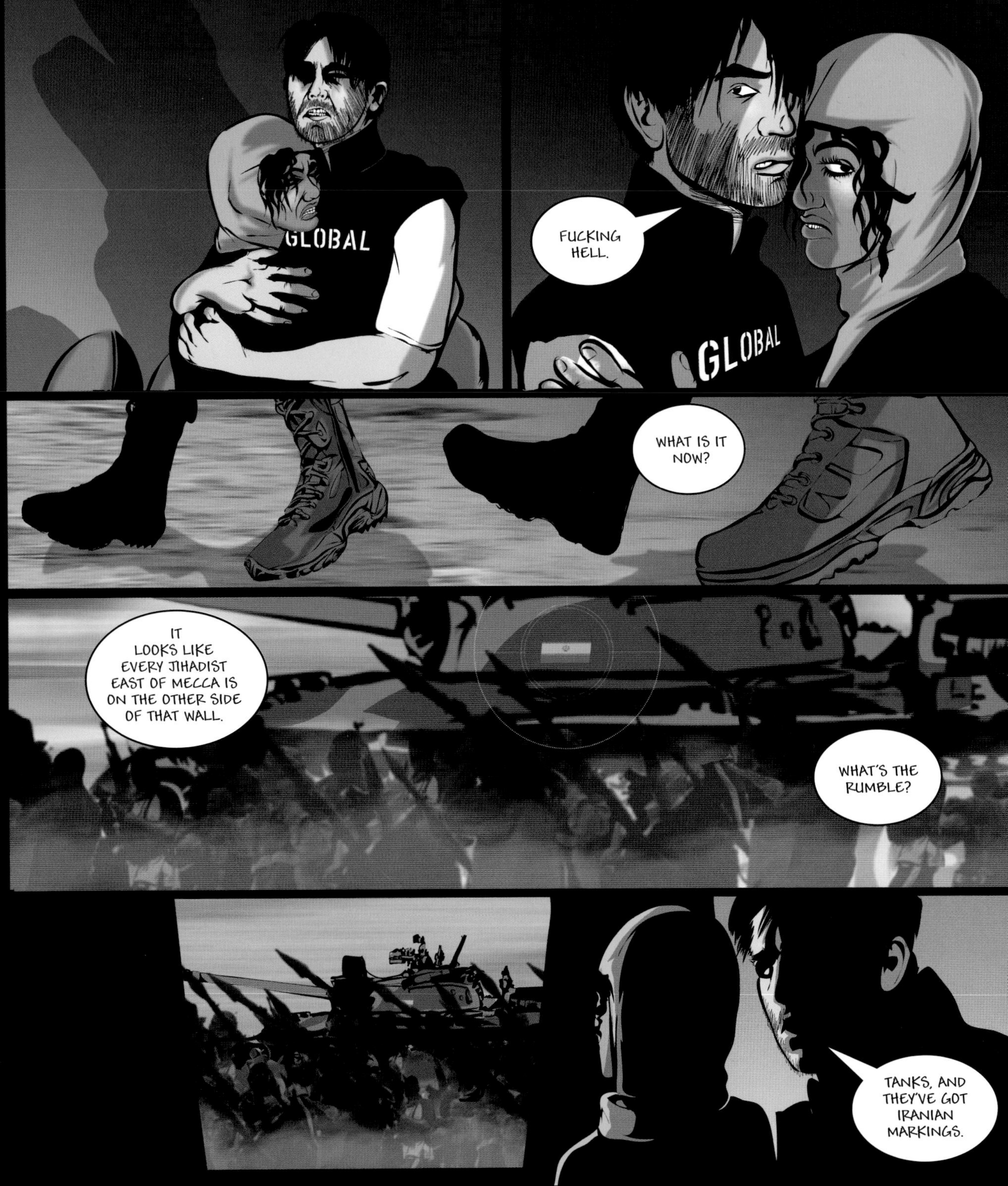
GLOBAL
FUCKING HELL.
GLOBAL
WHAT IS IT NOW?
IT LOOKS LIKE EVERY JIHADIST EAST OF MECCA IS ON THE OTHER SIDE OF THAT WALL.
WHAT'S THE RUMBLE?
TANKS, AND THEY'VE GOT IRANIAN MARKINGS.

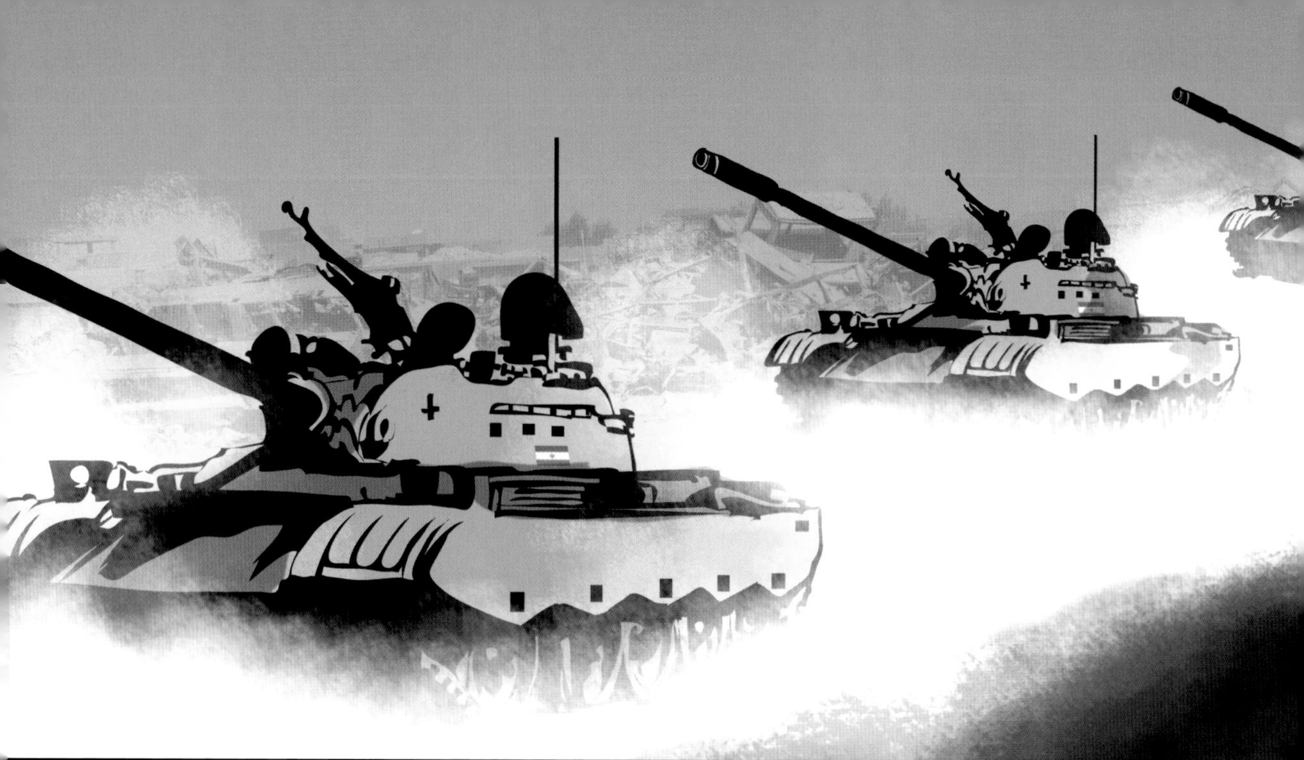

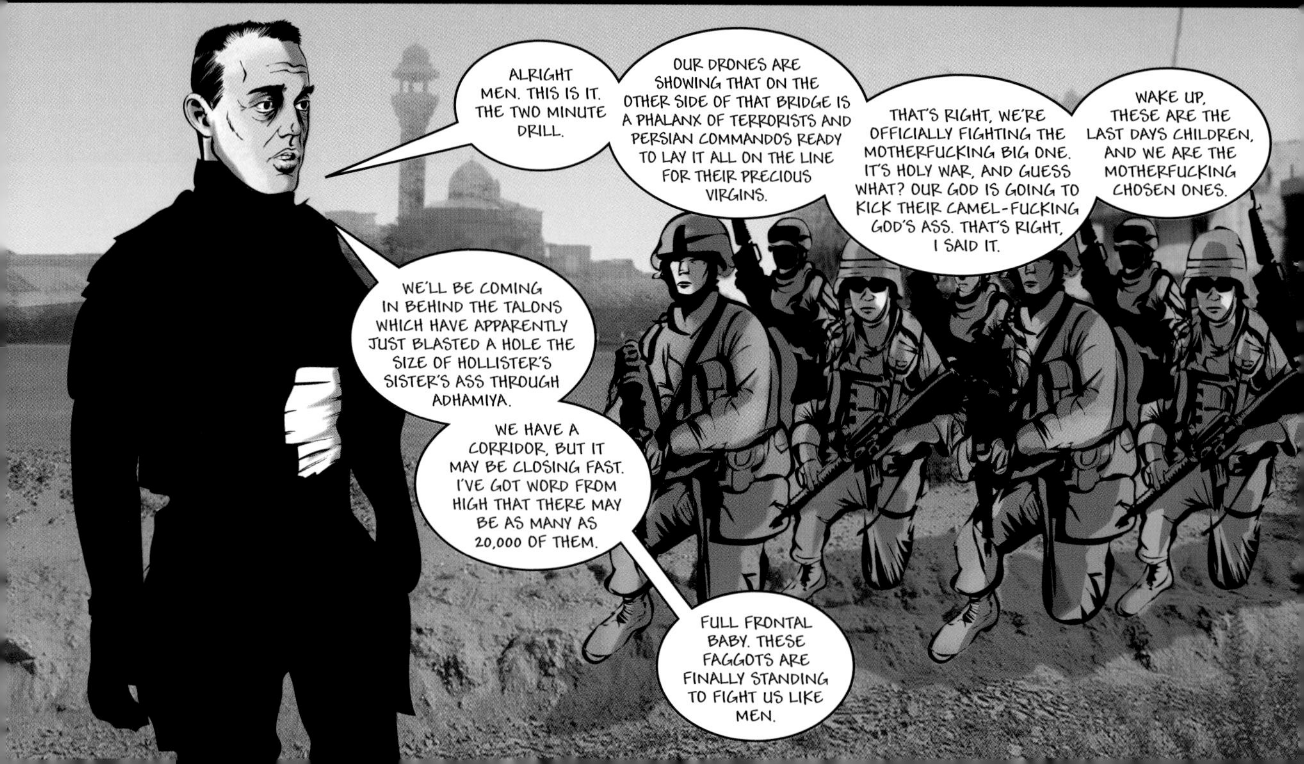

ALRIGHT MEN. THIS IS IT. THE TWO MINUTE DRILL.
OUR DRONES ARE SHOWING THAT ON THE OTHER SIDE OF THAT BRIDGE IS A PHALANX OF TERRORISTS AND PERSIAN COMMANDOS READY TO LAY IT ALL ON THE LINE FOR THEIR PRECIOUS VIRGINS.
THAT'S RIGHT, WE'RE OFFICIALLY FIGHTING THE MOTHERFUCKING BIG ONE. IT'S HOLY WAR, AND GUESS WHAT? OUR GOD IS GOING TO KICK THEIR CAMEL-FUCKING GOD'S ASS. THAT'S RIGHT, I SAID IT.
WAKE UP, THESE ARE THE LAST DAYS CHILDREN, AND WE ARE THE MOTHERFUCKING CHOSEN ONES.
WE'LL BE COMING IN BEHIND THE TALONS WHICH HAVE APPARENTLY JUST BLASTED A HOLE THE SIZE OF HOLLISTER'S SISTER'S ASS THROUGH ADHAMIYA.
WE HAVE A CORRIDOR, BUT IT MAY BE CLOSING FAST. I'VE GOT WORD FROM HIGH THAT THERE MAY BE AS MANY AS 20,000 OF THEM.
FULL FRONTAL BABY. THESE FAGGOTS ARE FINALLY STANDING TO FIGHT US LIKE MEN.

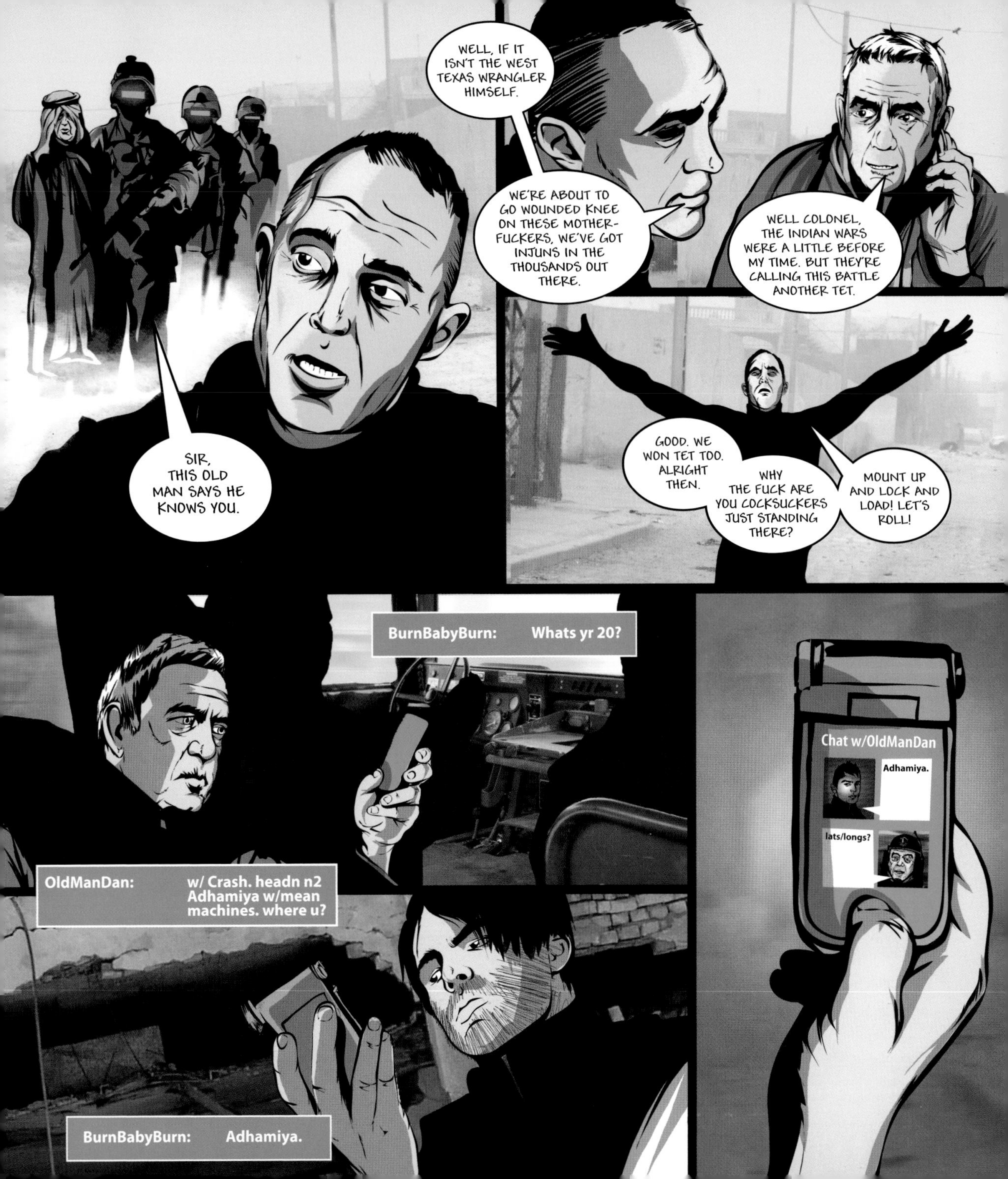
SIR, THIS OLD MAN SAYS HE KNOWS YOU.
WELL, IF IT ISN'T THE WEST TEXAS WRANGLER HIMSELF.
WE'RE ABOUT TO GO WOUNDED KNEE ON THESE MOTHER-FUCKERS, WE'VE GOT INJUNS IN THE THOUSANDS OUT THERE.
WELL COLONEL, THE INDIAN WARS WERE A LITTLE BEFORE MY TIME. BUT THEY'RE CALLING THIS BATTLE ANOTHER TET.
GOOD. WE WON TET TOO. ALRIGHT THEN.
WHY THE FUCK ARE YOU COCKSUCKERS JUST STANDING THERE?
MOUNT UP AND LOCK AND LOAD! LET'S ROLL!
BurnBabyBurn: Whats yr 20?
OldManDan: w/ Crash. headn n2 Adhamiya w/mean machines. where u?
BurnBabyBurn: Adhamiya.
Chat w/OldManDan
Adhamiya.
lats/longs?

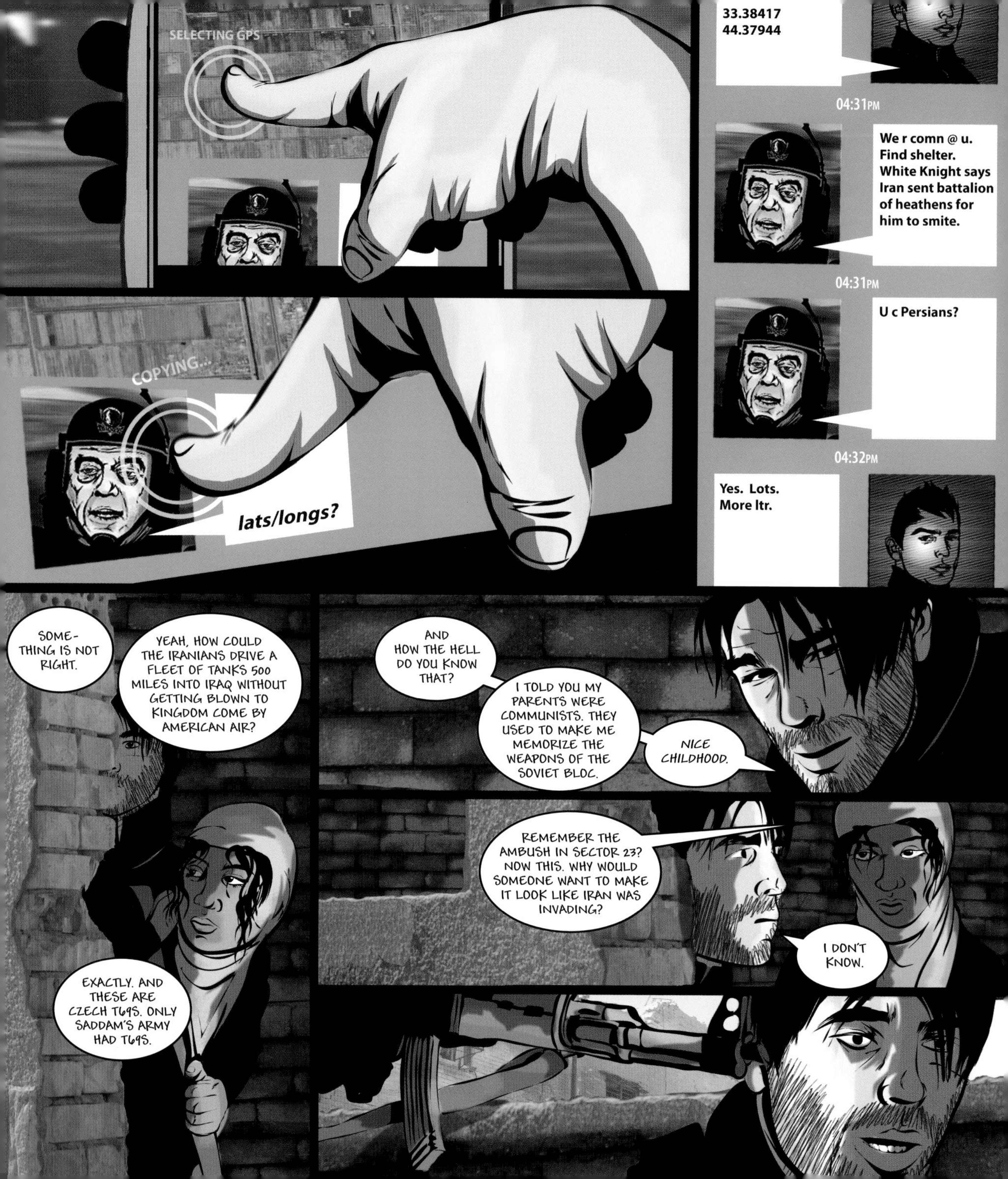
SELECTING GPS
COPYING...
lats/longs?
33.38417
44.37944
04:31PM
We r comn @ u. Find shelter. White Knight says Iran sent battalion of heathens for him to smite.
04:31PM
U c Persians?
04:32PM
Yes. Lots. More ltr.
SOME-THING IS NOT RIGHT.
YEAH, HOW COULD THE IRANIANS DRIVE A FLEET OF TANKS 500 MILES INTO IRAQ WITHOUT GETTING BLOWN TO KINGDOM COME BY AMERICAN AIR?
EXACTLY. AND THESE ARE CZECH T69S. ONLY SADDAM'S ARMY HAD T69S.
AND HOW THE HELL DO YOU KNOW THAT?
I TOLD YOU MY PARENTS WERE COMMUNISTS. THEY USED TO MAKE ME MEMORIZE THE WEAPONS OF THE SOVIET BLOC.
NICE CHILDHOOD.
REMEMBER THE AMBUSH IN SECTOR 23? NOW THIS. WHY WOULD SOMEONE WANT TO MAKE IT LOOK LIKE IRAN WAS INVADING?
I DON'T KNOW.

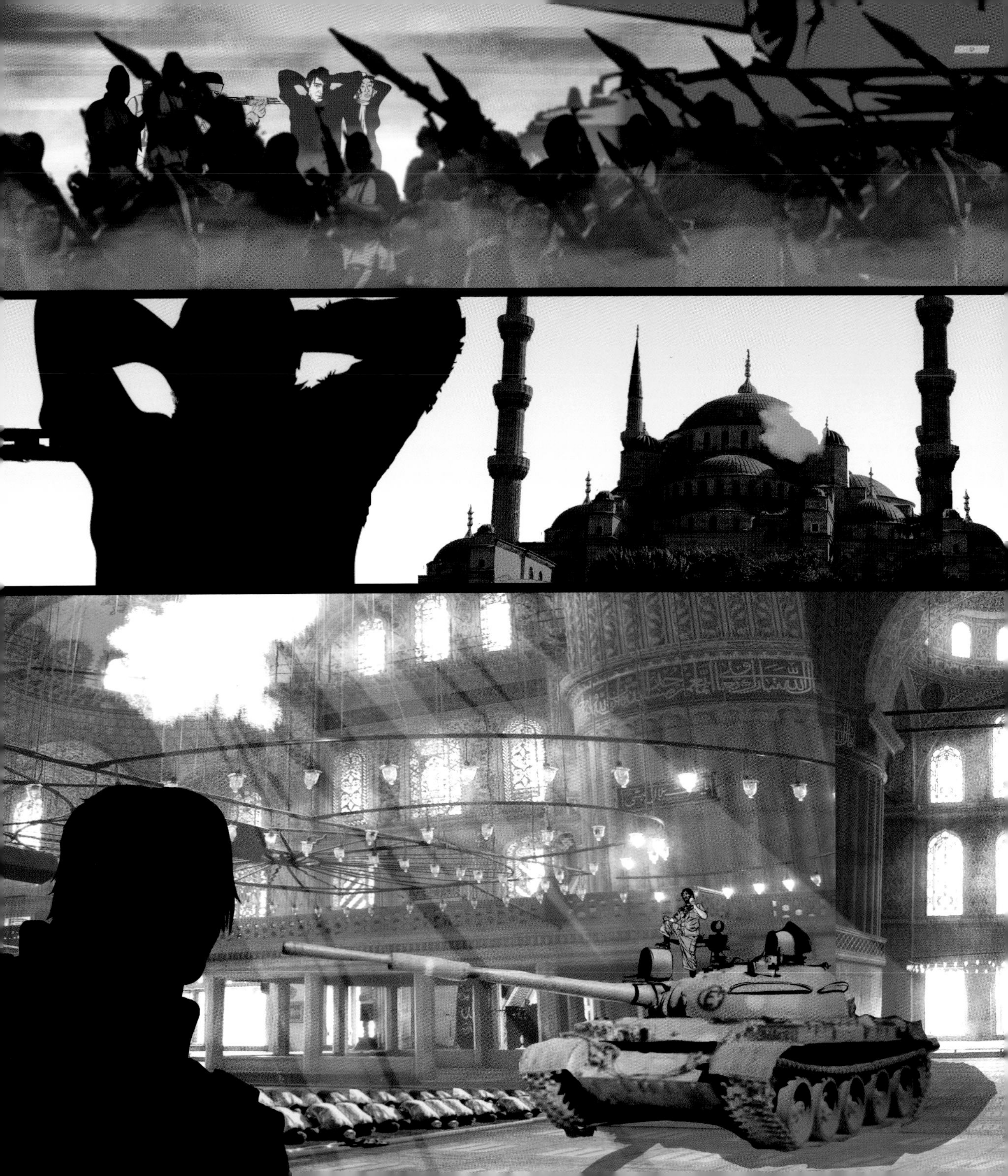

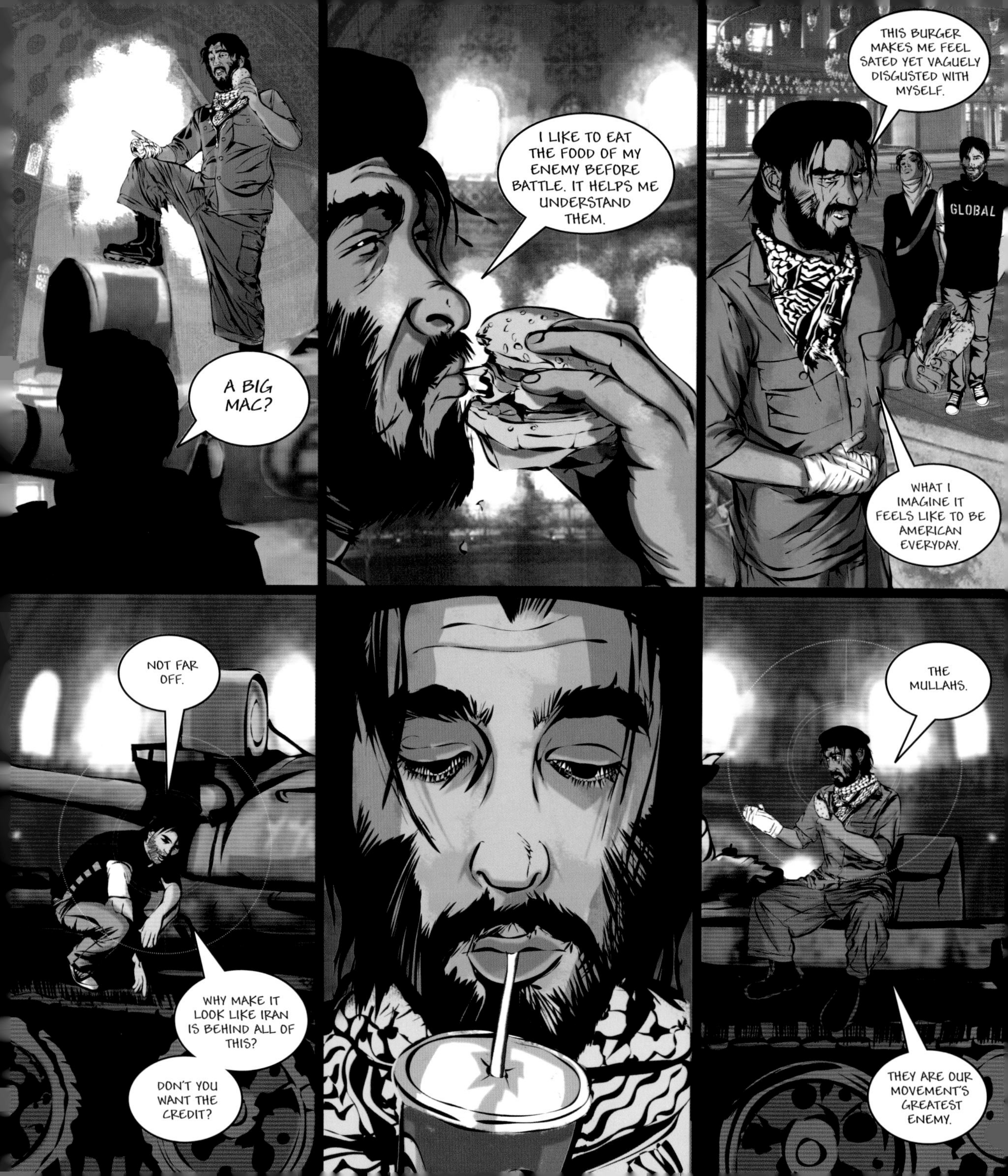
A BIG MAC?
I LIKE TO EAT THE FOOD OF MY ENEMY BEFORE BATTLE. IT HELPS ME UNDERSTAND THEM.
THIS BURGER MAKES ME FEEL SATED YET VAGUELY DISGUSTED WITH MYSELF.
GLOBAL
WHAT I IMAGINE IT FEELS LIKE TO BE AMERICAN EVERYDAY.
NOT FAR OFF.
WHY MAKE IT LOOK LIKE IRAN IS BEHIND ALL OF THIS?
DON'T YOU WANT THE CREDIT?
THE MULLAHS.
THEY ARE OUR MOVEMENT'S GREATEST ENEMY.

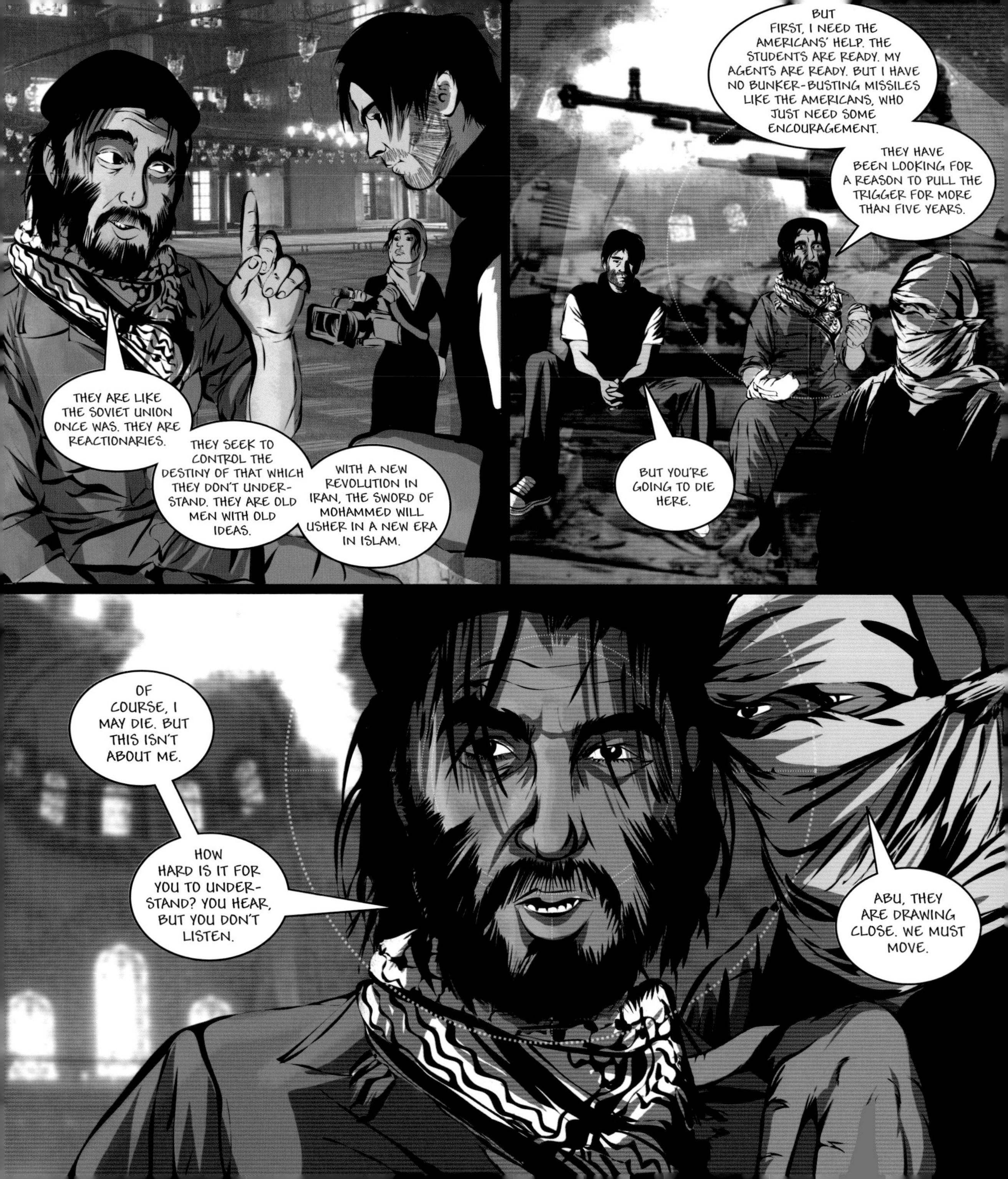

THEY ARE LIKE THE SOVIET UNION ONCE WAS. THEY ARE REACTIONARIES.
THEY SEEK TO CONTROL THE DESTINY OF THAT WHICH THEY DON'T UNDER-STAND. THEY ARE OLD MEN WITH OLD IDEAS.
WITH A NEW REVOLUTION IN IRAN, THE SWORD OF MOHAMMED WILL USHER IN A NEW ERA IN ISLAM.
BUT FIRST, I NEED THE AMERICANS' HELP. THE STUDENTS ARE READY. MY AGENTS ARE READY. BUT I HAVE NO BUNKER-BUSTING MISSILES LIKE THE AMERICANS, WHO JUST NEED SOME ENCOURAGEMENT.
THEY HAVE BEEN LOOKING FOR A REASON TO PULL THE TRIGGER FOR MORE THAN FIVE YEARS.
BUT YOU'RE GOING TO DIE HERE.
OF COURSE, I MAY DIE. BUT THIS ISN'T ABOUT ME.
HOW HARD IS IT FOR YOU TO UNDER-STAND? YOU HEAR, BUT YOU DON'T LISTEN.
ABU, THEY ARE DRAWING CLOSE. WE MUST MOVE.

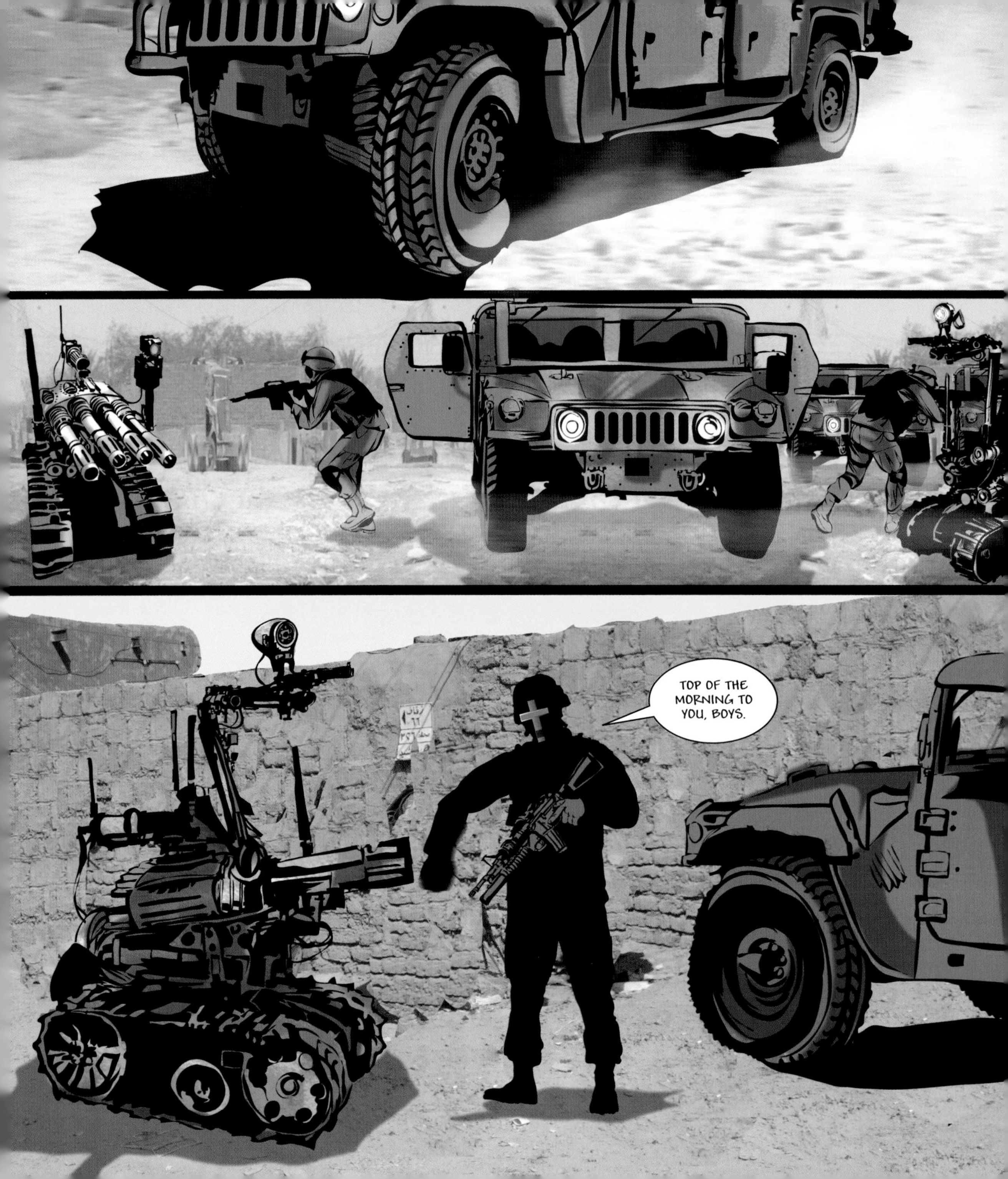
TOP OF THE MORNING TO YOU, BOYS.

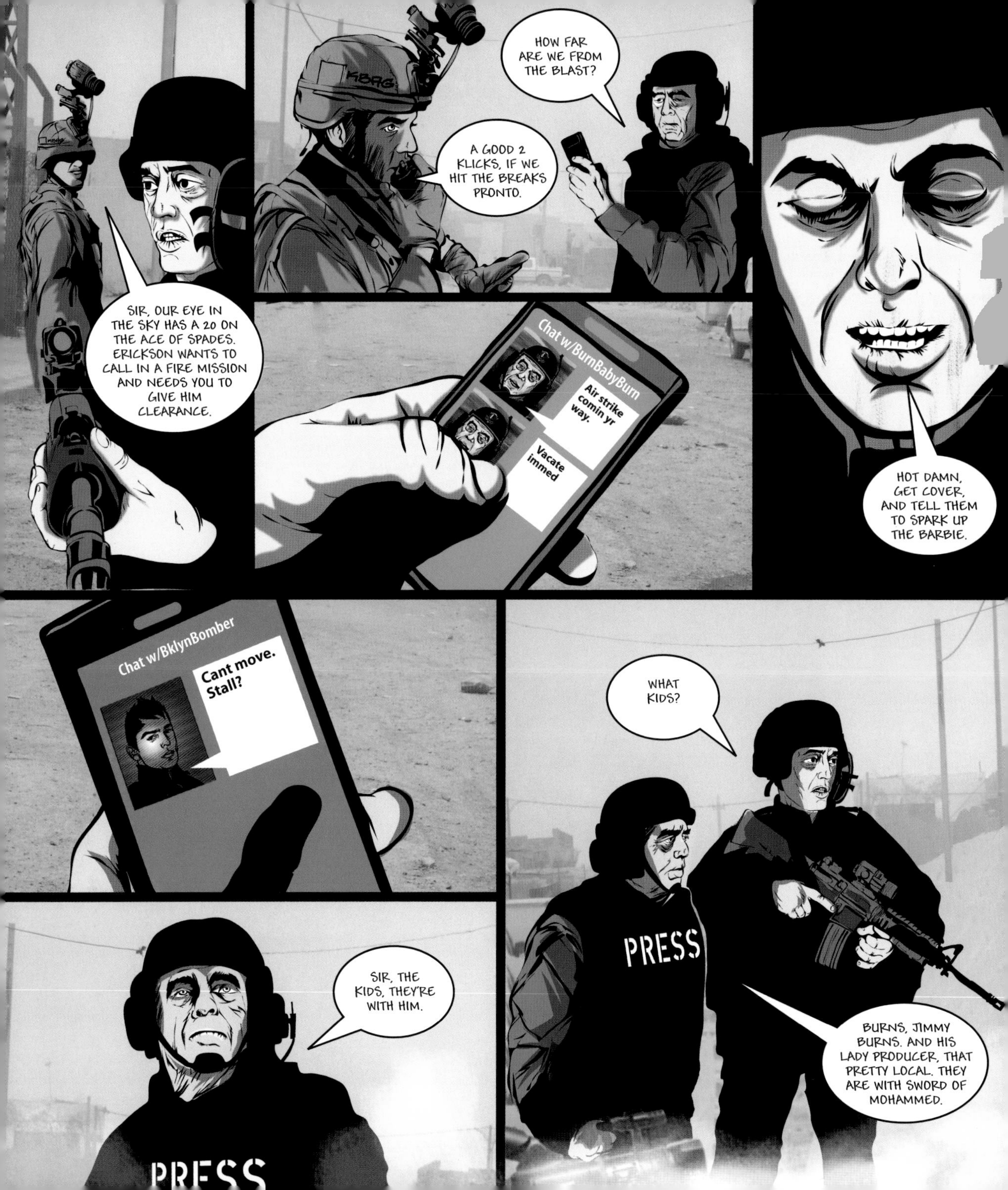
SIR, OUR EYE IN THE SKY HAS A 20 ON THE ACE OF SPADES. ERICKSON WANTS TO CALL IN A FIRE MISSION AND NEEDS YOU TO GIVE HIM CLEARANCE.
KBRG
HOW FAR ARE WE FROM THE BLAST?
A GOOD 2 KLICKS, IF WE HIT THE BREAKS PRONTO.
Chat w/BurnBabyBurn
Air strike comin yr way.
Vacate immed
HOT DAMN, GET COVER, AND TELL THEM TO SPARK UP THE BARBIE.
Chat w/BklynBomber
Cant move. Stall?
WHAT KIDS?
SIR, THE KIDS, THEY'RE WITH HIM.
PRESS
BURNS, JIMMY BURNS. AND HIS LADY PRODUCER, THAT PRETTY LOCAL. THEY ARE WITH SWORD OF MOHAMMED.
PRESS

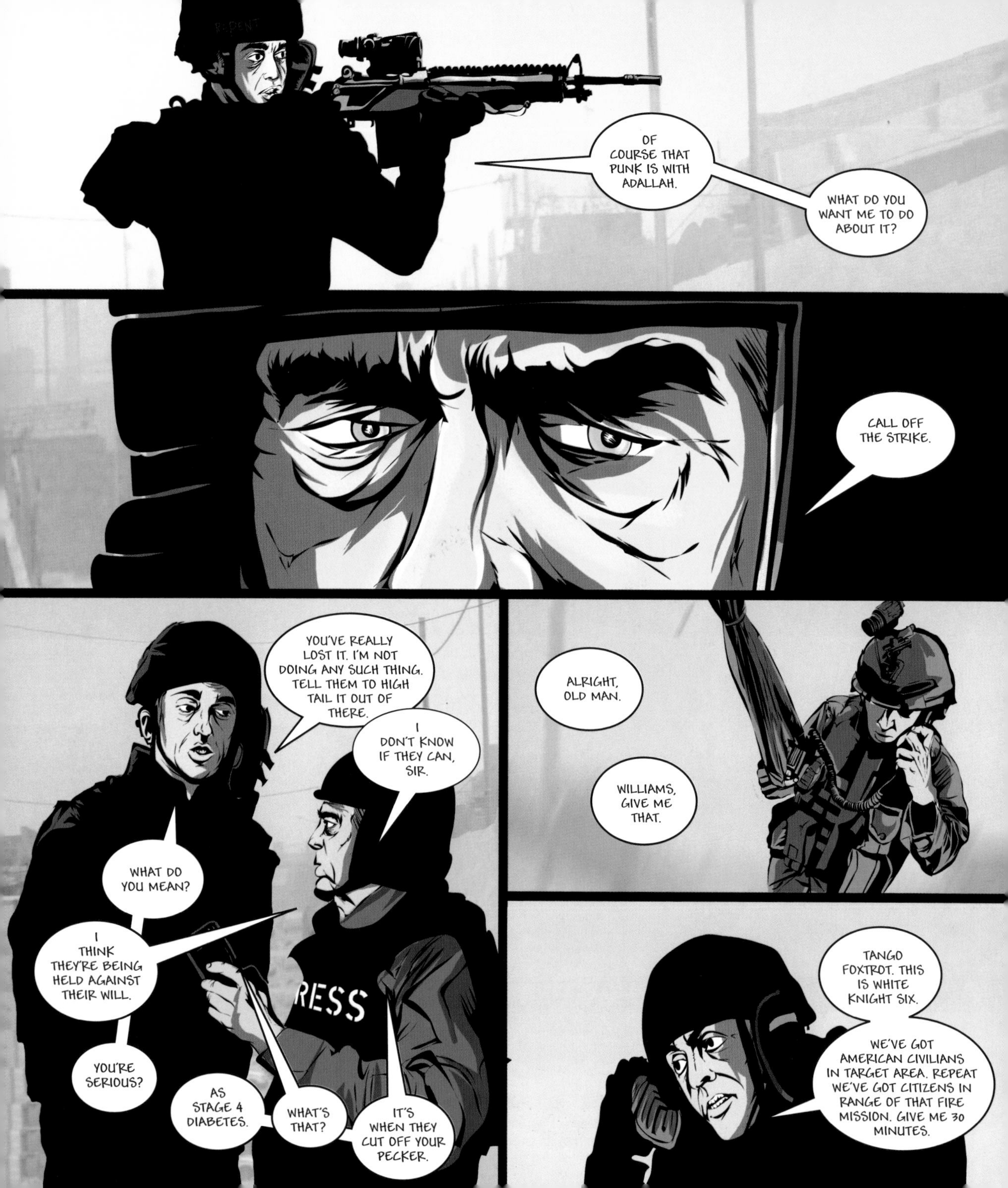
OF COURSE THAT PUNK IS WITH ADALLAH.
WHAT DO YOU WANT ME TO DO ABOUT IT?
CALL OFF THE STRIKE.
YOU'VE REALLY LOST IT. I'M NOT DOING ANY SUCH THING. TELL THEM TO HIGH TAIL IT OUT OF THERE.
I DON'T KNOW IF THEY CAN, SIR.
WHAT DO YOU MEAN?
I THINK THEY'RE BEING HELD AGAINST THEIR WILL.
YOU'RE SERIOUS?
AS STAGE 4 DIABETES.
WHAT'S THAT?
IT'S WHEN THEY CUT OFF YOUR PECKER.
ALRIGHT, OLD MAN.
WILLIAMS, GIVE ME THAT.
TANGO FOXTROT. THIS IS WHITE KNIGHT SIX.
WE'VE GOT AMERICAN CIVILIANS IN TARGET AREA. REPEAT WE'VE GOT CITIZENS IN RANGE OF THAT FIRE MISSION. GIVE ME 30 MINUTES.
RESS

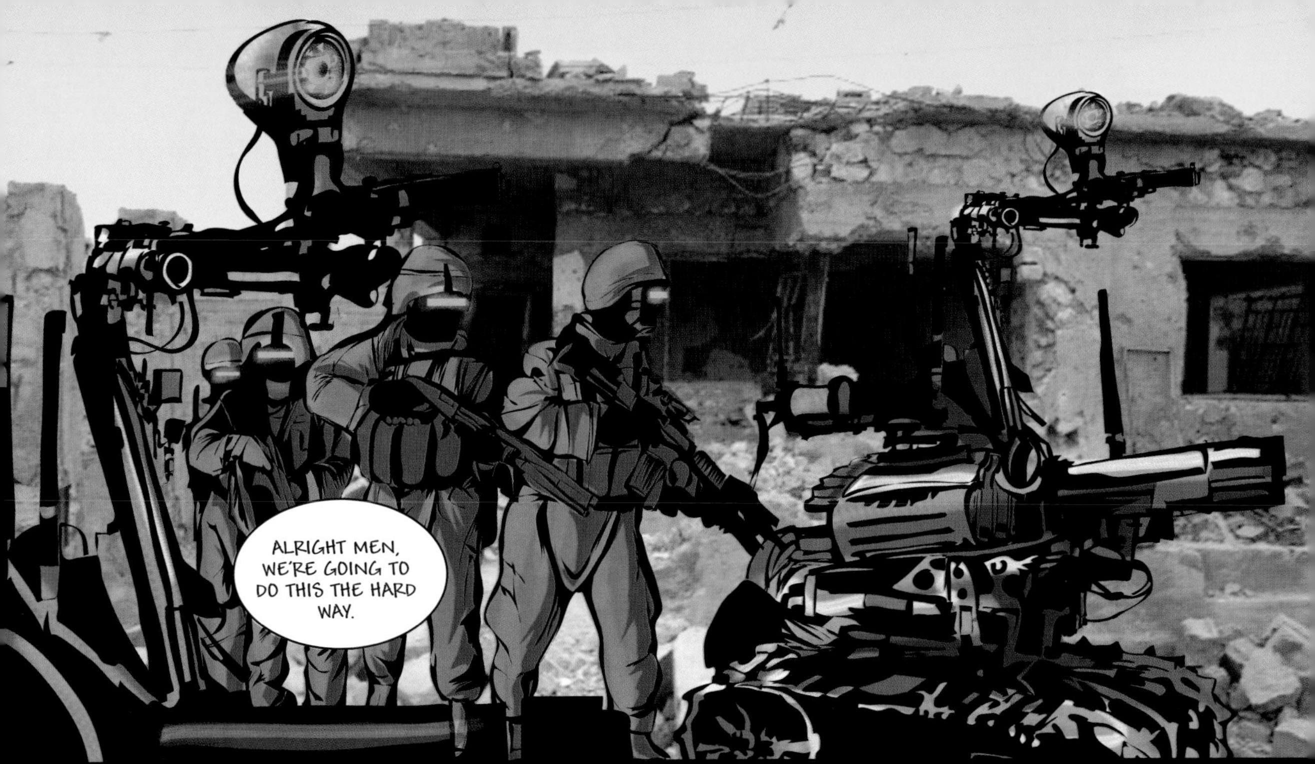
ALRIGHT MEN, WE'RE GOING TO DO THIS THE HARD WAY.

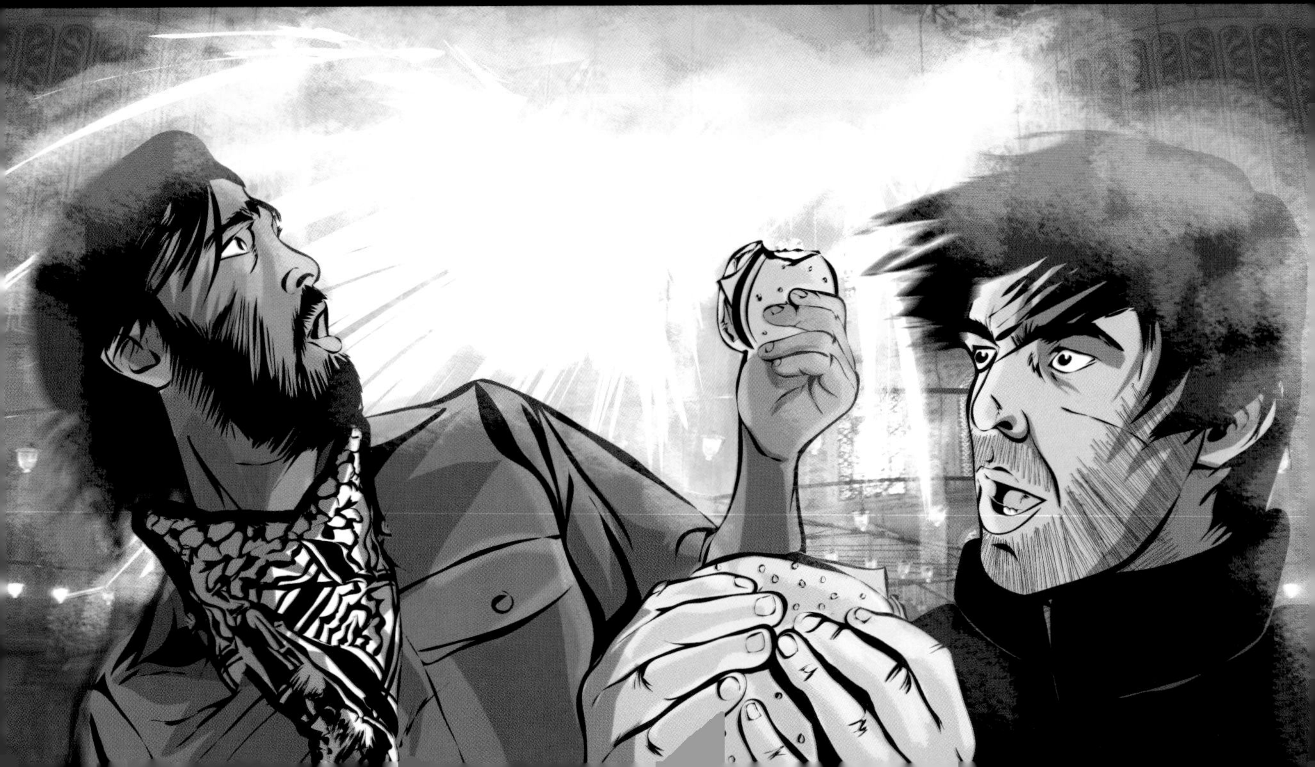

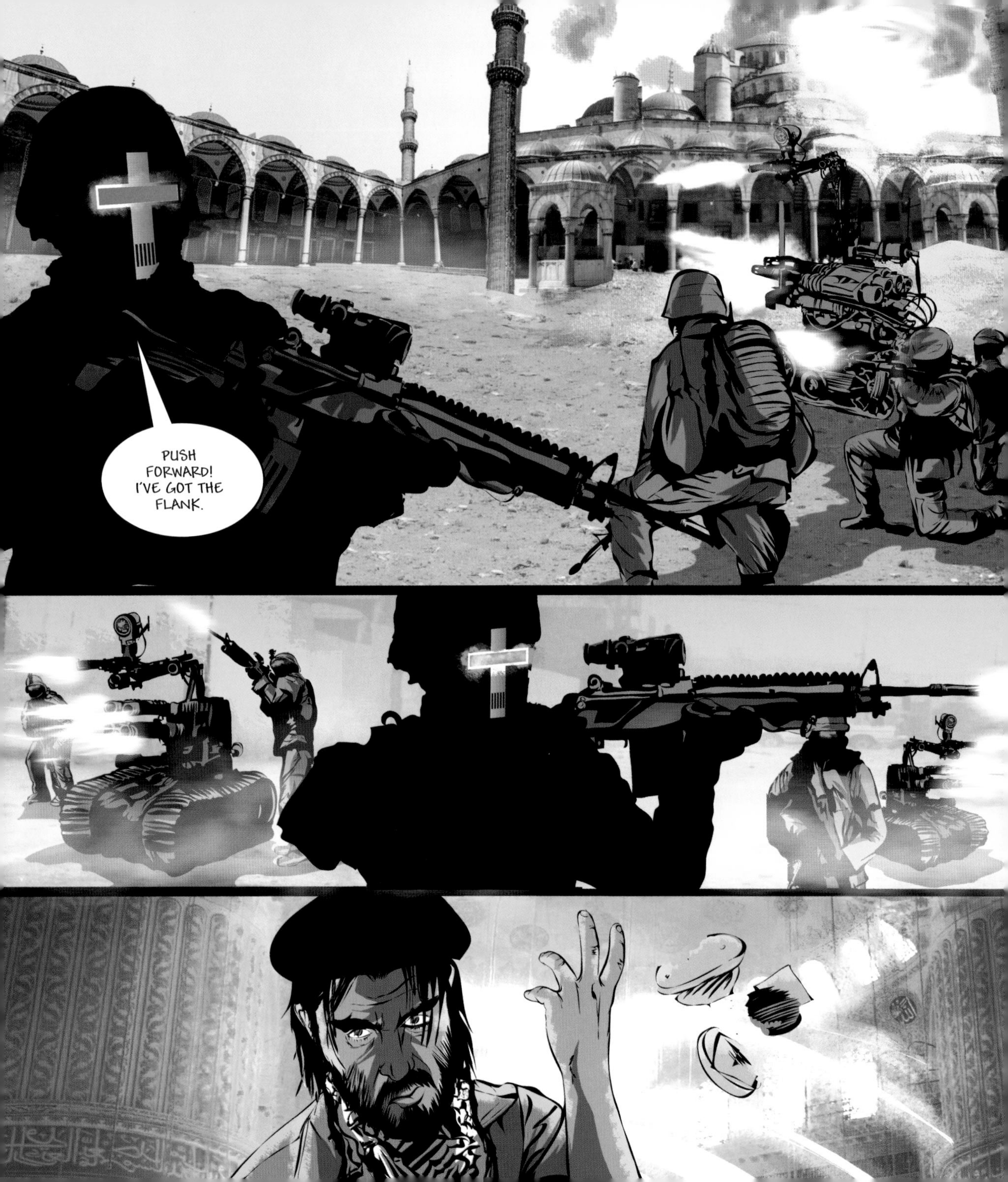
PUSH FORWARD! I'VE GOT THE FLANK.

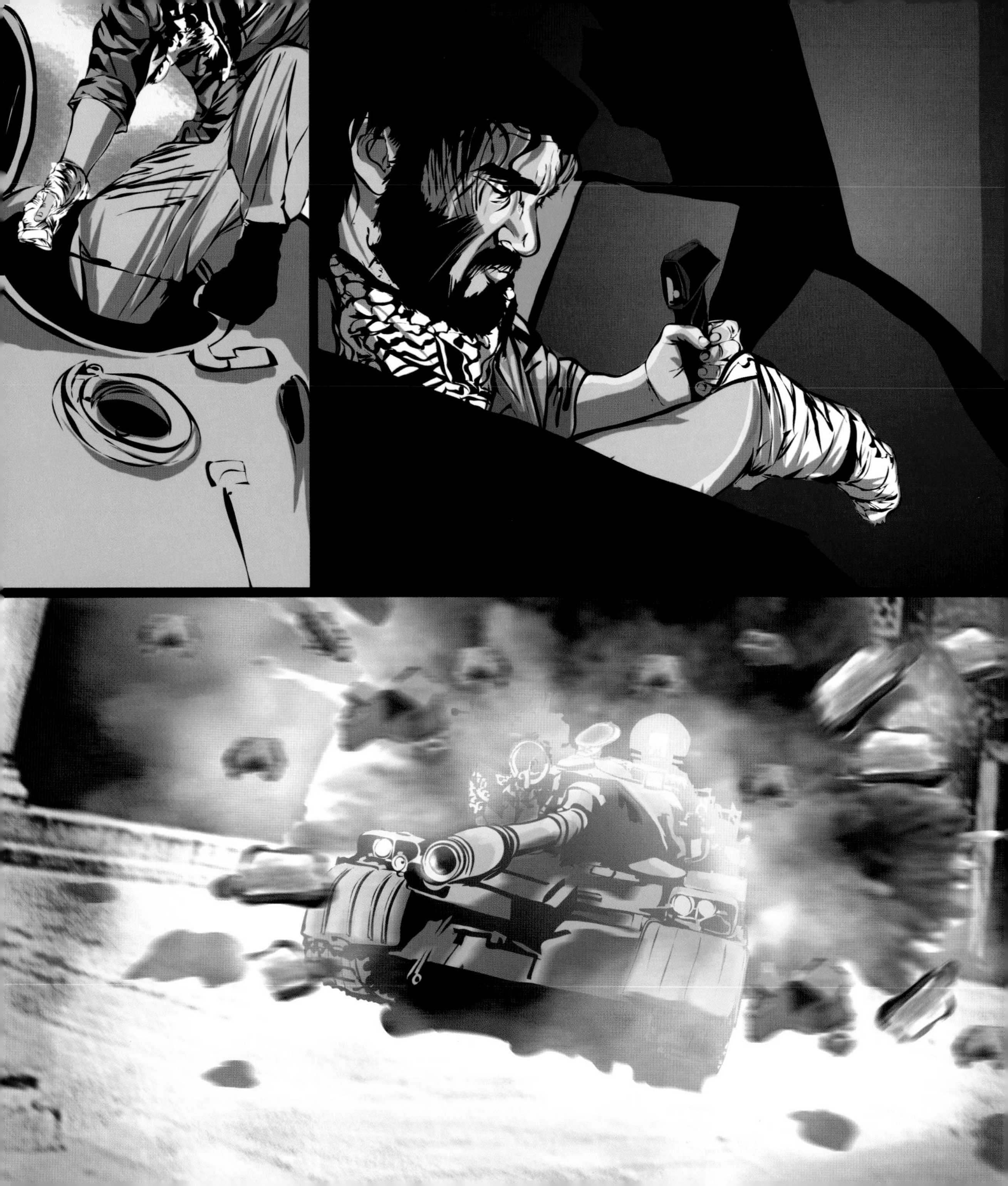

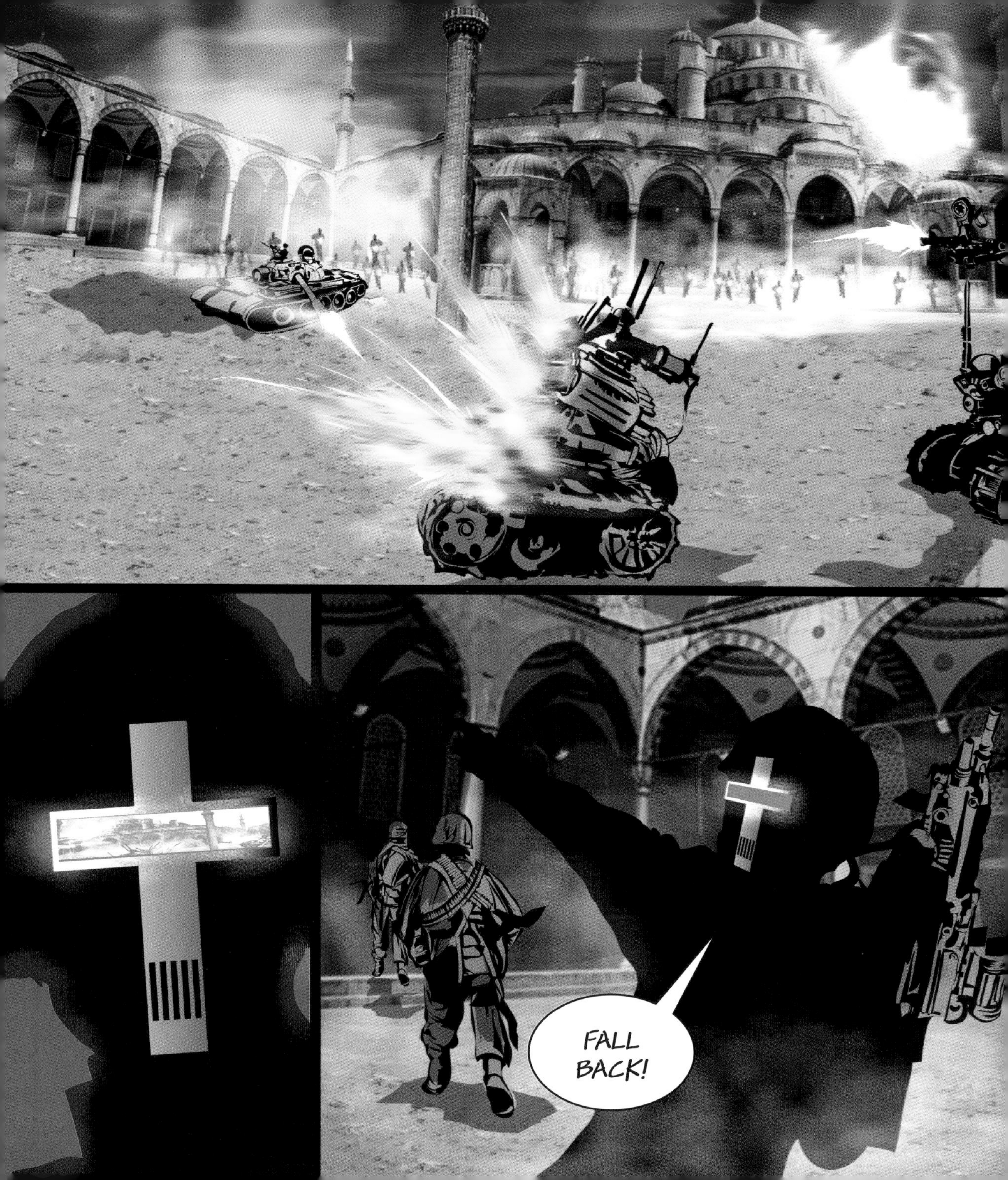
FALL BACK!

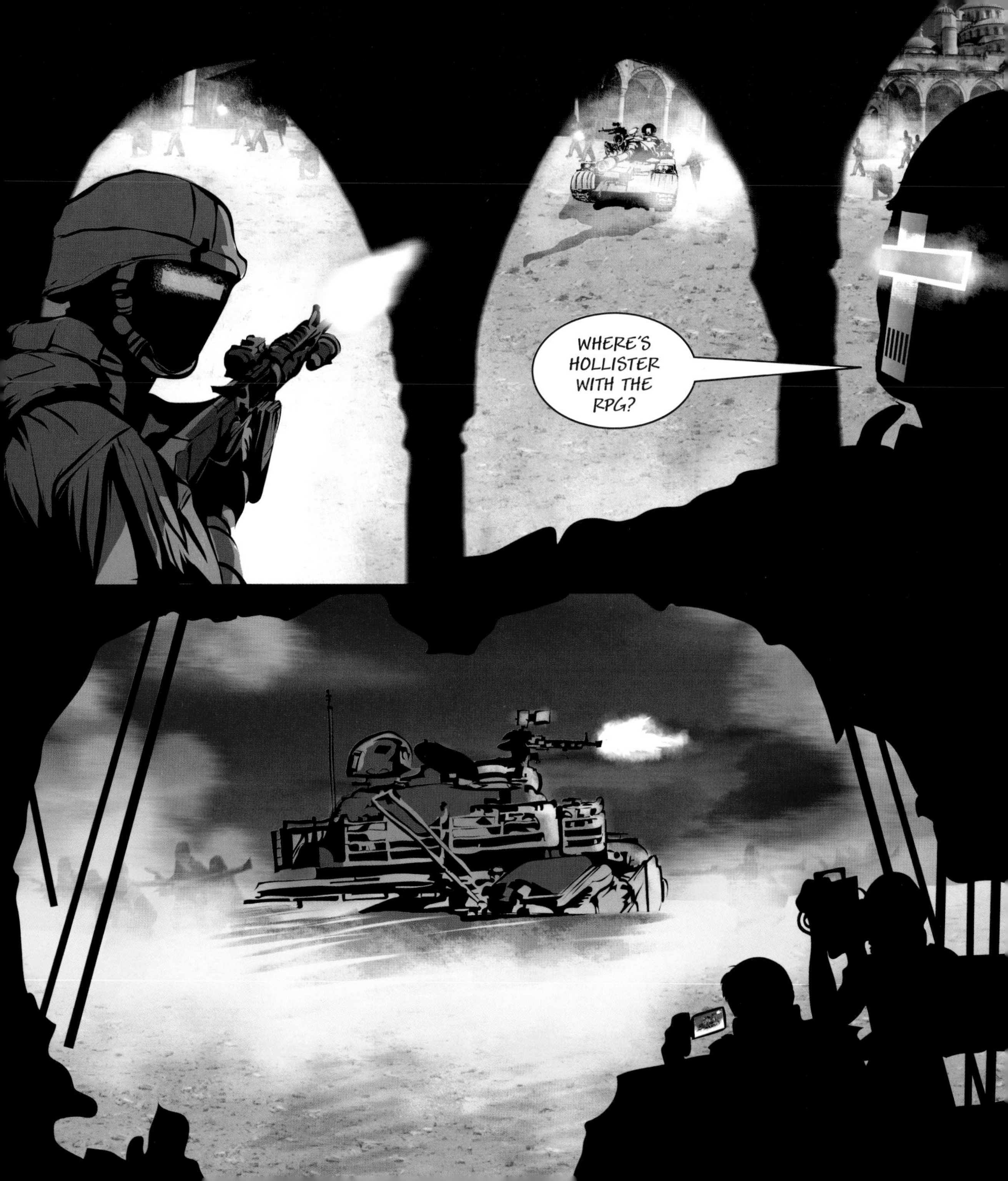
WHERE'S HOLLISTER WITH THE RPG?

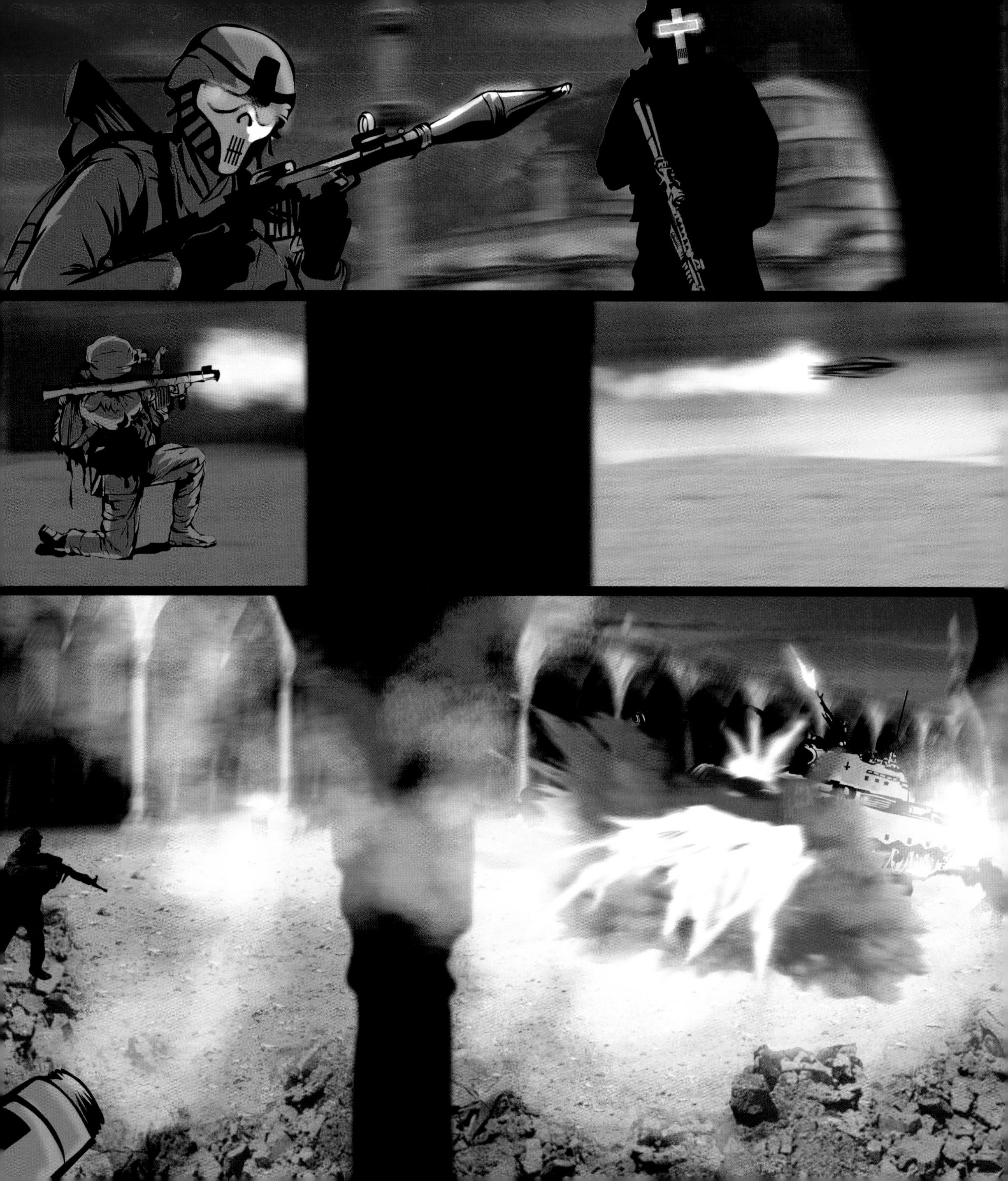

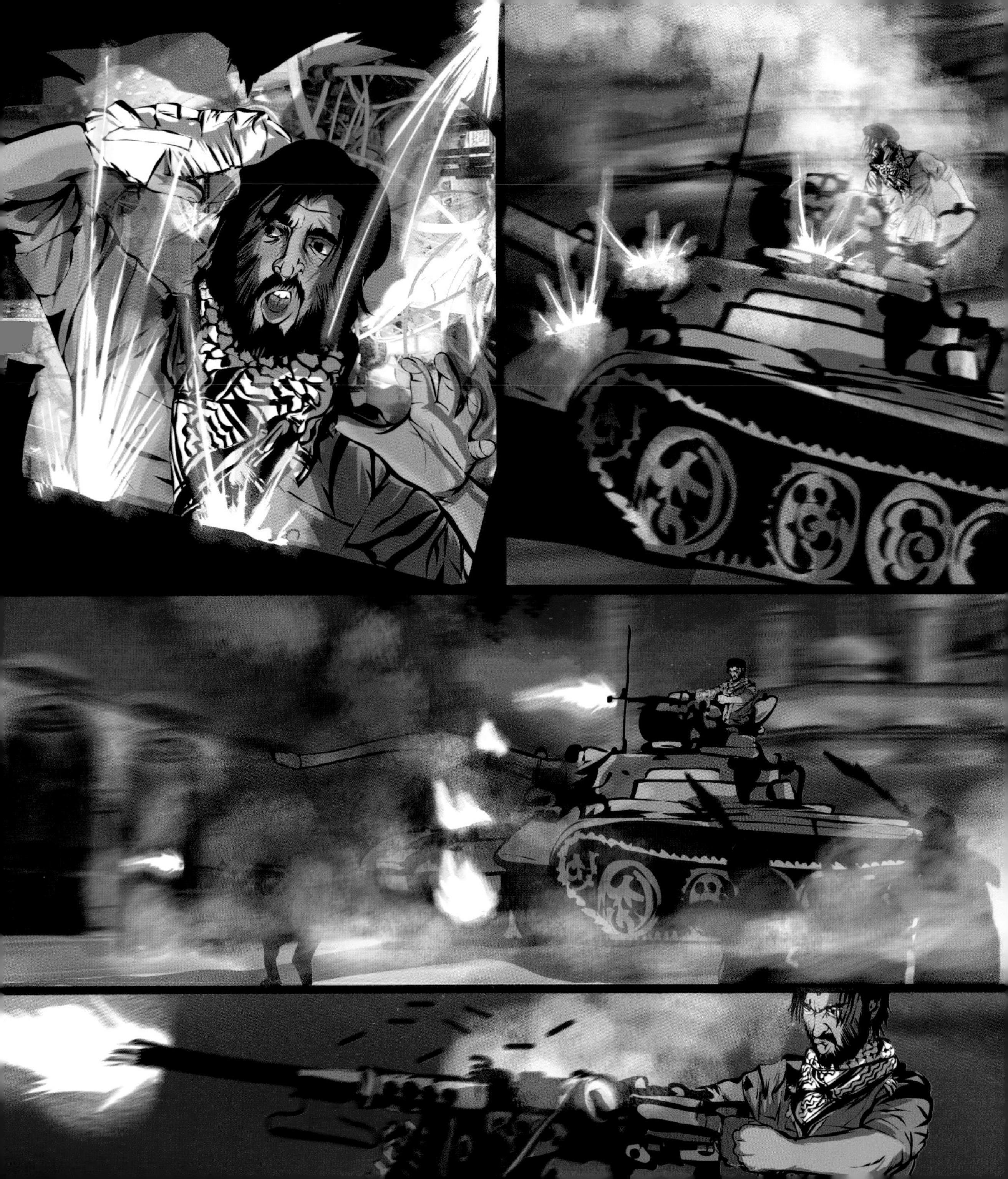

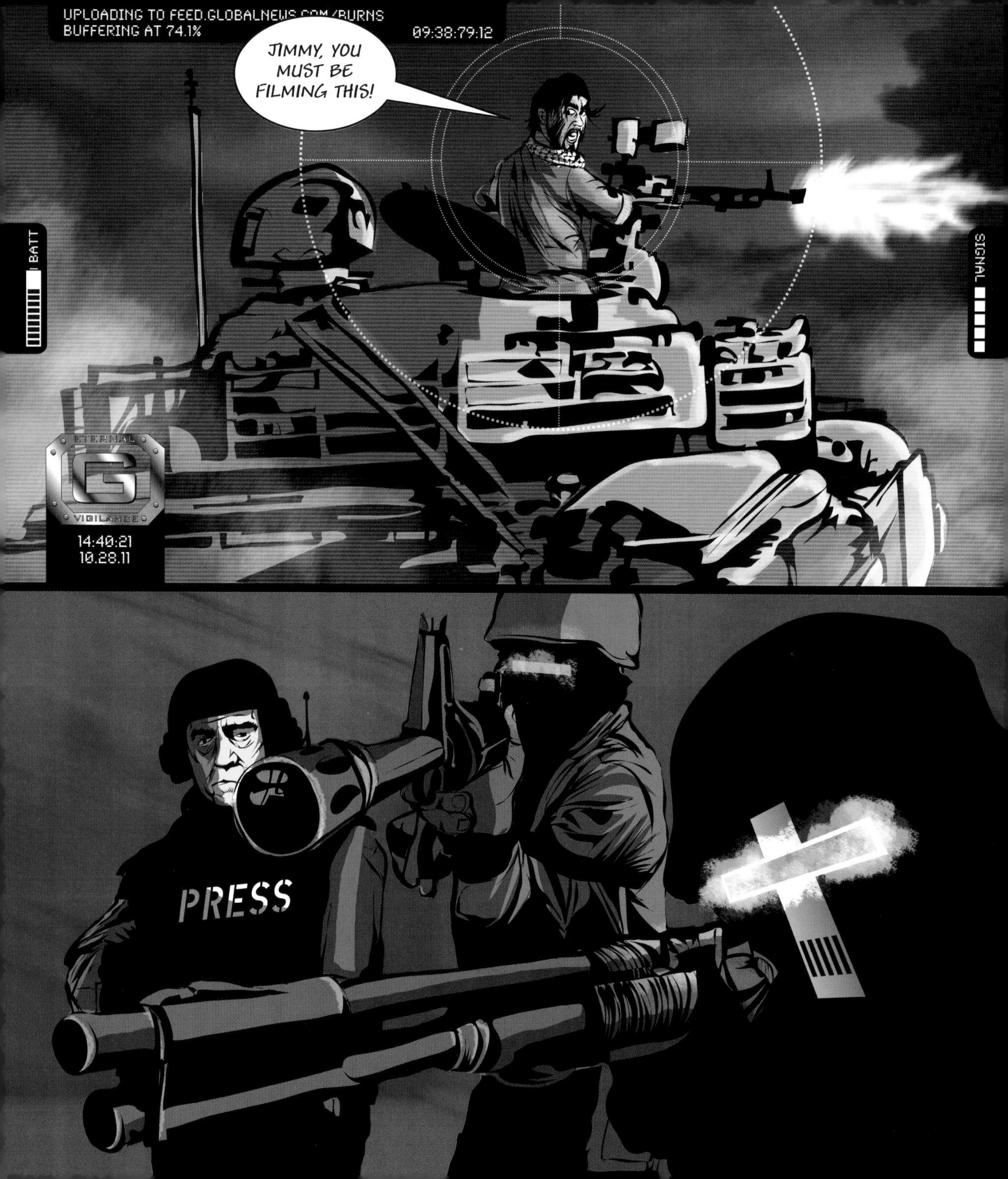
UPLOADING TO FEED.GLOBALNEWS.COM/BURNS
BUFFERING AT 74.1%
09:38:79:12
JIMMY, YOU MUST BE FILMING THIS!
BATT
SIGNAL
ETERNAL
VIGILANCE
14:40:21
10.28.11
PRESS

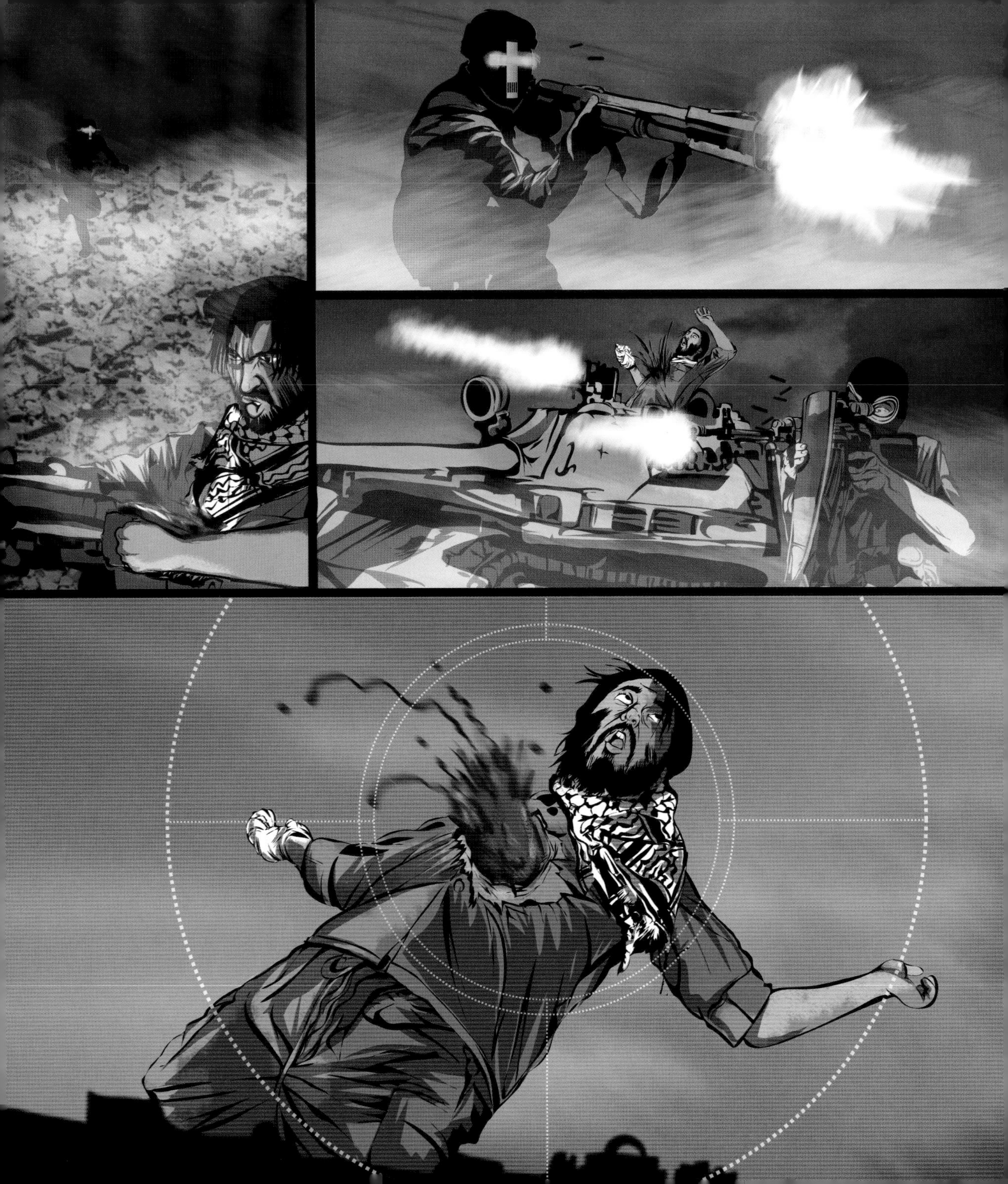

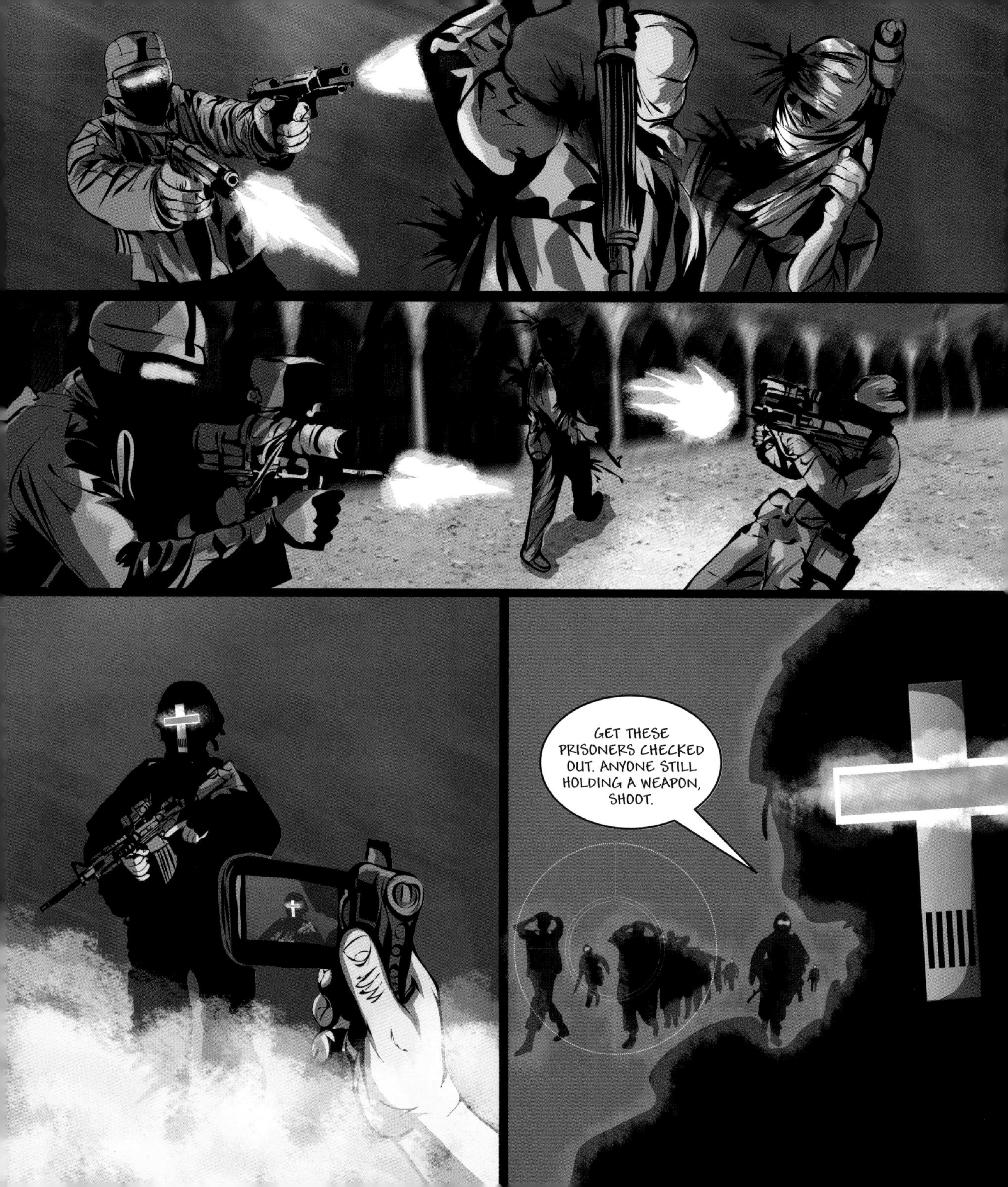
GET THESE PRISONERS CHECKED OUT. ANYONE STILL HOLDING A WEAPON, SHOOT.

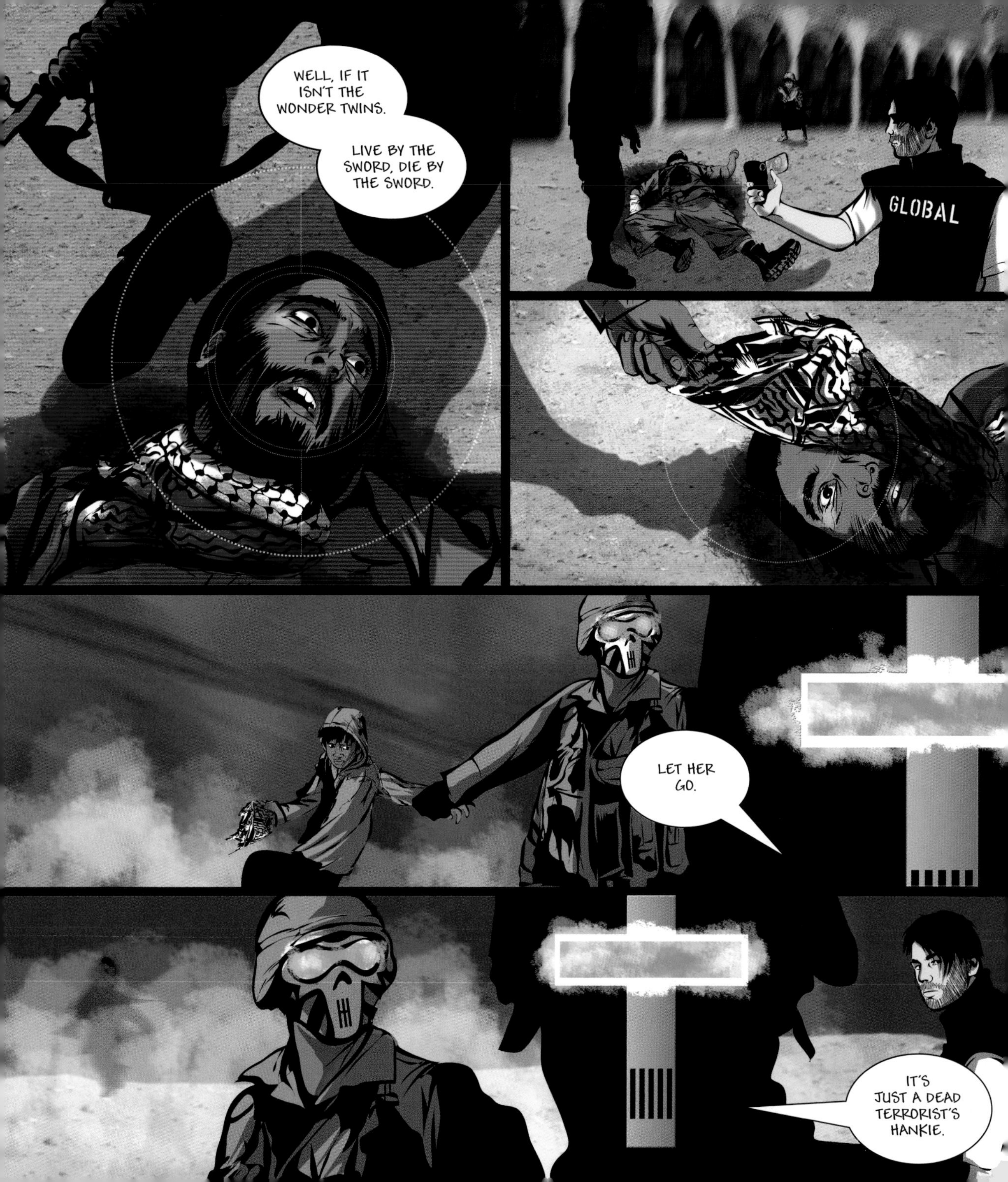
WELL, IF IT ISN'T THE WONDER TWINS.
LIVE BY THE SWORD, DIE BY THE SWORD.
GLOBAL
LET HER GO.
IT'S JUST A DEAD TERRORIST'S HANKIE.

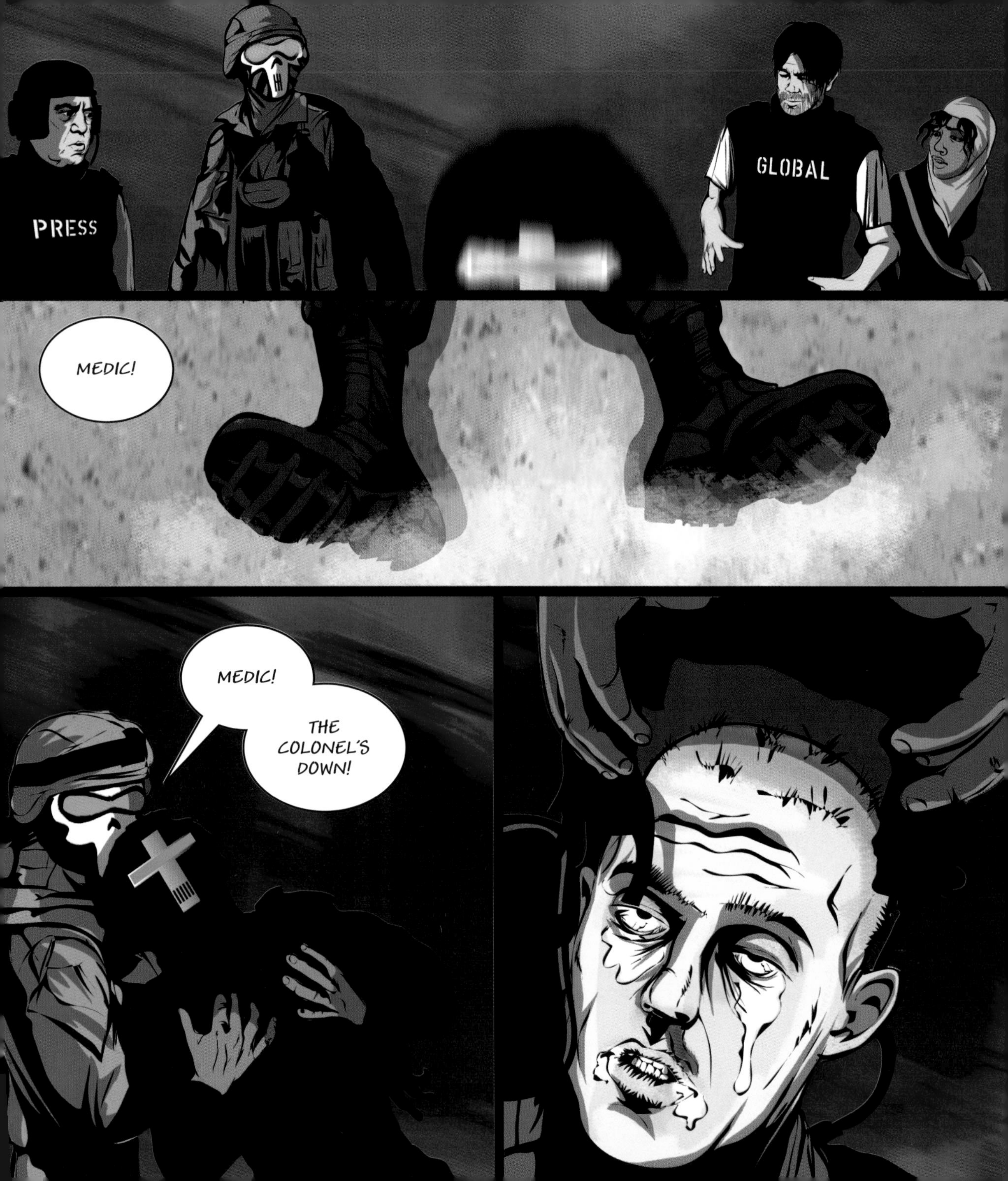
PRESS
GLOBAL
MEDIC!
MEDIC!
THE COLONEL'S DOWN!

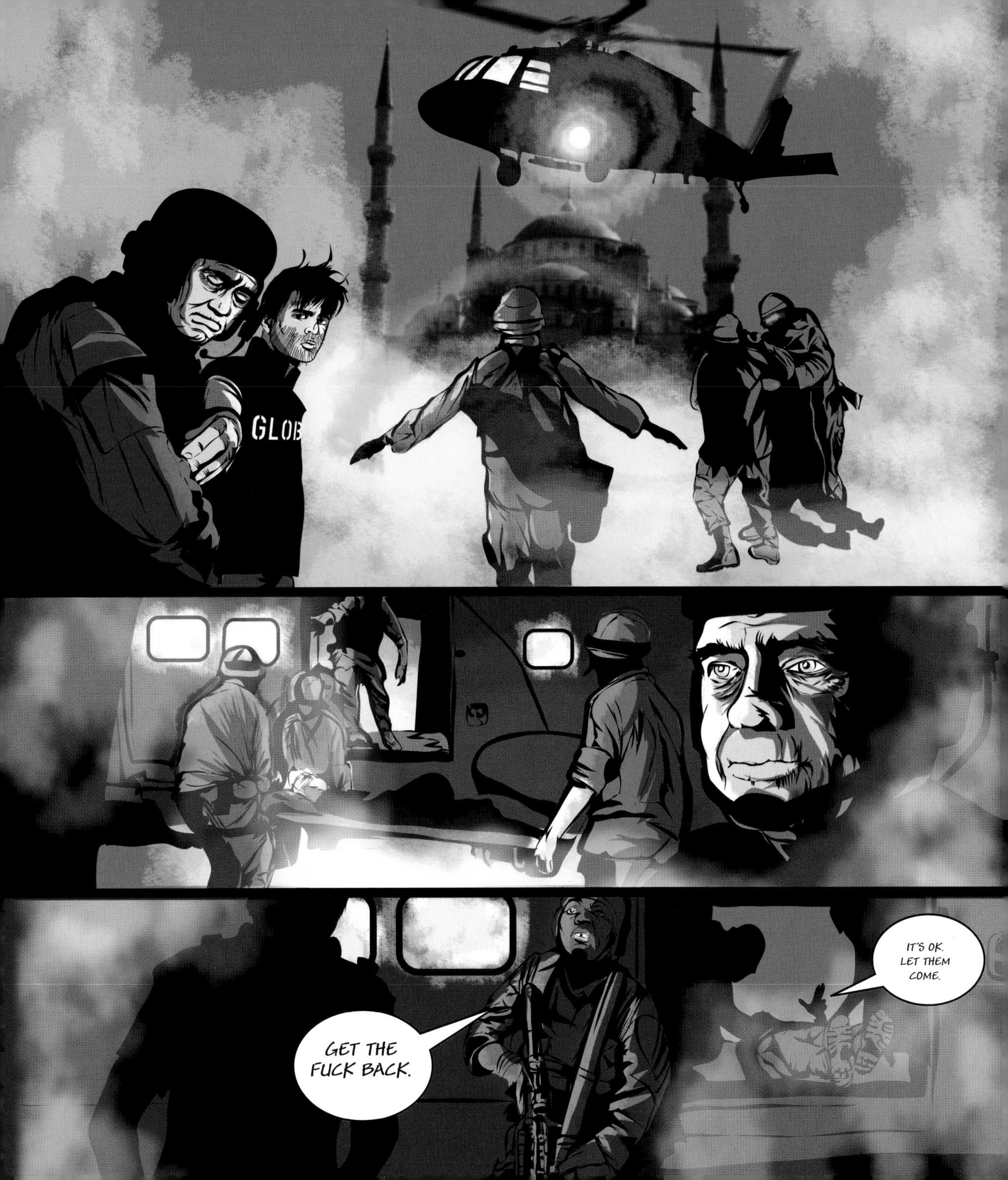
GLOB
IT'S OK. LET THEM COME.
GET THE FUCK BACK.

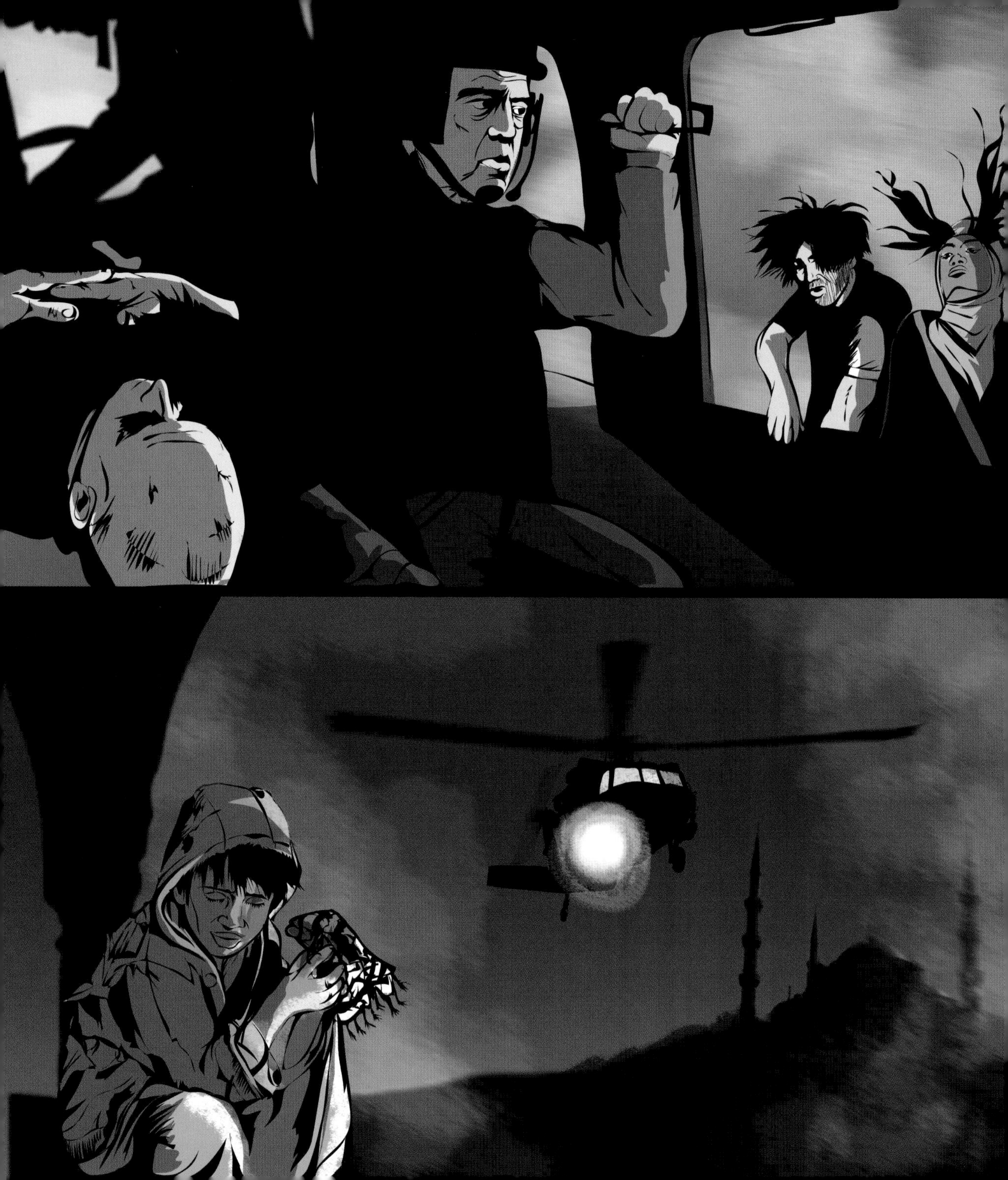

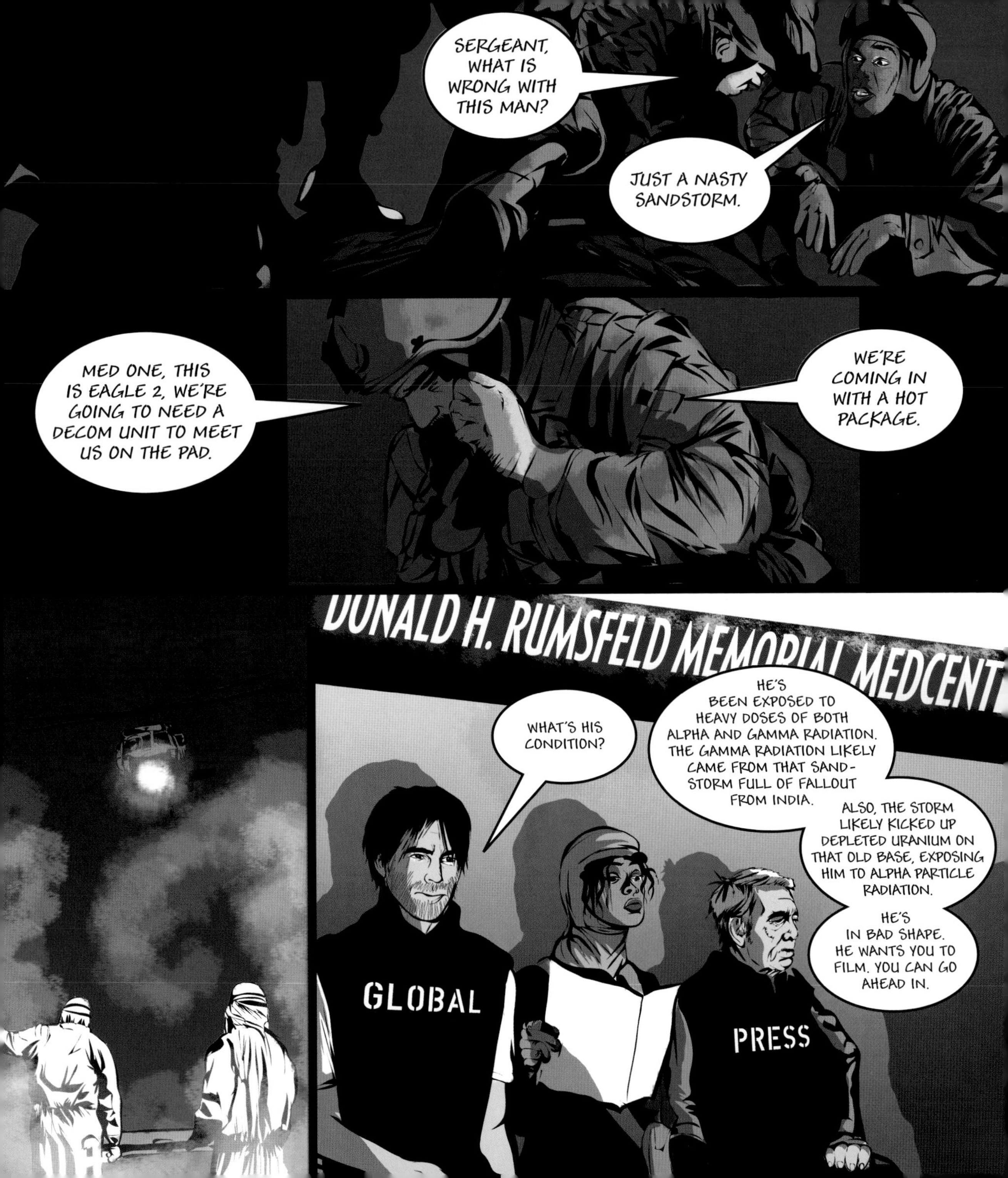
SERGEANT, WHAT IS WRONG WITH THIS MAN?
JUST A NASTY SANDSTORM.
MED ONE, THIS IS EAGLE 2, WE'RE GOING TO NEED A DECOM UNIT TO MEET US ON THE PAD.
WE'RE COMING IN WITH A HOT PACKAGE.
DONALD H. RUMSFELD MEMORIAL MEDCENT
WHAT'S HIS CONDITION?
HE'S BEEN EXPOSED TO HEAVY DOSES OF BOTH ALPHA AND GAMMA RADIATION. THE GAMMA RADIATION LIKELY CAME FROM THAT SAND-STORM FULL OF FALLOUT FROM INDIA.
ALSO, THE STORM LIKELY KICKED UP DEPLETED URANIUM ON THAT OLD BASE, EXPOSING HIM TO ALPHA PARTICLE RADIATION.
HE'S IN BAD SHAPE. HE WANTS YOU TO FILM. YOU CAN GO AHEAD IN.
GLOBAL
PRESS

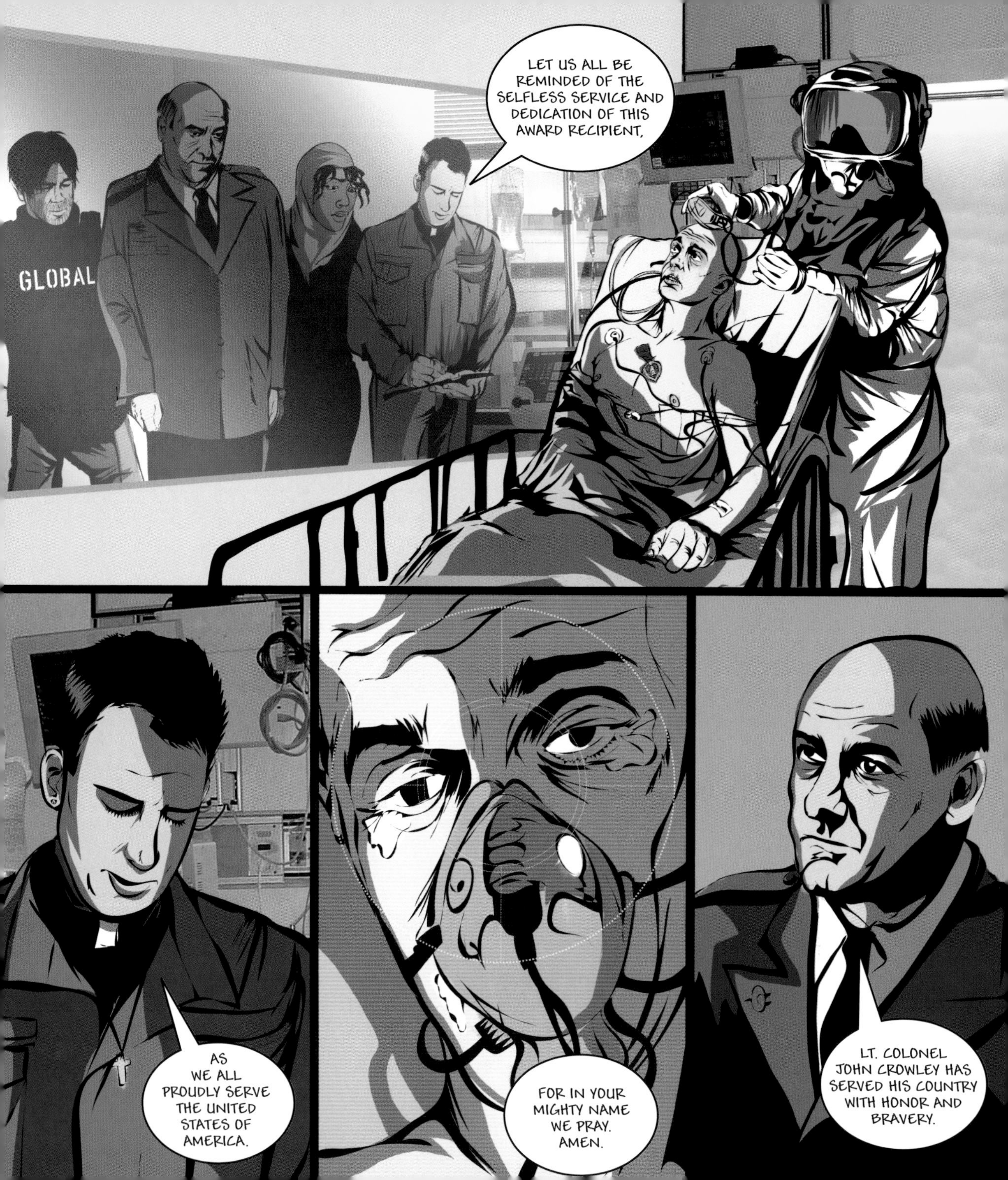
GLOBAL
LET US ALL BE REMINDED OF THE SELFLESS SERVICE AND DEDICATION OF THIS AWARD RECIPIENT,
AS WE ALL PROUDLY SERVE THE UNITED STATES OF AMERICA.
FOR IN YOUR MIGHTY NAME WE PRAY. AMEN.
LT. COLONEL JOHN CROWLEY HAS SERVED HIS COUNTRY WITH HONOR AND BRAVERY.

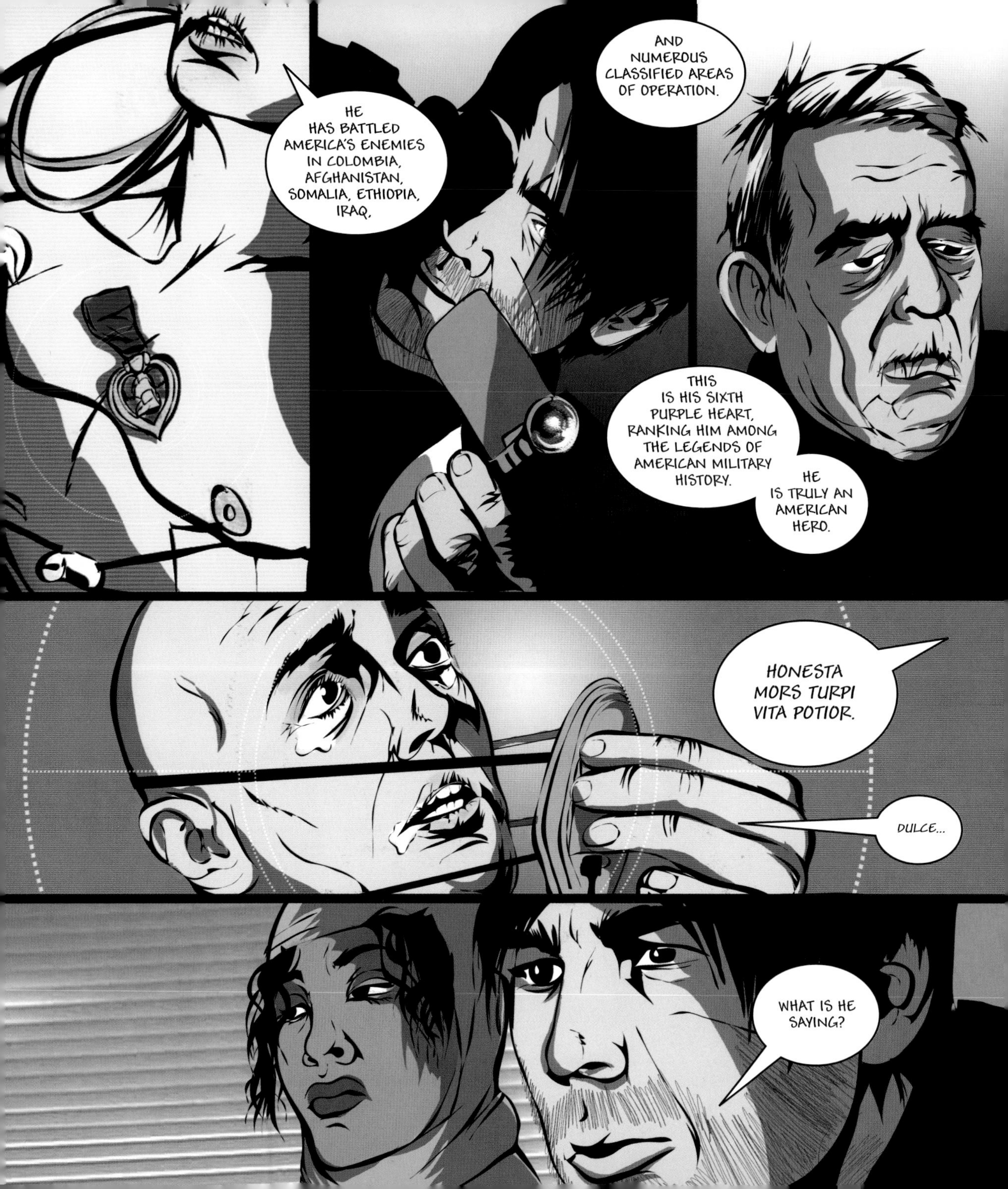
HE HAS BATTLED AMERICA'S ENEMIES IN COLOMBIA, AFGHANISTAN, SOMALIA, ETHIOPIA, IRAQ,
AND NUMEROUS CLASSIFIED AREAS OF OPERATION.
THIS IS HIS SIXTH PURPLE HEART, RANKING HIM AMONG THE LEGENDS OF AMERICAN MILITARY HISTORY.
HE IS TRULY AN AMERICAN HERO.
HONESTA MORS TURPI VITA POTIOR.
DULCE...
WHAT IS HE SAYING?

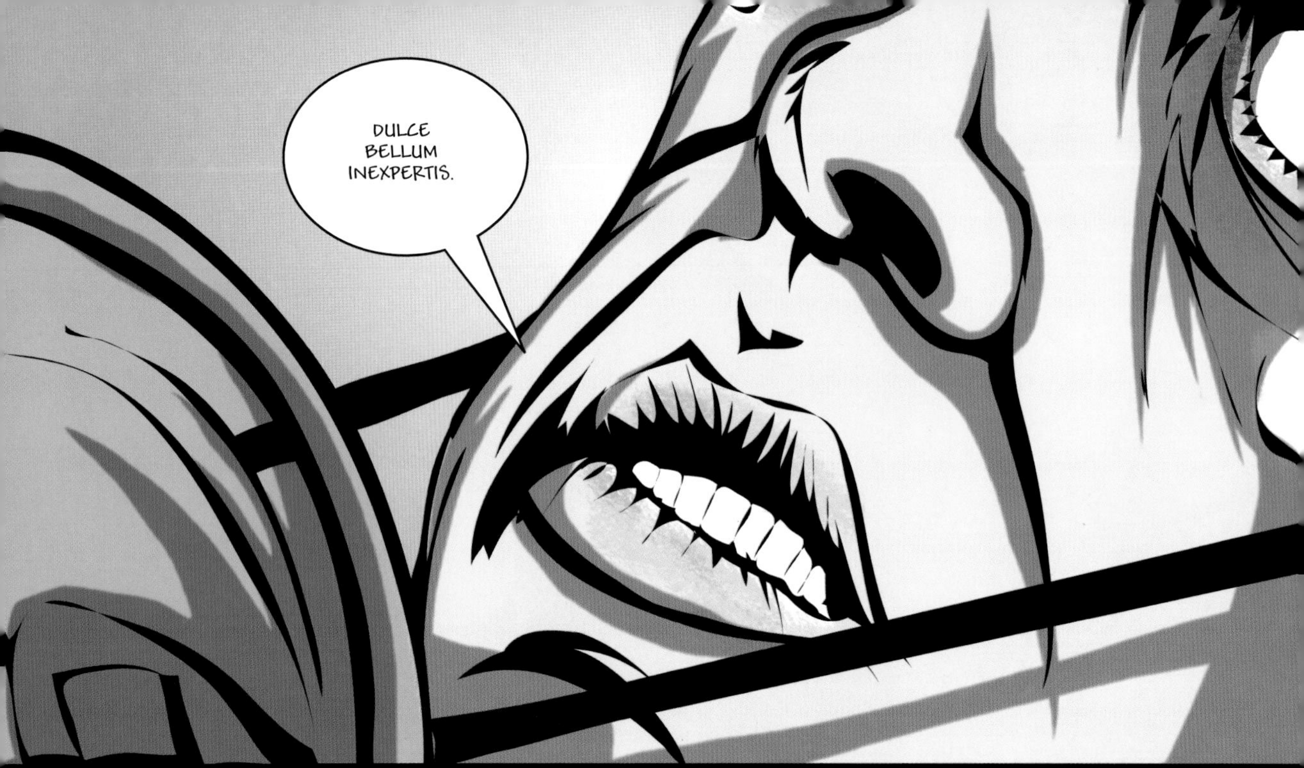
DULCE BELLUM INEXPERTIS.

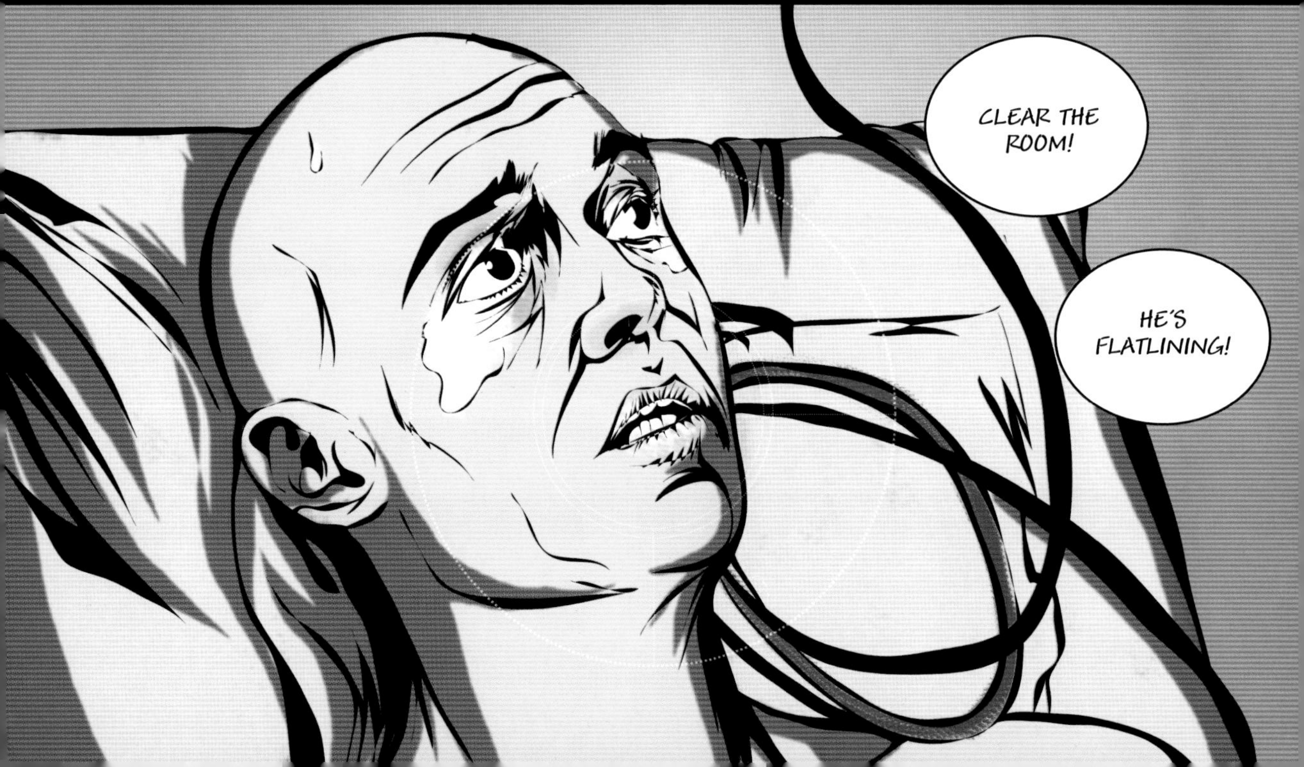
CLEAR THE ROOM!
HE'S FLATLINING!

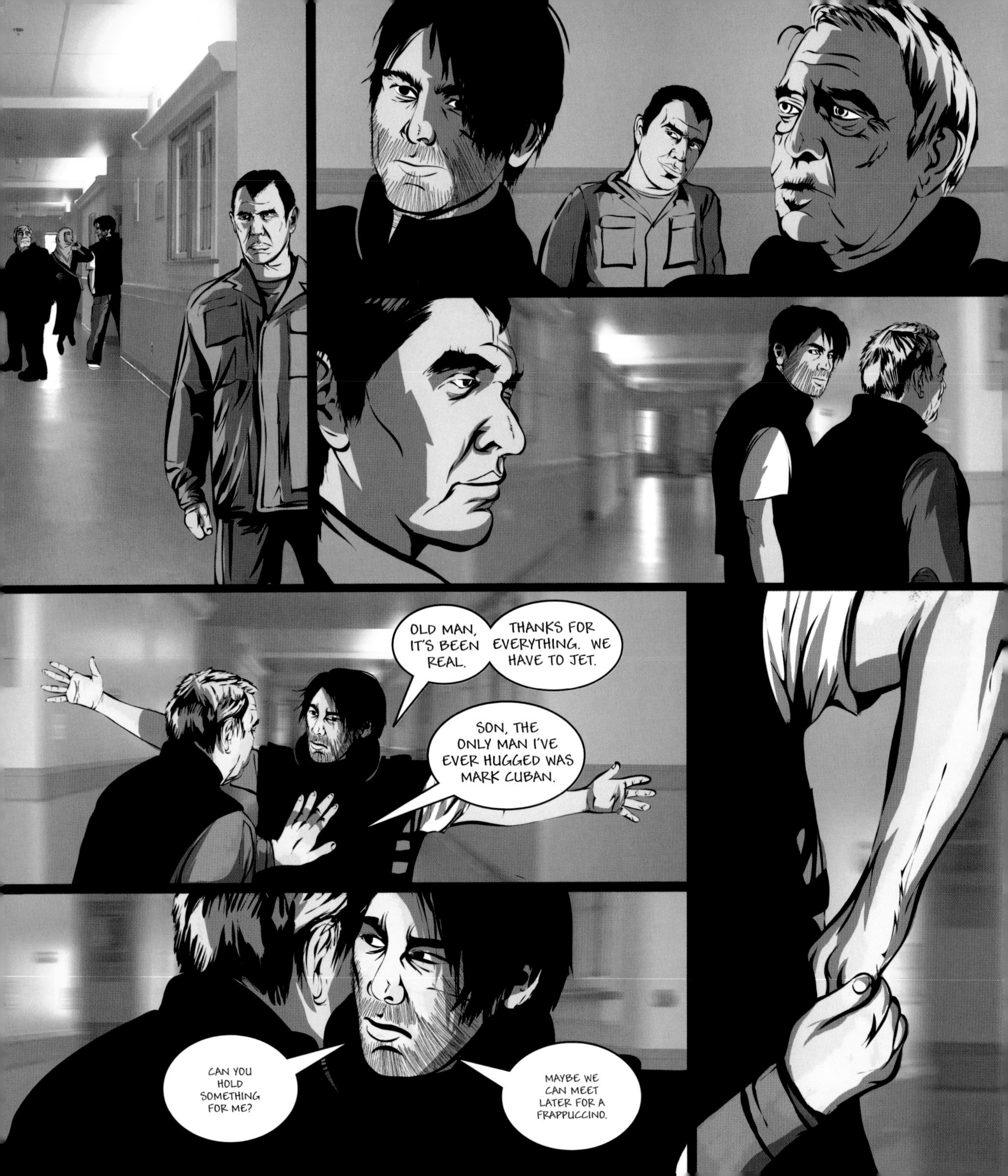
OLD MAN, IT'S BEEN REAL.
THANKS FOR EVERYTHING. WE HAVE TO JET.
SON, THE ONLY MAN I'VE EVER HUGGED WAS MARK CUBAN.
CAN YOU HOLD SOMETHING FOR ME?
MAYBE WE CAN MEET LATER FOR A FRAPPUCCINO.

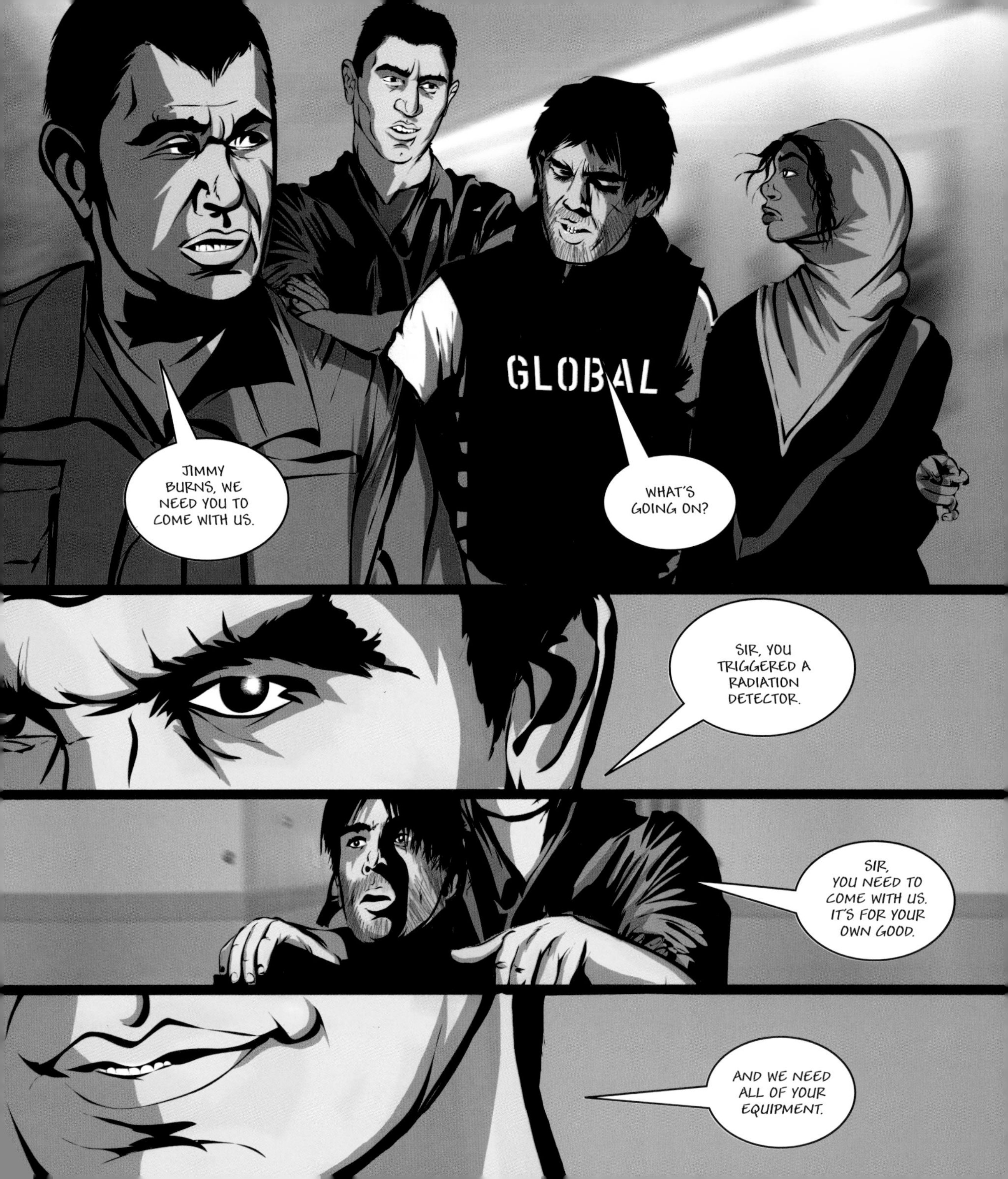
GLOBAL
JIMMY BURNS, WE NEED YOU TO COME WITH US.
WHAT'S GOING ON?
SIR, YOU TRIGGERED A RADIATION DETECTOR.
SIR, YOU NEED TO COME WITH US. IT'S FOR YOUR OWN GOOD.
AND WE NEED ALL OF YOUR EQUIPMENT.

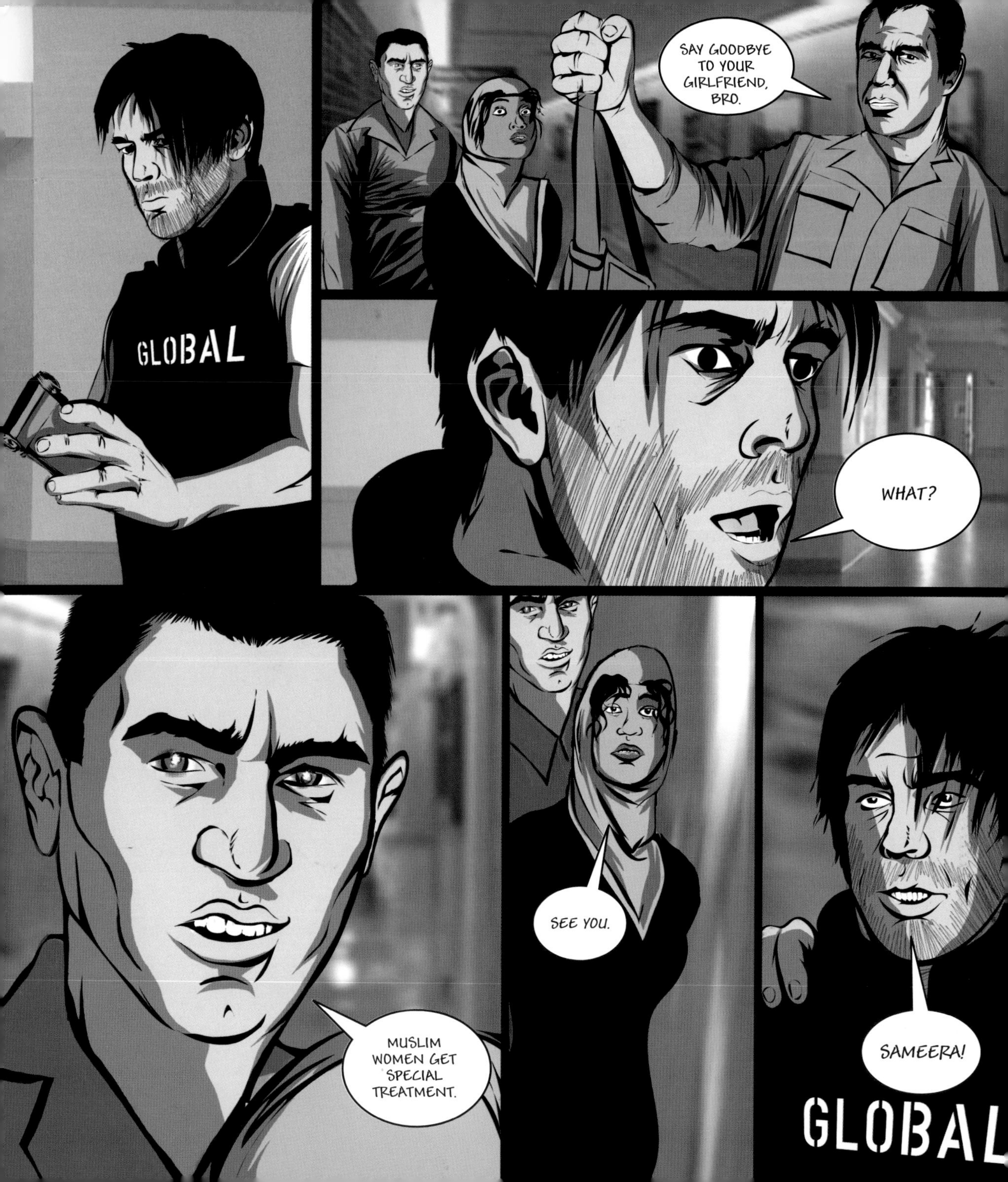
GLOBAL
SAY GOODBYE TO YOUR GIRLFRIEND, BRO.
WHAT?
MUSLIM WOMEN GET SPECIAL TREATMENT.
SEE YOU.
SAMEERA!
GLOBAL

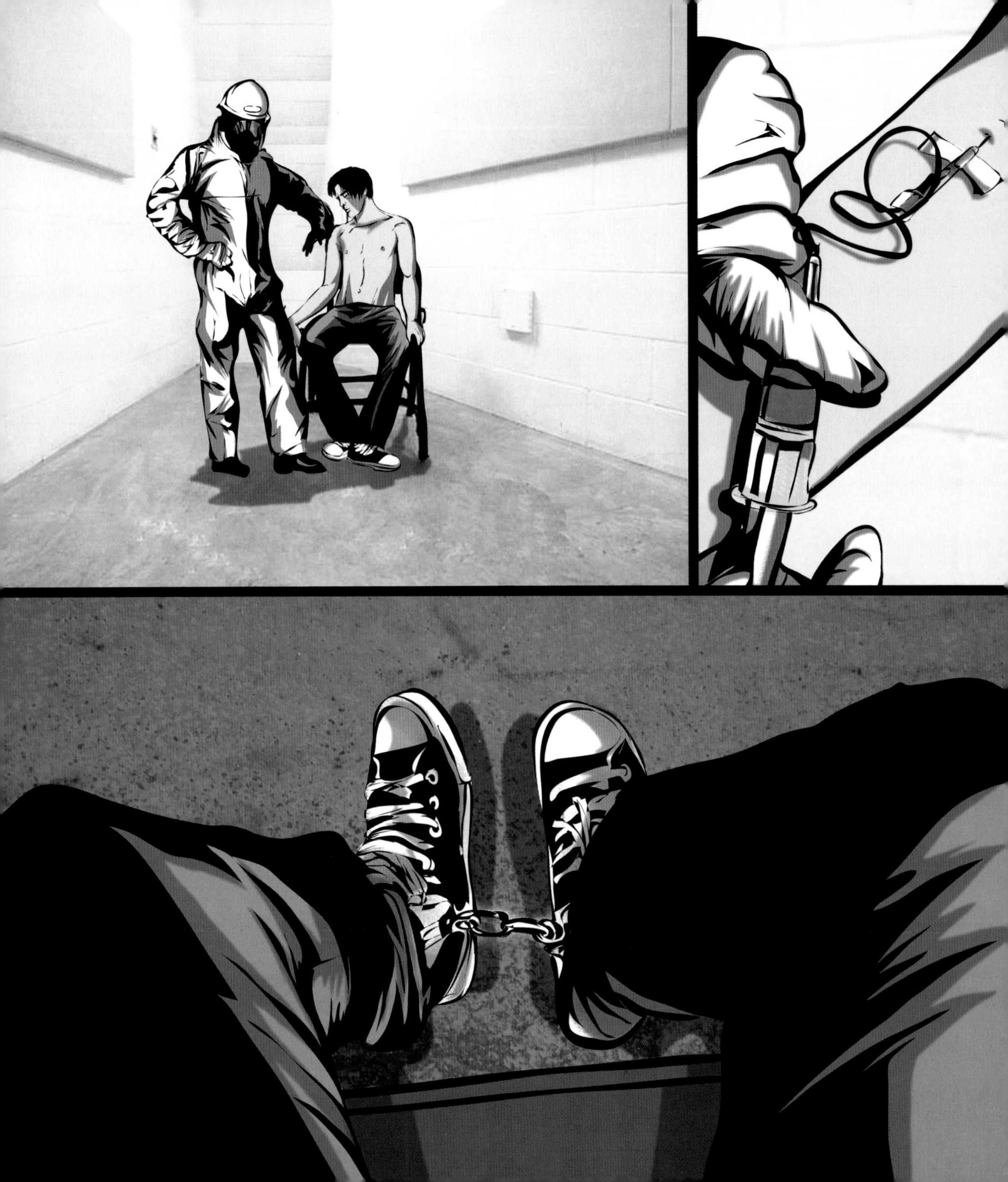

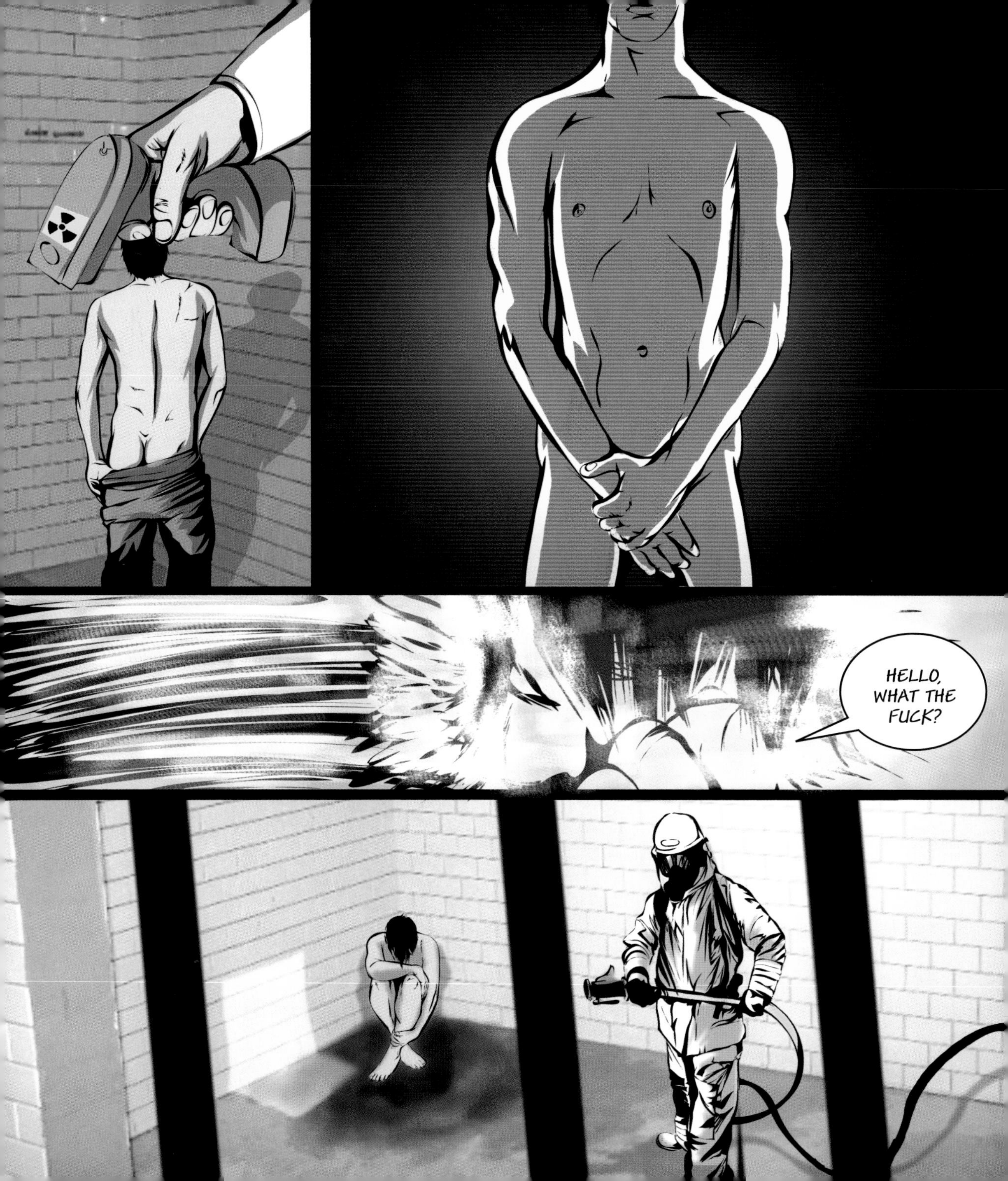
HELLO, WHAT THE FUCK?

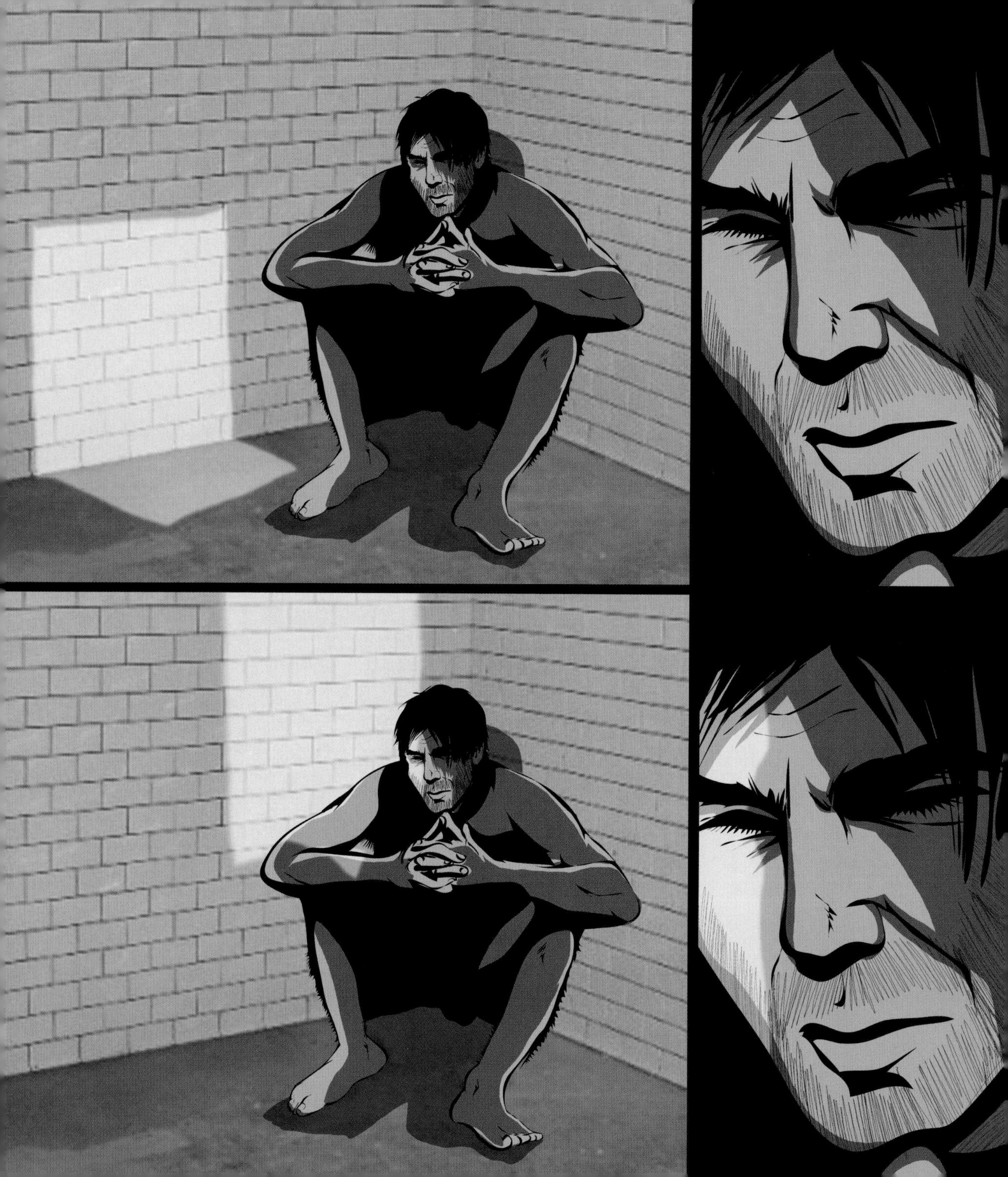

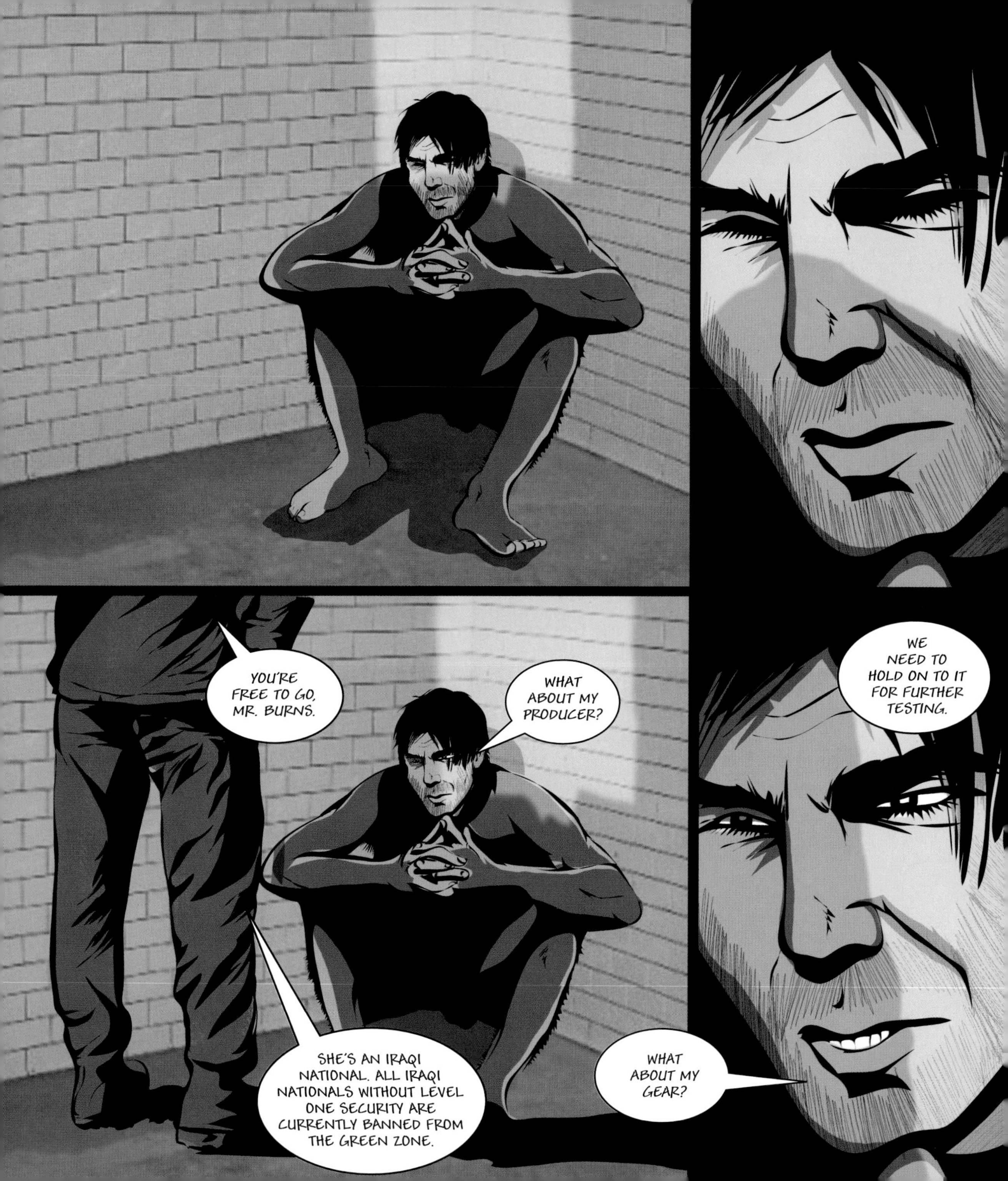
YOU'RE FREE TO GO, MR. BURNS.
WHAT ABOUT MY PRODUCER?
SHE'S AN IRAQI NATIONAL. ALL IRAQI NATIONALS WITHOUT LEVEL ONE SECURITY ARE CURRENTLY BANNED FROM THE GREEN ZONE.
WE NEED TO HOLD ON TO IT FOR FURTHER TESTING.
WHAT ABOUT MY GEAR?

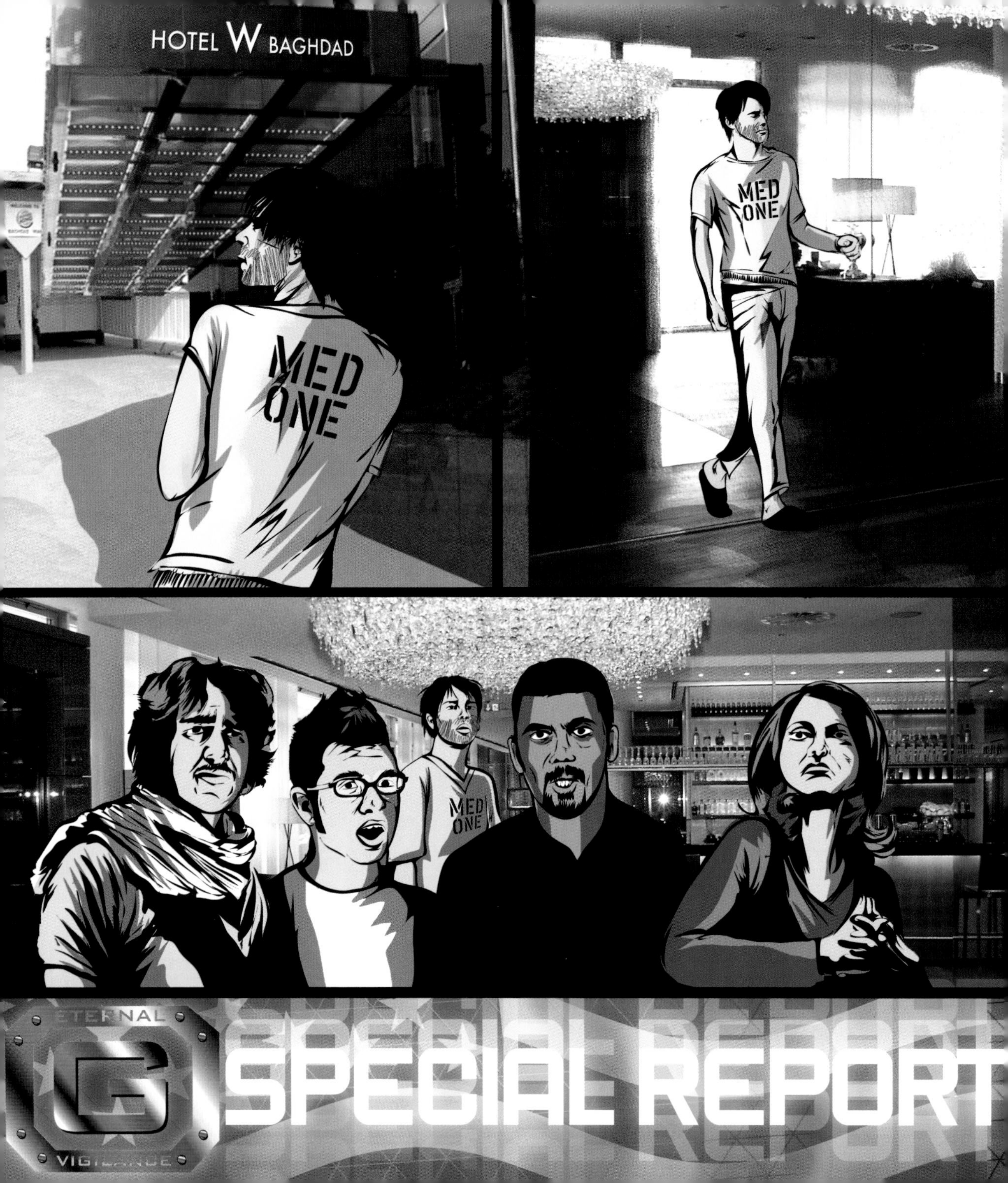
HOTEL W BAGHDAD
MED ONE
MED ONE
MED ONE
ETERNAL
VIGILANCE
SPECIAL REPORT

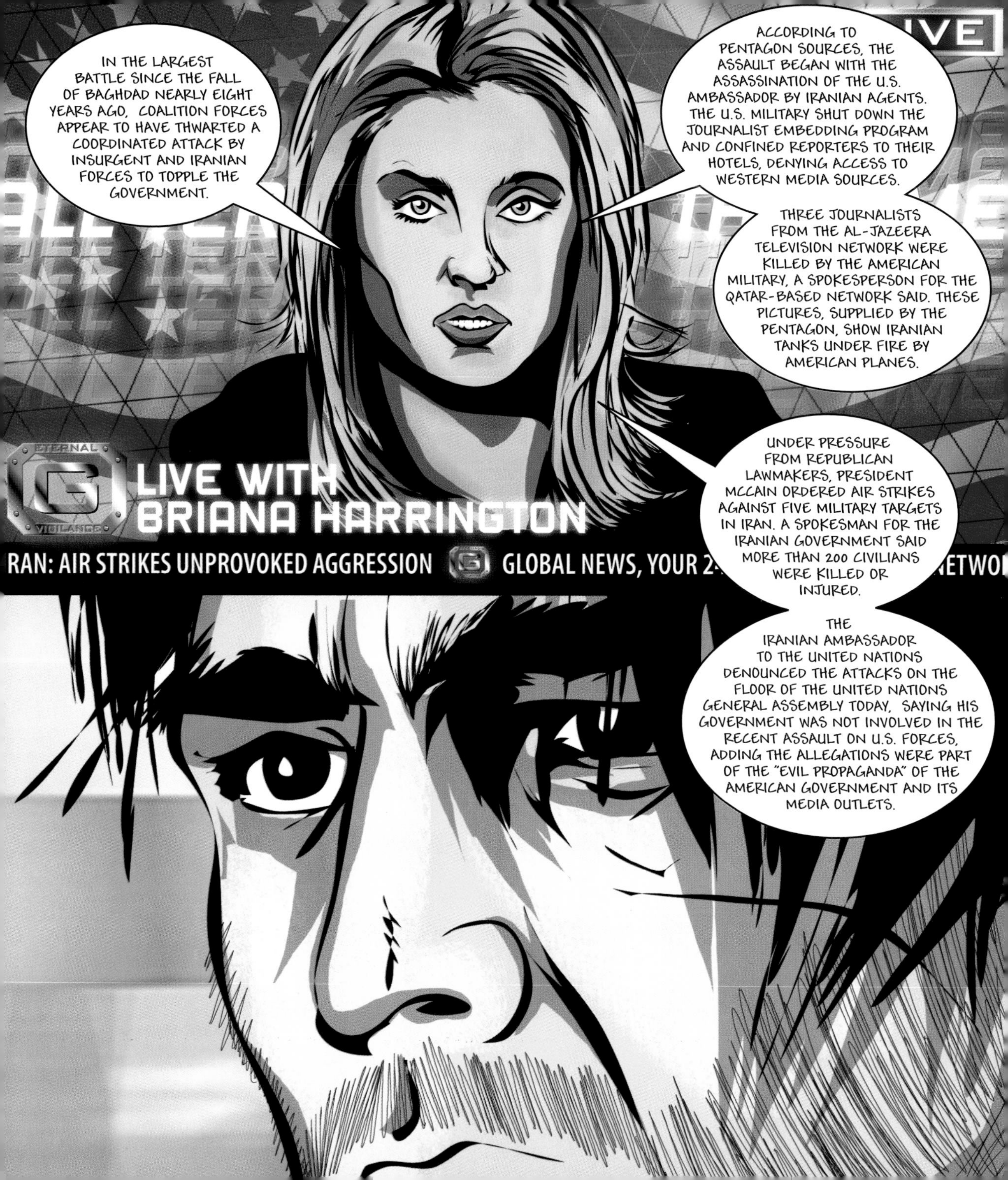
LIVE
IN THE LARGEST BATTLE SINCE THE FALL OF BAGHDAD NEARLY EIGHT YEARS AGO, COALITION FORCES APPEAR TO HAVE THWARTED A COORDINATED ATTACK BY INSURGENT AND IRANIAN FORCES TO TOPPLE THE GOVERNMENT.
ACCORDING TO PENTAGON SOURCES, THE ASSAULT BEGAN WITH THE ASSASSINATION OF THE U.S. AMBASSADOR BY IRANIAN AGENTS. THE U.S. MILITARY SHUT DOWN THE JOURNALIST EMBEDDING PROGRAM AND CONFINED REPORTERS TO THEIR HOTELS, DENYING ACCESS TO WESTERN MEDIA SOURCES.
THREE JOURNALISTS FROM THE AL-JAZEERA TELEVISION NETWORK WERE KILLED BY THE AMERICAN MILITARY, A SPOKESPERSON FOR THE QATAR-BASED NETWORK SAID. THESE PICTURES, SUPPLIED BY THE PENTAGON, SHOW IRANIAN TANKS UNDER FIRE BY AMERICAN PLANES.
ETERNAL VIGILANCE
LIVE WITH BRIANA HARRINGTON
UNDER PRESSURE FROM REPUBLICAN LAWMAKERS, PRESIDENT MCCAIN ORDERED AIR STRIKES AGAINST FIVE MILITARY TARGETS IN IRAN. A SPOKESMAN FOR THE IRANIAN GOVERNMENT SAID MORE THAN 200 CIVILIANS WERE KILLED OR INJURED.
RAN: AIR STRIKES UNPROVOKED AGGRESSION
GLOBAL NEWS, YOUR 2
NETWO
THE IRANIAN AMBASSADOR TO THE UNITED NATIONS DENOUNCED THE ATTACKS ON THE FLOOR OF THE UNITED NATIONS GENERAL ASSEMBLY TODAY, SAYING HIS GOVERNMENT WAS NOT INVOLVED IN THE RECENT ASSAULT ON U.S. FORCES, ADDING THE ALLEGATIONS WERE PART OF THE "EVIL PROPAGANDA" OF THE AMERICAN GOVERNMENT AND ITS MEDIA OUTLETS.

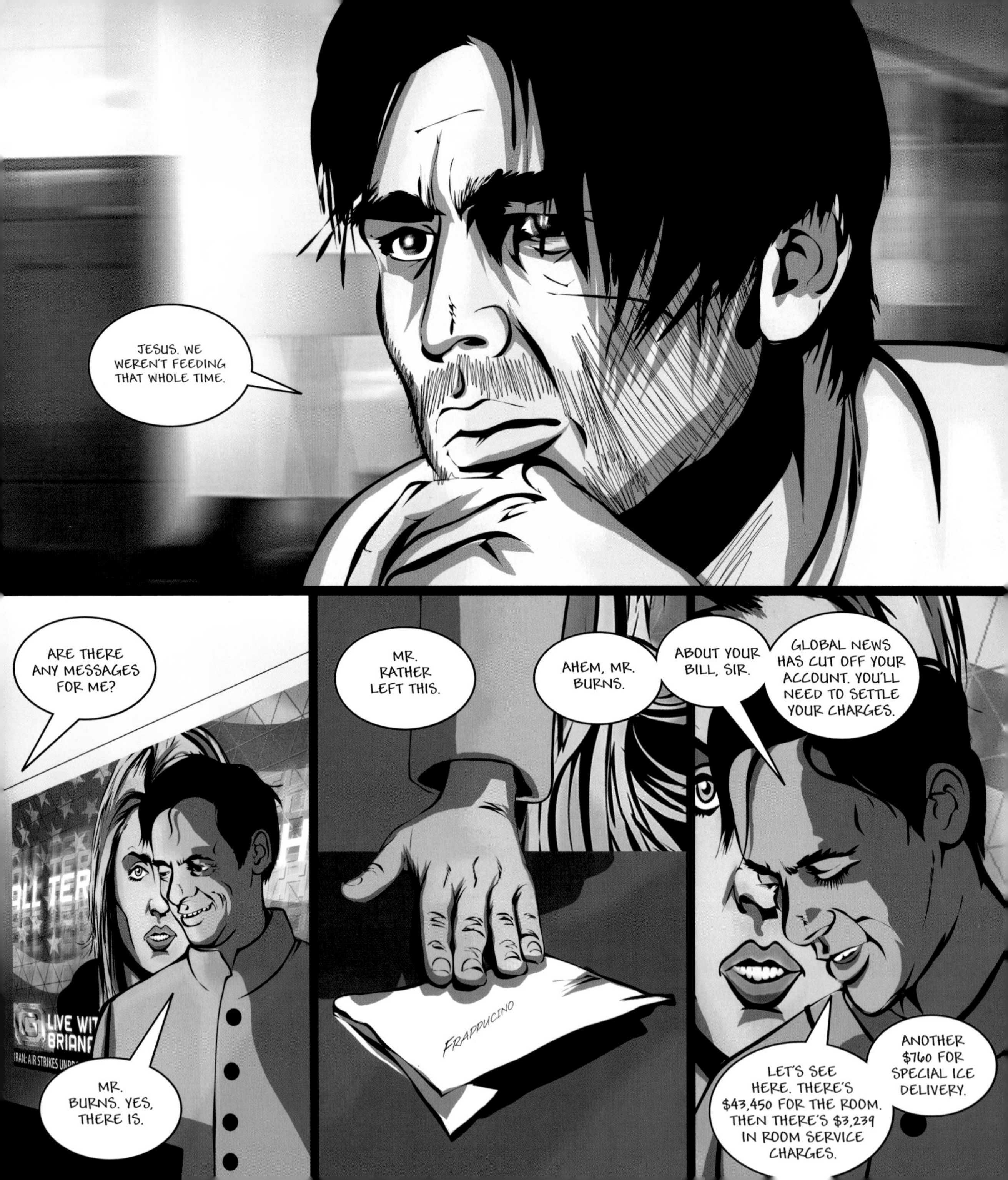
JESUS. WE WEREN'T FEEDING THAT WHOLE TIME.
ARE THERE ANY MESSAGES FOR ME?
ALL TER
LIVE WIT
BRIAN
IRAN: AIR STRIKES UNPR
MR. BURNS. YES, THERE IS.
MR. RATHER LEFT THIS.
FRAPPUCINO
AHEM, MR. BURNS.
ABOUT YOUR BILL, SIR.
GLOBAL NEWS HAS CUT OFF YOUR ACCOUNT. YOU'LL NEED TO SETTLE YOUR CHARGES.
LET'S SEE HERE. THERE'S $43,450 FOR THE ROOM. THEN THERE'S $3,239 IN ROOM SERVICE CHARGES.
ANOTHER $760 FOR SPECIAL ICE DELIVERY.

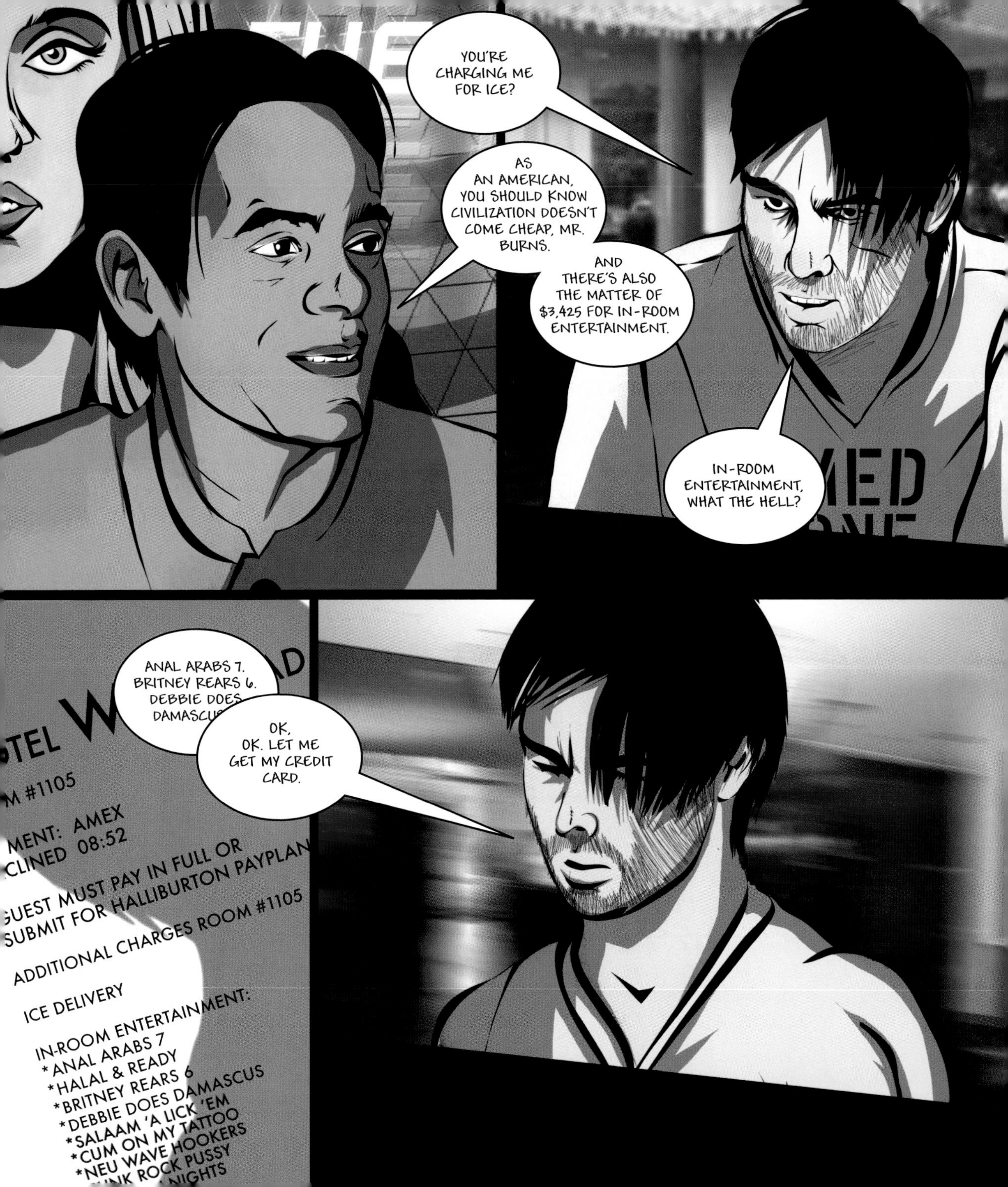
YOU'RE CHARGING ME FOR ICE?
AS AN AMERICAN, YOU SHOULD KNOW CIVILIZATION DOESN'T COME CHEAP, MR. BURNS.
AND THERE'S ALSO THE MATTER OF $3,425 FOR IN-ROOM ENTERTAINMENT.
IN-ROOM ENTERTAINMENT, WHAT THE HELL?
TEL
M #1105
MENT: AMEX
CLINED 08:52
GUEST MUST PAY IN FULL OR
SUBMIT FOR HALLIBURTON PAYPLAN
ADDITIONAL CHARGES ROOM #1105
ICE DELIVERY
IN-ROOM ENTERTAINMENT:
*ANAL ARABS 7
*HALAL & READY
*BRITNEY REARS 6
*DEBBIE DOES DAMASCUS
*SALAAM 'A LICK 'EM
*CUM ON MY TATTOO
*NEU WAVE HOOKERS
ROCK PUSSY
NIGHTS
ANAL ARABS 7. BRITNEY REARS 6. DEBBIE DOES
OK, OK. LET ME GET MY CREDIT CARD.

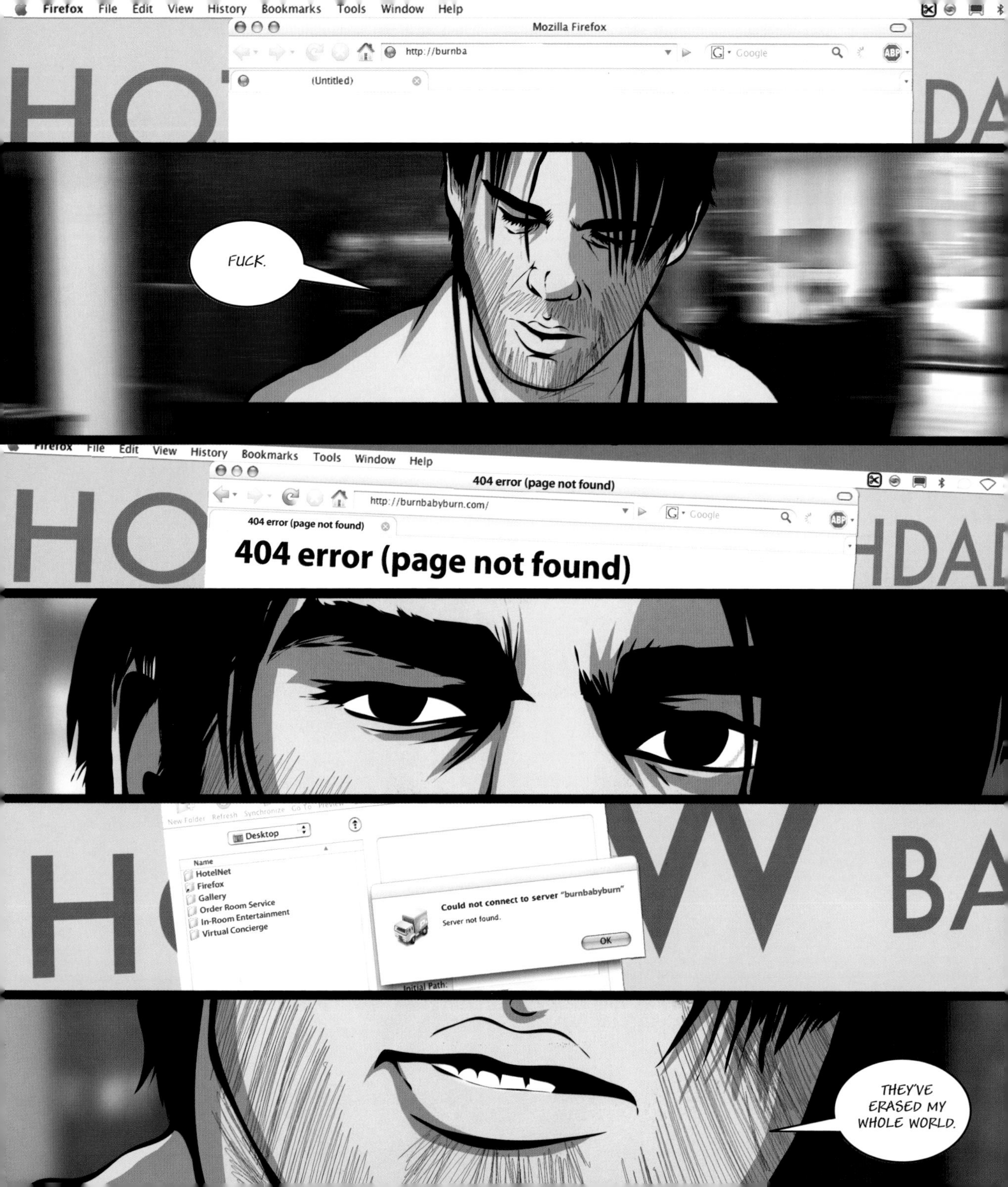

Firefox File Edit View History Bookmarks Tools Window Help
Mozilla Firefox
http://burnba
(Untitled)
FUCK.
404 error (page not found)
http://burnbabyburn.com/
404 error (page not found)
404 error (page not found)
Desktop
Name
HotelNet
Firefox
Gallery
Order Room Service
In-Room Entertainment
Virtual Concierge
Could not connect to server "burnbabyburn"
Server not found.
OK
THEY'VE ERASED MY WHOLE WORLD.

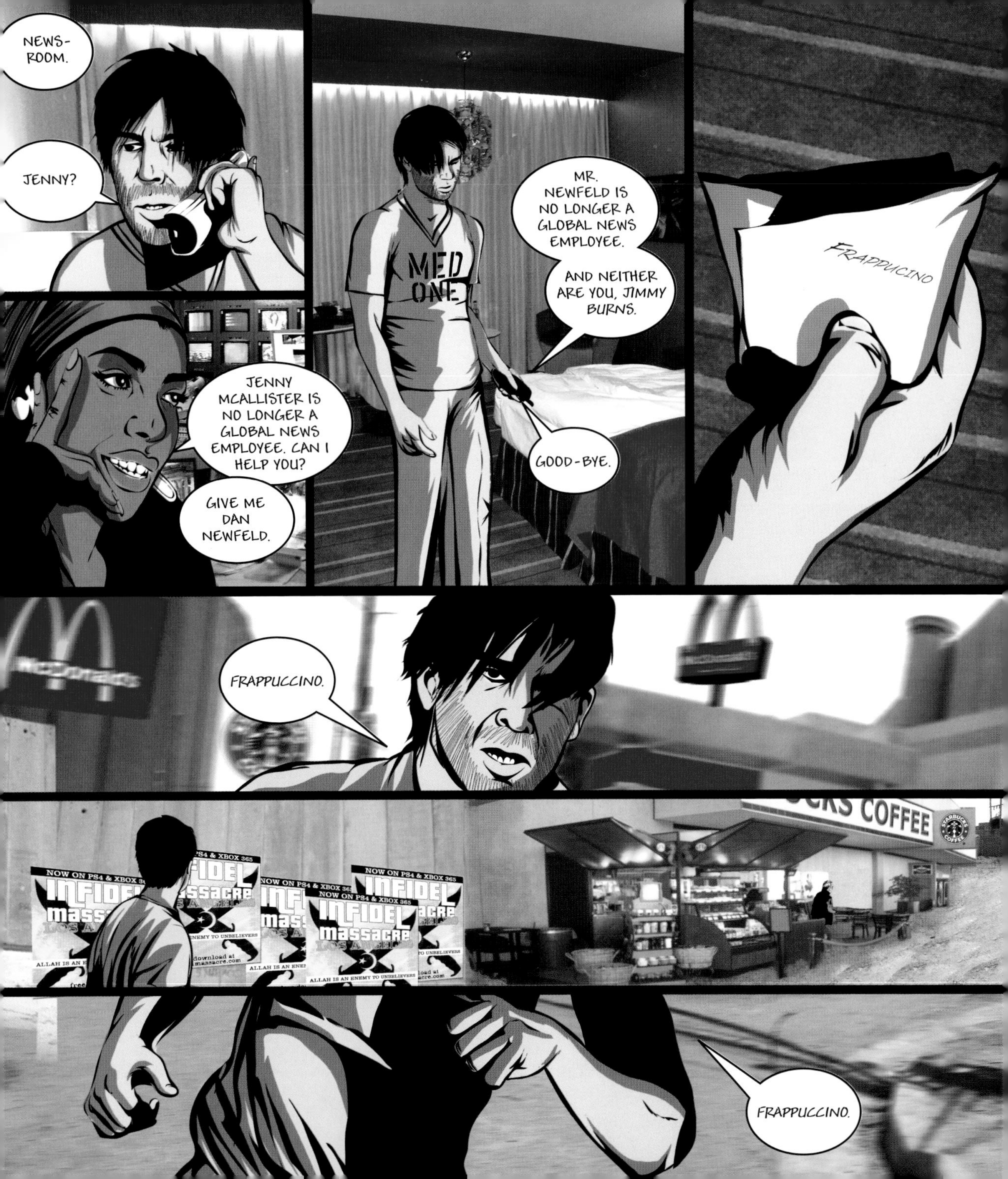
NEWS-ROOM.
JENNY?
JENNY MCALLISTER IS NO LONGER A GLOBAL NEWS EMPLOYEE. CAN I HELP YOU?
GIVE ME DAN NEWFELD.
MED ONE
MR. NEWFELD IS NO LONGER A GLOBAL NEWS EMPLOYEE.
AND NEITHER ARE YOU, JIMMY BURNS.
GOOD-BYE.
FRAPPUCCINO
FRAPPUCCINO.
NOW ON PS4 & XBOX 365
INFIDEL massacre
ALLAH IS AN ENEMY TO UNBELIEVERS
COFFEE
STARBUCKS COFFEE
FRAPPUCCINO.

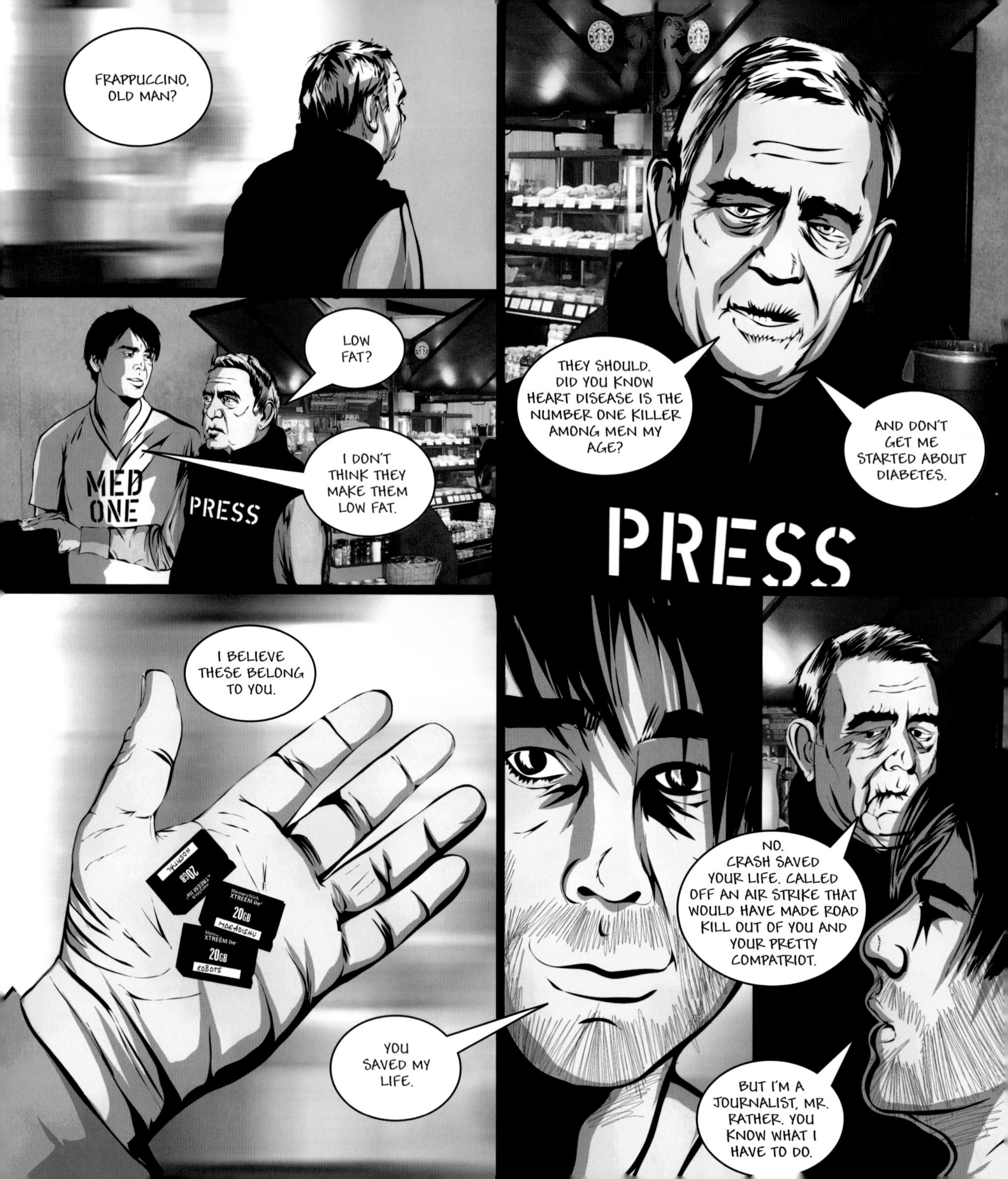
FRAPPUCCINO, OLD MAN?
LOW FAT?
I DON'T THINK THEY MAKE THEM LOW FAT.
MED ONE
PRESS
THEY SHOULD. DID YOU KNOW HEART DISEASE IS THE NUMBER ONE KILLER AMONG MEN MY AGE?
AND DON'T GET ME STARTED ABOUT DIABETES.
PRESS
I BELIEVE THESE BELONG TO YOU.
20GB
MemoryStick XTREEM IIe
20GB
MOGADISHU
XTREEM IIe
20GB
ROBOTS
YOU SAVED MY LIFE.
NO. CRASH SAVED YOUR LIFE. CALLED OFF AN AIR STRIKE THAT WOULD HAVE MADE ROAD KILL OUT OF YOU AND YOUR PRETTY COMPATRIOT.
BUT I'M A JOURNALIST, MR. RATHER. YOU KNOW WHAT I HAVE TO DO.

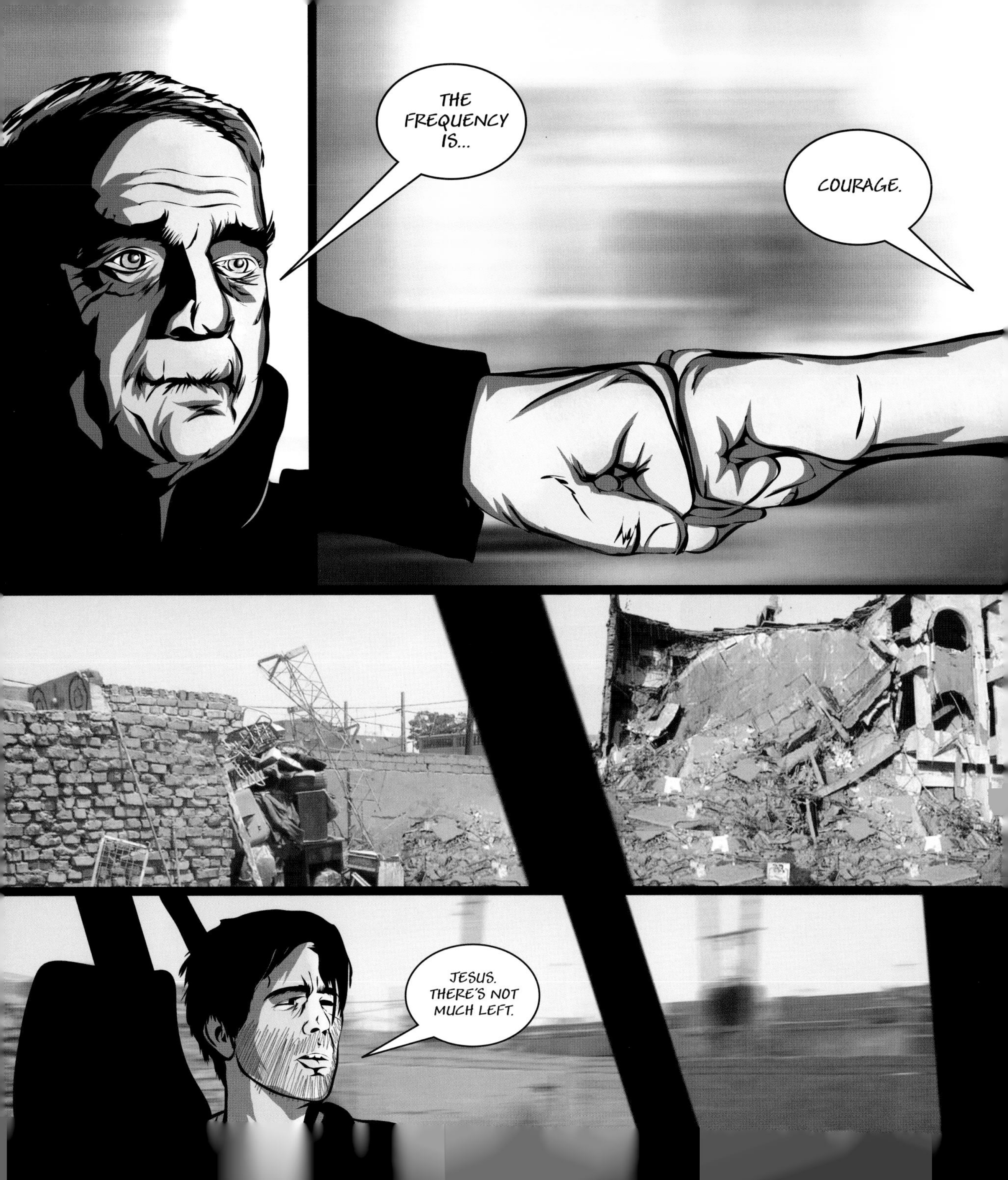
THE FREQUENCY IS...
COURAGE.
JESUS. THERE'S NOT MUCH LEFT.

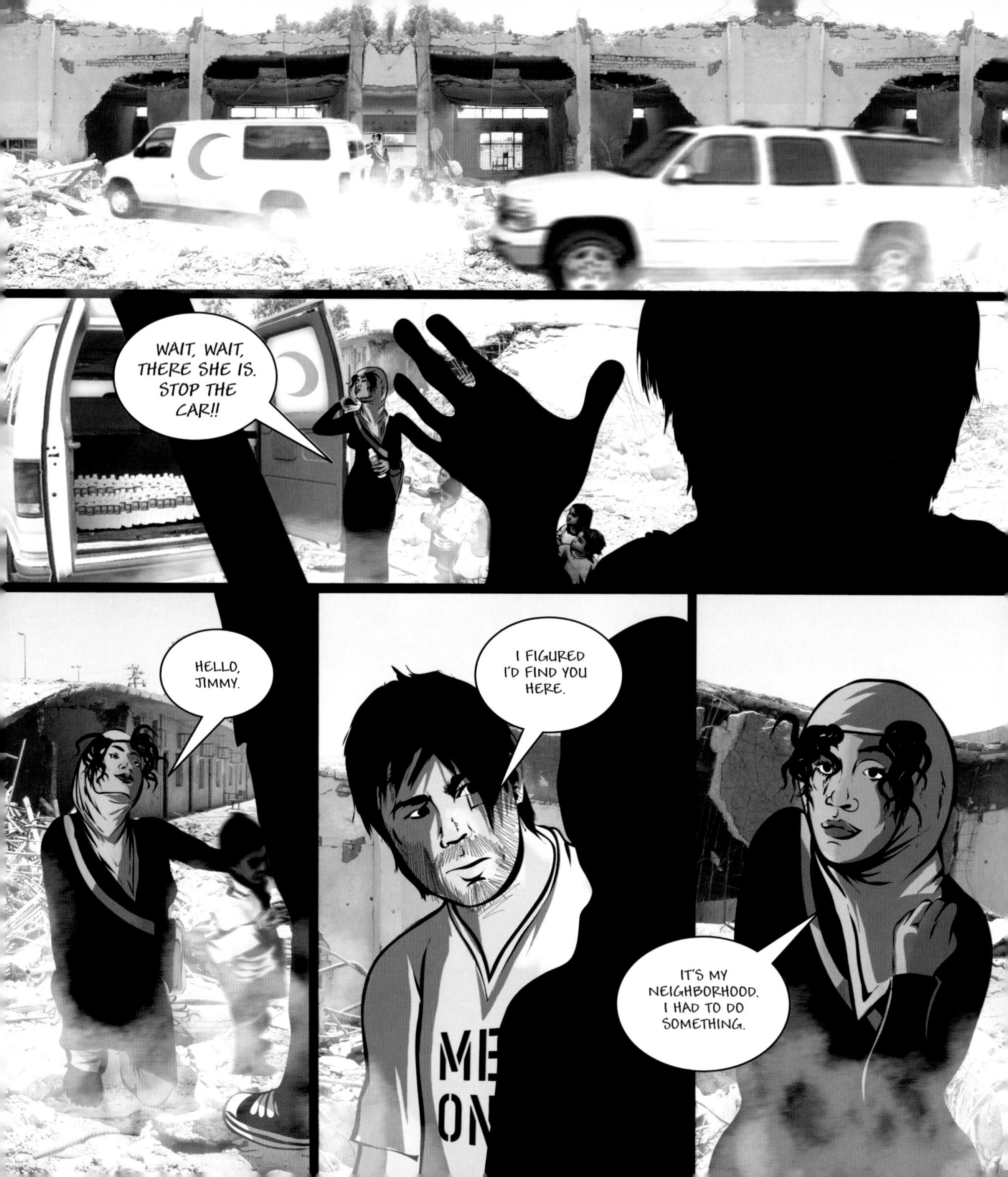
WAIT, WAIT, THERE SHE IS. STOP THE CAR!!
HELLO, JIMMY.
I FIGURED I'D FIND YOU HERE.
IT'S MY NEIGHBORHOOD. I HAD TO DO SOMETHING.
ME
ON

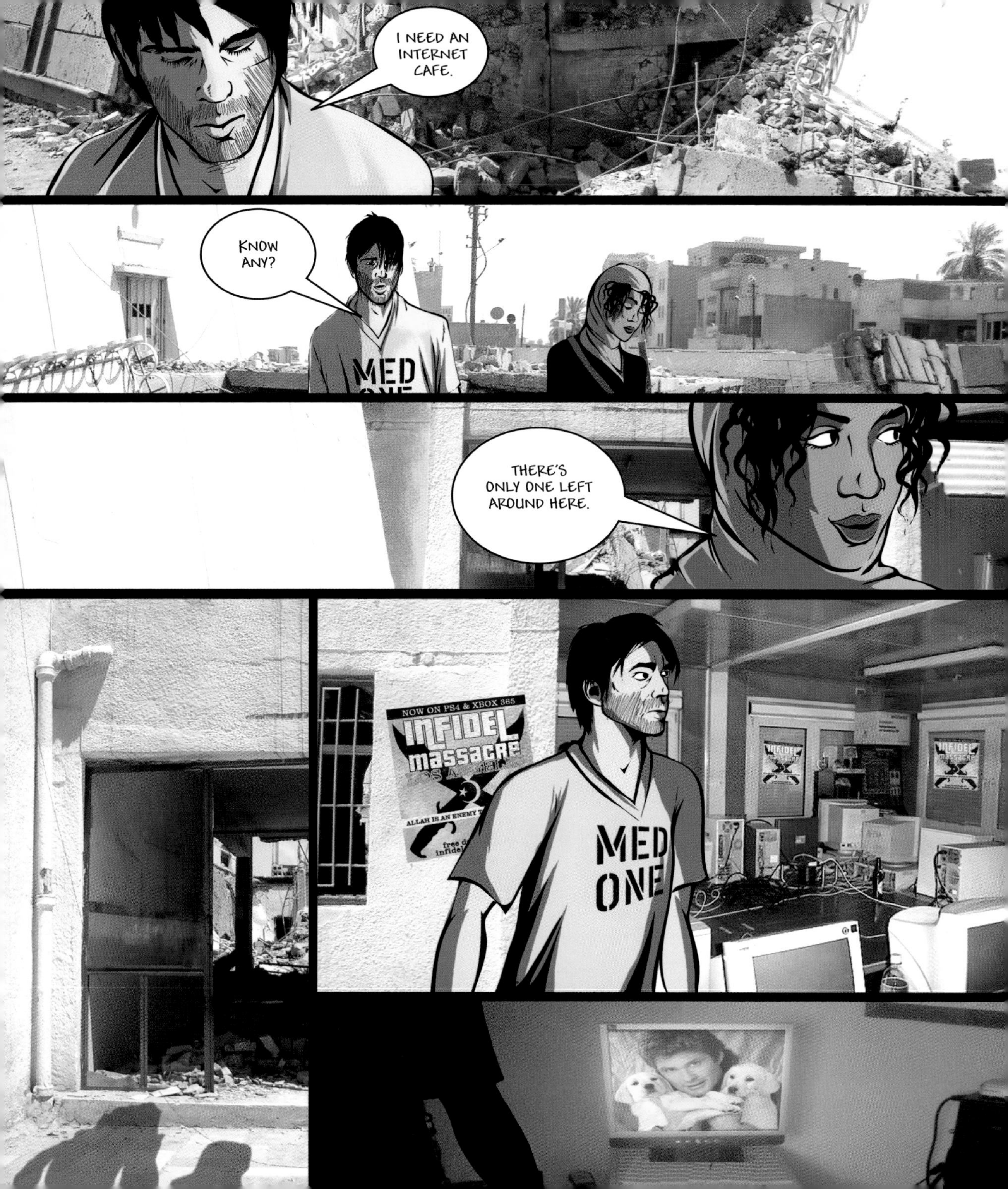
I NEED AN INTERNET CAFE.
KNOW ANY?
MED ONE
THERE'S ONLY ONE LEFT AROUND HERE.
NOW ON PS4 & XBOX 365
INFIDEL massacre
MED ONE

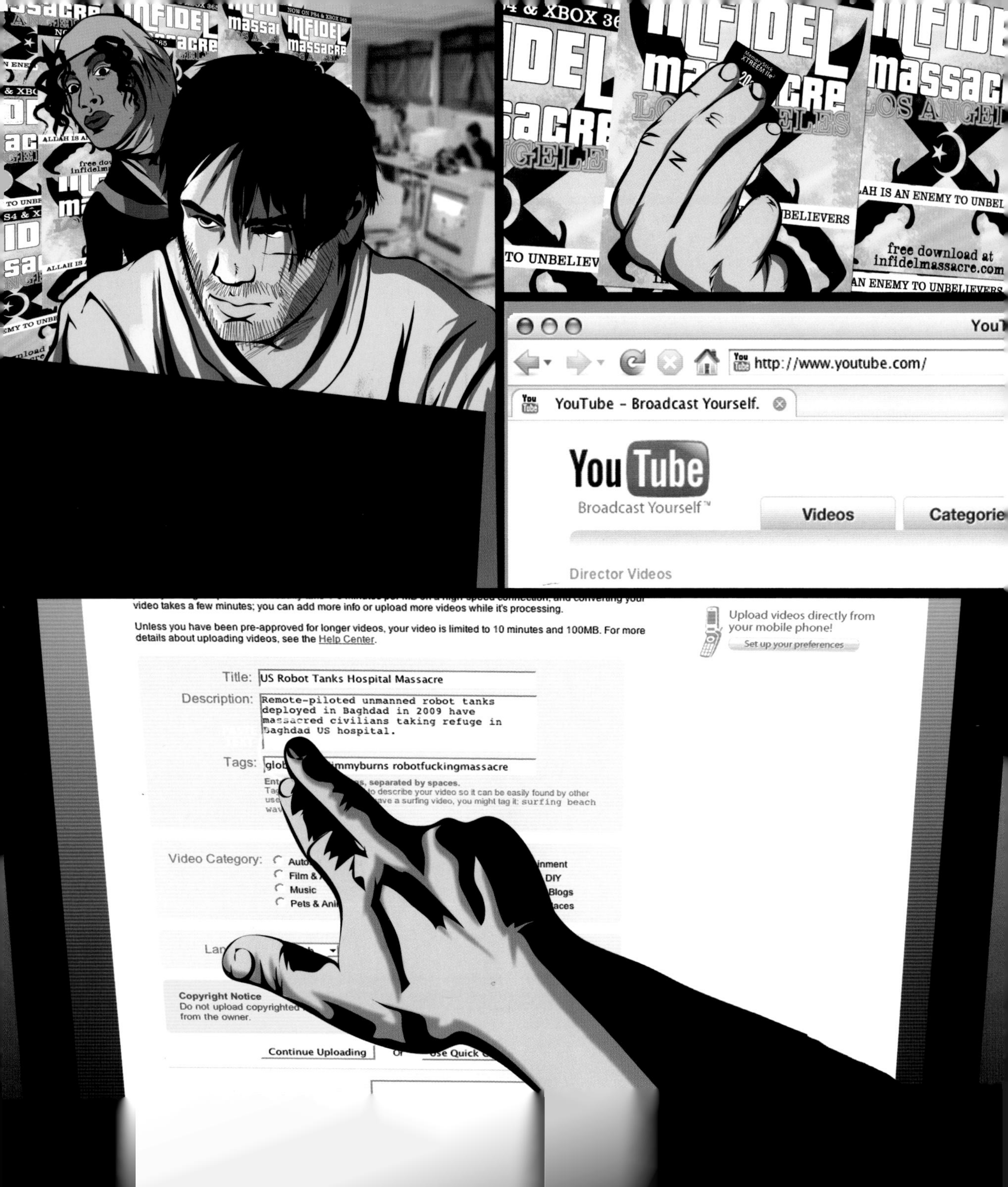
ALLAH IS AN ENEMY TO UNBELIEVERS
free download at
infidelmassacre.com
YouTube
http://www.youtube.com/
YouTube - Broadcast Yourself.
You Tube
Broadcast Yourself™
Videos
Director Videos
video takes a few minutes; you can add more info or upload more videos while it's processing.
Unless you have been pre-approved for longer videos, your video is limited to 10 minutes and 100MB. For more details about uploading videos, see the Help Center.
Upload videos directly from your mobile phone!
Set up your preferences
Title: US Robot Tanks Hospital Massacre
Description: Remote-piloted unmanned robot tanks deployed in Baghdad in 2009 have massacred civilians taking refuge in Baghdad US hospital.
Tags:
robotfuckingmassacre
Video Category:
Music
DIY
Copyright Notice
Continue Uploading

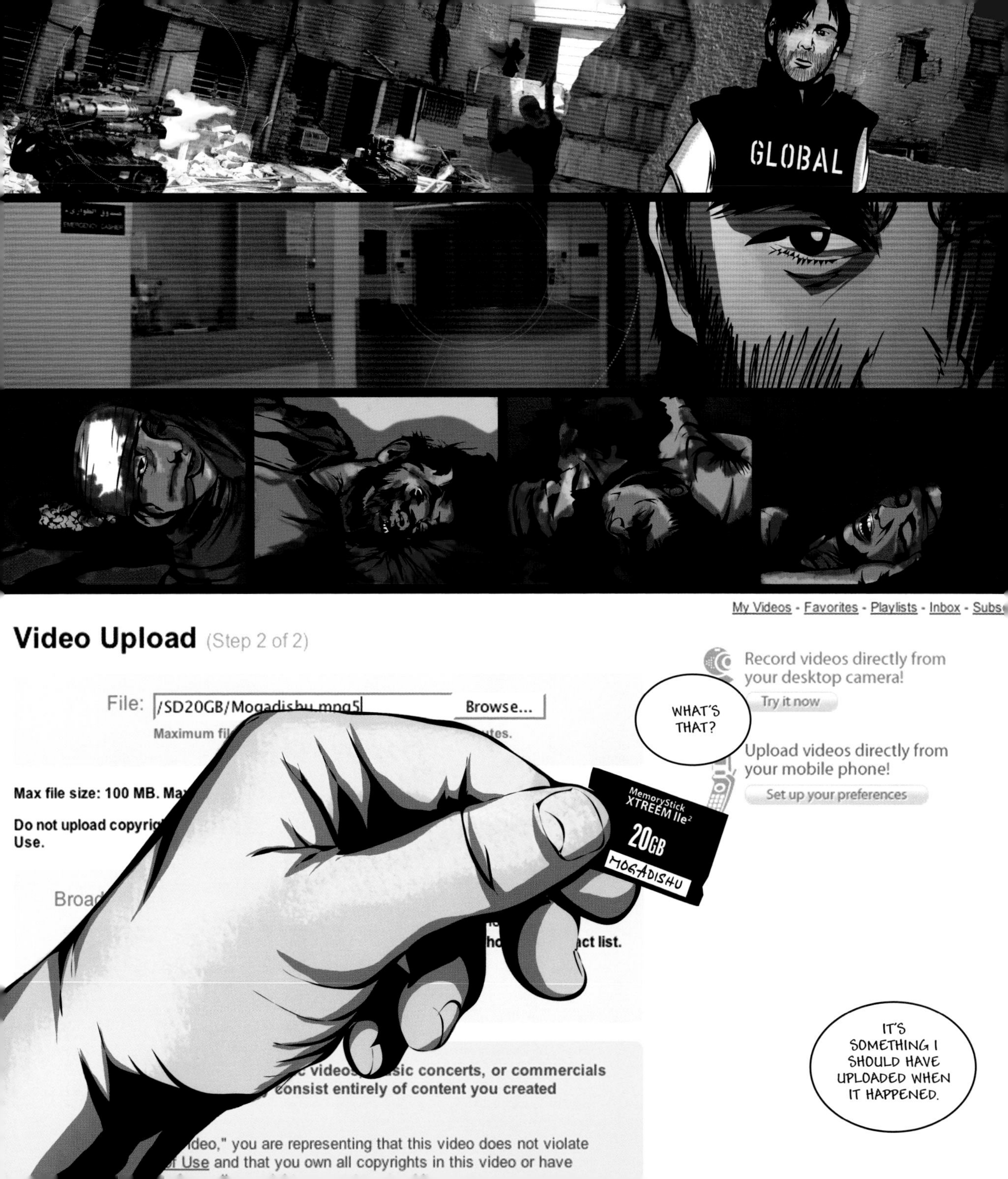

GLOBAL
My Videos - Favorites - Playlists - Inbox - Subs
Video Upload (Step 2 of 2)
File: /SD20GB/Mogadishu.mpg5
Browse...
Maximum fi
utes.
Max file size: 100 MB. Ma
Do not upload copyrig
Use.
Broad
ho
act list.
c videos, usic concerts, or commercials
consist entirely of content you created
ideo," you are representing that this video does not violate
of Use and that you own all copyrights in this video or have
Record videos directly from
your desktop camera!
Try it now
Upload videos directly from
your mobile phone!
Set up your preferences
MemoryStick
XTREEM IIe²
20GB
MOGADISHU
WHAT'S THAT?
IT'S SOMETHING I SHOULD HAVE UPLOADED WHEN IT HAPPENED.

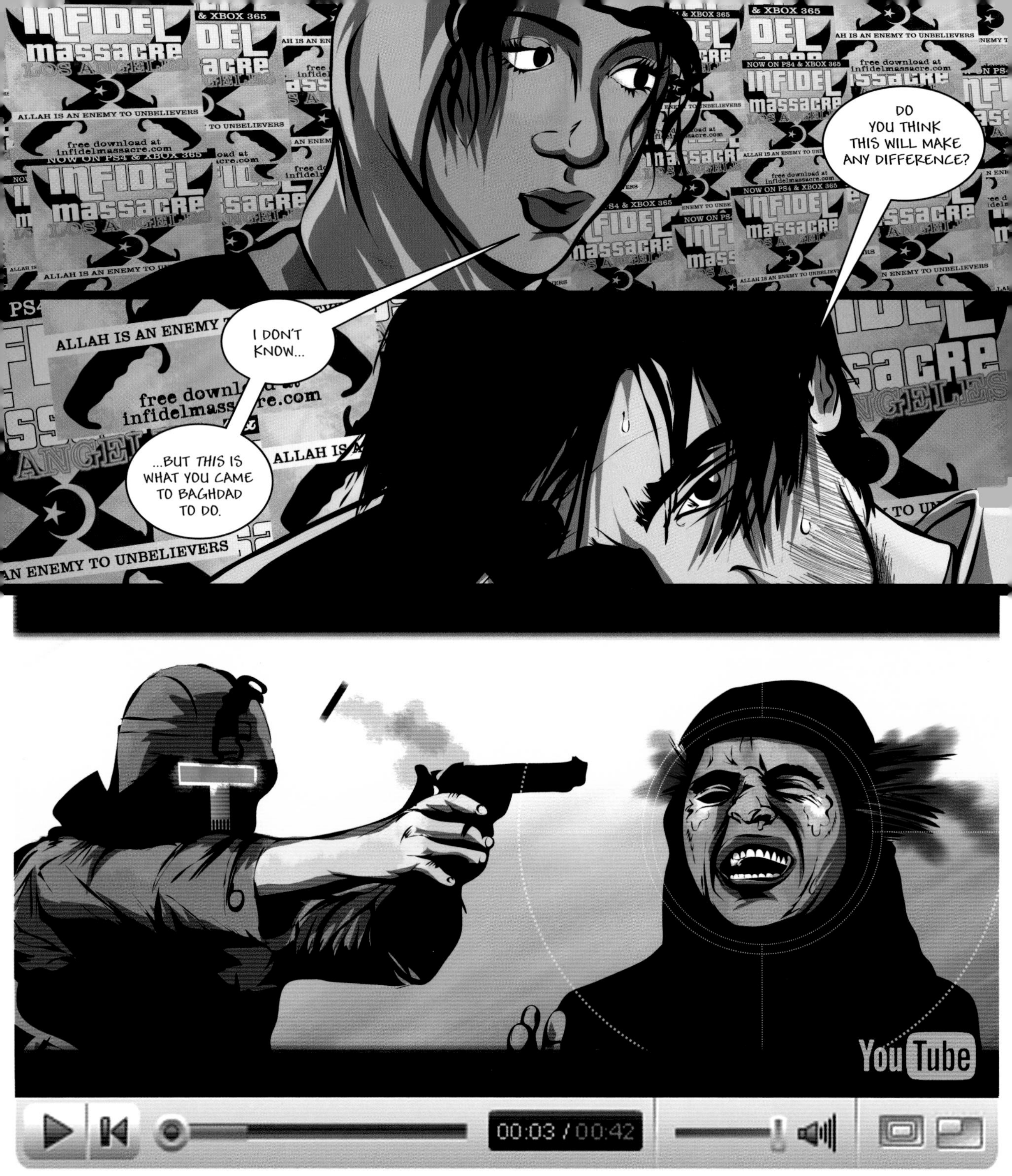
INFIDEL massacre LOS ANGELES
ALLAH IS AN ENEMY TO UNBELIEVERS
free download at infidelmassacre.com
NOW ON PS4 & XBOX 365
DO YOU THINK THIS WILL MAKE ANY DIFFERENCE?
I DON'T KNOW...
...BUT *THIS* IS WHAT YOU CAME TO BAGHDAD TO DO.
YouTube
00:03 / 00:42

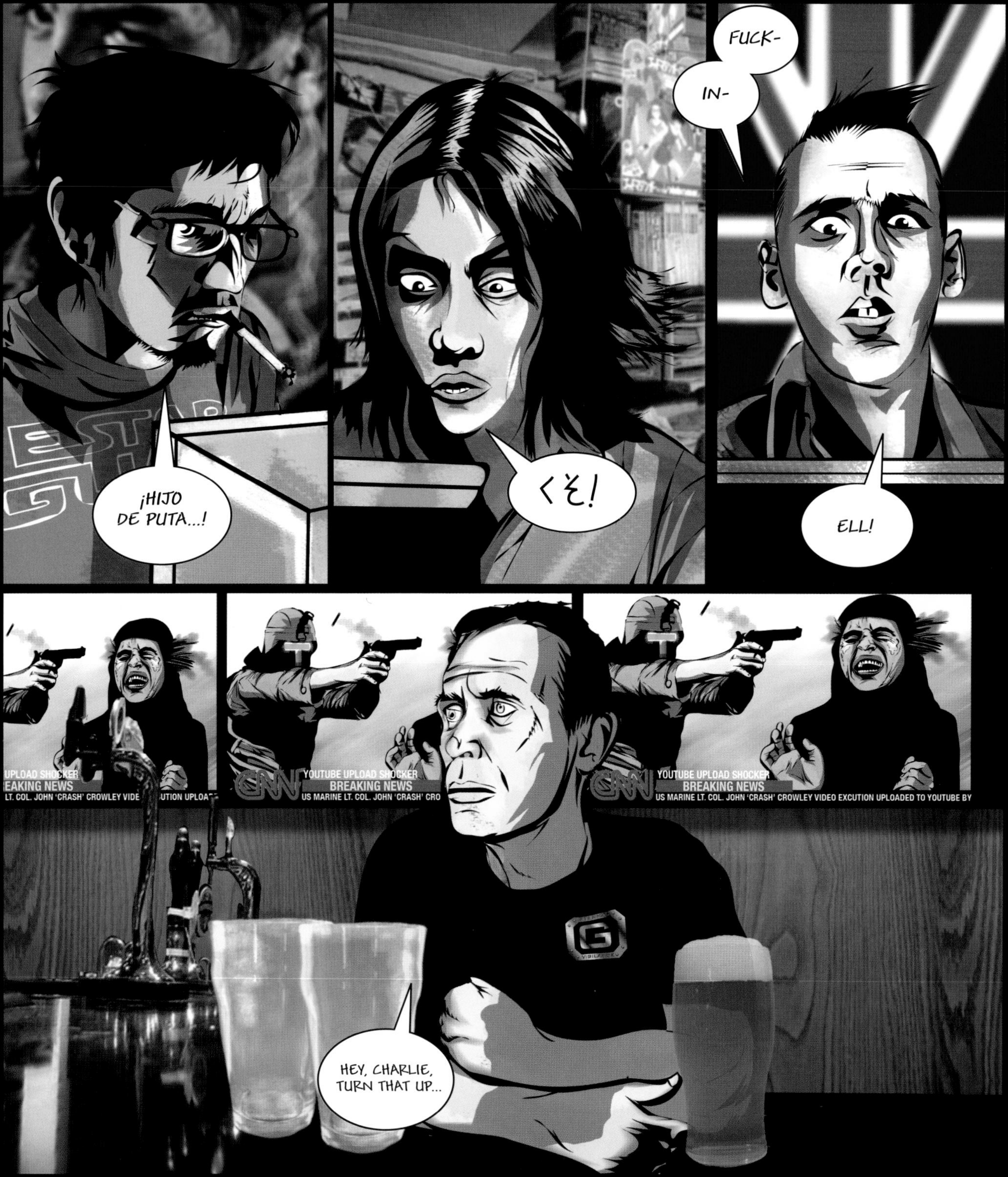
¡HIJO DE PUTA...!
くそ!
FUCK-
IN-
ELL!
YOUTUBE UPLOAD SHOCKER
BREAKING NEWS
US MARINE LT. COL. JOHN 'CRASH' CROWLEY VIDEO EXCUTION UPLOADED TO YOUTUBE BY
HEY, CHARLIE, TURN THAT UP...

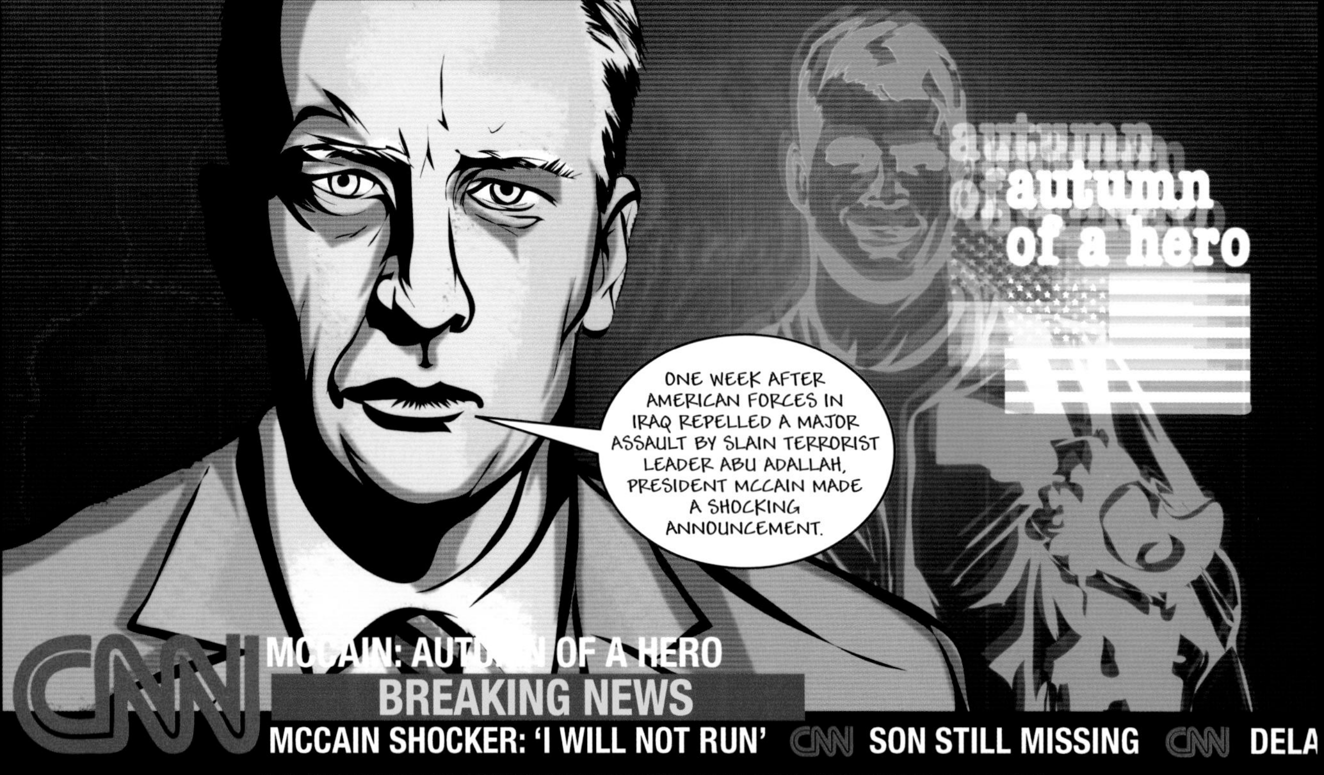
autumn
of a hero
ONE WEEK AFTER AMERICAN FORCES IN IRAQ REPELLED A MAJOR ASSAULT BY SLAIN TERRORIST LEADER ABU ADALLAH, PRESIDENT MCCAIN MADE A SHOCKING ANNOUNCEMENT.
CNN
MC AIN: AUTU OF A HERO
BREAKING NEWS
MCCAIN SHOCKER: 'I WILL NOT RUN'
CNN
SON STILL MISSING
CNN
DELA

EARLIER TODAY, THE PRESIDENT ANNOUNCED HE WOULD NOT SEEK RE-ELECTION AS THE REPUBLICAN NOMINEE IN 2012. WHITE HOUSE SOURCES TELL CNN THAT THE PRESIDENT HAD BECOME INCREASINGLY DESPONDENT OVER HIS SON'S ONGOING ABDUCTION AND THAT HE WAS DISTRAUGHT BY FRESH ALLEGATIONS OF AMERICAN WAR CRIMES.

THE IMAGES OF AN AMERICAN LT. COL. EXECUTING AN ELDERLY IRAQI WOMAN ON AN IRAQI STREET AND AMERICAN REMOTE CONTROLLED ROBOTS KILLING UNARMED CIVILIANS UPLOADED TO YOUTUBE BY FORMER GLOBAL NEWS CORRESPONDENT JIMMY BURNS WERE SAID TO HAVE ESPECIALLY DISTURBED THE VIETNAM VETERAN CHIEF EXECUTIVE.

THE ANNOUNCEMENT HAS LEFT THE NATION STUNNED. MANY COMMENTATORS COMPARED MCCAIN'S DEMEANOR TO A DEFEATED-LOOKING PRESIDENT LYNDON JOHNSON WHO SHOCKED THE NATION IN MARCH 1968 WHEN HE ANNOUNCED HE WOULD NOT SEEK A SECOND TERM IN OFFICE. MUCH HAD BEEN MADE ABOUT PRESIDENT MCCAIN'S MENTAL STATE IN THE LAST THREE MONTHS, WITH MANY WHITE HOUSE INSIDERS SAYING HE APPEARED TO BE SHOWING SIGNS OF DEPRESSION.

RUMORS HAVE CIRCULATED OF SESSIONS WITH THERAPISTS AND PRIESTS, AND EVEN AN ADDICTION TO ANTI-DEPRESSANTS. IT IS CLEAR THAT THE LAST THREE YEARS HAS TAKEN ITS TOLL ON THE 75-YEAR-OLD MAN WHO ENDURED MORE THAN FIVE YEARS IN A VIETCONG PRISON TO GO ON TO SERVE ONE TERM IN THE HOUSE OF REPRESENTATIVES AND FOUR TERMS IN THE U.S. SENATE BEFORE BECOMING THE 44TH PRESIDENT OF THE UNITED STATES.

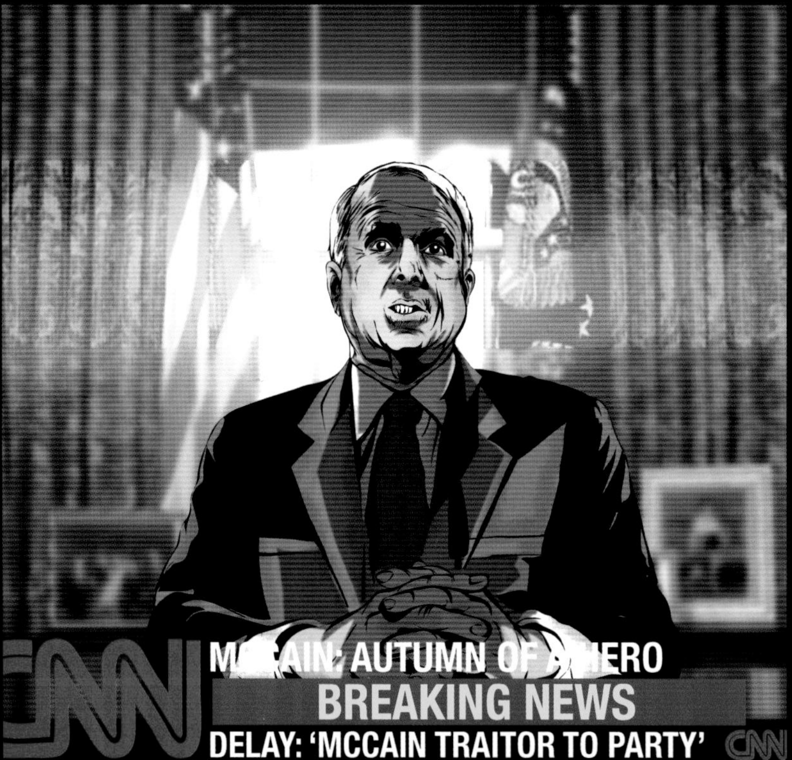
M AIN: AUTUMN OF ERO
BREAKING NEWS
DELAY: 'MCCAIN TRAITOR TO PARTY'

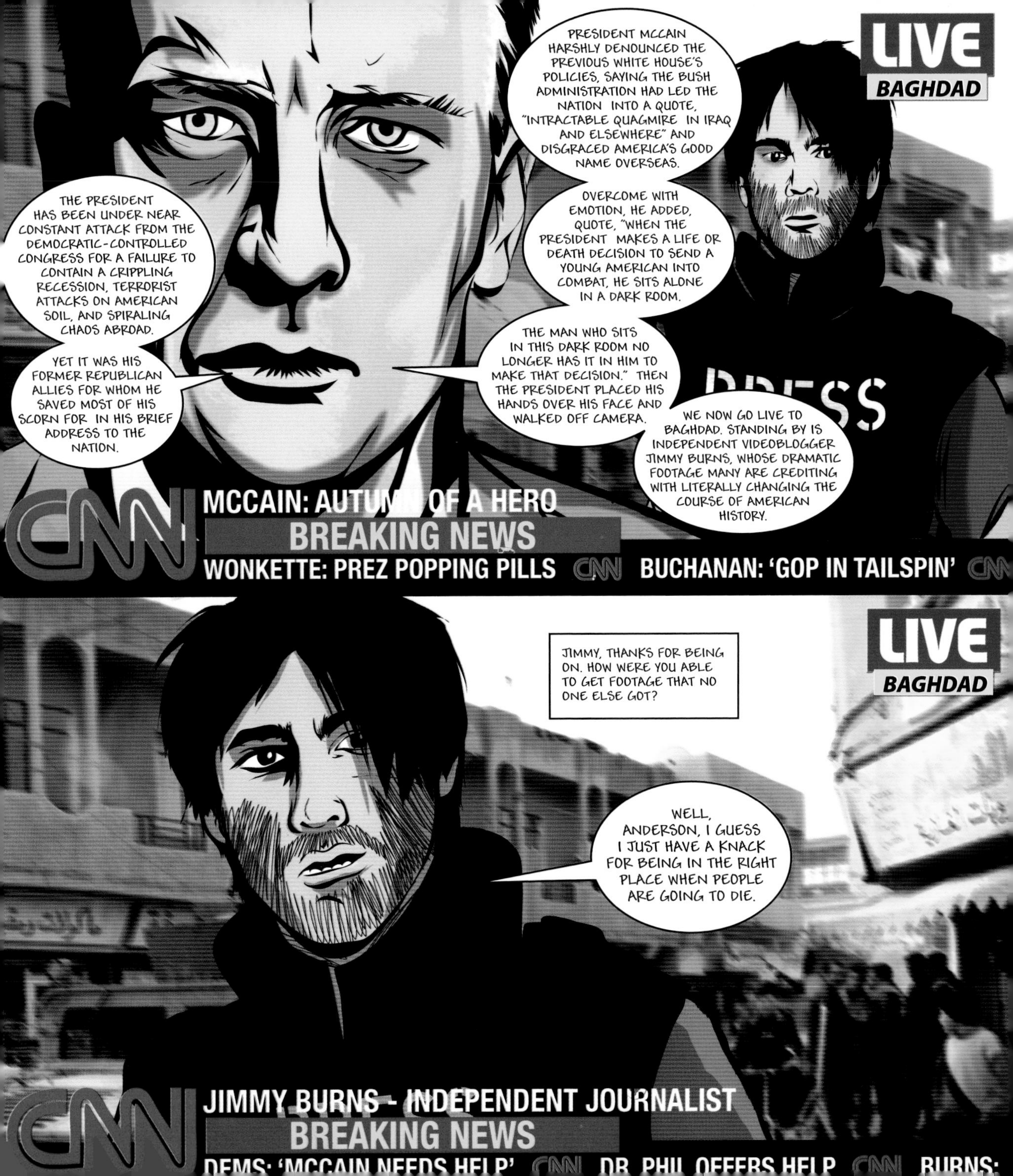
LIVE
BAGHDAD
THE PRESIDENT HAS BEEN UNDER NEAR CONSTANT ATTACK FROM THE DEMOCRATIC-CONTROLLED CONGRESS FOR A FAILURE TO CONTAIN A CRIPPLING RECESSION, TERRORIST ATTACKS ON AMERICAN SOIL, AND SPIRALING CHAOS ABROAD.
YET IT WAS HIS FORMER REPUBLICAN ALLIES FOR WHOM HE SAVED MOST OF HIS SCORN FOR IN HIS BRIEF ADDRESS TO THE NATION.
PRESIDENT MCCAIN HARSHLY DENOUNCED THE PREVIOUS WHITE HOUSE'S POLICIES, SAYING THE BUSH ADMINISTRATION HAD LED THE NATION INTO A QUOTE, "INTRACTABLE QUAGMIRE IN IRAQ AND ELSEWHERE" AND DISGRACED AMERICA'S GOOD NAME OVERSEAS.
OVERCOME WITH EMOTION, HE ADDED, QUOTE, "WHEN THE PRESIDENT MAKES A LIFE OR DEATH DECISION TO SEND A YOUNG AMERICAN INTO COMBAT, HE SITS ALONE IN A DARK ROOM.
THE MAN WHO SITS IN THIS DARK ROOM NO LONGER HAS IT IN HIM TO MAKE THAT DECISION." THEN THE PRESIDENT PLACED HIS HANDS OVER HIS FACE AND WALKED OFF CAMERA.
WE NOW GO LIVE TO BAGHDAD. STANDING BY IS INDEPENDENT VIDEOBLOGGER JIMMY BURNS, WHOSE DRAMATIC FOOTAGE MANY ARE CREDITING WITH LITERALLY CHANGING THE COURSE OF AMERICAN HISTORY.
CNN
MCCAIN: AUTUMN OF A HERO
BREAKING NEWS
WONKETTE: PREZ POPPING PILLS
BUCHANAN: 'GOP IN TAILSPIN'
LIVE
BAGHDAD
JIMMY, THANKS FOR BEING ON. HOW WERE YOU ABLE TO GET FOOTAGE THAT NO ONE ELSE GOT?
WELL, ANDERSON, I GUESS I JUST HAVE A KNACK FOR BEING IN THE RIGHT PLACE WHEN PEOPLE ARE GOING TO DIE.
CNN
JIMMY BURNS - INDEPENDENT JOURNALIST
BREAKING NEWS
DEMS: 'MCCAIN NEEDS HELP'
DR. PHIL OFFERS HELP
BURNS:

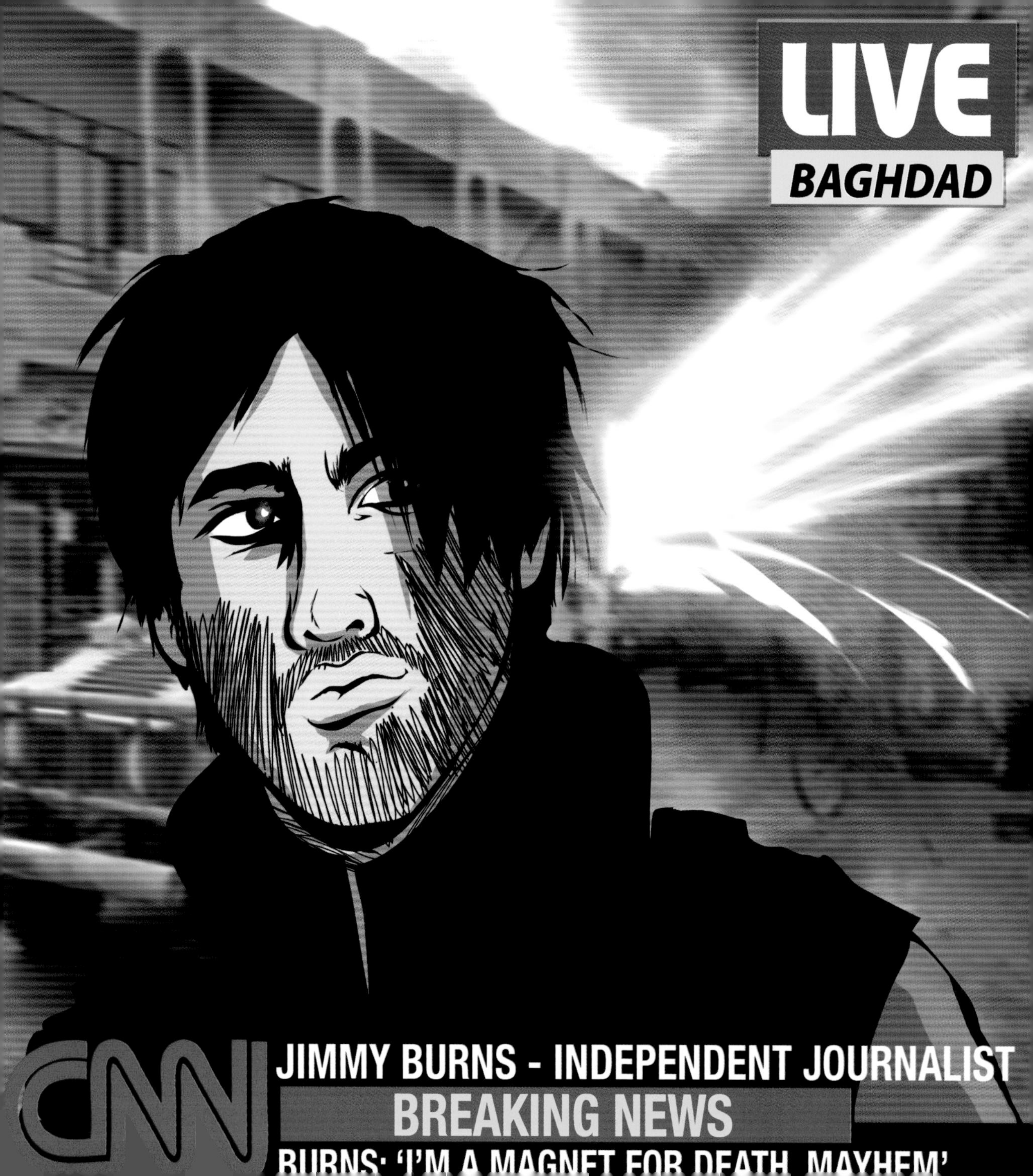
LIVE
BAGHDAD
CNN
JIMMY BURNS - INDEPENDENT JOURNALIST
BREAKING NEWS
BURNS: 'I'M A MAGNET FOR DEATH, MAYHEM'

THIS BOOK IS A WORK OF POLITICAL SATIRE. WE HOPE IT GETS YOU THINKING ABOUT SOME BIG QUESTIONS CONCERNING THE MEDIA, THE WAR IN IRAQ, AND AMERICAN FOREIGN POLICY IN GENERAL. WE ALSO HOPE IT MAKES YOU CHUCKLE.

FIRST AND FOREMOST, WE'D LIKE TO THANK THE INTREPID READERS OF SMITH MAGAZINE WHO HELPED MAKE THE ONLINE PREVIEW OF THIS BOOK A WEB PHENOMENON THROUGH THEIR SUPPORT, CONTRIBUTIONS, AND FEEDBACK. ESSENTIAL THANKS TO SMITH PUBLISHER LARRY SMITH FOR SEEING THE FUTURE AND TO TIM BARKOW FOR HELPING US BUILD IT; TO OUR AGENT IAN KLEINERT FOR HIS WISE CONSUL; AND TO JEFF NEWELT FOR CREATING THE CULTURAL PETRI DISH WHERE THIS AND MANY OTHER AMAZING PROJECTS LIVE AND BREED. BUT MOST SIGNIFICANTLY, WE'D LIKE TO EXPRESS OUR DEEPEST GRATITUDE TO OUR EDITOR, JAIME LEVINE, AND HER ASSISTANT TIMOTHY MUCCI FOR THEIR VISION AND GUIDANCE IN HELPING TURN A SCRAPPY ONLINE COMIC INTO A WORK OF LITERATURE.

IN ADDITION, WE'D LIKE TO THANK EVERYONE WHO HELPED SHOOTING WAR SPREAD FAR AND WIDE: HEIDI MACDONALD, JULIAN DIBBELL, BRIAN LAM, CALVIN REID, CHRIS ARRANT, JOE GORDON, RICH JOHNSTON, ANGELA GUNN, BRUCE STERLING, MARK FRAUENFELDER, DENNIS CROWLEY, TIM LEONG, MATT KOELBL, CAMILA VIEGAS-LEE, EDUARDO SIMOES, TERESSA IEZZI, T. CAMPBELL, DAN GILMOR, AND MICHAEL SLENSKE.

FINALLY, NONE OF THIS WOULD BE POSSIBLE WITHOUT THE SUPPORT, INSPIRATION, COLLABORATION, AND ENCOURAGEMENT OF DOUG JAEGER, MARK CREEL, THE HAPPY CORP, LVHRD, BOB MECOY, NICK BERTOZZI, SIMON FRASER, DEAN HASPIEL AND THE REST OF THE ACT-I-VATE CREW, DOUGLAS RUSHKOFF, MARY MAXWELL, PAUL POPE, CHARLES BROWNSTEIN, DJ SPOOKY, ADAM MATTA, RACHEL KRAMER BUSSELL, MICHAEL GESZEL, MILES VANMETER, DANNY FINGEROTH, RYAN ROMAN, ARIEL PALITZ, DAN LANTOWSKI, DOUGLAS LITTLE, MIDTOWN COMICS, FORBIDDEN PLANET, ROCKETSHIP, SAPPORO, SAMSUNG, TOBI ELKIN, JEFF AYERS, VANESSA ARRICO, DANIEL WHITE, KRISTIN JONES, PAUL RIECKHOFF, DAVID ENDERS, PHILLIP ROBERTSON, RICHARD ROWE, MORRIS GOLDMAN, CAROL GOLDMAN, FRANCES MOORE LAPPÉ, ANNA LAPPÉ, AND LAURA THOMAS.

WE WANT TO GRATEFULLY ACKNOWLEDGE THAT PHOTO SOURCES CAME FROM, AMONG OTHER SOURCES, CHRISTIAN PEACEMAKERS TEAMS, THE U.S. GOVERNMENT, AND **BATTLEGROUND: 21 DAYS ON THE EMPIRE'S EDGE.**

SHOOTING WAR WAS DRAWN DIGITALLY USING A WACOM CINTIQ 21UX INTERACTIVE PEN DISPLAY.

SHOOTING WAR WAS ORIGINALLY SERIALIZED ONLINE AT SMITHMAG.NET.

CREATIVE CONSULTANT: JEFF NEWELT

WWW.SHOOTINGWAR.COM
THE FREQUENCY IS COURAGE